Victor Amadeus II

MEN IN OFFICE

General Editor:
Professor Ragnhild Hatton

GEOFFREY SYMCOX

Victor Amadeus II

Absolutism in the
Savoyard State 1675–1730

with 35 illustrations

UNIVERSITY OF CALIFORNIA PRESS
Berkeley and Los Angeles

To Linda, who made it possible

UNIVERSITY OF CALIFORNIA PRESS
Berkeley and Los Angeles, California

© 1983 Thames and Hudson Ltd, London

**Library of Congress Cataloging in
Publication Data**
Symcox, Geoffrey.
   Victor Amadeus II: absolutism in the
Savoyard State, 1675–1730.
   Includes bibliographical references.
   1. Victor Amadeus II, King of Sardinia,
1666–1732. 2. Savoy (Duchy) – History.
3. Sardinia (Kingdom) – History. 4. Piedmont
(Principality) – History. 5. Savoy (Duchy) –
Kings and rulers – Biography. 6. Sardinia
(Kingdom) – Kings and rulers – Biography.
7. Piedmont (Principality) – Kings and rulers –
Biography. I. Title.
DG618.53.S95 1983   945´.907´0924
82–45904

ISBN 0-520-04974-8

Printed in Hungary

Contents

Preface

Victor Amadeus II of Savoy is almost unknown to students and scholars in the English-speaking world. From time to time he receives fleeting mention as a Machiavellian diplomat forever changing sides in the great conflicts of Louis XIV's later years, without apparent motive or effect; in the drama of war and diplomacy he is given a walk-on part – and an unsavoury one at that – if he gets anything at all. The extent and nature of the territories he ruled remain equally obscure. Known generally – but misleadingly – as the duchy of Savoy, although their real centre lay across the Alps in the Piedmontese plain of north-western Italy, the Savoyard domains figure in the historical atlases but have never formed the subject of research in English. Historians seem to have assumed that a small state like Piedmont-Savoy has little to teach us; they side unconsciously with the big battalions, evidently believing that the study of larger states reveals a higher historical truth.

In this book I shall try to correct these misconceptions. I believe that an analysis of the Savoyard state under Victor Amadeus II, in what was a critical epoch of its development, can tell us a great deal about the nature of absolutism and its impact on society. Between his assumption of power in 1684 and his abdication in 1730 Victor Amadeus carried through a programme of reforms which completely transformed the state he ruled, increasing its revenues, strengthening its military power, enhancing the central government's control over the periphery, and completing the process of drawing the privileged orders into the service of the state. In their audacity and thoroughness the changes that he wrought parallel and sometimes surpass the radical overhaul of government institutions under-.taken by contemporary rulers like Louis XIV in France, Karl XI and XII in Sweden, Peter I in Russia or the Great Elector and Frederick William I in Brandenburg-Prussia. As a result, by 1730 the Savoyard state was one of the most efficiently run monarchies in Europe. I would argue that the way in which Victor Amadeus formulated and then implemented his policies provides a definitive illustration of the methods and objectives of absolutism at work. The small size of the state he ruled makes it a purer 'laboratory' specimen of absolutism than larger states like France, where the development of absolute monarchy is usually studied: in Victor Amadeus's 'état tiré au cordeau' (as the marquis d'Argenson called it in the mid-eighteenth century) central authority was more clearly defined and institutional structure was simpler, so that the direction and purpose of transformation are easier to grasp, and the implications of the growth of state power are easier to assess. In the internal history of the Savoyard state Victor Amadeus II's reign set the seal on more than a century of prior evolution towards highly centralized absolutism and defined its structure and institutions for the rest of the Ancien Régime.

In external affairs too, his reign was a watershed. In two gruelling wars between 1690 and 1713, Victor Amadeus broke free from the domination of France, conquered significant territorial additions to his state and established himself as a valuable ally courted by the great powers. A better knowledge of his foreign policy and the motives behind it will thus add to our understanding of European international relations at a particularly complex moment when old empires and hegemonies were breaking down and new states – among them Piedmont-Savoy, whose rise recalls in some ways that of Prussia – were coming to the fore. And in the end these upheavals in internal and external affairs cannot be separated from the enigmatic character of Victor Amadeus himself, who always stood at the focus of power. Narrowly pragmatic in certain ways, imaginative and almost visionary in others; a model of bureaucratic diligence and a stickler for detail, yet given to paroxysms of rage and energy; brutally autocratic yet strangely hesitant in his methods, and capable of sensitive discernment and even charm when he chose; at once fascinating and repellent, he is I feel a prime candidate for psycho-biographical investigation, and the thrust of his forceful personality can be seen in all the great developments that marked his reign, and in the shaping of state and society until the end of the Ancien Régime.

English-speaking historians are not alone in neglecting these important themes; historians in Italy, where greater attention might have been expected to be devoted to Victor Amadeus II's reign, have had little to say about it until recently. The only biography of Victor Amadeus II – a fine work by Domenico Carutti, to which I at once confess my debt – is more than a century old. The central part played by the Savoyard state in the Risorgimento focused attention on its growth and development, giving rise to a number of general histories like those of Cibrario or Ricotti, but they did not pay special attention to this critical period which did so much to prepare Piedmont for the leading position it would assume in the struggle for national unification. Some historians touched on one or another aspect of Victor Amadeus's policies in the course of treating wider themes of Piedmontese history, without focusing on his reign; thus P. C. Boggio studied his conflict with Rome and Tommaso Vallauri examined his educational reforms, for both topics bore directly on the contemporary tension between the new Italian state and the Vatican. But for the most part the patriotic writers who dominated Italian historio-

most as a work of synthesis; at the present moment, given the lack of any modern study of Victor Amadeus II's reign in all its aspects, I feel there is a real need for an attempt to draw conclusions – which must perforce be provisional, and liable to correction – and to suggest possible lines of enquiry. These are the tasks that I have therefore set myself. The most salient difference between this book and the studies on which I have drawn lies in its attempt to treat Victor Amadeus's disparate territories as a single whole. The literature on the Savoyard state has up to now been national or regional; Italian scholars have written about Piedmont, French scholars have dealt with Savoy and Nice; there is an important tradition of local historiography covering the Val d'Aosta; Sardinia (and Sicily, which for a brief period formed part of Victor Amadeus II's domains) have always been treated separately. Such a division of labour is easily understandable, given the distribution of archival resources into so many regional centres, the tradition of local studies which is so valuable a part of Italian and French historiography, and the political destiny that separated Nice and Savoy from Piedmont in 1860 to make them part of France. But these conditions have also, unavoidably, made it impossible to see the Savoyard state for the composite whole it once was, multilingual and pre-national, and so to reconstruct it as it was when Victor Amadeus ruled it. Coming from the outside I have found it easier to survey this complex political organization without regional or national preconceptions. I hope that what I lack in detailed local knowledge I have made up, to some degree at least, by a readiness to take a broad view and to see Victor Amadeus II's work in the perspective not merely of one of the several segments of his state, but of the state in its entirety, and so to appreciate the impact of his political will and vision in its proper context.

Acknowledgments

Any piece of extended research such as this owes a great deal to the aid of archivists and librarians, whose indispensable but often unsung efforts make an author's work possible. I gratefully acknowledge the help I have received from the staffs of the Archivio di Stato, the Biblioteca Reale and the Biblioteca Nazionale at Turin; particular thanks are due to Giovanni Ajmar, at the Archivio del Comune in Turin, and to Janet Ziegler of the Interlibrary Loan service at UCLA Library.

My friends and colleagues at the University of Turin have helped me to clarify my ideas in discussion, through their specialized knowledge and well-informed comments; many of them have also read this work in manuscript. I should like to single out Franco Rosso and Giovanni Brino of the Faculty of Architecture, and Mauro Ambrosoli, Dino Carpanetto, Luciano Allegra, Angelo Torre, Giuseppe Ricuperati and Giovanni Levi of the Faculty of Modern History. If the book is still far from perfect, it is not for lack of their patient assistance.

A special debt is due to my friend Sandro Lombardini, also of the Faculty of Modern History, for his advice, and to Doctor Enrico Bertana, of the Soprintendenza per i Beni Ambientali ed Architettonici del Piemonte, for helping to procure some of the illustrations.

I take pleasure in recording my gratitude to the various bodies which have assisted me financially during the research and writing of this book: the Committee on Research at UCLA, the American Philosophical Society, for a grant in the spring of 1980, and above all the Guggenheim Foundation, which supported me during a year of study in 1977–8 with the disinterested generosity for which it is justly renowned, and for which my thanks here are only an inadequate response.

Finally I should thank Stanley Baron, of Thames and Hudson, and the editor of the series of monographs of which this book forms a part, Professor Ragnhild Hatton, who has waited with infinite patience during the protracted composition of the work. To her I owe a particular debt for her careful comments on the manuscript, and for her unfailing moral support through every phase of writing. She provided the initial impetus that led to the research and writing of the book, and without her aid it could hardly have been completed.

Los Angeles–Turin–London 1979–82   *Geoffrey Symcox*

I
The Growth of the State

NOTE *All dates are New Style unless otherwise stated.*

At Victor Amadeus II's accession the Savoyard state consisted of a mosaic of territories straddling the western Alps, pieced together in apparent defiance of the logic of geography and communications in a process of conquest, purchase and inheritance that had spanned six centuries. The state was roughly bisected by the formidable barrier of the Alpine chain; its provinces were not united by a common language or culture, and differed widely in their political traditions and levels of economic development. The common denominator that held them together was obedience to the same ruling house, and to the political institutions that were gradually taking shape under its direction.

The heart of the state was the principality of Piedmont; bounded to the south by the republic of Genoa, and to the west by the Alps, it embraced the upper Po valley and the hills to the east of it, as far as the border with Spanish Lombardy – the area centring on Milan which, conquered by Spain in the sixteenth century, was officially designated the Stato di Milano and is also known in English as the Milanese, or simply Milan. In this region of fertile plains and foothills lay the richest resources and the densest population of the entire state, and here too stood the capital, Turin. The predominance of Piedmont over the duchy of Savoy, lying west of the Alps and the original nucleus of the state and cradle of its ruling dynasty, had been symbolized by the transfer of the capital to Turin from Chambéry in 1560. The state's centre of gravity was now fixed on the Italian side of the Alps, for Savoy itself was a relatively poor territory, a largely mountainous region with much thinner economic and demographic reserves than its neighbour. Savoy was moreover a perpetual hostage to fortune, soon lost in a war against France, its French-speaking inhabitants increasingly susceptible to the political and cultural attractions of their powerful neighbour to the west. Between Piedmont and Savoy lay the duchy of Aosta in its remote valley, linked by a tenuous linguistic and cultural allegiance to Savoy, but in other respects a world apart, shut off from the rest of the state by the mountains that surrounded it on all sides. To the south-west the other major component of the state, the county of Nice, was almost as isolated. Barren and mountainous, turned in on itself, the county gravitated around its own capital, the city of Nice and its port of Villefranche, the state's only point of contact with the sea.

Just to the east of Nice lay the tiny Savoyard enclave of Oneglia, sand-wiched between Genoese fiefs along the rocky Ligurian coast. It offered no viable access to the sea, for its port was minuscule and its territory was cut off from the other Savoyard domains.

Profound divergences between its component provinces, aggravated by bad communications, thus remained a fundamental problem built into the structure of the Savoyard state. Yet this defect was by no means insuperable; communication between the different regions over the Alpine passes could be maintained at all seasons – albeit sometimes with difficulty – while the relatively small size of the state facilitated efficient administration. The whole state measured perhaps 300 kilometres as the crow flies, north-south from Nice to Geneva, and about 250 kilometres east-west, from Pont-de-Beauvoisin on the French frontier to the borders of Spanish Lombardy close to Vercelli. Even after the acquisition of Sardinia in 1720 the internal administrative problems facing the Savoyards never attained the scale and intractability that they did in larger monar-chies like France or Spain. Efficient government could do much to offset the adverse effects of geography, and perhaps Victor Amadeus II's most lasting achievement was the establishment of a highly centralized state apparatus that went far towards breaking down the regional autonomies that had prevailed before his reign.

Poor communications could have their advantages too. Trade funnelled through the mountain passes could be taxed more easily, and possession of the strategic routes between France and Italy made the dukes of Savoy much sought after as allies. Their traditional role as 'the gatekeepers of Italy' depended on their command of the few Alpine passes through which an army could march with its baggage-train and artillery: Tenda in the south, the Mont-Cénis and Mont-Genèvre close to Turin, the Great and Little Saint Bernards to the north. In a sense, therefore, the formation of the Savoyard state followed an underlying geopolitical logic, aimed at dominating the commercial and military routes across the Alps. Though the mountains divided the state and isolated its component provinces, they gave it a strategic *raison d'être* and formed a structural armature, a spine to hold it together.

The inflexible imperatives of Alpine geography thus worked both to the advantage and the disadvantage of the Savoyards. Within their domains the Alpine watershed marked a fundamental dividing line, whose implications were central to the historical development of the state. The original Savoyard lands, acquired in the mid-eleventh century by the dynasty's semi-legendary founder, count Humbert the White-Handed, consisted of territories west of the Alps: the county (later duchy) of Savoy proper, and the valley of Maurienne. Humbert won recognition as the secular overlord of the Val d'Aosta, thus securing a foothold east of the Alps as well. His descendants however for long proved unable to extend their dominions into Italy. Through the twelfth and thirteenth centuries they gradually expanded their holdings on the western slope of the Alps as far as Lake Geneva, and northward into the districts of Vaud and Valais. By the end of the thirteenth century the Savoyards had established their permanent capital at Chambéry; east of the Alps they now controlled a few cities, Turin among them, but these did not counterbalance the essential westward orientation that the Savoyard state had assumed. This westward dynamic was reinforced in the fourteenth century by the acquisition of Gex and Faucigny, while the voluntary submission of the county of Nice in 1388 extended the state to the south. The Savoyard lands west of the Alps were, however, still divided by a broad salient of hostile territory in Dauphiné stretching as far as the crest of the Alps at Briançon, which became an insurmountable obstacle to further Savoyard expansion when it was absorbed by the French monarchy in the fifteenth century.

A major stride towards integrating these disparate territories and an important extension of Savoyard power into Italy were accomplished during the reign of Amadeus VIII (1391–1436). He established direct rule over the Savoyards' scattered domains in Piedmont, added Vercelli to them and thereby extended his frontier as far as the river Sesia, where it would remain until 1713. He also secured the county of Geneva, and the enhanced importance of the Savoyard state was recognized by his elevation to the dignity of duke by the Emperor Sigismund in 1416. From this time the Italian possessions of the house of Savoy came to play an increasingly significant part in the political life of the state. To the pull of their economic potential was added the push of rising French power, threatening the Savoyards' western lands and precluding further expansion in that direction. The reorientation of the state towards Italy and eastward expansion would be completed during the sixteenth century.

The Savoyard state suffered heavily during the Franco-Spanish conflicts for control of Italy in the first half of the sixteenth century. 1536 was a catastrophic year. Geneva, long restive under Savoyard rule, declared its independence, adopted Protestantism, and, along with the provinces of Vaud and Valais, accepted the protection of the Swiss Cantons. In the same year French armies overran Savoy, Nice and western Piedmont, while a Spanish force invaded from Lombardy to oppose them. Twenty years of brutal armed occupation ensued. In 1538 the Emperor Charles V rejected duke Charles III's claims on the neighbouring marquisate of Monferrato, whose ruling dynasty had died out, and adjudged it to the duke of Mantua. Only slowly and painstakingly did the Savoyards later make good their claim on Monferrato: Victor Amadeus II finally secured it during the War of the Spanish Succession. At the peace of Câteau-Cambrésis in 1559 the Savoyard state was reconstituted, in part through the diplomatic and military skill of duke Emanuel Filibert, who had

succeeded the luckless Charles III in 1553, and in part because of the desire
of both France and Spain to preserve the Savoyards as a buffer between
them. Once restored, Emanuel Filibert embarked upon a full-scale
reorganization of his government, revived the state's shattered economy,
and turned his ambitions eastwards towards Lombardy, where lay the
best chances for future expansion, although here the power of Spain was
for long to present a formidable obstacle. Turin developed rapidly as the
new capital of the state, emphasizing the political and economic preponderance of the lands east of the Alps. In 1601 the treaty of Lyon
carved away part of the Savoyard domains west of the Alps – Bresse,
Bugey, Valromey and Gex – and awarded them to France. This loss was
compensated by French recognition of Charles Emanuel's conquest of the
marquisate of Saluzzo, an important enclave on the Italian side of the Alps
hitherto under French suzerainty. The Savoyards' Italian possessions were
further consolidated by the treaty of Cherasco in 1631, which transferred
part of the disputed territory of Monferrato to duke Victor Amadeus I.
This minor acquisition was bought at some cost, for in return the duke
was compelled to cede Pinerolo to Louis XIII, along with a corridor of
territory leading back from that fortress to Dauphiné. Until Victor
Amadeus II recovered this bridgehead in 1696 his state lay open to constant
French interference and was reduced to the status of a satellite.

From the sixteenth century, therefore, the Alps divided the political
heartland of the state, Piedmont, from what was increasingly regarded as
a useful but ultimately expendable zone to the west, in Savoy and the
county of Nice. This division was economic too: the western provinces
were orientated towards Provence, Lyon and Geneva, rather than towards
Turin and the Lombard plain. Language reinforced this distinction. From
1560 Italian became the official language of government, but in Savoy
French naturally continued to be used. We should be careful, however,
not to overstate this difference. The linguistic frontier did not coincide
with the line of the Alps, for the Val d'Aosta and various enclaves on the
Italian side (such as the Vaudois valleys above Turin) were French-
speaking, while the population of Nice spoke their own language, Nissart,
an offshoot of the Langue d'Oc. To all intents and purposes, therefore, the
Savoyard state was multilingual. Victor Amadeus II, like many of his
nobles, spoke both Italian and French – as well as Piedmontese dialect,
almost a language in its own right – and official or personal correspondence was carried on in either language. And in an age when most people
knew no speech beyond their local *patois*, the higher politics of language
mattered little. To a peasant in the backlands of Nice, for instance, official
French and official Italian were both foreign tongues. Linguistic diversity
was broadened still further by the acquisition of Sardinia in 1720; there
the population spoke its own language, distinct from Italian, and Spanish
(or Catalan) was the language of government.

Allegory of the birth of Victor
Amadeus II, 1666. On the daïs, his
parents, surrounded by cherubs
bearing the arms of the different
Savoyard domains.

Victor Amadeus II in childhood.

Marie-Jeanne-Baptiste of Savoy-
Nemours (1644–1724), Victor
Amadeus II's mother, known as
Madame Royale.

4 Marie-Adelaide (1685–1712), elder daughter of Victor Amadeus II, married to the duke of Burgundy, 1696.

5 Marie-Louise (1688–1714), younger daughter of Victor Amadeus II, married to Philip V of Spain, 1701.

6 Anne of Orleans (1662–1728), wife of Victor Amadeus II.

VITTORIO AMEDEO II.

7 Victor Amadeus II, with the battle of
Turin in the background.

8 Victor Amadeus II's younger son and
successor Charles Emanuel III (1701–73)
in young manhood.

9 Victor Amadeus, prince of Piedmont
(1699–1715), elder son of Victor
Amadeus II.

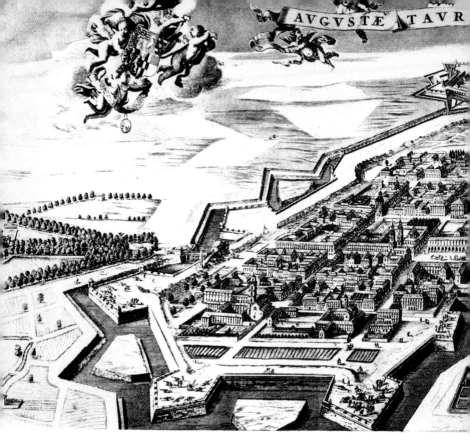

10 Turin in the 1660s looking west. In the distance, the citadel; in front of it the new quarter laid out in 1619: the older nucleus is distinguished by its denser housing and narrower streets. The royal palace is at bottom right: a new extension of the city would cover the open land in the foreground after 1669.

11 Garden front of the royal palace, begun in 1646 by Amedeo di Castellamonte. Guarini's dome of the chapel of the Holy Shroud is on the right.

12 Exposition of the Holy Shroud in front of the royal palace in 1737. The relic is the oblong displayed in front of the central pavilion: in front, a crowd fills the piazza.

SCENOGRAPHIA
ÆDIS ☩ REGIÆ
SACRATISSIMÆ SINDONI
DIC ☩ ATÆ.

13 The basilica of Superga b
Juvarra, 1717–31.

14 Project sketch by Juvarra
for Superga: note the
shallowness of the portico as
compared with the final
design.

15 Sectional view of Guarini
chapel of the Holy Shroud,
Turin, finished 1694. The
chapel was built to connect
royal palace (on the right) to
the cathedral. The dome is n
more than a cage of skeletal
ribs pierced by openings to
admit indirect light.

16 Interior of the dome of Superga with dedication by Victor Amadeus II, 1726.

17 Victor Amadeus II in early manhood.

18 The Comtesse de Verrue, Victor Amadeus II's mistress.

19 Juvarra's façade for the Palazzo Madama, Turin (1718), grafted onto a medieval castle, built around one of the city's Roman gates, whose roofs appear above the balustrade.

20 The royal hunting-lodge at Stupinigi, designed by Juvarra in 1729. The central pavilion is the ballroom: apartments radiate from it in an X-plan. The outer wings were added later.

(Facing page)
21 Interior of the great oval ballroom at Stupinigi. The frescoes are by the Venetian artists Giuseppe and Domenico Valeriani, from 1731.

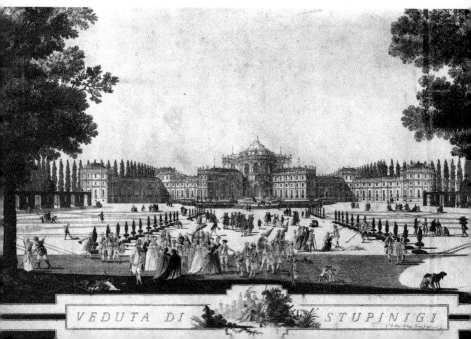

VEDUTA DI STUPINIGI

EDITTO
Marzo
N.°

EDITTO

DI SUA MAESTA

Per la Perequazione generale de'Tributi
del Piemonte.

In data de' cinque Maggio 1731.

TORINO, nella Regia Università, appresso GIO: BATTISTA CHAIS
Stampatore, e Libbrajo di S. R. M., degli Eccellentissimi
Magistrati, e della Regia Università.

22 Frontispiece of the edict reorganizing the land-tax in the
Piedmontese provinces, 1731 (the
perequazione), Victor Amadeus II's
most extensive and ambitious reform.

23 The difficulties of Alpine
communications: the main road
linking the county of Nice to southern
Piedmont, near Saorge.

24 Atrocities against the Vaudois,
which aroused horror in Protestant
Europe: this scene is taken from a
series published in England in 1655,
and directly recalls the imagery of
Milton's sonnet 'On the late massacres
in Piedmont'. Similar scenes were
repeated in 1686.

25 Silk-spinning machine, the basis of
Piedmont's industry and export trade.
The silkworms are killed in the vat of
a hot dilute alkali on the right and the
threads from the cocoons twisted
together and wound onto the frame at
left.

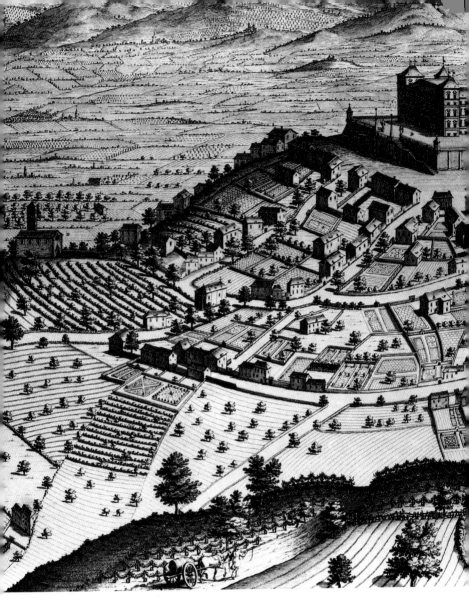

5 The Piedmontese landscape: in the foreground, terraced vineyards and orchards around the nobleman's country residence (note the vines trained along trees); in the plains in the background are fields of cereals.

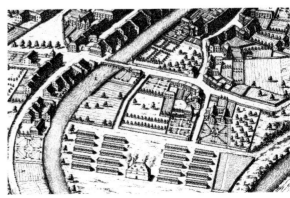

7 Salt production at Moustiers in Savoy. Water from the local saline springs is evaporated in the sheds.

28 The Alpine frontier: the town of Susa with its fortress controlling the principal route (via the Mont-Cénis and Mont-Genèvre passes) from France into the Piedmontese plain.

29 Montmélian, the chief fortress of Savoy, on its rock above the river Isère close to Chambéry. Its garrison held out for several years after French armies overran the duchy in 1690 and 1703.

30 Nice at the end of the 17th century, looking south-east: the river Paillon (foreground) was in fact only a rocky torrent. The old town clusters at the foot of the citadel, blown up by the French in 1706. Villefranche, the Savoyard state's only port, is on the bay to the left of the citadel.

31 The Fort of Bard, blocking the entry to the Valle d'Aosta from the Piedmontese plain.

32 (overleaf) The battle of Turin, 7 September 1706, seen from the north. In the background Turin, its citadel, surrounded by the French trenches (note how the farmhouses are incorporated into the besiegers' lines). The Po is the broad river to the left; the Dora Riparia and Stura flow into it. The French are fleeing from the allied army attacking from the right.

33 The castle at Rivoli, where Victor Amadeus II died in 1731.

35 Sketch by Juvarra for the catafalque of Victor Amadeus II, a temporary structure erected for the funeral service held in the cathedral of Turin.

34 Victor Amadeus II in old age

Language was hardly a divisive force within the state, for as yet no equation had been made between language and national culture, as would happen later in the eighteenth century – a point forcefully made by the dramatist Vittorio Alfieri in his *Memoirs*.[1] But the differences between the provinces of the Savoyard state were nonetheless profound; widely divergent systems of land-tenure and customary law operated on each side of the Alps, with innumerable local variations; Savoy and Piedmont had different weights and measures, and different monetary systems. Local administration and law were not uniform; the legal system in Savoy, as administered by the Senate at Chambéry, conformed fairly closely to French practice, and diverged from the legal norms followed by the Senates of Turin or Nice. This difference would persist even after the promulgation of Victor Amadeus II's new law codes in 1723 and 1729. Once again, however, it is important not to make too much of these differences, or to read back from the French annexation of Nice and Savoy in 1860 in search of earlier tendencies which seem to point towards a rift between the eastern and western regions of the Savoyard state. By the standards of the seventeenth and eighteenth centuries such internal divergences were by no means exceptional; provincial separatism and diversity was the rule rather than the exception in any state at that time. The importance of these infinite local differences of law, custom, and administrative practice lies in the obstacles that they posed – at least in the eyes of the sovereign and his ministers – to the smooth functioning of the governmental machine.

Since Emanuel Filibert's restoration of the government, successive Savoyard rulers had laboured to construct a single bureaucratic administration that would command obedience throughout the state, without distinction of local custom and privilege. Victor Amadeus II's sweeping reorganization of the entire structure of government forms an integral part of this process, even though his reforms were more far-reaching in their scope and swifter in their implementation than those of his predecessors. Like them, he strove to wring the utmost from the meagre resources at his disposal, spurred on by the exigencies of the most desperate war to face the state in a century and a half. In his drive for fiscal and administrative efficiency Victor Amadeus laboured to weld all his diverse territories into a single whole, establishing new institutions to transmit his will to the remotest parts of the state, and to bring into the orbit of the central power social groups and geographic regions hitherto barely touched by it.

II
The Regions of the
Savoyard State

This chapter will examine the four principal regions that composed the Savoyard state: the two transalpine territories – the county of Nice, with its tiny adjunct, Oneglia, and the duchy of Savoy – then the Val d'Aosta, midway between Savoy and Piedmont, and finally Piedmont itself, the economic and political heart of the state.

THE COUNTY OF NICE

This region embraced 3,600 square kilometres of precipitous terrain, from the abrupt cliffs of the coastline, threaded by slender alluvial plains as at Nice itself, to the high plateaus and gorges of the interior: a predominantly pastoral land of isolated villages and forested highlands, almost without roads. The magnificent corniche road that would later open the Riviera to tourism was not constructed until Napoleon's day; until then movement along the coast was by boat. The main road to Piedmont, across the pass of Tenda, was suitable only for mules. Only in the 1780s would a prodigious feat of engineering – the first complete opening of an Alpine pass to wheeled traffic – make it accessible to carriages and wagons. North of Tenda a few minor passes, mule-tracks at best, crossed the Alpine ridge. The most important of these, at La Maddalena, would be ceded along with the valley of Barcelonnette to France in 1713. On these lesser roads the traffic was almost exclusively local: pedlars, migrant workers, transhumant shepherds and their flocks. Within the county, communications followed the river valleys whenever possible, swinging up and over the intervening ridges on narrow, tortuous pathways. The small townships and villages of the backlands thus lived in isolation, largely self-sufficient and introspective. The littoral, broken up somewhat by the valleys of the lower Var and Paillon, was marginally more open; for some of its needs it gravitated to Nice and Villefranche, but self-sufficiency was still the rule.

The inadequacy of communications cut Nice off from its hinterland, and condemned the entire county to poverty. Here the classic pattern of an enclosed mountain economy prevailed, similar to many parts of Savoy or the Alpine valleys of Piedmont: a meagre agriculture heavily dependent on stock-rearing, incapable of supporting the whole population, which was thus compelled to resort to seasonal migration. Communications were better to the west, into Provence and France, and it was here that most of the migrants went in search of work. The roads sufficed for this: foot traffic was difficult but feasible. The movement of goods was another matter. On a tour of inspection of the county in 1693, Vauban reported to Louis XIV that the roads were:

> very difficult and made only for men on foot or on horseback, and for mules, which can go loaded, but not with pack-saddles, since the roads are not wide enough for the use of panniers or trunks; these roads are very narrow, rough, and stony.[1]

The city of Nice remained an isolated enclave, orientated as much towards the sea as to its hinterland, a capital largely divorced from its province. Vauban described it in his report with his customary solicitude for statistics:

> The city is densely populated in relation to its size, and may contain as many as 966 houses, all of four or five storeys, plus thirteen convents and monasteries and six confraternities: a total of 11,752 persons of all ages and both sexes, including 1,357 who inhabit the townships round about which form the city's suburbs. The city contains many nobles, but they are poor and do not live in style. There is very little trade.[2]

If we accept the estimate of the county's population in 1700 as being about 70,000, this means that about one-sixth of the total lived in Nice itself. In the hinterland the density of population was very low: in the mid-eighteenth century, when the first reasonably accurate census was taken, there were no more than about thirty-two persons per square kilometre. No other town approached Nice in size, and it was in fact after Turin the largest city in all the Savoyard domains.

Until the new harbour of Lympia was dug in the 1750s, under the promontory on which Nice's citadel stood, any traffic of importance passed through the port of Villefranche just down the coast. Vauban noted that it was 'large and spacious, and could be made suitable for all types of vessels'.[3] But despite a charter of 1612 liberating all merchandise in transit from the payment of duties, Villefranche remained little more than a coasting harbour, condemned to insignificance by the lack of a productive hinterland, or a good route over the Alps. In 1688 Victor Amadeus II, following the ideas of earlier Savoyard rulers, revived one of the perpetual schemes for developing the port, even seeking the advice of the English consul there, but finally took no action. Salt was imported through Villefranche for the state gabelles, mainly from Hyères, and a certain amount of timber, barrel-staves, hemp and fruit were exported. In the later seventeenth century a discreet but growing English commercial presence began to make itself felt, and by the middle of the next century the English were bringing cloth, salt fish and colonial goods to Nice, as the political entente between England and the Savoyards became an established fact. This traffic provided the Savoyard government with a small revenue, which was augmented by the levying of the traditional 'droit de Villefranche', a 2 percent duty on all passing ships, nominally for the upkeep of coastal defences and protection against pirates.

The city of Nice, however, lived more from the land than from commerce. Statistics from the mid-eighteenth century show that half of its dependent territory – the best land in the whole county – was given over to vineyards, but even so there was not enough wine for local consumption. About a third of the city's territory was devoted to pasture, or was simply heath; the rest consisted of woodlands and meadows. Producing hardly any grain, the city was dependent on supplies brought in from the hinterland, or by sea. There were a few modest local industries: soap and candle-making, tanning, cooperage, some textile manufacturing, silk-spinning. A small Jewish colony engaged in trade and had introduced some new industries, notably sugar-refining. Fishing contributed significantly to the city's wealth: part of the catch of sardines and anchovies was sold at the fairs of Provence.

The economy of Nice benefited from the city's position as the local capital and residence of many of the county's leading landowners. From 1614 Nice had been the seat of a Senate or high court with jurisdiction over the whole county, and even after the destruction of the citadel by the French in 1706 it remained a garrison town. The city boasted a college of law, established in the sixteenth century, and a Jesuit college. It had traditionally been the meeting-place of the county's representative assembly, but faced by the encroaching power of the central government, the assembly fell into decay after 1680. The mainspring of local government was the Senate, which carried out numerous executive functions besides acting as the supreme judiciary, until the last years of the seventeenth century, when Victor Amadeus II appointed the first intendants. Nice then became their headquarters; they rapidly established a tight hold over the life of city and county alike, whittling away the autonomy of the local communities and bringing the municipality of Nice under their tutelage. The arrival of the intendants in many ways marks a watershed in the history of Nice and its county, a shift from the easy, distant relationship that it had hitherto enjoyed with its sovereigns, and a new intrusiveness on the part of the central power.

For a while the municipal government of Nice managed to resist the inroads of Victor Amadeus's intendants, showing greater vitality than the moribund provincial Estates. The city government drew its strength from a tradition of autonomy dating back to the period before the *dédition* to the Savoyards in 1388. The urban population was divided into four classes or *gradi* (nobles, merchants, artisans and farmers), each of which elected a proportion of the city council and one of the four syndics. But during the seventeenth century the municipality had slipped further and further into debt, and financial weakness laid it open to interference by the central power. The crucial moment came, as we shall see, between 1699 and 1702 when Pierre Mellarède was appointed intendant of the city and county. Although he left the municipal institutions largely intact, much of the life had gone out of them; the steady erosion of local autonomy which is the dominant trend in the internal evolution of the Savoyard state in the eighteenth century had begun.

This trend was most marked in the city of Nice itself, but it was also felt in the self-governing communities of the hinterland. A survey of the county conducted by Mellarède in 1701 listed ninety-eight separate communities in the four vicariates of Nice, Sospel, Puget-Theniers and Barcelonnette, together with the marquisate of Dolceacqua and the lesser counties of Tenda and Beuil. The overwhelming impression left by the survey is one of dire poverty. Official statistics – never notable for their tendency to overestimation – classified forty-seven communities as 'poor'. A critical problem was the extent of communal indebtedness: only eighteen communities in 1701 could balance their budgets. The rest were weighed down by an accumulation of debts incurred during the wars and natural disasters of the preceding century. These debts could not be paid off except by the desperate expedient of selling some or all of the communal lands, which in turn reduced the communal revenues, since the income from leasing common lands and pasture was a basic element in their budgets. Payment of interest on the communal debt often swallowed up a third, sometimes over a half of most communal incomes.

Much of the work of Mellarède and the intendants who followed him was devoted to stabilizing the communities' tenuous finances. The War of the Spanish Succession delayed any attempted remedies, but in 1716 the intendant Cossato ordered that all communal budgets be submitted to him for annual audits, to eliminate fraud and mismanagement. Gradually the communities adopted a standardized form of budget, which was carefully scrutinized by the intendant. The institution of a new *catasto* or tax-register by Mellarède in 1702 tended to equalize the tax burden among the different communities, and helped to ease the lot of the poorest communes. But all the time the government's fiscal demands were increasing. Although the new *catasto* distributed taxation more fairly, it also allowed the government to levy taxes more efficiently than before, substituting a standardized *taille réelle*, which could be increased at will, for the fixed *donativo* formerly voted by the Estates. Moreover, all tax assessments, many of which dated back a century and more, were now revised and brought into line with the current value of money. The government calculated the difference owed since the previous assessment, because of the failure of taxes to keep pace with inflation, and demanded the payment of sizeable arrears. As was to be expected, these demands frequently could not be met; deeper indebtedness followed.

State fiscal policy also worked in another way to undermine the
financial stability of the local communities. Throughout the century the
government had adopted the expedient of 'infeudating' certain free
communes in order to raise money. A number of communes were independent of any seigneur, and owed allegiance to the Crown alone. The
government could declare them to be fiefs, under certain conditions, and
then sell the feudal rights over them to the highest bidder, usually some
local magnate eager for a title. The operation was profitable to the
government in the short run, but in the end represented a loss since the
community would be struck off the tax-register. From the point of view
of the community, infeudation meant subjection to an often rapacious
feudatory, and so whenever possible the commune itself would buy up
the newly created feudal rights. In September 1697 the government
declared certain communities in the district of Sospel and in the valley of
Barcelonnette to be feudal, offering the rights over them for sale; rather
than permit this, the communities of Barcelonnette raised 100,000 lire, the
people of the Sospel region 45,000, to be rid of any feudal dominion. This
example was repeated elsewhere, but when the communities were too
poor to buy up the new feudal rights they would have to accept an overlord. But whether the communities purchased the rights or not, the effect
on their finances was grave; either they had to pay a large lump sum to the
Crown, or they would suffer the heavy hand of a feudatory anxious to
squeeze the maximum from his new rights.

Sporadic infeudations were, however, only a minor part of the growing
fiscal weight imposed by the central government; the major part was the
steadily rising incidence of regular taxation, direct and indirect. In the
1680s the county of Nice as a whole paid direct taxes of 40,000 or 50,000
lire per year; by 1731 this had risen to 73,575 lire a year. In the same period
the yield from the gabelles rose too, reaching over 210,000 lire a year by
the end of Victor Amadeus II's reign.[4] But despite the growing efficiency
of the state's fiscal mechanism, poverty and backwardness set a limit to the
revenues that the county could be made to yield. Only so much could be
squeezed from self-sufficient communities living by subsistence agriculture, and only a minimum of liquid wealth could be tapped from what
was still essentially a pre-monetary economic system, where the absence
of trade and exchange networks gave the tax-collector little opportunity
to exercise his arts.

Climate and geography were the underlying reasons for the low level
of economic development in the county of Nice throughout this period,
and indeed down to the French annexation in 1860 and beyond. The
mountainous terrain offered few fertile valley bottoms for cultivation;
the scrub and forests of the pre-Alps lent themselves best to extensive
pastoralism. The forests themselves provided some timber for export, but
the absence of good communications prevented systematic development

of the timberlands. Deforestation was nonetheless proceeding at an ever-increasing pace, because of the demand for wood as fuel and the increasing pressure of grazing: a census of animals in 1754 listed 6,843 cattle and oxen, 4,486 horses and mules, and 86,790 sheep.[5] The largest concentration of flocks and herds was in the northern highlands, where their numbers were augmented in summer by large transhumant flocks of sheep from Provence: the traditional routes of transhumance orientated the interior of the county towards Provence rather than towards Piedmont. Barcelon-nette offers a striking example of this: besides providing pasture for large flocks from as far away as Arles, the valley also specialized in the rearing of mules, bought young in France, grazed in the uplands of the valley and then resold in Provence, the Lyonnais and Dauphiné. In the high mountains of the county of Nice the animal population outnumbered the human by two or three to one, and formed the basis of the inhabitants' livelihood. But the steady growth of the flocks, although perhaps marking an increase in prosperity in the upland communities, also led to a general degradation of the mountain pastures and forests, which would become critical by the nineteenth century. Wool from the flocks was woven into coarse cloth for local consumption, and a small surplus of this cloth was transported laboriously to the coast for sale. The rough local cloth's cheapness guaranteed it a market even at a time when imported cloth was beginning to penetrate through the port of Villefranche, but the profits from its sale were small, and were almost consumed by the costs of transport. The .manufacture of cloth was thus no more than a marginal addition to the subsistence agriculture of the interior.

The mountainous topography of the county ruled out any form of agriculture except extensive pastoralism and climatic factors reinforced this tendency, for the region's aridity made it unsuitable for many types of cultivation, including cereals. Rainfall was – and is – unevenly distributed from season to season, very little falling in the hot summer months, while after July the run-off from melting snow in the mountains ceases. At the same time the fluctuations in rainfall from year to year can be brutal; some years will be wet enough for the successful cultivation of cereals, while in other years the lack of rain will ruin the crop. On his tour in 1693 Vauban pointed out the benefits that would accrue if the land around Nice could be irrigated:

> The fields are cultivated very carefully, but the trouble is that the drought desolates them and often makes the labour useless. An outlay of ten or twelve thousand écus could provide them with irrigation, which would double the revenue from them.[6]

But formidable capital cost stood in the way of such improvements, and irrigation remained no more than a theoretical possibility. So in the coastal regions and in the warm valleys the principal crops were olives, vines and fruit trees, often oranges, with figs providing a staple for the population. Higher up in the mountains chestnuts were cultivated and formed the basic diet of many communities, and here too higher rainfall allowed for some cultivation of cereals and even produced a meagre surplus which could be sold in Nice and along the coast.

Such a thin economic base could support only a limited population, in fact even less than the county actually held. Migration remained the only way to balance a rising population against a limited agricultural base. Here we meet the familiar pattern of mountain communities throughout the Savoyard state: during the winter, when there was little agricultural work, many males would leave to seek a living elsewhere. Exact figures are hard to find, but it seems evident by the mid-eighteenth century that in some places half or more of the menfolk would be away from their villages during the winter months. One estimate suggested that of these migrants two-fifths went to Provence, another two-fifths moved down to the coast and the city of Nice, while the remaining fifth made for Piedmont. Few had any special skills; they worked as casual labourers, eking out a marginal existence, often reduced to begging. This way of life, dismal though it was, still provided some sort of livelihood, while relieving the impoverished home communities of the burden of feeding part of their population for half the year. Migrant labour might even bring in small savings, accumulated on the road, to supplement some households' resources. And as population pressure built up, seasonal migration would turn to permanent expatriation; each year a few men would follow their accustomed paths in search of work as winter drew on, and never return.

Migration thus functioned as a safety-valve preserving the economic and demographic stability of the village community, so that it remained a largely self-contained, self-governing political unit into the eighteenth century. But below the surface changes were making themselves felt. In part because of the rising demand for taxes to be paid in cash, the isolated villages were imperceptibly drawn into a system of monetary exchanges, and in the course of the eighteenth century what one authority has termed 'agrarian individualism' began to erode the base of communally organized agriculture which sustained the village economy and made it self-sufficient.[7] The arrival of the intendants and the mounting fiscal pressure of the state thus helped to hasten fundamental changes in the structure of peasant society. But in many ways the village communities of the county of Nice still functioned under Victor Amadeus II as they had in the Middle Ages, managing their internal affairs by themselves. Their contact with the outside world would be limited to brushes with the tax-collector and the local seigneur – if they had one – or boundary disputes with their neighbouring communities. The basis of authority within each community was the assembly of the heads of households, which met regularly

French Departments of Savoie and Haute-Savoie: its population, according to the first reliable census, that of 1723, numbered 337,184 – perhaps slightly exaggerated, but accurate enough.[9] The density of population at that time would have been about 30 to 32 persons per square kilometre, close to the average for the county of Nice in the mid-eighteenth century, and about half the average for the Piedmontese provinces.

The mountainous nature of most of the duchy, the sparseness of its population and its relatively low level of economic development thus make it similar in many respects to the county of Nice, even though significant differences in climate and agricultural methods set the two regions apart. Yet whereas the county of Nice was a blind alley, shut in by inaccessible mountains and an inhospitable coast, Savoy was a great cross-roads of trade: through its defiles passed a north-south axis from Marseille and the fairs of Beaucaire to Geneva, and an east-west route from Genoa and Lombardy towards Lyon. The raw silk that formed Piedmont's most important export was transported over the Mont-Cénis to the mills of Lyon, while the woollens of Dauphiné and southern France moved in the other direction towards Piedmont and the Lombard plain. The duchy thus formed the focus of a network of trade routes, but, as we shall see, it retained little of the wealth from this traffic, remaining backward and overwhelmingly agrarian.

A clear indication of the duchy's backwardness is given by the stunted growth of its towns, little urban islands in a vast rural sea. Most of their wealth came from agriculture and not from trade or manufacture. Chambéry, the largest city in the duchy and the ancestral seat of Savoyard power, was at best a middling-sized place: as late as 1774 its population was no more than 10,200. It was a town of magistrates and lawyers, of government functionaries and landed nobles. Its size and importance derived from its role as the administrative centre of the duchy and as the residence of many aristocratic families – about half the duchy's nobles lived in the city or nearby. Its commercial and industrial wealth was less significant. The same held good for the other towns: Annecy by 1774 could muster a total population of only 6,730. Here too wealth and power were concentrated in the hands of the magistracy, the clergy and the landed aristocracy. The other provincial centres were no more than rustic market towns with a thin élite of lawyers, notaries and a few nobles.[10]

The mercantile and commercial economy of Savoy was thus of minor consequence. The international trade that passed through the duchy was largely controlled from outside: the merchants of Chambéry were eclipsed by the more powerful interests of Lyon, Geneva, Milan and Turin. The fairs of Chambéry, though blessed by government privileges, remained insignificant. Furthermore, the routes through Savoy were not the only way for goods to cross the Alps, and in the later seventeenth century the duchy faced increasing competition from the Simplon route, longer, but

better engineered for the movement of goods, and not subject to the high
duties charged by the Savoyard fisc. The Mont-Cénis, although the only
legal route for goods moving between France and Italy, was already being
deserted by the big merchants of Lyon before the outbreak of war in 1690
halted most of the trade that passed along it. The official monopoly
enjoyed by the Mont-Cénis route was restored at the treaty of Utrecht
in 1713, but by then a great deal of traffic had been lost permanently to the
Simplon. In the north of the duchy the export of agricultural products –
mostly wine and grain from Chablais – was hampered by an embargo imposed in the 1660s by the Canton of Berne, while traffic between Lyon
and Geneva increasingly followed an easier route through French territory west of the Rhône, barely touching Savoy at all. All this meant that
one of Victor Amadeus's basic concerns would be to maintain control of
the arteries of trade, to stimulate traffic and to discourage the use of competing routes. But since these considerations had to be balanced against
the lure of the tariffs levied on goods moving through the duchy, duties
remained high, deterring trade. And the desire to improve the roads and
passes to facilitate trade had to be balanced against the need to keep them
militarily defensible, and thus difficult of access. The Savoyard rulers
never managed to find a satisfactory compromise between these different
demands.

Savoy thus remained a passive channel of communication between
more powerful economies. Its own economy was integrated more closely
with south-western France than with Piedmont: political boundaries did
not coincide with economic reality. The tax-farmers who managed the
gabelles of Savoy were usually French, sometimes acting through a straw
man from Chambéry, more often using their own names. The currency
in Savoy was tied to the movements of the French money market; the
monetary reform of 1632 kept the livre used in Savoy separate from the
Piedmontese lira, so that whereas the lira followed the monetary movements of Milan and Genoa, the livre of Savoy was tied to the trajectory of
the French *livre tournois*. All this reflected a state of dependence on the
French economy which reinforced strong cultural and linguistic ties, and
which was to be further emphasized by two long French occupations
between 1690 and 1713. Small wonder therefore that the aristocracy of
Savoy tended to look westwards rather than across the Alps, and betrayed
an underlying resentment against Piedmontese rule in occasional velleities
of Francophilia.

With little or no industry, Savoy exported next to nothing apart from
agricultural produce. Such industries as did exist were small in scale and
largely rural. The nail manufactures of the plateau of Les Bauges which
had begun to develop in the mid-seventeenth century, using local iron-
ore, produced their wares for the internal market. Annecy in the seventeenth century possessed a few silk-spinning workshops, which never

really flourished since they were overshadowed by the more powerful silk industries of Piedmont and Lyon. There were sporadic attempts to develop the duchy's mineral resources. A few nobles mined the iron-ores on their domains; later on, the state would intervene, and in 1740 most of the mining in the duchy was turned over to a syndicate of English and Walloon entrepreneurs. None of these operations was of sufficient scale to make any real impact on the economy, which remained agrarian: the majority of the duchy's exports consisted of grain, some wine, cheese and other dairy products. But in general, agriculture meant subsistence farming rather than cash crops; as Jean Nicolas observes in his recent study of eighteenth-century Savoy, 'essentially, the countryside lived off its own resources'.[11]

Within this general pattern we must however be careful to distinguish some important regional differences. The Alpine provinces of Maurienne and Tarentaise were more isolated than the flatter regions of Savoy proper, of Genevois, or the northern edges of Faucigny and Chablais close to Lake Geneva. The bulk of the population was concentrated in the valleys where there was more cultivable land; the Alpine regions were overwhelmingly pastoral, with a more diffuse economic base and a much sparser population. Feudalism had hardly penetrated the less rewarding mountain areas, and the concentrations of noble and clerical property were situated in the central and western parts of the duchy, away from the Alpine chain. Taking the duchy as a whole in about 1730, the nobility drew roughly 17 percent of all revenues from the land, but this was unevenly distributed. In Savoy proper about 22 percent of the landed wealth was controlled by the aristocracy; in Genevois about 19 percent. But in the province of Maurienne the nobility's share fell to a scant 3½ percent of the landed wealth. In the Alpine zone of Maurienne and Tarentaise, with its vast mountain pastures and its isolated villages, the overwhelming proportion of the land – 72 percent – was communally owned. In Savoy proper, by contrast, some villages no longer possessed any common lands, and only 28 percent of the landed wealth, in terms of revenues, was communally owned.[12] A broad dichotomy therefore existed between the mountain regions, which although more thinly populated were generally more prosperous, and the villages of the lower lands where the greater productivity of the soil was more than outweighed by the burden of seigneurial exactions.

The pastoralism of the upland regions depended on a form of transhumance, and there was even a certain movement of flocks over long distances: herders from Provence would drive their sheep as far north as Savoy to pasture them for the summer. The grazing of animals from outside formed one source of income for the peasantry in the mountains; the sale of dairy products and livestock formed another. But this pastoral economy was fundamentally inelastic. Although the rainfall was far higher than in the county of Nice, the absence of intensively cultivated meadowlands imposed a strict upper limit on the number of animals that the mountain pastures could support. So in Savoy, as in the county of Nice, the natural complement to pastoralism was seasonal migration.

The large numbers involved in this seasonal movement indicate how crucial a part migration played in maintaining the fragile balance between population and resources. An enquiry conducted in the province of Faucigny in 1726 revealed that 2,981 men and youths out of a total male population of 24,329 were absent from their homes for several months or more: in some communities well over half the male population emigrated.[13] Some migrants were specialists who could command fairly good salaries – the stonemasons of the Giffre valley for instance, who ranged far afield in search of work, or at a lower economic level the traditional chimney-sweeps of Parisian folklore, with their forlorn troupes of little apprentices. Certain villages specialized in the trade of pedlar, hawking lace, cloth, ironmongery and gewgaws into France, Switzerland, even southern Germany. Most migrants, however, were unskilled farm workers, or porters seeking casual employment in Paris and other French cities: men like these earned the Savoyard his traditional reputation for abject poverty. Often, as in the county of Nice, seasonal migration was the prelude to permanent expatriation, compensating for the high birthrate of the mountain communities.

Emigration was by no means a monopoly of the Alpine regions of Savoy: large numbers of seasonal or permanent migrants also came from the villages in the lower-lying lands. In part this was the result of backward methods of cultivation and poor use of the soil; in part it was the result of seigneurial exactions, which took away a greater share of the meagre agricultural surplus than in the high mountain zone. Throughout Victor Amadeus II's reign, and in fact until the close of the eighteenth century, agriculture in Savoy remained backward and unproductive. Barely able to feed itself in a normal year, the duchy was particularly vulnerable to climatic setbacks, and frequently had to import grain in the bad years between about 1690 and 1730, despite strenuous efforts to maximize cereal production. Grain was cultivated wherever it could be made to grow, even in unsuitable soils or high in the mountains where the growing season was perilously short. The lower regions of the duchy were something close to a cereal monoculture, for every peasant farmer strove to produce enough grain – wheat in the lowlands, rye higher up – to meet his own needs, whatever the cost. All this added up to poor yields. As late as 1774 an observer commented: 'In Savoy a piece of land is esteemed good if for every sack of seed it yields three of grain; one for the new season's seed, the second for the tenant, and the third for the landowner. Most land yields only two to one; one sack for seed, the other to be divided between the tenant and the owner.'[14]

Cereal production thus dominated agriculture except in the highlands, but in a few places agrarian specialization was becoming apparent, notably in regions which concentrated on wine production, like parts of the Val d'Isère, the most advanced agricultural area in the duchy. Although zones of more intensive cultivation were growing up around the towns, large-scale commercial agriculture was still ruled out by inadequate communications. Some river transport was possible, but the duchy lacked a network of good routes linking the local mini-economies to large markets, so that most agricultural production remained autarkic, trapped within the limits of local consumption. Even timber, which Savoy produced in abundance, was not marketed on a large scale because of the difficulties of transport. About one-fifth of the area of the duchy in 1700 was woodland, over half of this being real forest rather than mere scrub. Little of this vast forested area was accessible, however, and already by 1700 forests that were within easy reach of roads or waterways had been devastated by indiscriminate exploitation. Most of the timber exported from Savoy was used to build ships for the French navy. In an endeavour to halt the destruction of the forests, the government banned the export of timber and required that any felling be first authorized by the intendants. But these restrictions were impossible to enforce, and the destruction of the forests for timber, fuel and charcoal increased during the eighteenth century.

It would nevertheless be a mistake to regard the agrarian economy of Savoy as completely static and unmoving. Change was taking place, sometimes almost imperceptibly, but the transition to an economy of exchanges was under way. In the more fertile valleys aristocrats and urban notables owned a number of large estates with permanent workers, supplemented by seasonal labour, producing a surplus which could be sold on the market. Most land was still farmed by tenants on three- or six-year leases, usually paying their rent in kind, but paying an increasing proportion in cash as the century wore on. There was always a certain amount of trade between regions: the mountainous areas depended on the valleys for the grain they could not grow, exchanging cheese and livestock for cereals. The pull of the urban markets was growing stronger; the limited demands of towns like Chambéry or Annecy were far out-stripped by the needs of Geneva – whose population had risen to about 18,500 by 1711 – which drew much of its food from the provinces of Faucigny and Chablais. In the south, Maurienne and Tarentaise exported a certain quantity of grain to Dauphiné. In Savoy, more than in the county of Nice, the isolation of rural life was beginning to break down as some sectors of the agrarian economy began to be commercialized. Even the remote mountain communities felt the pressure of change as they traded their cheeses and livestock in the lowlands, and their migrants brought back the tiny savings they had scraped together. By the middle of the eighteenth century, for instance, the peasants-turned-pedlars of the Pays des Villards in Maurienne constituted a modestly prosperous local élite, borne up by the profits of their trafficking in France. Although the mountain regions of Savoy were the last part of the duchy to feel the inroads of a market economy, they too were being gradually drawn into it.

These economic pressures were seconded by the intrusion of the state. In Savoy, as in the county of Nice, Victor Amadeus II's reign marks a watershed, for with the appearance of the ubiquitous intendants the state could intervene in local affairs and impose a degree of control as never before. For Gabriel Pérouse, one of the great historians of Savoy, 1713 opens a new era in the life of the duchy.[15] The presence of the intendants now became an established fact and their tutelage grew steadily more invasive. Even the remotest village councils felt their heavy hand, and the municipalities of Chambéry and the other towns lost their autonomy. The intendants examined communal accounts, overruled decisions about the use of common lands, and sapped the foundations of fiscal and administrative autonomy. The village ceased to be a voluntary, personal association and became an administrative division existing for the convenience of the state. Its syndics and councillors were no longer elected by the heads of households to represent their collective interests, but were appointed by the emissaries of the central government from a narrow oligarchy of the more substantial inhabitants. The communal assemblies, already threatened, fell into irreversible decline, and the local government reform of 1738 completed this process by abolishing whatever vestiges remained of popular election. From this time onwards, significantly, the village syndics swore their oath of office to the king, and no longer to the community, as they had traditionally done. The peasant community, and the peasantry in general, were faced at the same time by another kind of threat from the landed aristocracy and the new notables who were acquiring lands and titles. Jean Nicolas has detected a 'revival of seigneurialism' in the years around 1680, and this aggressive thrust was to continue for the duration of Victor Amadeus II's reign and beyond.[16] Forgotten feudal dues were claimed, arrears were demanded, land-registers were brought up to date. The resurgence of seigneurial fiscalism coincided with a long-term agricultural depression, and may well have been provoked by it, at least in part.

From about 1690 agricultural productivity declined, and conditions were aggravated by the effects of war and recurrent subsistence crises. Intensified seigneurial pressure, coming as it did just when times were getting harder, was bitterly resented by the peasantry and was contested at every turn. In the face of this mounting tension between lord and peasant, Victor Amadeus II's government at first adopted an ambiguous attitude, but then moved to confront the whole issue of seigneurial rights. Here the intendants played the key role, since they provided the instrument, hitherto lacking, by which the government could intervene in relations between the aristocracy and the peasantry. After the Peace of Utrecht restored the duchy to him, Victor Amadeus mulled over projects for abolishing parts of the seigneurial system; then with the great cadastral survey begun in 1728 he contemplated dismantling the system piecemeal. In fact the state in Victor Amadeus's later years was starting to assume the role of a social mediator, a policy which was to culminate in the Edicts of 1762 and 1771 enfranchizing the Savoyard peasantry, an act almost without parallel in the history of the Ancien Régime.

The state's attack on their privileges left the Savoyard nobles profoundly resentful. Their grievances stemmed in part from a sense that they and their duchy, the cradle of the dynasty and the original nucleus of the state, had been eclipsed by Piedmont. Victor Amadeus II's reforms dealt this wounded *amour-propre* another blow, besides threatening them with a serious loss of income from the reduction in feudal dues and the disallowing of many of their fiscal exemptions. Small wonder that in some cases their loyalties wavered and occasional grumbling was heard against the 'tyranny' of the king. Such disloyalty was rare, however; resignation was more the rule, or indirect signs of disapproval like the welcome accorded to the French invaders in 1690, 1703 and 1742. But the aristocracy of Savoy nevertheless remained a powerful class, enjoying unchallenged supremacy within the duchy. A survey taken in 1702 counted 795 families of noble rank, or roughly 3,400 persons – just over 1 percent of the population of the duchy – but this restricted group enjoyed about 17 percent of the landed wealth. Within this class a small élite numbering only 22 percent of the whole aristocracy controlled more than two-thirds of the landed wealth of the class as a whole; on the other hand about a third of all the nobles were relatively poorly off, owning less than a hundred hectares of land.[17] Taken as a whole, despite the disparities within its ranks, the aristocracy of Savoy wielded vast power and influence, and dominated the social edifice. So although the nobles might grumble at the slights inflicted on them by Victor Amadeus's officials – who were almost always Piedmontese – they could not detach themselves from the structure of royal authority that sustained them and guaranteed their ascendancy. And Victor Amadeus could not afford to antagonize them too deeply, for fear of their power as a class. His reforming policies, anti-aristocratic though they undoubtedly were, in the end had to accommodate themselves to the social and political realities of the duchy.

The nobles of Savoy, besides encompassing wide differences of wealth and status, exhibited corresponding variations of political outlook. The greatest families, with an easy entrée to the court at Turin, and a certain cosmopolitanism of mind, aspired to careers in government or diplomacy; the rustic *hobereaux*, on the other hand, rarely left their farms and lived within very narrow political horizons. A superficial unity was conferred on the nobility as a group by their readiness to choose a military career:

about half of them in 1701 had served or were serving as soldiers, most frequently in the duke's army, but also under foreign colours, usually those of France. But this common pursuit of a military vocation cannot conceal the fact that the nobility was a heterogeneous class. Many nobles were of comparatively recent vintage: of those whose origins can be traced with certainty, about 54 percent in 1700 had only acquired their titles since the mid-sixteenth century.[18] The newer families had usually risen through magistracies and government offices in a wave of social advancement that seems to have peaked about 1640, followed by a period of consolidation and stasis: in the later seventeenth century the aristocracy of Savoy became more like a closed caste, no longer recruiting itself from below.

The nobility was closely intertwined with the high magistracies of the duchy, and several of the most distinguished noble houses pursued careers in the judiciary, generation after generation: the Costa, Lescheraine, Milliet and others. Savoy possessed two sovereign courts, the Senate and the Chambre des Comptes. The Senate was a judicial body, with some political and administrative functions, similar to those of a French Parlement. As we shall see in greater detail later, Victor Amadeus curbed its right of remonstrance and handed over many of its non-judicial functions to his intendants. The Chambre des Comptes, which supervised fiscal and economic policy in the duchy, adopted a more resolute stance, at times refusing to register ducal edicts and acting more overtly as the protector of privileged interests. Victor Amadeus finally abolished it in 1720, delivering another blow to the battered sensibilities of the duchy's nobles. With the Chambre des Comptes abolished and the Senate muzzled, the aristocracy of Savoy lacked a firm institutional bastion to defend it against Victor Amadeus II's reforming centralization.

The nobility of Savoy was also closely linked to the upper echelons of the clergy. For example, in the diocese of Geneva (whose bishop had resided at Annecy since the Reformation), 8.9 percent of all the clergy between 1700 and 1750 were of aristocratic origin, but in the upper and middle ranks of the clergy this proportion rose to 21 percent.[19] Although the clergy as a group held no more than 4 to 6 percent of the landed wealth of the duchy, in some places they owned significant concentrations of lands, like the estates of the archbishop of Tarentaise, or those of great abbeys like Tamié or Hautecombe. The ecclesiastical organization of the duchy remained a source of concern to Victor Amadeus II, as it had been to his predecessors, since so much of Savoy came under the jurisdiction of French prelates, the archbishop of Vienne and the bishop of Grenoble. French influence made itself felt in the numbers of French clerics appointed to benefices in Savoy, and in the close conformity of the local church to Gallican usages. As a rule the clergy obeyed its sovereign docilely enough, for instance in the Jansenist controversy after 1713, or during Victor

Amadeus's long jurisdictional dispute with the Papacy. The only clash came over the issue of taxation. In 1721 the clergy of Savoy were forced to pay a special levy to combat the plague spreading from Marseille, despite their outraged protests. Subsequently the cadastral survey begun in 1728 disallowed a number of tax exemptions formerly enjoyed by the clergy, for clerical immunities were as much a target of Victor Amadeus II's fiscal reforms as were the more extensive noble exemptions. In a general way he pursued a similar policy in his dealings with all the privileged orders in Savoy: while limiting their power and curbing their fiscal exemptions, he preserved their structures intact, for they were indispensable props for his rule.

One reason for Victor Amadeus's relative circumspection in dealing with the clergy in Savoy was his knowledge of the wide respect and popularity that they commanded. The religious vitality infused by the Counter Reformation was still a powerful social force. Savoy was after all the country of Saint François de Sales and Sainte Jeanne de Chantal, who personified the movement of spiritual and institutional renewal, not merely within the confines of the duchy, but throughout Catholic Europe. Furthermore, the proximity of Geneva was a constant admonition to the clergy of Savoy: with the Protestant Rome on their doorsteps they could not afford to relax. In the mid-sixteenth century, following the loss of Geneva, some northern districts had embraced Protestantism. But already by about 1580, and certainly by 1600, there were clear signs of renewal within the church in Savoy: Saint François de Sales and a host of other missionaries re-Catholicized the areas lost to Protestantism; reforming bishops enforced the decrees of the council of Trent; benefices were no longer monopolized by scions of the local nobility; the duties of residence were enforced; pluralism and nepotism were curbed. Seminaries raised the moral and intellectual level of the clergy, and a growing number of clerically run schools and colleges provided for the education of pious laymen. By the later seventeenth century virtually every parish was regularly served either by its own curate or vicar or by peripatetic priests who ministered to several scattered mountain villages together. The clergy seem to have been relatively numerous – in Tarentaise, for instance, there was roughly one priest for every 220 inhabitants, and when we include the monastic clergy the proportion becomes even more impressive.[20]

The most obvious indication of the continuing effects of these ecclesiastical reforms was a remarkable level of popular devotion, revealed in concrete form by a wave of church-building and decoration that reached its peak in the late seventeenth and early eighteenth centuries. Archbishop Milliet de Challes of Tarentaise was a great builder and rebuilder of churches throughout his diocese; during his long episcopate (1659–1703) he consecrated no less than thirty-three new or reconstructed churches. The chief glory of these churches lies in the decoration commissioned by the parishioners: retables and altars of sculptured wood, vigorous statues and crucifixes, a true popular art, deriving from baroque prototypes, but rendered in a vernacular mode by local craftsmen. Its vigour and vitality attest to a popular piety deeply rooted in the everyday life of the local community. Other manifestations of popular devotion are to be found in the spread of confraternities and pious foundations, and in the staging of mystery plays by certain villages, usually in the mountains where the vogue for decorated churches was also strongest. The people's year was punctuated by the feasts of the church, by processions and banquets organized by the confraternities, accompanied by a distribution of alms and food to the poor. Although the fervour of these processions never reached the levels attained at Nice in 1716, when crowds of Flagellants stirred up by Jesuit preachers had to be dispersed by force, they attested to the strength of popular piety in Savoy and the enormous influence wielded by the church at all levels of society.

For the duchy of Savoy the reign of Victor Amadeus marks a critical period of historical development. The long French occupations between 1690 and 1713 were succeeded by a sustained spurt of growth in the power of the state that affected every segment of the duchy's population, privileged and non-privileged alike. The force of the royal will accelerated a process of administrative centralization that had been under way for most of the seventeenth century, and now began to affect the traditional balance of forces within society. The resurgence of seigneurial authority was met and countered by a powerful thrust of state power which effectively contained it; the privileged orders were bound more closely than ever to the machinery of the state, and subjected to greater control. The mass of peasant society, hitherto largely untouched by the state, began to feel increasing fiscal and administrative pressures as the intendants interposed themselves between the seigneurs and the communities, saw to the collection of taxes and took charge of village administration. The entire relationship between the duchy and the government at Turin was being restructured. One consequence was to turn the duchy, like the rest of Victor Amadeus II's domains, into one of the most efficiently run states in Europe, where the central government's writ ran even at the lowest levels of political activity. And the way was opened for the continuance of reforming activity under Victor Amadeus's successors, in a way hardly equalled elsewhere in Europe at the time. But the deeper imprint of the central authority, and the harsher side to its reformist zeal, left scars. While Victor Amadeus's reforms tightened the administrative links that integrated the duchy into the rest of the state, they also alarmed and alienated many members of the privileged orders, estranging them psychologically and feeding their particularist sentiments.

THE DUCHY OF AOSTA

If there was an undercurrent of particularist sentiment in the duchy of Savoy, it was even more ingrained and obtrusive in the Val d'Aosta across the Alps to the east. Of all the territories that made up the Savoyard state, the Valley had most successfully preserved its own institutions, and in many ways it was still, even in the early eighteenth century, a kind of fossilized specimen of medieval autonomy. Alone among the Savoyard domains it still possessed a functioning representative assembly, the Estates, which met every five years to vote taxes. In the intervals between meetings of the Estates, it was administered by a small committee of the assembly, the Conseil des Commis. The Valley formed a self-contained diocese under its own bishop who resided at Aosta, the capital and the only town of any consequence. A high court, the Cour des Connaissances, judged all cases in first instance: its right to judge all cases within the Valley was jealously guarded by the Conseil des Commis against the pretensions of the Senates of Piedmont and Savoy.

Particularist feeling in the duchy of Aosta was hallowed by centuries of tradition and grounded in a firm foundation of local institutions. It is no accident therefore that it should have produced the most articulate and tenacious upholder of local autonomy against the centralizing tendencies of Victor Amadeus II's government: Jean-Baptiste de Tillier, secretary of the Conseil des Commis from 1700 until his death in 1744, tireless delver in the local archives, erudite, using the power of his office and his unequalled knowledge of local laws and traditions to fashion an eloquent defence of the Valley's liberties against the intrusion of the state. For Tillier, the duchy of Aosta was a political unit entire and of itself, neither *ultra montes* and thus dependent on the duchy of Savoy, nor *citra montes* and forming part of Piedmont: it was *intra montes*, a region defined by nature and geography for autonomy. 'The duchy of Aosta has always been a state, forming a single undivided body. The seventy-eight church-towers, or rather the cities, towns, parishes and separate communities which exist in the Valley, are the members of this state.'[21] To call it a 'state' in this way had far-reaching implications: Tillier argued that it had existed as a political entity long before the Savoyards acquired it, and that it had given itself voluntarily to them in a free act of *dédition*. The corollary of this was of critical importance: by the terms of the *dédition*, the Savoyards were obliged to respect and uphold the Valley's liberties. Tillier was in fact putting forward, with proofs adduced from the local history he knew so well, a theory of contractual sovereignty in direct opposition to the concept of absolutism that Victor Amadeus and his ministers were imposing on the state. For Tillier, royal power was strictly circumscribed by the traditional rights of established orders and institutions, and by the liberties of the different territories that comprised the state. It is hardly surprising therefore that the government did its best to suppress his writings, which remained almost unknown until the late nineteenth century.

Tillier's work illustrates in the sharpest way a tendency discernible to a lesser degree in Savoy. Particularist sentiment was inseparable from aristocratic privilege; local liberties and personal liberties were part and parcel of the same system. An attack on either was an attack on both. The institutions that enshrined local autonomy were staffed by members of the privileged orders, and functioned as the front line of defence against the inroads of state power. To defend the Conseil des Commis and the Estates of the Val d'Aosta, as Tillier did, was also to defend the monopoly of political power enjoyed by his own class and exercised through these very institutions. To allow the agents of the state to dismantle the Valley's ancient system of government would be to admit them to the citadel of local power and open the way for them to modify the hierarchical organization of society, as they were beginning to do in Savoy. Some of Victor Amadeus II's officials saw this just as clearly as did Tillier. The *vibailli* of Aosta, Grésy, reported in 1722 that the privileged classes shifted the whole burden of taxation on to the peasants. Privilege had been abused. The organs of local government, monopolized as they were by the nobility, had become an obstacle to efficient administration. 'This country was formerly very badly governed, though they say that it governed itself well. . . .'[22] Here the battle-lines were sharply drawn between two conflicting views of what constituted 'good government': the régime of local and caste privilege, enshrined in the institutions of the Valley and so fervently defended by Tillier, and Savoyard absolutism with its constant search for more effective ways to tap the state's fiscal resources, and thereby to undermine privilege.

The duchy of Aosta was thus a point of extreme tension between the forces of local particularism and reforming centralization. Here the opposition to Victor Amadeus II's restructuring of the state manifested itself in its most obvious form. But the resolution of this tension would not come for another generation or so: Victor Amadeus left the institutions of the Valley much as they were. The officials whom he appointed to run it along with the Conseil des Commis might draw attention to the manifold problems stemming from an archaic system of local and aristocratic privilege, but the king himself was content merely to raise larger revenues by vote of the Estates, and the duchy of Aosta was left out of the general scheme of reform that so profoundly affected the other parts of the state. Victor Amadeus sent no intendants to the Valley. The cadastral survey that restructured the land tax in the county of Nice, in Piedmont and in Savoy was not extended to Aosta until 1767. The Estates continued to function until 1766; the Conseil des Commis outlived Tillier, lasting until 1758; the first reform of the communal administrations came only in 1762. The pattern of reform in the rest of the state operated by a kind of delayed action in the Val d'Aosta, an aftershock that completed the massive upheavals of Victor Amadeus II's reign.

The duchy of Aosta was thus an anomaly within the emerging system of centralized power that Victor Amadeus had constructed by 1730. The most likely reason for this is the combination of small fiscal rewards and great difficulties that would have faced the king if he had sought to impose a more centralized system of government there. Later on, it would be a different story. By the end of Tillier's life, as he himself sadly admitted, the vitality had gone out of the Valley's peculiar institutions; the Estates barely functioned, and the Conseil des Commis was felt to be irrelevant. By the 1760s these institutions could safely be abolished, for they had essentially collapsed of their own weight. But in the earlier part of the century they were still vital enough to put up a good fight, so with typical pragmatism Victor Amadeus remained content to use the existing system of local government, with all its contradictions and inequities, to squeeze whatever he could out of an inelastic tax-base.

The Val d'Aosta was more effectively isolated from contact with the outside world than any of the other Savoyard domains. Even today it is a region apart, encircled by a ring of mountains that includes some of the highest peaks in the entire Alpine chain. Communication with Piedmont and Savoy was restricted to two routes. The Little Saint Bernard pass led from the western end of the Val d'Aosta into the upper valley of the Isère in Tarentaise. Once a highway of considerable importance, the Little Saint Bernard was by the seventeenth century only a minor route; most traffic passed over the Simplon to the east or the Mont-Cénis and Mont-Genèvre to the south. A more significant route crossed the northern rim of the Valley via the Great Saint Bernard; here a certain volume of traffic passed between Aosta and the Swiss Cantons, for economically the duchy was more closely linked to them than to either Piedmont or Savoy. By this route the merchants of Aosta transported Piedmontese rice, wine and livestock to the Cantons. The one link to Piedmont was via the only real gap in the girdle of mountains that surround the Valley, where the river Dora Baltea breaks through to the plain at Ivrea. Here stood a customs post where duties were levied on all goods entering or leaving the Valley; a constant source of recrimination taken up regularly by the Estates, which sought in vain to have the tariffs reduced to favour the export of the Valley's products.

Geography thus defined the duchy of Aosta as a self-contained economic and political unit. The peculiarity of its institutions and the survival of its traditional privileges were to a large degree the result of centuries of seclusion. The Valley was formed by the basin of the Dora Baltea and its tributaries, torrents springing from the surrounding mountains; its shape is an elongated saucer with steep sides. The basis of its economy was Alpine farming, with a heavy reliance on stock-rearing: in this respect it resembled the high valleys of Savoy. At some places in the mountains there were mineral deposits, which yielded some iron and copper – as at Cogne where the commune owned and exploited the iron mines – but these resources never provided any real complement to the pastoralism that formed the basis of the Valley's economy. As in the other mountain regions, population pressure was alleviated to some extent by seasonal migration. But the Valley remained desperately poor, with little possibility of economic expansion or improvement. Its population was sparse: the census conducted in 1729 revealed a total of 61,906 persons, which by 1774 had risen to 65,481. The city of Aosta itself had a population of 2,718 in 1734, rising to 5,106 forty years later.[23] The slow growth in population, the lack of urban centres and the low density – about 19 or 20 persons per square kilometre in 1729 – suggest that a limit had been reached in what the meagre resources of the Valley could be made to support.

The duchy of Aosta functioned as a separate world; its claim to constitute an independent state *intra montes*, repugnant as this might be to the government at Turin, nonetheless corresponded in a large measure to political and economic realities. Only the governor and his immediate subordinate, the *vibailli*, were appointed by the prince. From the early seventeenth century these offices had been filled by outsiders, Savoyards or Piedmontese, but the Conseil des Commis still retained a wide freedom of action. During the French invasions of 1691 and 1704 it was the Conseil that arranged terms with the conquerors, and on the outbreak of war in 1690 the Conseil had opened secret negotiations with the French to maintain the neutrality of the Valley, following a long tradition of similar actions in the past – at least since the French occupation of Piedmont and Savoy in 1536–59. And although Victor Amadeus II began to bring the Valley into the political orbit of Piedmont, linguistically and culturally it was closer to Savoy. Its language was French; this was the language in which Tillier wrote. The bishop of Aosta came under the jurisdiction of the archbishop of Tarentaise, and his diocese conformed to the Gallican usages of Savoy rather than to the ecclesiastical practices of Piedmont. Throughout Victor Amadeus II's reign therefore the Val d'Aosta remained effectively autonomous, balanced between the countervailing political attractions of Piedmont and Savoy, unassimilated by either, and largely untouched by the great movement of reforms that changed the face of the rest of the state.

THE PRINCIPALITY OF PIEDMONT

Long before Victor Amadeus II ascended the throne, Piedmont had become the vital nucleus of the Savoyard domains. Although its mountainous fringes could be as poor as the uplands of Savoy or the county of Nice, it was by far the most fertile and most populous region in the state;

it had a higher concentration of towns and cities, with a significant artisan and manufacturing economy, and important internal trade. It contained the only large city in the whole state, Turin, whose position as capital emphasized the political predominance of Piedmont. The dynasty could easily survive the loss of Savoy or Nice, but the loss of the Piedmontese provinces would have been disastrous, for they provided the bulk of the revenues and manpower that kept the state going. The Piedmontese aristocracy enjoyed an unchallenged ascendancy within the state, providing most of the personnel for the government. And the process of governmental centralization further enhanced the preponderance of Piedmont over the other regions, rendering the transalpine provinces ever more peripheral. In one sense, centralization meant the assertion of Piedmontese dominance at the expense of the other parts of the state.

Piedmont was also the springboard from which any expansion of the state would take place. Aggrandizement was only practicable to the east, in Lombardy. No territory stood to be gained to the west against the military might of France: Savoy and Nice were blind alleys, and a liability in time of war, falling easy victims to French invasion. The acquisition of a small part of Monferrato in 1631 marks the timid beginning of a process of eastward aggrandizement that would continue down to 1748 – and indeed into the nineteenth century – gradually extending the Savoyards' Italian possessions. Victor Amadeus II was therefore following an established maxim of dynastic policy when he resumed territorial expansion into Lombardy after 1690.

Piedmont's strategic value also derived from its position controlling the outlets from the main passes that traversed the western Alps. The principal route was over the Mont-Cénis, with its subsidiary the Mont-Genèvre, passing through the Val di Susa and issuing into the Piedmontese plain close to Turin. In 1631 Richelieu's acquisition of Pinerolo gave the French access to this vital route; Louis XIV's acquisition of Casale in 1681 further tightened their hold, placing Turin between two French garrisons and laying the entire Piedmontese plain open to attack. Victor Amadeus II consequently sought to oust the French from their two enclaves on the Italian side of the Alps, and to reassert undivided control over the Mont-Cénis–Mont-Genèvre route; only then, with his rear secure, could he prosecute the long-standing Savoyard ambition for expansion into the Lombard plain. But this policy, though rich with potential benefits, was also fraught with risk: Piedmont's strategic position made it a target for invasion, and between 1690 and 1706 it was constantly ravaged by French armies. Piedmont in fact became a crucial theatre in the European conflicts of the later seventeenth and early eighteenth centuries, a theatre where Louis XIV's enemies hoped to stage his downfall. As a result it suffered far more from the wars than did Victor Amadeus's transalpine possessions. Savoy and Nice fell with little resistance in 1690–1 and 1703, and though they had to bear the weight of occupation, they were spared the damage caused by protracted campaigning. Piedmont, on the other hand, paid a heavy price in lives and resources before it would make good its potential as the point of departure for territorial expansion.

At the centre of the Piedmontese plain stood Turin, straddling the chief routes of communication, north-south along the line of the Po, and east-west between Lombardy and the Mont-Cénis. The city was the strategic focus of the state, as well as its political and economic centre. Situated at the narrowest point of the upper Po valley, where the hills of Monferrato come to within about twenty kilometres of the Alps, Turin could interdict movement from north to south, while at the same time denying access to the Mont-Cénis. The city was therefore the most heavily fortified point in the entire state, the hub of a defensive ring that encompassed all the approaches to the Piedmontese plain. In the north, Vercelli and the fortress of Verrua commanded the route up the Po from Lombardy; the fort of Bard sealed the entrance to the Val d'Aosta; Susa and its citadel guarded the Mont-Cénis; to the south, Cuneo formed the principal strongpoint covering the passes into the county of Nice, while Asti and Alba controlled the routes from the south-east.

None of these places rivalled Turin in defensive strength. Since the thirteenth century the city had been the seat of the Savoyards' power on the Italian side of the Alps, and once it became the capital of their entire state in 1560, they encouraged aristocrats and officials to make it their residence, selling building sites at a nominal price or donating them to favoured courtiers and magistrates. Through the seventeenth and eighteenth centuries the Savoyards set an example of architectural patronage for the wealthy and powerful to emulate, supervising the expansion of the city according to a strict grid plan, and decorating it with palaces, churches, monasteries and public buildings – government offices, theatres, hospitals and poorhouses. The carefully maintained rectilinearity of the city's plan, and the great public buildings in a dramatic baroque style counterpointing the austerity of the urban fabric, were consciously intended to turn the city into a showplace for the régime, a concrete image of centralized order and a mirror of the prestige and magnificence to which its rulers aspired. This use of architecture and urban planning as political propaganda crystallized in the publication of a fine series of engravings of the Savoyard domains, the *Theatrum Sabaudiae*, in 1682.[24] The views of Turin in the *Theatrum* (see plate 10) reveal the intention behind it: they exaggerate the scale, the symmetry and the elegance of the city, creating an impression of controlled magnificence and almost military regularity that were far from being achieved in reality. The Savoyards also made Turin an immensely powerful fortress. Each time the city's perimeter was extended, in 1619, 1669 and finally around 1700, the fortified enceinte was strengthened, until by the time of Victor

Amadeus II's wars against France the city was protected by a formidable carapace of bastions and outworks, with a maze of subterranean counter-mines radiating out from its citadel. These defences made Turin one of the strongest places in Europe and enabled it to survive the siege of 1706.

Turin's rising importance as the capital of the state seems to have been the principal reason for its rapid growth from the later sixteenth century, as the ruling élite and their dependents were attracted to the focus of power. While other cities in Piedmont grew relatively slowly, Turin doubled in size between about 1560 and 1700, and then doubled again by the end of the eighteenth century.[25] Already in the sixteenth century Piedmont was more highly urbanized than the rest of the Savoyard state, but it was a region of small-to-middling towns, among which Turin figured merely as *primus inter pares*. By 1700, however, Turin had com-pletely outgrown the other Piedmontese towns, drawing population and wealth to itself, stunting the other urban centres and reducing them to the status of satellites. In the same way it dwarfed the other regional capitals across the Alps, or Cagliari in Sardinia when it was acquired in 1720. By the reign of Victor Amadeus II Turin was the dominant city not only of Piedmont, but of the state as a whole.

Turin's growth is attributable to economic factors, as well as to its favoured position as capital. Its original modest industrial base grew in the seventeenth century as new crafts made their appearance and older trades expanded, often with active encouragement from the state. The mainstay of the city's economy was the silk industry. Since the sixteenth century the government had helped foster silk-production, and by the later seventeenth century Piedmont was producing large quantities of high-quality spun silk, or 'organzines', some for export to the great factories of Lyon, but a growing amount to support the manufactures of silken fabrics that were springing up at Turin and elsewhere in Piedmont. The ready availability of water-power from the canals just outside the city walls encouraged the establishment of spinning-plants and manufactures of silken and woollen textiles, as well as a number of fulling-mills, ropewalks, tanneries and dyeworks. These canals also provided the motive power for trip-hammers and furnace-bellows to work iron, and the growth of a metallurgical industry in the city was stimulated by the presence of the main state arsenal, rebuilt on a much larger scale in 1659 to meet the Savoyard army's growing demand for weapons. Turin also possessed its share of luxury trades: gold- and silversmiths, weavers of cloth-of-gold and fine brocades, cabinet-makers, printers and engravers. A significant Jewish minority – 774 persons in 1702, or about 1.8 percent of the city's population, representing the largest Jewish colony in the state – con-tributed to its economic growth. Most Jews were small retailers, money-lenders and artisans, but a few were bankers, involved in transactions with the state, or prosperous wholesale merchants dealing in grain and other commodities. The city boasted a few banking houses which by the beginning of the eighteenth century commanded the capital to advance substantial loans to the government or to handle the transfer of subsidies from Victor Amadeus's allies.

The power of Turin's economy gave it a pivotal role in government finance, for the state's credit was underwritten by the municipality, in the same way that French government *rentes* were secured by the city of Paris. Government loans were raised by a special bank, the Monte, originally set up in 1653, and re-founded in 1682 under the protection of the city's patron saint, St John the Baptist. Interest on the debts contracted by the Monte was paid out of city revenues set aside for this purpose, the city in its turn being reimbursed by the government. Whenever the state required extra funds, the Monte would issue a new series of bonds at rates ranging from 4 percent in normal times to 8 percent in periods of crisis (as in 1705–6). Creditors were punctually repaid, and with the city's aid the government seemed a good credit risk, even in the tense years of war.

It remains true nonetheless that, despite the growth of Turin's economy, the city still could not rival the power of the great mercantile and industrial centres around it – Milan, Genoa, Lyon, Geneva. To a considerable extent, even in 1700, Turin and Piedmont remained dependent on these other concentrations of economic power, and particularly on France. In 1699 the English envoy Richard Hill reported that 'the merchants and shopkeepers of Turin are but the factors of those of Lyons, who furnish almost everything for these countries'. He went on to describe how Victor Amadeus's government was trying to remedy this: 'the Duke has endeavoured to set up a manufactory of cloth at Turin, and has brought several workmen from Holland and Flanders. His Highness has already spent 50,000 crowns upon this project. . . .'[26] State subsidies and protection would play a key part in Victor Amadeus's plans for economic development, for neither Turin nor Piedmont possessed a strong middle class capable of initiating and sustaining development on its own, especially in the face of competition from older established and more powerful centres abroad. Much of the stimulus for growth therefore had to come from the state. Turin's banking firms likewise depended heavily on state contracts. Until the end of the seventeenth century they took second place to French syndicates in farming the taxes, but the long wars helped to break the state's reliance on French financiers, and from the first years of the eighteenth century Turinese banking houses assumed control of the tax-farms. But the establishment of economic independence was a slow process. The government's policies helped to achieve greater self-sufficiency than before, but their success was by no means complete.

While state policy deliberately stimulated the capital's growth, it also curbed its autonomy. The city government of Turin resembled that of most other Piedmontese cities: a council, filled by co-optation, from which in turn were chosen the various executive officers, headed by two syndics. A special officer appointed by the state, the Vicario, handled many administrative matters – police, sanitation, industrial regulation and so on. During the seventeenth century the central government seems to have assumed a greater share in municipal decision-making, and this erosion of municipal autonomy was also evident in other spheres. Whereas in the sixteenth century architecture, planning and construction had been largely the city's own affair, in the seventeenth century such decisions were being made by the ruler. The duke rather than the city council regulated the expansion of the city, exercising his control in person or through a committee of architects and military engineers, the Congresso delle Fabbriche e Fortificazioni, originally set up in the 1630s to supervise architecture and fortification throughout the state. And behind the curtailment of Turin's autonomy – as in the other communities and municipalities throughout the state – loomed the lengthening shadow of debt. Successive crises – plague, famine, war – had burdened the city's finances during the seventeenth century, and to these were added the increasing fiscal exigencies of the state. Debt made the municipality depend more and more on the central government and its treasury. Nor was the city's commercial and manufacturing sector powerful enough to form the base for real municipal autonomy; as we have seen, much of Turin's economic development was sponsored by the government, and remained tied to it. The guilds were weak and unassertive, functioning mainly as a mechanism for economic regulation. In 1687 Victor Amadeus undertook a sweeping reform of both the guilds and the municipal council. The guild statutes were rewritten; the city council's composition was strictly defined, and the executive officers chosen from it were made subject to ducal approval. Later reforms would further reinforce government control and the tendency to oligarchy, until by the late eighteenth century municipal autonomy was little more than a name.

Although Turin represented the greatest concentration of economic strength in Piedmont, it was by no means the only centre of trade and manufacture. The silk-spinning industry was widely distributed throughout the region, often in the countryside, where water power and wood for fuel were more readily available. Most towns had a plant or two to spin locally produced cocoons into thread. The small town of Racconigi was the largest centre of silk-spinning in Piedmont, with far more machines than Turin: it benefited from the patronage of the princes of Carignano (a collateral branch of the Savoyard house), who helped set up the factories. By 1708 the town's silk-spinning machines already employed 2,525 workers – a far larger number than at Turin – out of a total of 6,990 workers in 378 plants throughout Piedmont.[27] New silk-spinning works were frequently set up; in 1685, for instance, at Cuneo, where a local chronicler noted that 'it proved of great utility to the poor people of the

city, who now to the number of several hundred had the means to earn
their bread, for which formerly they had had to go begging, blushingly,
with their daughters in no small danger of losing their virtue'.[28] At
Pinerolo silk-spinning plants were established in 1702 and 1713, with the
support of the municipality, and powered by water from the local canal.
The government also worked to build up a silk-weaving industry, in
order to reduce imports of French silks, and create employment. A state
manufacture of silken cloth had been set up just outside Turin at Venaria
Reale in 1671; by the time its privileges were renewed in 1680 it was
equipped with 50 looms. Victor Amadeus would lavish especial care on
this industry, granting privileges to craftsmen and entrepreneurs who
introduced new techniques or improved existing processes. The government also paid close attention to the silk-dyeing industry, and subsidized
and protected the manufacture of luxury textiles made from a mixture of
silk and gold or silver thread.

Piedmont also possessed an extensive woollen industry which had been
in existence for centuries and had in some places reached a high level of
efficiency, particularly in the district around Biella in the north. By the
early eighteenth century the industry there, much of it dispersed in the
nearby mountain villages, was producing an impressive quantity of cloth,
some of high quality. Here an important textile industry – more significant than that of the capital – had appeared spontaneously, benefiting from
local conditions, notably the large pool of labour in the overpopulated
mountain region. It was largely run on a putting-out system, by local
entrepreneurs who furnished capital and materials, marketed the finished
product, and had an eye for technological improvements. The geo-
graphical distribution of the woollen industry in the rest of the state
followed the same general pattern as in the Biellese, being more evident
in the mountainous provinces of Ivrea, Susa and Pinerolo, where the
population depended upon rural industry to supplement their meagre
agricultural resources. For the most part this led to a characteristically
decentralized structure, with small family workshops predominating,
usually with one or two looms.

A different type of textile industry was the cotton and fustian manufacture of Chieri, which had achieved greater concentration under the
control of the town's guild of merchant clothmakers. Until 1713 they
enjoyed a monopoly in the production of cottons, and had the sole right,
reaffirmed by the government in 1686, to buy the finished cloth from the
artisans who wove it. The industry operated on the putting-out system,
spinning and weaving being performed by a labour force in Chieri itself
and its surrounding villages. Cotton production however was a small,
specialized industry compared to the production of hemp and canvas.
Most production was still at a household level, but there was a tendency
towards concentration and specialization; statistics for the period 1716–9

show that Carmagnola was by far the most important centre for the production of hemp with Carignano and Savigliano as distant competitors.

The Alpine regions of Piedmont provided deposits of various ores – iron, copper, lead, and even small veins of gold and silver – but mining and metallurgy formed only a small element in the economy of the region as a whole. There were few large, productive mines: most were small, undercapitalized and worked by relatively primitive methods, and operations were limited by a growing shortage of timber for fuel, as the forests were depleted by neglect and abuse. The government attempted to make the state self-sufficient in metals, by granting concessions to individuals, or by founding companies to prospect and exploit mineral resources. A number of metallurgical enterprises were headed by members of the nobility, who were in a good position to raise the large amounts of capital needed, and who claimed the right to operate trip-hammers as a feudal privilege. The conte di Scarnafigi, for instance, owned iron-foundries in the area around Mondovì, while the marchese del Borgo was proprietor of others in the mountains near Saluzzo. But Piedmont never produced enough metals to meet its own needs, and in the middle of the eighteenth century was still importing roughly three-quarters of its annual requirements. In the later seventeenth century the production of iron was concentrated mainly in the provinces of Ivrea, Biella and Saluzzo, while a large number of furnaces and trip-hammers was also to be found in the province of Turin, stimulated by demand from the capital, and by a spillover effect from the state foundries and arms factories there.

Yet despite these incipient industrial concentrations, the economy of Piedmont remained overwhelmingly agrarian and rural. Land was by far the most important source of wealth, and the vast majority of the population were farmers: even in the mid-eighteenth century only about 12 or 13 percent of the Piedmontese population lived in towns, and in the late seventeenth century this percentage was undoubtedly lower still. The preponderance of the land is illustrated in a schematic analysis of the Piedmontese economy in the early eighteenth century conducted by Luigi Einaudi, who assessed the weight of its different sectors like this:

Income from land	42,769,625 lire p.a.
Income from buildings and city property	2,000,000
Income from trade and manufacture	5,892,000
Total	50,661,625 lire p.a.

Such estimates are at best approximate, but they indicate that, in round figures, agriculture generated more than four-fifths of the total wealth.[29]

Figures for the population of Piedmont are hard to ascertain before the census of 1734, the first to be conducted with any degree of statistical rigour, and current estimates vary widely.[30] Between the 1620s and 1650s the population declined under the impact of plague, war and economic depression, recovering thereafter until in the 1690s another cycle of war and famine wrought fresh havoc. Sustained growth seems to have resumed only after the passing of the great famine of 1708–9 and the end of the War of the Spanish Succession. One authority (S. J. Woolf) suggests that the population of Piedmont in 1700 may not have numbered more than 700–800,000, which is fairly close to the estimate of G. Prato (800,000) but appreciably lower than that of K. J. Beloch who places the total at 950,000. With the census of 1734 we are on firmer ground: it gives a figure of 1,075,318 for the original Piedmontese territories, excluding those conquered in the War of the Spanish Succession, which bring the total up to 1,377,670. This population was far denser than that of the duchy of Savoy or the county of Nice. In 1700 the principality of Piedmont measured about 16,500 square kilometres in extent. Victor Amadeus II's conquests in Lombardy and along the Alps added another 4,700 or 4,800 square kilometres, so that by the end of the reign his Italian domains totalled roughly 21,300 square kilometres in area. Using the 1734 census figures, this gives an average density of about 64–65 persons per square kilometre for the Piedmontese territories. An aggregate figure like this, however, conceals wide differences in the density of population from province to province, due in large part to divergences in the level of agricultural productivity.[31] The most sparsely populated provinces were the marshy regions of Vercelli and the Lomellina – the latter conquered in 1707 – or mountainous areas like the Val Sesia or the Val di Susa. But not all mountain regions were thinly settled: the province of Biella was the most densely populated province of all, largely because of its rural textile industry. This diversified economic base permitted some mountain communities to maintain a high degree of internal cohesion, despite the high mobility of much of their male population. Families kept a foothold on the land, working partly as small farmers even when they also engaged in household textile-weaving or migrant labour – the Biellese region was famous for its skilled masons who travelled widely in search of work. The tendency to hold on to a small farm helped to anchor a population which in other respects was becoming increasingly dependent on non-agricultural labour. The same pattern of migrant work and rural industry probably helps to account for the high density of population in the adjoining province of Ivrea, much of which was also barren and mountainous.

The agricultural heartland of Piedmont was formed by the fertile plains of the Po valley, stretching northwards from the province of Cuneo through the central region around Turin as far as the Vercellese and the border with Lombardy, and embracing the foothill regions of Monferrato, eastwards as far as Alessandria and south to Alba. Here the dominant crop was cereals, giving way in the hill-country to vines; the region was destined to become one of the great wine-producing areas of Italy. Wine formed the most important cash crop, while cereal production generally took the form of subsistence farming. Although Piedmont produced enough grain to feed its cities in a normal year, as in Savoy, the over-bearing need for grain to meet the farmers' immediate needs led to over-cropping and the cultivation of marginal lands, with a correspondingly low yield. In view of the marginal nature of agriculture in much of Pied-mont, Victor Amadeus's conquest of territory in Monferrato and Lombardy represented an important addition to the agrarian resources of the state.

Cereal yields were low, in part because of primitive techniques and inefficient systems of rotation, but also for lack of fertilizer and irrigation. The Piedmontese plain is well watered by the run-off from the Alps, and since the Middle Ages a system of canals had developed, notably in the regions around Vercelli and Saluzzo. Nevertheless in the late seventeenth and early eighteenth centuries most of the plain was still unirrigated. The hill country of Monferrato in particular suffered from drought, for it lacked substantial rivers and could not draw on the water from the Alps. The Alpine foothills to the west, on the other hand, were plagued by erosion and flooding, since the local communities were too poor to con-struct dykes. In 1728, for example, floods devastated farmland around Pinerolo and in the Val di Susa. Much of the course of the Po itself lacked dykes, and the river meandered, often overflowing its bed.

The abundance of water from the mountains turned much of the pro-vince of Vercelli into a region of stagnant ponds and marshes, interspersed with large tracts of scrub. Here conditions favoured the cultivation of a special crop: rice.[32] Originally introduced about the middle of the fifteenth century, in Victor Amadeus's reign it was still being produced by the old methods. Marshy land was sown in the spring, and the rice was left to grow almost untended until harvest time. (The vast canals and rice-paddies characteristic of the region today, and the intensive tending of the rice crop by a large labour force, were developments of the nine-teenth century.) In 1710 about 7 percent of the province of Vercelli was given over to rice: by 1800 this proportion had risen to 26 percent. The spread of the rice-fields engendered malaria, and from the sixteenth century the government sought to banish rice cultivation from the vicinity of the towns, but under pressure from the owners of rice-fields it had gradually reduced the statutory distance. In 1728 an edict, summing up the previous legislation, permitted the cultivation of rice outside a radius of four miles from any town. Specialization in rice cultivation was a consequence of the low density of population and peculiar topography of the Vercellese, and led to the development of the most advanced form of capitalist agriculture in the state. Rice would grow on soggy land unsuited to other crops, and required only a minimum of labour, performed by migrant workers; it constituted a cash-crop of increasing importance, which enriched the large landowners of the region. Because the province was so sparsely populated, periodic attempts were made to colonize it during the reign of Victor Amadeus: in 1687, as we shall see, over a thousand converted Vaudois were forcibly settled there, and in 1699 it was the turn of 564 rebel families exiled from the district of Mondovì. Neither of these endeavours prospered. The Vaudois pined away or escaped, and the Monregalesi were allowed to return home after a few years. A different venture in 1700, pioneered by the Swiss colonel Redingh, who tried to settle his soldiers and their families on land assigned to them by the government, was obstructed by the local villagers and foundered during the turmoil of the War of the Spanish Succession.

In the province of Vercelli the shortage of labour therefore remained a serious obstacle to agricultural development. In certain other provinces of Piedmont, however, the reverse was true, for the population exceeded the level that the existing agricultural techniques and organization of production could support. To some extent this was because the land itself was not fully utilized. As late as 1750 a survey revealed that about one-quarter of the land in Piedmont served merely as rough pasture, or was waste, and in many regions the arable lay fallow for extended periods. Under-utilization of the land seems to have occurred most frequently where big estates predominated; where small peasant ownership was the rule – as in the Alpine foothills – cultivation was more intensive. But demographic pressure on the land was increasing everywhere, and as demand rose, the price of land increased; a government analysis of land sales between 1680 and 1718 showed a general increase in prices, which would continue steadily through the coming century.[33] Increasing demand allowed landowners to raise rents and grant leases on less advantageous terms. Indirect evidence of mounting demographic pressure is also provided by the steady destruction of the forests. Already in the later seventeenth century the government was concerned about the shortage of wood for fuel, and the consequent rise in its price. A number of surveys were made of the forests, and in 1729 a comprehensive edict laid down rules for their conservation, summarizing earlier enactments, in order to assure the supply of fuel and building timber, and combat erosion. But this failed to halt the inexorable process of deforestation; as in Savoy and the county of Nice, a growing human and animal population was making massive inroads into the woodlands.

Forms of land tenure varied widely from one region to another in Piedmont. The last vestiges of serfdom had disappeared in the sixteenth century, and the peasants farmed the land as leaseholders or sharecroppers. Small peasant holdings predominated in the uplands. The high mountain villages, like their counterparts in Nice or Savoy, were still largely self-sufficient, living by pastoralism or subsistence farming – in which the cultivation of chestnuts often provided the staple food – and frequently possessing vast communal lands, used chiefly for pasture. But the foundations of these self-contained mountain economies were being sapped by fiscal pressure from the state and by the development of closer ties with the more advanced economy of the plains. The effects of this transformation were revealed most dramatically in the revolts that convulsed the district of Mondovì in the 1680s and 1690s. In the plains large estates were more common, although peasant proprietors survived in many places. Some estates were cultivated by a nucleus of permanent workers, supplemented by casual labour at certain times of the year, but most were too fragmented for this type of organization; it was more efficient to lease them out to tenant-farmers or sharecroppers, often under the direction of a factor responsible to the lord. Leaseholds were generally for a period of nine years, while sharecropping contracts were customarily for three or six years, with the lord providing the farm buildings, tools and seed, and taking one-third or half the crop. Leaseholders generally paid part of their rent in kind, so that in many ways renting and sharecropping tenures were similar.

A recent study of the fortunes of three great landowning families emphasizes the diversity of conditions in different parts of Piedmont, and the wide disparity of wealth within the nobility as a class.[34] One of these families, the Falletti di Barolo, with lands mainly in the south-east of Piedmont, steadily extended their holdings during the troubled years from the late seventeenth to the early eighteenth centuries, and diversified their investments by making large loans to impoverished rural communities. The rise in their fortunes was made manifest in their purchase of feudal titles and was crowned by the building of a great palace in Turin, begun in the 1690s. Another family, the Paesana of Saluzzo, likewise profited from the upheavals of the seventeenth century to acquire more land and extend their power over neighbouring communities through large loans. They too celebrated their ascent by building on a grand scale, but too ambitiously: the cost of their palazzo – the largest private building in Turin – finally ruined them. The upward trajectory of these two families was not necessarily typical for the nobility as a whole: the Valperga di Rivara grew poorer through this period and had to sell off most of their lands. The different branches of the Radicati clan, one of which produced the philosopher Alberto Radicati di Passerano, varied widely in their wealth. This impression of wide diversity within the Piedmontese nobility is corroborated by an inquiry conducted in 1734 for the levying of a capitation tax, which revealed the existence of a small élite of very wealthy nobles; a total of fourteen fiefs were worth over 200,000 lire a year each, and the richest of all, the marchese del Pozzo's fief of Vettigne, brought in no less than 500,000 lire a year. This élite was, however, counterbalanced by a sizeable stratum of relatively impecunious nobles, and by a middling group of several score families with incomes of over 10,000 lire per annum.[35]

Despite its heterogeneity, the nobility clearly dominated Piedmontese society. Great power and prestige still attached to feudal titles, and they were eagerly sought after. Infeudation, which we have already observed in the county of Nice, was common in seventeenth-century Piedmont too, until Victor Amadeus discontinued the sale of fiefs just after 1700. Only ancient fiefs, however, carried legal and political jurisdiction; new titles did not, for the state was careful not to alienate such powers. The main advantage offered by the purchase of feudal rights was immunity from taxation: strictly speaking, this exemption would take effect only fifty years after the creation of the fief, to prevent the tax-burden from being shifted immediately onto the rest of the district, but in practice exemptions were claimed from the start. Feudal dues brought in a certain income, but the value of a fief was chiefly honorific – the indefinable aura of prestige and authority that went with possession of a feudal title. Aristocratic families sought to preserve their patrimonies from generation to generation, and to prevent their dispersion, by the legal device of entailment, or *fedecommesso*. This formed a potent instrument for the conservation of a family's wealth, and for the maintenance of the social and political ascendancy of the nobility as a whole; Victor Amadeus II would take a first tentative step towards weakening it in the new law code of 1723.

The actual proportion of land owned by the Piedmontese nobility and clergy was fairly modest when compared to the proportion in certain other Italian states – in the kingdom of Naples, for instance, the barons alone controlled about one-third of the land. But the proportion was still impressive, and it assured the political and social preponderance of the privileged classes. It has been estimated that around 1700 approximately 10 percent of all income from land in Piedmont went to the aristocracy, and 20 percent to the Church. The nobility comprised about 3,000 families, or roughly 15,000 people, while the clergy numbered perhaps 20,000 persons all told. Three or 4 percent of the population of Piedmont therefore controlled close to one-third of the landed wealth.[36] Much of this land, moreover, paid no taxes: fiefs and certain categories of ecclesiastical property enjoyed legal immunity from taxation, and in many cases the other – supposedly tax-paying – lands belonging to the clergy or the nobility benefited from spurious exemptions. Fraudulent immunities had multiplied during the troubled years of the seventeenth century, further increasing the wealth of the privileged orders, at the same time as the shrewder or more fortunate landowners, both noble and clerical, had profited from the effects of war and natural catastrophes to extend their holdings at the expense of the smaller farmers.

The dominance of the privileged orders is confirmed by statistics for landownership in the province of Vercelli – the only area so far studied systematically.[37] The province is not completely typical, since latifundism was more general here than in the rest of Piedmont. About 1700 the land was distributed like this:

Common lands	13.2 percent
Small proprietors (less than 10 *giornate* each)	7.9 percent
Medium proprietors (10–1000 *giornate* each)	21.6 percent
Big proprietors (over 100 *giornate* each)	57.3 percent

In general, the nobility owned perhaps one-quarter of the land in the Vercellese, the clergy one-third. The predominance of great estates is further emphasized by the fact that a group of only nineteen owners controlled a quarter of the entire landed area of the province. Concentration into larger and larger estates would go on through the eighteenth century, and it is significant that among the biggest landowners there are no members of the middle class: in the Vercellese the biggest properties were a clerical and noble monopoly.

In the present fragmentary state of research it is impossible to say whether Piedmont witnessed a wave of resurgent seigneurialism like that discerned by Jean Nicolas in Savoy at the end of the seventeenth century, although the evidence from the Vercellese seems to point in the same direction. But it seems clear that the economic dislocation caused by war and subsistence crises after 1690 impoverished many communities and ruined many small proprietors, enhancing the power of the bigger landowners, as the wars and economic crises of the early seventeenth century had done. And in any case, even if we cannot assume that a 'seigneurial reaction' was taking place, the wealth and power of the privileged orders in Piedmont constituted a problem of the first magnitude for Victor Amadeus II. It thus becomes easier to understand why his policy concentrated to such a degree on curbing the power of the clergy and nobility, and on rooting out the illicit fiscal exemptions that they claimed. The growth of intrusive state authority, and the fundamentally anti-aristocratic direction of his policy which so alarmed the nobles of Savoy, was felt just as banefully by the privileged orders in Piedmont. Victor Amadeus II's reforms thus accomplished a crucial social, economic and political transformation, grounding the central authority on a firmer economic base, and extending its wealth and power at the expense of the only rivals that could challenge it.

III
The Institutions of Government

The various territories forming the Savoyard state were held together by a system of institutions that were becoming progressively more uniform and centralized in the course of the seventeenth century. Victor Amadeus II's administrative reforms thus continued a process that had long been in motion, as regional distinctions were broken down, and unified direction was imposed from the capital. Nevertheless important regional differences persisted; the most obvious divergences were to be found between the institutions of Savoy and Piedmont, while the county of Nice conformed more to Piedmontese practice, and the duchy of Aosta remained a political anomaly outside the mainstream of state development. And although a century of expansion in the state administration had tended to concentrate power at Turin, the regional capitals still maintained considerable local influence.

The imposition of central control from Turin faced fresh difficulties as a result of the conquest of territory in Lombardy after 1707, and the acquisition of Sardinia in 1720. The assimilation of the Lombard lands, with their different legal and fiscal institutions, was not completed in Victor Amadeus II's reign, while the absorption of Sardinia was hardly begun until the middle of the eighteenth century. Despite the very definite centralizing tendency of Victor Amadeus's policies, and the success that they undoubtedly achieved, a pattern of underlying regional differences persisted in the institutions of the Savoyard state.

At the lowest level of local government, however, a certain uniformity had always prevailed. For the village community in Piedmont or Savoy, the Val d'Aosta or the county of Nice, government was represented by the local castellan. This office dated from the twelfth century and had originally been mainly concerned with the administration of the rulers' demesne lands. But with the virtual disappearance of the ducal demesne the position of castellan had declined in importance; once a prize for the local nobility, by Victor Amadeus's time the office had become the preserve of local notaries. The castellans saw to the execution of the government's instructions and cooperated with the syndics of the communities, always being present at meetings of the village assemblies. The communal organization of the village did not really constitute a part of the state's administrative structure. It had evolved separately and spontaneously, long before anything like a state mechanism appeared in the high Middle Ages, and was only now being transformed (as Gabriel Pérouse noted in Savoy) into an administrative and fiscal unit serving the central government. Until the seventeenth century the castellans functioned as the liaison between the ruler and the local community, but from about 1620 this began to change; first – as we shall see – with the creation of the provincial *direttori* or *referendarii*, and then with the arrival of the intendants. The castellany however remained the basic district of local government, and a group of castellanies together formed a wider administrative area under the direction of a bailiff, whose office dated from the thirteenth century but who – like the castellan – had now declined in importance.

Justice at the local level was in the hands of judges appointed sometimes by the ruler (in the rare instances where a locality still formed part of the Crown lands) but usually by the local seigneur. They judged only minor cases; more serious matters were referred to the higher courts. The appointment of seigneurial judges had to be approved by the Senate under whose jurisdiction they came, and their conduct was subject to review by state-appointed provincial judges. In Savoy each province had a *juge-mage*, with his assistant, and an *avocat fiscal* who watched over the state's interests. In Piedmont the provincial justices were known as *prefetti*, instituted in 1560 and reorganized in the 1620s. By then each of the six provinces of Savoy, plus the *bailliages* of Ternier and Gaillard, had its *juge-mage*, while Piedmont was divided into twelve *prefetture*, with Nice and the duchy of Aosta forming two more. The provincial *juges-mages* and *prefetti* in turn came under the authority of the Senates of Turin, Chambéry or Nice.

The Senates constituted the supreme judicial authority – save in the few cases where their decisions could be appealed to the Crown – and acted under the direction of the Chancellor. Together with the other sovereign courts, the Chambre des Comptes at Chambéry and the Camera dei Conti at Turin, which dealt with fiscal matters, the Senates exercised a wide variety of administrative powers, in addition to their judicial functions. They also registered the laws issued by the ruler and enjoyed the right to remonstrate if they believed that these contravened established legal practice or the fundamental laws of the state, acting for most of the seventeenth century as a limited restraint on the sovereign's authority. The sovereign courts were the most venerable institutions in the state, deriving from the old *curia* of the counts of Savoy, which had fixed its residence at Chambéry in the later thirteenth century. By 1389 the Chambre des Comptes had become a separate court, supervising the levying of taxation, while another court acted as the supreme judiciary, handling civil and criminal cases. Subsequently a similar judicial tribunal was established at Turin. During the French occupation from 1536 to 1559 these courts were remodelled on the pattern of the Parlements, and after Emanuel Filibert was restored to his duchy he retained much of the French institutional structure, although he re-baptised the supreme courts with the more sonorous title of Senates. In 1577 he created the Camera dei Conti at Turin as the counterpart of Chambéry's Chambre des Comptes, with jurisdiction in fiscal and economic matters over the Italian domains and the county of Nice. In 1614 another Senate was established at Nice. These sovereign courts were not large; the Senate of Savoy in 1713 comprised only twenty-four magistrates and a few ushers, while the Chambre des Comptes numbered forty-eight members all told.[1] This was typical of the entire Savoyard administration, which tended to be small and compact; a minimal personnel discharged an enormous volume of official business, as the masses of documents in the archives eloquently attest. The Savoyard state was not burdened by the luxuriant proliferation of office-holders to be found in France, and in certain other Italian states. The magistrates of the sovereign courts epitomized the virtues – and some of the shortcomings – of the Savoyard system of government. They were studious, indefatigable, characterized by an austere rectitude that might sometimes verge on intellectual narrowness, and by a tradition of devoted service to the state that on occasion could take precedence over independence of judgment.

The various sovereign courts differed subtly in their relationship to the central power. The Senate and Camera of Turin rarely opposed Victor Amadeus II's orders, and submitted without overt protest to the restrictions he imposed on their right of remonstrance. They were not, however, completely submissive; in 1697 the Camera dei Conti refused for months to register an edict removing some of the restrictions on rice cultivation around Vercelli, and in 1723 the second president of the Senate of Turin was banished to his country estate for two years for rendering a verdict contrary to Victor Amadeus's specific instructions. But these are isolated instances. As a rule the Senate and Camera loyally supported government policy, and were rewarded by the grant of powers stripped from other courts – the Camera took over the jurisdiction of the small fiscal court of Casale in 1713, and of the Chambre des Comptes in 1720; the Senate inherited the functions of the lesser Senates of Pinerolo and Casale when they were suppressed in 1730. In fact the sovereign courts at Turin seem to have lived in satisfactory symbiosis with the government. The Senate of Nice too showed little sign of restiveness, carrying out the government's orders without protest, and never setting itself up as a mouthpiece of local interests. This docility was due in some measure to the fact that the senior magistrates at Nice were always Piedmontese; native-born senators found their advancement blocked unless they were willing – like Caissotti, who left the judiciary at Nice to rise to ministerial rank – to move to the capital.

The sovereign courts of Chambéry were rather more independent, and were alone in offering serious resistance to Victor Amadeus's authority. This may have been due, in part at least, to pride of tradition in being the state's oldest-established judicial institutions. It may also have been due to differences in legal practice and outlook: the Senate at Chambéry followed procedures closer to those of a French Parlement than to those of the Senate of Turin, and this sense of separateness was no doubt reinforced by the long French occupations, during which the Senate and Chambre became the real governing agencies of the duchy. But whatever the reason, the magistrates of Chambéry were more willing than their colleagues at Nice or Turin to carry out their traditional duty of limiting the arbitrary use of ducal authority. Between 1696 and 1702 the Senate of Savoy refused to register the edict imposing the *tabellion*, or compulsory recording of deeds by state-approved notaries. After this Victor Amadeus seems to have circumvented its opposition by simply bypassing the formality of registration, by a little judicious flattery – in 1713 the *présidial* court of the province of Genevois was abolished and merged with the Senate – and by leavening the Senate's membership with his own appointees, many of whom were Piedmontese. Of thirty-eight new magistrates between 1700 and 1750 who can be identified, only twenty-five were natives of Savoy.[2]

The Chambre des Comptes was more openly hostile to the central government, probably because it felt more threatened by encroachments on its jurisdiction. The first intendant appointed to Savoy in 1686 took over the Chambre's traditional functions of supervising roads, bridges, military lodgings and a wide range of economic matters, so that a report of 1700 noted with official understatement that 'the Chambre does not view with pleasure the establishment of the intendancy'.[3] Faced with the loss of its fiscal jurisdiction to the intendant, the Chambre naturally made common cause with the disaffected nobles of the duchy and saw itself as the citadel of threatened privilege and particularist sentiment. It skirmished constantly with the government, refusing to approve a new land-survey – which threatened noble tax-exemptions – and opposing new customs tariffs. In 1720 Victor Amadeus abolished the Chambre des Comptes and transferred its powers – those not already taken over by the intendants – to the more pliant Camera at Turin.

The abolition of the Chambre des Comptes provides a spectacular demonstration of the general trend to limit the sovereign courts' authority, which had begun well before Victor Amadeus's reign. But this development has wider implications. It formed part of a pervasive tendency towards administrative specialization discernible throughout the Savoyard government in the seventeenth century. New agencies and new officials were created to discharge political and economic duties formerly assigned to the sovereign courts. And in another sense the erosion of their powers can be seen as a 'functionarization of justice', as Jean Nicolas calls it – a shift away from the high moral and ethical vision of judicial office towards a concept of the magistrate as judicial bureaucrat, following prescribed norms.[4] This implies a loss of intellectual autonomy, which had its political dimension too. By the end of Victor Amadeus's reign the sovereign courts no longer acted in the traditional way to restrain the executive power, or in the language of contemporary political theory, to prevent absolutism from degenerating into tyranny. They had been transformed from independent checks on the ruler's power into judicial cogs in a larger government machine; instead of standing apart from the central power, they had been absorbed by it.

The sovereign courts' traditional pre-eminence within the government was vanishing too. The high magistrates and the Chancellor – traditionally the senior minister, who presided over the ducal council of advisers – had always held the dominant position in the hierarchy of state officials. As late as 1647 the sovereign courts of Chambéry asserted their right of precedence over the other courts and functionaries, and the Senate of Savoy proudly claimed the privilege of automatic ennoblement for its members, although this was contested. But during the seventeenth century this traditional ordering of rank began to change. Prestige passed increasingly to the financial agencies, which grew in size and importance, overshadowing the judiciary. The Chambre des Comptes and the Camera dei Conti, the traditional keystones of the fiscal edifice, participated in the general eclipse that overtook the older judicially based organs of the state. The reforms undertaken by Victor Amadeus II and his finance minister Gropello, culminating in the complete reorganization of the state's financial administration after 1717, set the seal on a process of institutional development that had started a century before. The suppression of the Chambre des Comptes, which can be viewed in one light as a blow against particularism and privilege, or as the triumph of the central power over a stubborn opponent, should also be regarded as a further step in the emergence of a new, centralized fiscal system, staffed by new men and following new methods.

The new fiscal institutions, and the taxes that they levied, are traceable to the changes in the system of state finances effected by Emanuel Filibert in the 1560s. Prior to that date the Savoyard government had relied on periodic subsidies levied with the consent of the local Estates, bolstered by the proceeds of justice and the ducal demesne, and by revenue from the Alpine tolls. But from 1560 something like a revolution overtook the state's fiscal institutions. The Estates of Piedmont and Savoy met in that year for the last time, disbanding after voting a subsidy, which was then prolonged into a permanent tax by ducal authority. The Estates of Nice lingered on, as we have seen, until 1680, while those of Aosta survived into the eighteenth century. But the principle of taxation by the sovereign's will had been established in the provinces where it really mattered, and was extended to the marquisate of Saluzzo after it was annexed in 1588; there too the Estates ceased to meet and vote taxes. Isolated local Estates in outlying parts of Piedmont like the Val Maira or the Val Varaita withered and died in the first half of the seventeenth century. As the old machinery of consent disappeared, the state's fiscal institutions expanded and the burden of taxation increased.

Emanuel Filibert had originally conceived of his new tax as a salt gabelle, but the difficulties involved in levying it soon led to its replacement by a land tax – in Piedmont the *tasso*, in Savoy the *taille* – imposed district by district. The assessments for the *taille* and *tasso* were based on the registers compiled for the abandoned salt gabelle; they represented at best only crude approximations to a balanced and fair apportionment, and since they were never revised they soon lost any semblance of equity. The incidence of taxation varied enormously from place to place, and within each district some taxpayers were burdened unjustly while others paid little or nothing. At the same time the new tax system implied a fundamental change in the nature and purpose of the village community. From the 1560s it became the unit for levying taxation; tax-collectors were appointed from each village, and its syndics were held responsible for any failure to meet its quota. The autonomous village community was now becoming an administrative division of the state, in a process to be completed by the intendants and the reforms of local administration after 1713.

The *taille* and the *tasso* were the largest direct taxes levied by the Savoyard government; the donatives voted by the Estates of Nice and Aosta were levied in the same manner, according to a fixed assessment, district by district. These taxes were augmented by a series of other levies: the *comparto dei grani*, a tax in grain for the army instituted in 1572, the *sussidio militare*, a war tax imposed in 1659 as an emergency measure, which gradually mutated into a permanent supplement to the *tasso*, and the *quartiere d'inverno*, ostensibly a payment in lieu of the billeting of troops, collected only in wartime. In the course of the seventeenth century the weight of direct taxation rose, partly through the imposition of these new taxes, partly because of a gradual increase in the incidence of the *tasso*. By 1700 direct taxation was contributing just under half the state's revenues: 4,377,517 lire out of a total of 10,917,442 lire.[5] The remainder came from customs revenues like the *dacito di Susa* levied on Alpine traffic – by now only a minor element in the state budget – and from indirect taxes, the most important of which was the salt gabelle.

Although Emanuel Filibert in the 1560s had transformed his original scheme for a salt tax into a direct levy on the land, he soon returned to this idea and imposed a salt gabelle in addition to the *taille* and the *tasso* which had initially replaced it. The salt tax then became the prototype for a burgeoning array of other taxes on consumption – on wine, on meat, on hides and on a variety of other commodities. These gabelles were collected by tax-farmers – not by the state itself, as was the case with the *tasso* and the other direct taxes. The salt gabelle differed from the other indirect taxes since it was compulsory almost everywhere; any person over the age of five was obliged to purchase a quota of salt, fixed in 1680 at eight *libbre* (roughly 2.6 kilos) per person per year, at a price of four soldi per *libbra*. This represented a heavy burden, particularly since peasants with farm animals had to buy salt for them as well; small wonder that the salt gabelle was universally detested, and that smuggling and evasion were rampant. Because the revenues from this tax formed one of its principal sources of income, the government devoted close attention to the procurement of adequate supplies of salt. There were salt-mines in Savoy but these never supplied enough to meet the government's needs, while problems of transport made it more economical to export this salt to the Swiss Cantons rather than to consume it within the state. Most of the salt consumed in the Savoyard state came from France, and during the wars with Louis XIV the import of salt through the port of Villefranche was interrupted, with grave consequences for the hard-pressed state finances; Victor Amadeus had to bring in emergency supplies with the help of a small English squadron based at Nice.

The weight of taxation varied considerably from region to region. Piedmont, the most economically advanced part of the state, was also the most heavily taxed. Twenty-three different gabelles were levied there, as compared to eight in Savoy and the county of Nice, seven in Oneglia and only five in the duchy of Aosta. Direct taxation also bore more heavily on the Piedmontese provinces; with roughly two-thirds of the population they paid over three-quarters of the direct taxes.[6] But at the same time the fiscal system operated to Piedmont's advantage, since much of the revenue from the other regions was forwarded to Turin and spent there. It has been estimated that of the 2,750,000 lire collected in Nice, Savoy and the other parts of the state in 1700, about 1,500,000 lire were sent to the capital. This constant financial drain aroused resentment, especially in Savoy where it added another grievance to the list of complaints against Piedmontese ascendancy.[7]

The financial machinery that collected these taxes was, in the later seventeenth century, a bewildering multiplicity of overlapping agencies, beset by grave internal contradictions. It is probably fair to say that until the reforms of 1717 Victor Amadeus had no exact idea of what his revenue totalled, nor of how much money was in the state treasury at any given moment. Much of this confusion resulted from the rapid growth of the state's financial system in the seventeenth century, in response to the pressing needs of war in an age of economic depression. As new taxes were imposed, new departments were created to collect them; instead of being integrated into the existing system, the new agencies were grafted onto it, to coexist in a limbo of ill-defined functions. The Savoyard administration, like other governments in early modern Europe, tended to grow by a process of accretion, in which obsolete departments lingered on beside the newer agencies designed to replace them; nowhere was this as true as in the financial institutions, where successive overlays of newer officials and departments covered what was still a polycentric medieval structure. A certain measure of unity was however imposed from the centre, where the ducal Council of Finances (set up in 1588) determined fiscal policy, decided the annual assessments of *taille* and *tasso*, imposed new taxes, and planned the annual budget. Further uniformity was assured by a single system for auditing the numerous accounts rendered each year by the different financial agencies. All were reviewed by the controller-general, and then given final approval by the Chambre des Comptes or the Camera dei Conti.

The most serious obstacle to efficient financial administration lay in the lack of a central fund through which all revenues had to pass. Different sources of revenue were earmarked for different purposes and paid to different treasurers or receivers, or sometimes to several government agencies at once. For example, funds for the army came from the *tasso*, paid to the various provincial treasurers of Piedmont, from the *sussidio militare* and the *quartiere d'inverno*, collected by a special military treasurer, and from the *comparto dei grani*, levied by its own receiver. There was a treasurer-general for the whole of Piedmont, who represented the closest approximation to a central fund, but a good deal of tax-revenue never passed through his hands, being transferred straight from the local treasurers to one or another government agency. There were other provincial treasurers for Savoy, Nice, Aosta and Oneglia, along with various subsidiary treasurers and receivers of minor revenues from these regions. Indirect taxes were collected by the farmers of the *gabelle generali* – a grouping of the major consumption taxes including the salt tax – and various other tax-farmers who handled the lesser gabelles. As with the direct taxes, some revenue from the gabelles was paid straight to one of the government departments, and never passed through a central treasury. It was therefore impossible to keep track of the state's revenues, or to know precisely what funds were available. Furthermore, since particular sources of revenue were earmarked for a specific purpose, when a fund became exhausted moneys had to be diverted to it from other sources by juggling and borrowing.

More complications arose from the number of different government agencies that actually spent the revenue – the households of the duke and the duchess-regent, the director of the mint, the Ufficio del Soldo which handled most military expenditure, the separate bureaus for artillery and fortifications, and so on. The complexity of the system for collecting revenue was thus matched by an almost equal degree of complexity in the institutions for spending it. Victor Amadeus's reforms of 1717 remedied these defects by establishing centralized control over the collection and disbursement of state revenue through a single fund under a treasurer-general. The result was to simplify the institutional structure of state finance, to eliminate waste and increase efficiency to a degree equalled by few other European states at the time. But the wars against France, which strained the state's capabilities to the limit, had to be sustained by the old, unreformed fiscal system.

A further requirement for the efficient operation of the financial machine, and of the whole administration, was a more flexible and comprehensive linkage between the central government and the localities where the revenues were collected. As the state's fiscal demands grew, the existing system of castellans and bailiffs proved inadequate, necessitating a new echelon of intermediate officials at the provincial level, between the local community and the central government. After some experimentation, an edict of 1624 established a *referendario* in each of the Piedmontese provinces, charged with the local administration of justice, and with a wide variety of economic and fiscal functions: these officials were also known as the *direttori* of their provinces. By the 1650s there were eighteen *referendarii* or *direttori* in the various Piedmontese provinces.[8] The office of *referendario* seems, according to most authorities, to have anticipated the intendants appointed under Victor Amadeus II, although with certain significant differences: the *referendarii* seem to have been restricted to Piedmont, their term of office was unspecified, giving them a temporary and *ad hoc* character, and their powers were less comprehensive than those of the later intendants. We shall describe the establishment of the intendants in greater detail later on, for it constitutes, along with the reordering of the state's finances and the land-survey, the chief administrative achievement of Victor Amadeus II's reign. With the creation of the intendants, even more than with the *referendarii*, the government set up a flexible and responsive group of intermediate officials to assure the flow of taxation and to convey its orders to even the remotest regions of the state.

For the century or so since the reign of Emanuel Filibert the institutions of the Savoyard state had been growing steadily in size and in the range of administrative functions that they could perform. Quantitative assessments are difficult to make, but the most rapid period of growth was probably from about 1580 to 1650. The sale of offices was used to raise money at times of financial emergency, but the Savoyard rulers never used this method on anything like the scale that it was used in France, which helps to explain why their bureaucracy remained comparatively lean and trim. Only a few minor non-political offices were venal and hereditary in the French manner: public notaries, *procureurs* of the sovereign courts in Savoy, apothecaries, and *insinuatori* or keepers of the archives of notarial acts. In all these instances a fixed number of posts was created and sold, ostensibly to permit regulation for the benefit of the public. These were the only offices which actually constituted a form of property transmissible from generation to generation without restriction: every other type of venal office in the Savoyard state was transmissible for a maximum of one generation. This limitation formed a fundamental distinction setting Savoyard office-holding apart from the French type.

The Savoyard rulers thus retained a wide discretion in their choice of officials, which was further enhanced by the absence of any perpetual ownership and heritability of state office. The Savoyard state never had an equivalent of the French *paulette* which permitted the free disposition of offices by their owners. A system of guaranteed successions did exist, but was much more restricted in its scope. From the 1620s the Savoyard rulers had granted a right of succession – the *sopravvivenza* – to certain favoured office-holders, and this custom was enshrined in law by an edict of 1681 giving the right of succession for one generation to the magistrates of the sovereign courts, in return for a fee. But the *sopravvivenza* was a privilege, granted by the ruler as a reward for good service, and not purchasable at the will of the office-holder. Moreover, it permitted the transfer of the office only from father to son, and not to any third party, as in the French system.[9] Bureaucratic dynasticism thus never reached the proportions that it did in France.

Certain families nonetheless managed to carve out a lasting position for themselves within the Savoyard administration, and the acquisition of office formed the best avenue of social advancement for most of the seventeenth century. The rise of these new state servants can be exemplified through the history of one family, in many ways the most successful: the Carron de Saint-Thomas.[10] The family originated in Bugey but moved at some point in the sixteenth century to Chambéry, where Claude Carron was described as a 'citizen'. The first member of the family to achieve prominence was Claude's son Jean, born about 1570, who moved to Turin and worked in the office of the Chancellor from about 1590. In 1625 Jean Carron purchased the position of first secretary of state to duke Charles Emanuel I, an office which he shared with another functionary. He went on to acquire titles and estates, becoming conte di Buttigliera and seigneur of Saint-Thomas-de-Coeur. He had four sons. In 1637 one of these, Guillaume-François, was granted the right of succession to the secretaryship, and helped discharge the duties connected with it until in 1643 his father retired and he assumed full control. In 1649 Guillaume-François purchased the other secretaryship of state to unite the two offices, and secured his family's possession of them by obtaining the combined *sopravvivenza* for his son, Carlo-Giuseppe. In the meantime other members of the family were making their way in the provincial administration: to cite one example, Guillaume-François's younger brother became *vibailli* of Aosta in 1656, acquired the title of marquis de la Tour de Courmayeur, and finally retired with the rank of *referendario* in 1673. The senior branch of the family retained unbroken control of the first secretaryship of state for another two generations. Guillaume-François died in 1677, passing on his office and titles to his son; this was the marquis de

Saint-Thomas who was Victor Amadeus II's adviser on foreign affairs until his retirement in 1696. The office was then inherited by his son, Giuseppe-Gaetano, for whom the *sopravvivenza* had been secured. Victor Amadeus retained him despite his relative lack of aptitude for foreign affairs, apparently to deal with the everyday business of the office, while reserving his confidence for other advisers. Finally the reorganization of the government in 1717 provided Victor Amadeus with a pretext for disposing of his unsuitable minister as decorously as possible. Saint-Thomas's departure from the first secretaryship closed a cycle of ministerial dynasticism that had spanned almost a century.

The rise of the Carron de Saint-Thomas clan offers a generalized illustration of how the Savoyard administrative élite developed at this time. As the state's judicial and financial institutions grew, a new nobility of office emerged, blending with elements of the old feudal class to form a service nobility. The two groups remained distinct at first, but assimilation seems to have been quite rapid; two or three generations sufficed for a new family to merge with the old élite through the purchase of fiefs and titles. This phenomenon is discernible in Piedmont and Savoy alike; the rise of the Trucchi family was paralleled by that of the Lescheraine across the Alps. Certain families that had attained nobility through judicial office, like the Costa in Savoy, continued to serve in the magistracy for generations, bridging the gap between the new élite and the old. The judiciary, however, remained virtually inaccessible to the old nobility because entry to it required a doctorate in law, which few aristocrats bothered to acquire. For many non-noble families the financial administration became the ladder for social ascent. Financial expertise provided a ready entrée into state service, while the profits from tax-farming, army contracts or government loans could be used to buy offices and titles. The growth of the central government meant that by the end of Victor Amadeus II's reign state service offered the only sure means of advancement for aspiring nobles; aristocratic influence at the local level had been drastically curtailed, power and preferment were concentrated at the capital. An outward sign of this trend was the wave of palace-building at Turin in the early eighteenth century, as many noble families forsook their country seats in order to live close to the court and the focus of political power. The old aristocracy, reinforced by a new élite of functionaries, magistrates and financiers, had been harnessed to the service of the state.

The timing and mechanics of this process, however, remain obscure, and recent work on the growth of the Savoyard state and its ruling élite leaves us with conflicting views of how the transformation was actually accomplished. A quarter of a century ago Luigi Bulferetti suggested that the Savoyard state in the seventeenth century was dominated by what was still very largely a feudal aristocracy; new families quickly adopted the values of the traditional nobility, while land remained the basis of political power and the only real source of wealth, under what he termed (some-what confusingly) 'feudal capitalism'.[11] Subsequently Guido Quazza argued that (by the early eighteenth century at least) the ruling elements in the Savoyard state were composed overwhelmingly of 'bourgeois or the newly-ennobled'.[12] New men had taken over the state; they were the energetic officials who carried out Victor Amadeus II's reforms. In the last few years Enrico Stumpo and Jean Nicolas, each tackling the problem from a different angle (the former deals only with Piedmont, the latter only with the duchy of Savoy), have shown that the rise of this new élite goes back much further than Quazza implies, and must be placed in the first half or two-thirds of the seventeenth century. Both authors detect a slowing-down in the creation of offices and the grant of new titles by about 1670. Nicolas in fact describes the later seventeenth century as a 'period of social contraction', in which the ruling élite consolidated itself.[13] While the new men may have risen from a financial and professional bourgeoisie, as Stumpo argues, they do not seem to have ousted the older nobility; Nicolas stresses the continuing ascendancy of the landed aristo-cracy (in Savoy at least), and sees the late seventeenth and early eighteenth centuries as a period of seigneurial reaction, in which the landed class reasserted itself.

The discrepancies between these different analyses pose a number of problems. Whereas Bulferetti emphasizes the predominance of a feudal aristocracy, albeit leavened with newcomers, Quazza postulates a power-ful wave of low-born office-holders who came to dominate the state in the early eighteenth century, at a time when Stumpo and Nicolas suggest on the other hand that the pace of social and political transformation had slowed down. While all four authors agree on the critical importance of office-holding as the way in which the dominant class recruited itself, the stages in the process, and the social and political consequences that flowed from it, are far from clear. Was Victor Amadeus II's reign dominated by the rise of aggressive new men, or was it an age in which the noble-bureaucratic élite was closing itself off to recruitment from below and the feudal nobility was reasserting its authority? What was the exact nature of the social and political élite that dominated state and society at this time? These questions have important implications. For Quazza, much of the dynamism in Victor Amadeus's reform programme came from the personnel who implemented it; their humble origins made them willing collaborators in a policy directed against the old aristocracy, to which they felt little or no allegiance. But while Quazza stresses the radical, anti-aristocratic tone of Victor Amadeus's reforms, Nicolas sees them as essentially hesitant and cautious, unwilling to challenge the reality of feudal privilege. Nicolas implies that the ruling élite, although perhaps of recent vintage, was already too close to the feudal nobility to contemplate attacking its privileges, so that Victor Amadeus's policies have to be judged comparatively timid and incomplete. And Nicolas's delineation of the revival of the landed aristocracy in Savoy suggests that Victor Amadeus's efforts to curb the nobility should be seen as defensive in intention, a kind of rearguard action against a resurgent landed class, rather than the offensive onslaught against privilege that Quazza says they were.

These differences in interpretation leave unresolved the real nature and direction of Victor Amadeus II's policies, and of the ruling élite that carried them out – problems that are central to any understanding of the Savoyard state at this critical moment in the evolution of its absolutist structure. Victor Amadeus's reign is the most rapid and dramatic phase in the growth of an absolutist system that had been developing for more than a century and that would continue down to the revolution, although at a more relaxed tempo. And when we assess this development we must also take into account another factor that contributed powerfully to it: the character and intentions of the sovereign who directed this increasingly powerful governmental machine of dedicated state servants, and who summed up in his own person the aspirations to rigid centralized control that they embodied.

IV
The Ruler

Victor Amadeus II, as Guido Quazza observes, 'is really the chief mover and author of the reorganization of the state'.[1] But his autocratic will made itself felt with such effect only because the Savoyard state had already evolved into a system of highly centralized authority, making the exercise of power truly personal. The ground had been prepared for Victor Amadeus by a century of bureaucratic development which forged an obedient mechanism for transmitting the ruler's orders, while at the same time weakening the institutional restraints on his exercise of power. The mainspring of this machine was the duke and his small council of ministers; policy originated at the top. Victor Amadeus's relationship with those who served him, nobles or functionaries, was highly personal, founded on contact renewed at public ceremonies or in the daily running of the departments of the state. In these conditions his towering personality was decisive; brooking no contradiction, he would bring to bear the full force of his terrible displeasure on the recalcitrant. He was readily obeyed, even when he outraged the sensibilities of the privileged and rode roughshod over their traditional rights. His imperious, brutal personality overawed potential *frondeurs* and thus helped assure the success of his reforms. And as he concentrated political power in his own hands he transformed the traditional relationship between the Savoyard rulers and their nobles, de-personalizing it and distancing the sovereign from his privileged subjects. He impressed his own personal stamp on the development of the state, exploiting its structure of centralized personal power in order to effect far-reaching changes. The force of his relentless will penetrated to the outermost reaches of the state, setting a tone of hard work, frugality, punctuality and rigid subordination. Jean-Jacques Rousseau, lowliest of functionaries in the land-survey office at Chambéry in the 1730s, felt (and detested) these all-pervasive pressures, this model of disciplined efficiency that was Victor Amadeus II's legacy.[2]

His character recalls that of other contemporary rulers who sought to bend their subjects to accept fundamental change: one thinks of Frederick William of Prussia, or even Peter the Great. But in fact we know very little about Victor Amadeus II as a man; pathologically secretive, he had no real confidants, and always spun a web of mystery about his feelings and intentions. His correspondence tells us little; concerned with matters of policy, it gives few clues to personal motive. Our main source for trying to understand this enigmatic, contradictory man who dominated the Savoyard state for forty-six years, moulding it to his own harsh image, has to be the reports of foreign observers; his own subjects, who knew him better, were less given to recording their impressions, knowing that his eyes and ears were everywhere. Testimony from foreign diplomats and travellers, however, comes laden with its inherent defects. These observers arrived at the Savoyard court with preconceptions that inevitably coloured their assessments. For their analysis of his motives they depended on the gossip of the few privileged informants with whom they were permitted to converse, since court etiquette tightly restricted all contacts with foreign diplomats. In a very real sense therefore foreign visitors picked up 'official' explanations for transmission to their masters, and so to posterity. Much of our knowledge about Victor Amadeus's character comes from successive French ambassadors, who were naturally disposed to place a hostile construction on his words, and to follow a prescribed reasoning in accounting for his actions: consciously or unconsciously they would write what they knew to be acceptable at Versailles.

The correspondence of the maréchal de Tessé, French envoy at various times in the 1690s, is one of the most frequently quoted sources for understanding Victor Amadeus's character, yet it bears all the flaws that beset any official observer's account, while in addition being self-consciously aphoristic. Tessé was a renowned letter-writer and was composing for a wider audience than the immediate recipient of his despatches: he wrote to be quoted, and we must read his sparkling periods with a certain reserve. Richard Hill, the English envoy during the dark years of the War of the Spanish Succession, confessed himself mystified by Victor Amadeus, and refused to believe that he could be the loyal ally that he really was. Nevertheless accounts like Tessé's and Hill's remain, for better or for worse, a principal source for understanding Victor Amadeus as a man. Of all these accounts by foreign observers, one stands apart by reason of the circumstances of its composition: this was the long personal memoir written by Blondel, the French chargé d'affaires at the end of the reign, who was treated with a familiarity that no other observer achieved. Yet even here one remains dubious, remembering that Blondel wrote down his recollections long after the event, and wondering if perhaps his intimacy with Victor Amadeus had not dazzled him. His narrative is in many ways the truest to life, the most revealing portrait that we possess, yet it depicts the king at the very end of his reign, knowing his work was done and ready to hand over power: there is therefore a suspicion that the old man was seeking to transmit a particular version of himself to posterity, and that Blondel became the unwitting vehicle for the desired image.

The main lines of Victor Amadeus's personality, on which all observers agreed – an overbearing will, bursts of violent temper, an almost automatic recourse to dissimulation – were formed in his earliest years. His childhood was dominated by a distant, unloving mother and a father who alternately indulged him and beat him to break his spirit. This lack of parental affection, notable even by the standards of the time, combined with the unstable political atmosphere of a faction-ridden court to inculcate the character traits that would distinguish him for the rest of his life. He was born on May 14, 1666, the only legitimate offspring of his father. His first years were punctuated by severe illnesses; early in 1668, when his life was despaired of, the Holy Shroud (a famous relic possessed by the Savoyards) was displayed at Turin to invoke divine intercession, and pilgrimages were undertaken to secure his recovery. Constant illness no doubt reinforced the loneliness of his childhood and made him more withdrawn. Once grown to manhood, however, he would develop robust health, toughened by his favourite sport of hunting, and by years of campaigning.

From the first he displayed acute intelligence; when he was five years old an observer noted his precocious talent for repartee.[3] But his chief childhood passion was for soldiers; he was taken to reviews of his father's troops, learned the details of their arms and uniforms, and later organized war-games at a miniature fort in the park of the Valentino palace just outside Turin. Like all the princes of his day, he was brought up to command and to the profession of arms, and this training lay behind the meticulous attention that he would later expend on the improvement of his army. Of his formal education we know relatively little. His tutors were Emanuele Tesauro, Aristotelian scholar, compiler of histories and recondite philologist, and the reverend Pietro Gioffredo, who wrote a history of his native province of Nice. But Victor Amadeus seems to have had little interest in scholarship for its own sake. His mind ran to the severely practical and eschewed speculation. His tutors probably gave him the standard courtly education judged necessary for a future ruler: instruction in the Catholic faith, dynastic history and chronicles of past rulers, some geography, mathematics, Latin and other languages. His formal education, however, was a less significant factor in his upbringing than practical experience of politics and court life in his youth.

In June 1675 his father duke Charles Emanuel II died at the early age of forty-one, leaving Victor Amadeus as nominal ruler of the Savoyard state under the protection of his mother, who was proclaimed regent. Marie-Jeanne-Baptiste of Savoy-Nemours, Madame Royale as she was known, had married Charles Emanuel in 1664.[4] Since then she had presided at court festivities, produced a son and heir, and endured her husband's well-publicized infidelities. Her life had so far offered little gratification for her ambitions or scope for her considerable intelligence. As regent she found power to her taste, continuing some of her husband's multifarious projects and adding some of her own, like the foundation of an academy of art in

1678. She spent her time in state business and paid little heed to her son, who was brought in to visit her formally each evening and then dismissed. As we shall see, she delayed as long as possible before handing over power to him, and sought to prolong her personal rule indefinitely, until in the end he was obliged to wrest power from her. This perhaps helps account for his lack of capacity for real affection, and for the difficulties that marked his relationships with women. His mother's treatment of him in these early years was also a principal cause of his love of dissimulation. She spied on him and watched closely over the friendships he formed, in order to prevent him from assuming power. To combat this, Victor Amadeus resorted to duplicity, hiding his intentions behind an impenetrable exterior, brooding long hours alone: in order to emancipate himself from his mother's tutelage he was forced to don the mask that he would never again let fall. The relationship between mother and son was marked by a total lack of tenderness; occasional reconciliations were merely for effect, momentary truces in a perpetual cold war that ended only with Madame Royale's death in 1724.

Victor Amadeus's relationship with his mother was also replete with political overtones. Much of his hostility was attributable to her excluding him from power after he came of age in 1680, and when he finally took over in 1684, he banished her forever from affairs of state. But here Victor Amadeus had to contend with more than just his mother's desire to retain power; behind her loomed the figure of Louis XIV, who supported her as a convenient puppet. Victor Amadeus's struggle to free himself from his mother was thus also a struggle to free himself from the power of France. The process of subterfuge and manoeuvre that finally enabled him to escape his mother's tutelage made him acutely aware of Louis XIV's influence in Savoyard affairs. His goal of personal autonomy thus merged with a fundamental maxim of Savoyard policy: to undo the treaty of Cherasco, end French influence, and regain sovereign independence.

A further political dimension to the relationship between Victor Amadeus and his mother derived from her position as the storm-centre of the factions that divided the court. For this she was not really to blame; as a woman, and the temporary ruler of the state, she lacked the authority to curb the play of faction. Furthermore she had inherited a court riven by feuds, exacerbated by a lost war with Genoa in 1672 and the ensuing hunt for scapegoats. The nobility was traditionally split into pro-French and pro-Spanish factions, and always looked upon a regency as a time for open rivalry. All this made the regent's position insecure, but she added to her difficulties by her attachment to a succession of favourites, whose ascendancy in her affections brought political advancement for their families: her love-affairs helped to polarize the factions at court. Victor Amadeus, Hamlet-like, detested his mother's favourites.[5] In his eyes they degraded her while at the same time undermining the state. His mother's indulgence of personal affection thus took on a political dimension for him; apart from any revulsion her conduct may have caused him in the sensitive years of adolescence, he also saw that she was committing serious political errors. Here perhaps – in part at least – is the origin of his later uncompromising separation of personal emotion from matters of state. Some idea of the gulf between mother and son emerges from the description of Victor Amadeus's behaviour that the regent wrote to Louis XIV's minister Louvois in March 1683:

> I have noticed that His Highness is afflicted with melancholy, deep secretiveness and a perpetual restiveness of spirit, which I judge sometimes to be caused by the lingering effects of his illness or some instability of temperament, as much as by secret scheming. He has an incorrigible fondness for persons of low birth and spends most of the day with them. He wants to be informed of everything secretly; he is extremely curious; he loves the gossip of the town, out of which he draws false conclusions in his own mind. He spends a great deal of the day in the cellars or on his bed; nothing pleases or entertains him. He has almost given up hunting which was his greatest delight. He affects in a childish way to be above passion, and he is very ostentatious in what he says and does. He seems to have an aversion for those persons who are attached to my interests. Regretfully I see in him a nature inclined to harshness and rigour, with little tenderness and forthrightness.[6]

By the time he came to power in 1684, at the age of eighteen, Victor Amadeus's character was already formed: solitary, imperious, violent, perpetually veiled by an inscrutable public front. Behind that blank exterior a host of contradictory passions struggled for predominance, a welter of projects stood ready to burst forth. Single-minded in the pursuit of his objectives, he wavered endlessly in the choice of means to achieve them, incapable of leaving a project well alone once it was completed, returning compulsively to re-do the same task over and over again. His moods constantly changed: 'Proteus' was the epithet that Tessé used of him, and it is apposite, even when we remember that Tessé's dealings with Victor Amadeus led him to exaggerate the latter's instability and fickleness.[7] In many respects Victor Amadeus was a classically neurotic personality, and at the end, as age and sickness wore him down, he would degenerate into a state very close to madness, if it was not madness itself. But this instability had its productive side. His fertile mind was ever open to new ideas, and his imagination ranged freely, making bold leaps of invention, bursting the bonds of convention and tradition. Without this intellectual audacity – which contrasts so profoundly with the inconsequentiality of his father, or the stodginess of his son – Victor Amadeus would not have initiated reforms that challenged the accustomed order of things and radically transformed both state and society.

Yet his daring had its limits: in many ways Victor Amadeus remained supremely conventional and unimaginative – witness his attitude to religion, or his dealings with intellectuals. Only in certain prescribed areas was he venturesome, above all in his conception of state power and the means to extend it. Here his inflexible will and restless imagination were complemented by an unremitting appetite for work: Hill in 1699 described Victor Amadeus as 'loving business more than pleasures, or ease'.[8] Like his model Louis XIV, Victor Amadeus gloried in the *métier du roi* and devoted most of his waking hours to it. Some of his attention to detail sprang from an unwillingness to delegate authority and a mistrust of subordinates, which led him to perform an undue amount of routine work himself. An officer collecting his pay from the French military treasurer at Turin in 1696

> ... found Monsieur the duke of Savoy there; he had come to collect the pension that His Majesty [Louis XIV] paid him. He was alone, his coat buttoned up to his nose, and saw to his payment. A fine example of a great prince's attention to his business . . .[9]

Victor Amadeus's conception of government was essentially personal, and he summed it up for Blondel in this way:

> You should know that good government requires that one should either do everything oneself, or leave it completely alone; one must be the absolute master, without regard for proprieties and personal considerations that are usually contrary to equity, justice and the good of the state. . . .
> Sovereigns are born for an active life, and not for an idle or contemplative existence. They must devote a constant, serious attention to matters of government, although it is not unseemly for them to pursue some passion or other . . .[10]

Victor Amadeus always followed these maxims. Tessé characterized him, in a judgment echoed by other observers, as 'an eloquent prince of penetrating mind, a great asker of questions, in whose head all the affairs of Europe, and his own as well, turn over at least once each day'.[11] Much of his success was the result of his energy and penetrating intelligence, but it also depended on his careful choice of the functionaries who served him. The selection of loyal and efficient subordinates was an essential element in Victor Amadeus's system of government. He kept a close watch on them, for as Blondel noted, 'All his life he has looked on his ministers not so much as the secretaries of state, but rather as mere clerks for carrying out his orders.'[12] He kept them on a tight rein, allowing them no latitude to initiate projects of their own. He never met his council of ministers as a group, but consulted them separately and then decided alone what course to pursue; sometimes he encouraged the rivalries between them, for as he explained to Blondel, one should keep one's majordomo and head cook at odds if one wishes to be served honestly. But this point should not be taken too far. He also told Blondel that:

once one has chosen good ministers known for their skill in making plans, for their ability, their loyalty and their exactitude in carrying out instructions, they must be supported and given credit . . . the more a minister is secure, the greater the confidence that reigns both at home and abroad, the greater the solidity of one's projects, the greater the scope of one's enterprises . . . I have found that by following this maxim I reign more sovereignly in my little state than in the days when I made frequent changes.[13]

His actual treatment of his ministers bears this out: once they had proved themselves, they retained his confidence and received constant favours. Gropello served him for a quarter of a century; Mellarède for more than thirty years; Ormea for twenty-four, after which he went on to become chief minister to his son and successor. Victor Amadeus surrounded himself with a team of experienced, efficient subordinates, competent in every aspect of state business and ruthless enough to carry out any order. And though their loyalty was to Victor Amadeus himself, by his example he inculcated an ideal of service to the state rather than to the individual ruler, transcending old concepts of private fealty and substituting for them a sense of higher duty to the impersonal public entity of the state. Although his ministers were never permitted to decide matters on their own account, Victor Amadeus delegated wide administrative powers to them. Acting under his immediate supervision, they formed the core of the structure of centralized power by which he transformed the state and rendered it an extension of his own energetic and determined self.

Perhaps the search for discipline and order that informed all Victor Amadeus's actions, and which left its indelible stamp on state and society, can be seen as some kind of externalization of his inner struggle to curb and channel the passions that constantly agitated his mind. He was a man of volatile emotions, which had originally focused on his mother and later dominated his relations with all who were close to him, his family and his mistresses. In 1684 he married Anne, daughter of the duke of Orleans, in a typical dynastic arrangement. He does not seem to have loved her, and frequently treated her with studied neglect or outright callousness. She for her part remained devoted to him until her death in 1728, a model wife by the standards of her time and class: pious, undemanding, her horizons circumscribed by family duties, court functions and devotions. She bore him eight children in all, four of whom survived infancy: Marie-Adelaide, born in 1685 and later married to the duke of Burgundy, and Marie-Louise, the bride of Philip V of Spain, born three years later; Victor Amadeus, prince of Piedmont, born in 1699, heir-apparent until his premature death in 1715, and Charles Emanuel, born in 1701, who succeeded his father in 1730. Victor Amadeus's favourite was undoubtedly the young prince of Piedmont, his namesake, born when he had begun to despair of a male heir, and the embodiment of all his hopes for the future.

Tessé records Victor Amadeus's emotions following the birth of his son:

> ... I never thought that a father so little disposed by temperament to tenderness could find in his heart the emotion of fatherly love, the manifestations of which, in his case, are almost more akin to frenzy than to normal emotions.[14]

The last phrase is especially telling: for Victor Amadeus, emotion – even love – could only be violent. Starved of affection in his childhood, he could never express the emotions that welled up within him, save in an exaggerated or tortured way. When his cherished elder son died, Blondel records, Victor Amadeus was beside himself for a week, wandering in a frenzy through the palace until in a paroxysm of rage and grief he took his sword and butchered a horse as it stood in the stable. Then at last he became calm again. The young Charles Emanuel never aroused his affection; Victor Amadeus treated him with cold disdain, called him dull-witted, and neglected him until the elder son's death compelled him, reluctantly, to concern himself with this despised second son. Charles Emanuel was given a functional grounding in the business of state and subjected to a tight personal regimen. Victor Amadeus forced him to give up hunting, his chief pleasure, and even regulated his relations with his wife. Blondel claims that Victor Amadeus disapproved of his son's evident passion for his wife, 'only permitting him to sleep with her once a week', and that on one occasion, in October 1728, he publicly reproached his son for his conduct with her. Charles Emanuel, in a rare show of independence, replied that at twenty-seven years of age he knew how to behave himself, only to be overwhelmed by furious reproaches: 'look at you, presumptuous youth, you are nothing but a fool with no idea of how to behave or how to control yourself'. Charles Emanuel broke down in tears. Normally, however, he bore these reproaches in silence, or responded in monosyllables, 'without questioning, interest, familiarity or tenderness'.[15] His father's bullying must have robbed Charles Emanuel of his self-confidence, yet, surprisingly, it did not completely crush him: he became an efficient and conscientious sovereign, though understandably less venturesome than his father, given to the security of routine.

The same pattern of unstable emotions characterized Victor Amadeus's relations with his various mistresses. In his early manhood he seems to have had a series of longer or shorter liaisons with ladies of the court: mademoiselle de Priè, the marchesa di Cumiana – to whom he would return at the very end of his life – and apparently others. His marriage seems to have caused only a brief interruption in this progression of mistresses. The longest and most profound of all his love-affairs was with the comtesse de Verrue, a lady of aristocratic lineage married to one of the most distinguished Piedmontese grandees. The affair became public knowledge in the summer of 1689, when Victor Amadeus and the comtesse travelled to Nice together, and the attachment persisted with violent ups and downs until the end of 1700, when she fled to France to take refuge from her unpredictable, tyrannous lover. In the interim she had borne him a son and a daughter, who were legitimized in 1701 and later married into the flower of the Savoyard aristocracy. This passionate affair was probably the most profound emotional experience of Victor Amadeus's mature life, but it was far from happy. Madame de Verrue complained to Tessé (who was her close confidant) that Victor Amadeus 'is intolerable to those who love him best and who see him most often'. Tessé described their relationship in the following terms:

> The prince's love has turned into transports of tyrannical jealousy which makes them both unhappy . . . Yet although he believes he hates her he still comes back to her, and does not feel content or at ease save in her company. They spend their lives in mutual recrimination and reproach, and yet she knows everything, for he can hide nothing from her.[16]

This suggests that for Victor Amadeus the relationship with madame de Verrue rested on some form of psychological dependence, in contrast to his habitual imperiousness and self-sufficiency, and that the endless cycle of scenes and reconciliations was both frustrating and deeply satisfying to him at the same time. In the end it was the comtesse de Verrue who terminated the relationship, and after this Victor Amadeus does not seem to have formed any similar attachments.

The fragmentary picture that we possess of Victor Amadeus's emotional life leaves an impression of a continual ferment of passions barely under control. To some extent he seems to have found relief in strenuous physical activity, particularly hunting, and also in the thrill of physical combat. Contemporary observers, friend and foe alike, paid tribute to his courage; on the field of battle he was always at the head of his troops, at Staffarda, La Marsaglia or Chiari, at the siege of Chivasso and at the climactic battle of Turin. He was a resourceful general, who learned from his mistakes – as at Staffarda – and who immersed himself in the detail of military organization. His pursuit of *gloire* on the battlefield was in line with the behaviour expected of a prince of his day, yet the clash of wills, the ruses and stratagems, the physical danger all seem to have been especially satisfying to him, and he threw himself into the fighting with a zest that few contemporary rulers could equal. Perhaps the violence of combat provided some form of release for his inward turmoil; all we can say with certainty is that he chose to lead his troops in person, and sought the heat of the action, when convention would have been satisfied by his presence in a safe position towards the rear.

Victor Amadeus may perhaps have gone beyond the conventions of princely behaviour too in his interest in the supernatural.[17] To modern eyes there is a contradiction between the unrelenting rationalism of his *Realpolitik* and his recourse to astrologers and soothsayers, but this is a false distinction, which did not exist for him or his contemporaries. The invocation of supernatural forces or the search for favourable astrological predictions should perhaps be seen as an attempt to confer greater validity on a chosen course of action, a kind of insurance to overcome feelings of doubt. Throughout his life he maintained an interest in the occult. He corresponded with a celebrated astrologer, Giobbe Fortebraccio, a quack with contacts among dabblers in the occult throughout Italy, who produced horoscopes and predictions and conducted secret missions for his patron. On occasion Victor Amadeus would consult other soothsayers, as in 1709 when he went in disguise to seek counsel of a famous fortune-teller passing through Piedmont. At times of crisis he took comfort from the prophecies of a visionary nun at Turin. He was also reputed to be well versed in poisons and their antidotes. When madame de Verrue fell ill in 1697, Tessé records, Victor Amadeus supposedly saved her life with one of his secret potions.

Victor Amadeus's religious convictions seem to have been formed along much the same lines: there is little difference between the way he sought the advice of astrologers and fortune-tellers, and his search for conventional religious comfort. His religious outlook seems to have focused on external ritual. In May 1693 he made a pilgrimage to the mountain sanctuary of Oropa to fulfil a vow made during an attack of smallpox; in 1696 he undertook a pilgrimage to Loreto, apparently to pray for a male heir – about the same time as Giobbe Fortebraccio was sent to Iesi to consult a famous astrologer on the same topic. All this was supremely conventional; for Victor Amadeus, religion seems to have been a matter of concrete favours sought and granted, a strictly pragmatic affair without deep spiritual resonance. He was not given to speculation on theological questions; what concerned him was the function of religion in securing his subjects' obedience, or the political threat that the Papacy posed to his authority. His ideal, he once remarked, was the simple faith of the charcoal-burner; this was what his subjects should cultivate, spurning divisive theological controversies, and leaving the question of Papal authority to their prince. Typically, his reaction to the Bull *Unigenitus* (1713) and the blossoming dispute over Jansenism was to ban all debate and forbid even the mention of the Bull; to his mind that was enough to settle the matter once and for all.

This essentially practical, non-theological view of religion clearly influenced his conduct in the long dispute with the Papacy from 1694 to the end of the reign. Doctrinal issues were never ventilated, and the dispute was confined to questions of legal rights and political jurisdiction. His dealings with his small minority of Protestant subjects – the Vaudois inhabiting the Alpine valleys west of Turin – were similarly marked by an absence of real religious ardour. Brought up in a devout – not to say bigoted – court, and carefully schooled in his duties as a Catholic prince, Victor Amadeus evidently mistrusted these heretics. Yet the persecution that he launched against them in 1686 was not motivated by crusading conviction; it sprang from the political pressures to which he was subjected, both inside and outside the state. In 1694 – again for political reasons – he restored them to the limited toleration they had formerly enjoyed, and thereafter his policy towards them was dictated by the existing framework of laws defining their status, which he followed to the letter. For Victor Amadeus the question of the Vaudois was an affair to be regulated not by Catholic dogma but by reason of state.

His attitude to intellectual speculation was equally cut and dried: the limitations of his outlook can be seen in the reform of the university of Turin which he initiated in 1713, or in the recodification of the laws which produced the *Costituzioni* of 1723 and 1729. The function of the university was construed in the narrowest terms, as a mechanism for turning out competent bureaucrats; obedience was the prime virtue to be inculcated, intellectual independence was discouraged. The *Costituzioni*, as Mario Viora has shown in his study of their codification, were inspired by a very tradition-bound view of legal reform, becoming a compilation – albeit a good one – of existing laws, rather than a radical fusion and reformulation of precepts into a new code.[18] Victor Amadeus possessed an imaginative side that could envisage problems in a broad and sometimes original way. But the ideal that he set before himself in all his reforms was the enhancement of his own authority, and all other considerations were subordinated to it. This rigidly hierarchical, authoritarian conception of the state ruled out the luxury of intellectual independence for his subjects.

In one area, however, Victor Amadeus exhibited greater breadth of vision, and this was in his artistic patronage.[19] He was an intelligent but frugal patron, who took a close interest in the work that he commissioned and revealed an enlightened taste. The musical life of the court at Turin maintained its high standards during his reign. The Austrian painter Daniel Seyter executed a fine series of decorations for the newly completed gallery of the royal palace, and in 1697 Le Nôtre laid out the royal gardens as the last commission of his life. But architecture was Victor Amadeus II's chief passion; in this he followed his family's tradition for expressing their political aspirations in ambitious schemes of building and urban planning. In 1714 he brought the Sicilian architect Filippo Juvarra to Piedmont, at the moment when the Savoyard state had emerged victorious from its long wars with France. Juvarra had developed a lofty and grandiose baroque style during his formative years at Rome, and in Piedmont his genius flowered under Victor Amadeus's discerning patronage. He appeared at the moment when the impulse imparted to Piedmontese architecture by Guarino Guarini's audacious experiments had largely spent its force: Guarini died in 1683, and his great façade for the Palazzo Carignano (1679), his church of San Lorenzo and his chapel for the Holy Shroud (completed 1694) had no lineal successors. The scene was now occupied by a number of competent local architects such as Michelangelo Garove, working in a style that owed relatively little to Guarini. Juvarra invigorated this regional tradition with the powerful force of Roman high baroque, into which he wove something of Guarini's structural ingenuity and imaginative use of space and light. The great basilica at Superga (begun 1717) continues his grandiloquent Roman manner, with its classical portico and soaring dome, but some of its details – for instance the skeletal pierced arches of the interior – reveal a debt to Guarini. In his later work, like the church of the Carmine in Turin (completed in the 1730s) and the pleasure palace at Stupinigi, just outside the capital (begun in 1729), the use of open elements and the dramatic play of light become more evident. Juvarra worked at a prodigious pace for his royal patron, rebuilding the palaces at Venaria Reale and Rivoli, making additions to the Royal Palace in Turin, and laying out new streets and piazzas. He also designed palaces for aristocratic clients, while for Madame Royale, the king's mother, he produced the magnificent façade across the front of the old Palazzo Madama, with its grand ceremonial staircase (1718) which would become the prototype for so many baroque *Treppenhäuser* in Austria and Germany in the century to come.

Juvarra assembled a team of assistants to help with these multifarious projects, and in this way he trained a new generation of architects and decorators to continue the distinctive school of Piedmontese baroque for another generation, after he departed to end his days as chief architect to Philip V of Spain. His influence was of paramount importance in moulding the styles of the two greatest architects of the succeeding decades, Benedetto Alfieri and Bernardo Antonio Vittone, both of whom – though little known today outside their native region – were of European stature. Juvarra's sumptuous, refined style made Piedmont a centre of late baroque architecture which profoundly influenced later developments, particularly the rococo of southern Germany. Victor Amadeus was well aware that Juvarra's reputation enhanced his own: to him the money paid out for all these commissions was well spent. Aesthetically as well as politically Piedmont had come to occupy an important place in European affairs; it was no longer a provincial backwater but a centre where international influences converged. Victor Amadeus must be given credit for recognizing Juvarra's talent and for giving him commissions worthy of his genius and creative imagination. The political motives that lay behind this patronage in no way detract from the superb aesthetic achievement that it produced. Through Juvarra's high-flown, elegant architecture Victor Amadeus II attained his political goal: to celebrate the rising power of his state with éclat, and to create a lasting monument to himself.

V
The Regency and the
'Salt War' at Mondovì
(1675–1684)

Duke Charles Emanuel II died on 12 June 1675, leaving Victor Amadeus in the care of a special regency council headed by his mother, evidently hoping in this way to minimize the dangers that always beset a regency; no doubt he remembered his own minority (1638–1663) during which the state had been torn apart by civil war. But the new duchess regent, Madame Royale, quickly dispensed with the regency council bequeathed by her late husband and ruled alone, relishing the exercise of personal power so long denied her. As her chief advisers she chose the marquis de Saint-Thomas, until his death in 1677, when he was followed by the son who would serve as Victor Amadeus's first secretary of state, and the marquis de Saint-Maurice, until recently ambassador to France, and an intimate of many of the powerful figures at Versailles. Most observers connected the choice of Saint-Maurice to the special favours the regent accorded to his son, rumoured to be her lover. His ascendancy was to last four years, until the younger Saint-Maurice was displaced by a new favourite, the conte di Masino, while his father was succeeded by a new chief minister, the marchese di Pianezza, Masino's uncle. Within the regent's scheme of personal power there was no place for her son. He posed a threat to her ambitions to rule magnificently and to cut a figure in European affairs, and so she sought deliberately to exclude him from power. But by trying to deprive him of his place at the head of the state, especially after he officially came of age in 1680, the regent turned him into a rallying-point for opposition, both at court and in the state at large.

In the tangled politics of the regency such a complication was hardly needed. A ruler's minority was always a time of instability during which the grandees jockeyed for advancement. Cabals flourished, ministers rose and fell, feuds flared up with brawls in the streets of Turin and skirmishes in the countryside. In this atmosphere of intrigue and governmental weakness Victor Amadeus grew to manhood. Such an experience must have reinforced his autocratic tendencies; when he finally came to power he was determined to be master in his own house, and to discipline his insubordinate nobles. But his mother, as temporary head of the state, could not do this. She could only juggle the opposing factions and dispense pensions to buy support. As a result she was criticized for extravagance, but much of the money she spent was to placate the grandees, while her lavish pageants and masques might be construed as a system of upper-class bread and circuses to distract her courtiers from their perpetual intrigues.

Charles Emanuel II's death left the state in disarray. During the decade or so that he had ruled in person (1663–75), with the aid of his finance minister Trucchi he had set in motion a host of projects calculated to place the state on a firm economic footing and to expand its trade and industry in accordance with the precepts of orthodox mercantilism. After his death most of these plans foundered and Trucchi no longer dominated the government. But the new direction of economic policy was not entirely forgotten; after an interval it was resumed by Victor Amadeus II, more thoroughly than before. A far more troubling legacy than these half-finished mercantilist projects lay in the baleful consequences of the war that Charles Emanuel had launched against Genoa in 1672, which ended in swift and humiliating defeat; a bitter search for scapegoats followed, and was still going on when the regent assumed power. Pianezza had played a leading part in the disastrous campaign of 1672 and was accused of treason. He fled to France and in May 1675 was condemned to death *in absentia*, despite Louis XIV's intercession. But in the long run the power of his family's name and Louis XIV's demands for his reinstatement were too much for the regent to resist. Early in 1679 she permitted him to return from exile, and in December 1680 he came back in triumph to Turin, to assume the leading place in the regent's counsels, supplanting his rival Saint-Maurice. The rise and fall of these ministers is partly attributable to factional rivalries at court, but the real determinant was the influence wielded by Louis XIV, who in both cases secured the advancement of a minister devoted to his interests. In the same way the regent herself depended on Louis XIV's goodwill because of the inherent weakness of her position, and he backed her as long as she offered the best means for upholding his interests. The Savoyard state under the regency was a French satellite, so that Victor Amadeus II grew up imbued with the need to free his state from the influence of Louis XIV.

After the peace of Nijmegen in 1678 Louis XIV made the most of his superiority over the other European powers to pursue a policy of limited aggrandizement, aimed chiefly at improving the strategic situation on his northern and eastern borders, but with Italy also occupying an important place on his agenda. He began secret negotiations to take over the duke of Mantua's fortress of Casale in Monferrato, a key strongpoint on the frontier between Piedmont and Lombardy. In return for a pension to defray the cost of his spectacular debaucheries the duke agreed to let the French occupy the town and its powerful citadel. In January 1679 the regent learned of the plan through the indiscretion of conte Mattioli, the duke of Mantua's agent, who was passing through Turin to complete the arrangements. The alarming implications of the scheme were at once apparent to the regent and her advisers: from Casale Louis XIV would hold Piedmont in a vice, overawe the lesser princes of northern Italy, and be able to attack Spanish Lombardy at any time. From Turin word of the negotiations spread swiftly to Milan, and the Spanish governor there arrested the officer sent by Louis XIV to implement the plan. The French king immediately suspected Mattioli as the source of the leak and had him imprisoned at Pinerolo; nor did he abandon his designs on Casale. Slowly he resumed the negotiations with the duke of Mantua, until in July 1681 the latter was persuaded to sign a treaty handing over the fortress. At the end of September a French force marched from Pinerolo across Piedmont and occupied Casale.

From this moment the regent was even more a captive of French power. Although she had tried to thwart Louis XIV's plan to occupy Casale, and never willingly gave in to his demands, she and her ministers were believed to be tools of French policy. Her government thus grew more unpopular, while her freedom of action was restricted by the presence of another French garrison on her borders. In January 1682 the French ambassador warned his master that 'there are few countries in the world where the French are less loved than they are here, and where Your Majesty's power arouses greater fear and suspicion, especially since your taking possession of Casale'.[1] High-handed actions by French envoys and continual pressure from Versailles added to the tensions besetting the regent's government. Open criticism was voiced against her at court, and the factions hostile to her and to French influence naturally tended to gravitate around the young Victor Amadeus, particularly since his minority had ended more than a year before, on his fourteenth birthday in May 1680. In October 1681 Louis XIV's minister Louvois commented that the regent ought to welcome the occupation of Casale, which strengthened the French military presence in her domains,

> since her authority in Piedmont can only be maintained through the active assistance of His Majesty [Louis XIV]. It is impossible that Madame Royale should so misunderstand her own interests as not to be glad to see the king in a position to ensure that she is obeyed in Piedmont, even against her own son, if he should league himself with her enemies.[2]

Shortly afterwards Louvois reaffirmed his master's intention of supporting the regent:

> The king desires nothing more than the continuation of the conduct that madame the duchess has been following for some time, and the maintenance of the government in her hands. As long as her authority lasts the king will consider his interests there better served than if his troops were stationed in the chief fortresses of the country.[3]

Louvois, however, was sounding a note of concern, reflecting his appreciation that the regent's political ascendancy was now very shaky. Her weakness stemmed not merely from her supposed subservience to French influence, but also from policies of her own which were unleashing a storm of opposition: most of this resentment focused on the project she had recently unveiled for her son's marriage. Since her first days in power the regent had been secretly pursuing a plan to marry Victor Amadeus to the Infanta of Portugal, daughter of the regent's sister. As the plan proceeded another dimension was grafted onto it: a scheme in the tradition of Trucchi's mercantilist projects for a company based at Nice to trade with the Portuguese empire. Once married, Victor Amadeus would reside at Lisbon and eventually succeed to the throne there, since there were no male heirs to the Portuguese crown. This arrangement would leave the regent in effective control of the Savoyard domains, ruling as her son's nominal viceroy. In December 1678 she secretly communicated her scheme to Louis XIV, who declared his approval. On 15 May 1679 the marriage contract was signed at Lisbon. But the project soon aroused widespread hostility among all levels of Savoyard society, and especially from the young duke himself, who perceived that the real purpose of the marriage was to remove him permanently from the centre of affairs at Turin. The French ambassador reported that when Victor Amadeus was first told of his impending marriage, on 22 July 1679, he sulked for two days.[4] His attitude encouraged the undercurrent of opposition to the regent's plan, and she was forced to proceed more cautiously. In the meantime disagreements arose with the Portuguese over the proposed trading company, further delaying the negotiations. The company was not set up until January 1681, with capital partly from the Savoyard government and partly from influential financiers and courtiers whom the regent obliged to contribute: heading the list was Pianezza.[5]

Once the trading company was established the regent pushed ahead with her plans for Victor Amadeus's marriage. In January 1681, at the same time that the commercial agreement was signed, he formally consented to marry the Infanta and promised to leave for Lisbon in the summer of 1682. But by this point a fresh obstacle had appeared, making the conclusion of the marriage increasingly problematical. In August 1680 simmering peasant discontent in the district of Mondovì had flared up in open rebellion. The insurrection had little to do with the Portuguese marriage, but the regent's enemies fanned the flames in order to embarrass her and checkmate the scheme. From time to time the rebels demanded that the regent abandon her plans to send her son away to Portugal, but contemporary observers believed that these protests were largely the work of powerful figures at court rumoured to be in league with the insurgents. The French ambassador singled out the marchese di Parella for blame; he was the leader of the pro-Spanish faction at court, a declared foe of the

Portuguese marriage, and known to have clients and followers at Mondovì. The regent made every effort to bring the troubles to a speedy end, knowing that if the revolt spread the Portuguese authorities would think twice about an alliance with the strife-torn Savoyard state. But her attempts to crush the revolt were unsuccessful, and by the summer of 1681 she faced a crisis: her authority was being openly flouted by the rebels, cabals were proliferating at court, the Portuguese marriage was in jeopardy, and Louis XIV had been offered a fresh opportunity to intervene in Savoyard affairs under the guise of aiding in the suppression of the revolt.

The immediate cause of the rebellion at Mondovì in 1680 was the imposition of a *donativo* to pay for Victor Amadeus's forthcoming marriage, but the momentum behind the revolt was generated by opposition to the salt gabelle: the name by which the revolt is generically known – the 'Salt War' – reveals the decisive importance of the salt tax as a catalyst of rebellion. Mounting fiscal pressure from the state was felt with particular force in a province which had traditionally enjoyed immunity from new taxes, based on a charter granted in 1396 when it accepted Savoyard suzerainty. But this charter was more than just a guarantee of fiscal immunity; to the people of Mondovì it was the cornerstone of a whole system of political and judicial liberties, which added up to a broad freedom to run their own affairs. The 'Salt War' therefore marks the moment of collision between the expanding authority of the state and the tradition of local autonomy, in a region more strongly attached to its ancient independence than perhaps any other in Piedmont.

The district of Mondovì was traditionally a turbulent region, where the authority of the central government enjoyed little respect. Feud and vendetta were common; smuggling was rampant. Lying on the Genoese frontier, the region was a natural haven for contrabandiers who moved with impunity along the pack-trails of its rugged hinterland. They went armed, to defend themselves from rival bands or the customs officials, and in fact the carrying of weapons was general among the peasantry of the whole region. Frequent prohibitions by the government against the bearing of arms had no effect. Smuggling and vendetta threw up a constant stream of outlaws who took to the hills, and groups of bandits and smugglers played an important part in keeping the rebellions going. But they were notoriously volatile: the promise of a reward or a pardon could turn them against their fellow rebels. For the smugglers, the salt tax was a crucial matter. They bought salt in Genoese territory in defiance of the fisc, or carried it from Mondovì, where it was cheap, to the surrounding provinces where the salt gabelle made it far more expensive. Any attempt by the government to tighten up the administration of the salt gabelle or to restrict the flow of contraband salt was a direct threat to the smugglers' livelihood, and they reacted accordingly.

But it is not enough to write off the long series of revolts in the Monregalese (as the district was called) as the work of smugglers and des-
perados. The turbulence of the region, the bands of outlaws that it
sheltered, were the expression of a wider reality: Mondovì was accustomed to living more by its own laws than by the state's. Even the local
clergy were riotous and undisciplined, constantly at odds with the law.[6]
Bandits and outlaws survived and flourished because they enjoyed the
protection, or at least the implicit tolerance, of the populations of the
isolated mountain villages, which lived their own life apart from the rest
of the state, and distrusted outsiders. Such fierce independence could be
the source of great internal strength and formed the mainspring of revolt;
in the face of the state and its officials, the villagers banded together and
fought tenaciously side by side. But isolation also narrowed the rebels'
political horizons and prevented them from building more broadly-based
resistance. So one village fought against another, out of traditional
enmity or for momentary advantage, and the central government was
able to exploit their differences in a classic policy of *divide et impera*.
Disunity would finally prove fatal to the rebels' cause, and their watch-
word 'se fossimo uniti le cose anderebbero meglio' (if we were united
things would go better) expresses a clear realization of their irreparable
divisions. The mountain villagers shared little sense of common interest
with the inhabitants of the lowland communities, where a more commercialized form of agriculture and an incipient economy of exchanges were
dissolving the bonds of communal solidarity; they shared even less of a
sense of purpose with the citizens of Mondovì, who lived largely by trade
and manufacture under an oligarchy of lawyers and merchants. The
upland communities south of Mondovì resembled the isolated villages of
the county of Nice or the backlands of Savoy. They were self-contained,
living off their meagre resources, and their economic base of subsistence
farming and autoconsumption had its political counterpart in a pro-
nounced feeling of local autonomy. Much of the land belonging to these
villages was given over to vast stands of chestnut trees which provided the
staple food for the population; many of the chestnut plantations were
owned in common by the communities, or by local confraternities. The
latter served as the dispensers of charity in hard times, thus performing a
vital economic function, as well as reinforcing the social bonds within the
community. The importance of the village confraternities is indicated by
the fact that in 1699, when the government finally crushed the revolt, they
became a prime target for repression: the communal stands of chestnuts
were cut down and the ceremonial and social activities of the confraternities were discouraged.

By the later seventeenth century the economy of the mountain communities was being stretched to its limits, especially in the highest valleys,
where climatic fluctuations were felt most brutally. Recurrent food

shortages – as in the 1670s – forced the population to turn to other means of subsistence like petty trade, smuggling or increased seasonal migration. The isolation of the village economies began to break down, differences of wealth within each community were magnified, and divergencies of interest grew more apparent. The stress of sustained revolt in the 1680s accelerated the formation of rifts within the rebel communities; the tiny élite of the better-off was willing to compromise with the government and abandon its fellows. Internal dissension as much as military repression was to prove the rebels' undoing in 1699.

The city of Mondovì was a place of some significance at this time, a centre of the tanning industry and a staging-post on the road to Genoa. The war with Genoa in 1672 and the Piedmontese government's efforts to levy tolls on goods passing through the territory of Mondovì provoked severe unrest, contributing to the rebellious mood of the entire region. Mondovì was the centre of provincial government and the seat of a bishopric; it also boasted a Studium or college of law, the symbol of its civic pride, which it vigorously defended against Turin's claims to a monopoly of higher education for its own university. The running battle with Turin over the Studium was part of a rearguard action fought not only by Mondovì, but by all the lesser cities of Piedmont against the rising power of the capital. In 1680 the syndics of Mondovì took the lead in the initial revolt, and their defiance can perhaps be seen as a last assertion of civic independence against the growth of the central power. But the municipal oligarchy was too weak to pursue its course for long, and eventually came to terms with the state. Its power had been undermined in part by debt. Decades of war and natural catastrophes had overwhelmed the city's finances, while the state had taken over many of the local gabelles which formerly provided the revenues to fill the city treasury. One of the chief remaining sources of income for Mondovì was its own salt gabelle, which the city administered; it bought the salt on the open market – not from the state tax-farmers – and resold it to its citizens at a price much lower than that prevailing in the rest of the state. This privilege was distinctly advantageous to the municipality and to the population of the whole district, so that the government's threat to establish the salt gabelle mobilized resistance on a broad front, in city and countryside alike. But in the long run the city of Mondovì could not command the loyalties of its dependent territory. The surrounding villages felt, with good reason, that the city oligarchy used its dominant position to shift a disproportionate share of taxes onto their shoulders. So they constantly demanded changes in the structure of government in the district in order to distribute power – and taxes – more equably. But remodelling the local administration had little effect; real power remained in the hands of the leading citizens of Mondovì. These resentments divided the city from its hinterland, and provided a fertile source of discord for the state to exploit.

The roots of the 'Salt War' thus go back long before 1680; the district had been in a condition of endemic rebellion for decades, and the outbreak of insurrection in August 1680 was merely one episode in a continuing saga of revolt. In 1654 the government's first attempt to extend the salt gabelle to Mondovì had provoked an uprising, since it meant not only that the local population would have to pay far higher prices for its salt, but also that the government would enforce an obligatory quota of salt for each taxpayer, and would draw up tax-rolls to ensure that this quota was purchased. The apparently simple procedure of 'dividing the register', as the process of establishing a roll of individual taxpayers was called, would revolutionize the relationship between the local population and the state. Instead of buying his salt – and only as much as he wanted – from his local community, the taxpayer would now have to submit to the investigation of a census-taker and buy an obligatory quota of salt from the *gabellieri*. Every village, instead of acting as a single community, as before, would be reduced to a list of individual taxpayers, each in direct contact with the fisc. The government's periodic efforts to draw up tax-registers and establish quotas for the salt gabelle, as in 1667, thus met with evasion or outright opposition. Further fiscal demands coincided with a period of economic setbacks for the region; the war with Genoa in 1672 disrupted trade, troops devastated the border area, and a sequence of bad harvests eroded the narrow margin of subsistence on which the population lived, particularly in the mountains. Smuggling increased and public order virtually broke down. In 1675 the regent – who had just assumed power – appointed the marchese Pallavicino to pacify the district; in the following year he was given the formal title of *direttore* of the province. The choice of Pallavicino was by no means felicitous. He was a local feudatory, lord of the village of Frabosa, and was therefore mistrusted; moreover he was reputed to have profited from speculations on the city debt of Mondovì. He soon became enmeshed in conflict with the leading citizens of Mondovì over his plans for reorganizing the system of local government, and his high-handed efforts to collect taxes from the clergy, who claimed exemption from them, led to another wave of armed resistance.

Mondovì and its district were therefore seething with discontent in the summer of 1680 as news spread of Victor Amadeus's impending marriage, and of the special *donativo* to pay for it. The local authorities, headed by Giovanni Grasso, syndic of Mondovì, apportioned the payment of the *donativo* between the dozen or so communities of the district, including the village of Villanova which had recently been infeudated to the conte Faussone. The latter refused to allow Villanova to pay its share of the *donativo* and insulted the officials sent from Mondovì to collect it. The citizens marched out in force and a riot broke out as Faussone was made to publish the order for levying the *donativo*.

This rebellion in August 1680 was the start of a new cycle of revolt. The regent ordered Pallavicino and the military governor of Mondovì to suppress the disorders and arrest the leaders, notably Grasso. The latter took sanctuary in a monastery and from there directed a widening campaign of resistance; the council ceased meeting, local administration came to a standstill, taxes went unpaid. The people of the surrounding villages rallied in support of Grasso and the council, gathering in large armed bands to deter intervention by the garrison of Mondovì, or any other forces that the government might send to enforce its will. The regent now faced a crisis, just as the negotiations for Victor Amadeus's Portuguese marriage entered their most delicate phase. At first she sought to negotiate, but by the early months of 1681 she and her advisers became convinced that the only solution was to suppress the rebellion by force, before it could spread to other parts of the state, and before her opponents at court could exploit the unrest for their own purposes, and prevent Victor Amadeus from departing for Lisbon as planned. Early in May 1681 a force of about 2,500 troops advanced on Mondovì, temporarily overawing the rebels; municipal elections were resumed and taxes began to be collected once more. This success encouraged the government to proceed with its old plan for doing away with the district's privileged fiscal status: on 23 May Pallavicino issued orders for levying the salt gabelle and set up a special tribunal to try the leaders of the rebellion.

The focus of resistance now shifted to the countryside; Mondovì itself was cowed, and some of its leading citizens were declaring their willingness to act as collectors of the new salt gabelle. But the mountain communities – especially the village of Montaldo – remained unsubdued, and the government troops now faced the difficult task of reducing them by force. On 24 June the army attacked Montaldo, driving the peasants into the forests, and forcing the syndics to acquiesce in the establishment of a tax-register for the salt gabelle. But the troops had suffered heavy losses fighting their way through the defiles towards Montaldo against peasant sharpshooters lurking among the trees, and their commander Don Gabriele di Savoia warned the regent that the rebels could not be easily put down. Nevertheless, heartened by this apparent success, the regent withdrew half the troops from the district, leaving only about 1,000 men to levy the salt gabelle. This proved to be a serious mistake. The resistance of Montaldo had rekindled the revolt, and once the harvest was gathered the peasants were free to counter-attack. In the first days of August 1681 well-organized bands of rebels began to close in on Mondovì, and on 14 August they occupied the lower suburb of Mondovì-Breo, sacking the houses of the wealthier citizens who were suspected of being government tax-collectors. The revolt was now taking on distinct overtones of a war between the poor peasants of the hinterland and the better-off city-dwellers, and seemed likely to spread to the neighbouring provinces. In this emergency the government recalled its forces to Mondovì. On 20 August they recaptured Breo and pacified the surrounding area. But they did not venture into the hinterland, leaving the rebels there undisturbed.

Military force had not crushed the rebels or imposed the salt tax. The entire district was in an uproar; taxes could not be collected; disorder reigned. The regent's attempts to quell the revolt by military force had failed, and she was forced to adopt a more conciliatory policy. This change was hastened by Louis XIV's occupation of Casale at the end of September, which was immediately followed by an offer of French troops to help put down the rebels. The real meaning of this proffered assistance was clear: Louis XIV was seeking new ways to intervene in the internal affairs of the Savoyard state, and the rebellion at Mondovì provided him with an excellent opportunity. It was therefore imperative to end the revolt, so early in October 1681 the regent appointed the marquis de Senantes to command the district of Mondovì, with orders to negotiate a settlement. But by spring 1682 a settlement still had not been reached, and the time for Victor Amadeus's departure for Portugal was approaching. Rumours circulated that the rebels would try to prevent him from travelling to Nice to embark. Faced by this threat to her plans the regent had to give in and meet all the insurgents' demands. On 5 April 1682 a full pardon was granted, the compulsory quotas of salt were abolished and all arrears of taxation were cancelled.

Outwardly the peasants of Mondovì had won an impressive victory and had shaken the regent's authority to its foundations. But this was as far as their limited conception of revolt could take them. They were disunited, and the violence they had directed against the government and its troops now increasingly turned inwards upon themselves: the countryside fought against the city, one village against another, family against family. The revolt had lost whatever cohesion it originally possessed; its success was due less to the rebels' strength than to the extreme weakness of the regent's government, undermined by aristocratic faction and beset by external pressure. Despite the amnesty the troubles went on: when Victor Amadeus II assumed power in his own right in 1684 one of his first actions would be a renewed attempt to suppress the disorders around Mondovì, and the unrest there would continue with varying intensity until he finally crushed it in 1699.

In June 1682 a Portuguese squadron anchored off Nice, ready to transport Victor Amadeus to Lisbon. But he did not embark. On learning of the squadron's departure he had fallen ill, and through the summer of 1682 his condition worsened until for a while his life was thought to be in danger. His illness may have been genuine; a special French envoy sent to investigate believed that it was, although its timing naturally aroused suspicion.[7] Perhaps his early childhood maladies had recurred; perhaps he was afflicted by a psychosomatic reaction brought on by repugnance for the marriage forced upon him by his detested mother. But genuine or not, the illness proved to be the final stumbling-block that put an end to the Portuguese marriage. In September the Portuguese squadron sailed away from Nice and the Portuguese ambassador left Turin in disgust. Almost at once Victor Amadeus's health began to improve.

Through the summer of 1682 as Victor Amadeus lay ill and the Portuguese negotiations broke down, the aristocratic opposition to the regent erupted in an insurrection headed by the marchese di Parella. For some time he had been plotting against the regent, and as we have seen he was suspected of being in league with the rebels at Mondovì. In January 1682 he approached the Venetian envoy at Milan with a proposition: he would capture the French fortresses at Pinerolo and Casale, overthrow the regent, stop Victor Amadeus's marriage to the Infanta of Portugal and form a new government at Turin which would take the lead in creating a league of Italian states, with the Emperor's backing, to keep the French permanently out of Italy. Parella's plans soon leaked out. In July 1682 he asked the Venetians for immediate help to raise a revolt at Ivrea and to stir up more trouble around Mondovì, but before he could act the plot was discovered. On 15 August he fled to his estates near Biella where he raised a band of several hundred armed peasants as the nucleus of his planned insurrection. But no outside help materialized and after a few days he prudently took refuge across the border in Milan. The revolt fizzled out: his men at Biella did not join forces with the insurgents around Mondovì, as the regent initially feared they might, and there were no repercussions among Parella's friends at court. The conspiracy had failed, but it had administered a nasty shock to the regent, again revealing the insecurity of her position.

Louis XIV and Louvois now exploited the regent's growing weakness to conclude a formal alliance with her: by this time French support was the only prop that sustained her and she could not refuse their demands. The origins of the alliance go back to a renewed offer of military assistance made by Louis XIV in May 1682, when the rebels at Mondovì seemed to threaten Victor Amadeus's passage to Nice.[8] The regent turned this offer aside by suggesting the possibility of a permanent military commitment to protect herself and safeguard French interests in Piedmont. Negotiations proceeded inconclusively through the summer, until Parella's abortive rising brought home to the regent how insecure her position was. On 24 November 1682 she signed a treaty along the lines dictated by her protector. The stated purpose of the alliance was to protect the Savoyard domains from attack, and to secure the French border, Pinerolo and Casale. But its other aim, left unstated, was equally important: to keep the regent in power. As Louis XIV explained to his ambassador, 'as long as His Majesty keeps Casale and has a corps of 3,000 horse on the other side of the Alps, that princess's authority will be secure against both foreign and domestic foes'.[9]

Just how necessary such protection had become was demonstrated by another aristocratic plot less than a month later. This time the instigator was none other than Pianezza, the regent's chief adviser. Always an astute politician, he had concluded that the regent's days were numbered, for there were signs that Louis XIV was ready to abandon her and throw his influence behind Victor Amadeus, whose claims to rule the state were becoming harder for his mother to deny as he grew older. As soon as the alliance had been concluded Louis XIV proposed that the young duke be married to the daughter of the duke of Orleans – an old idea originally put forward at the start of the regency, and opportunely revived now that the Portuguese marriage had collapsed.[10] Pianezza was privy to these overtures and understood their significance: once Victor Amadeus was married it would be impossible for his mother to exclude him from power any longer; he would be an adult in every sense of the term and head of his own household, while Louis XIV would hardly permit the husband of his niece to rule as a mere figurehead. The details of Pianezza's man-oeuvres remain obscure, but in the middle of December 1682 his nephew, the conte di Druento, approached Victor Amadeus with a secret proposal from Pianezza to overthrow the regent.[11] Victor Amadeus listened to this proposition with apparent sympathy, but then informed his mother. On 21 December Pianezza and Druento were arrested and imprisoned. By betraying their plot Victor Amadeus displayed a precocious talent for duplicity and a cool sense of his own interests. He recognized that Pianezza's real purpose was to perpetuate his own ascendancy as chief minister after the regent's fall; the young duke would merely have ex-changed his mother's tutelage for that of a powerful minister. This he never accepted, even in the earliest days of his personal reign: one of his fundamental maxims was to rule alone, like Louis XIV whom he so admired. Furthermore, he knew that the discussions for his marriage to a French princess meant that he must soon come to power in his own right; Pianezza's aid was superfluous. French influence which had so long main-tained his mother in power was now working in his favour, and he was prepared to wait while events took their course.

Sensing his new strength, Victor Amadeus began to assert himself more openly and at last received a place in his mother's council of ministers. Quarrels between him and his mother grew more frequent and more public. In the meantime he carefully cultivated Louis XIV's support. On 13 May 1683 the French ambassador reported that the young duke had declared his undying admiration for the French monarch, and had asked for a French princess to be his bride.[12] Such dutiful protestations were a necessary part of the role that Victor Amadeus was called upon to play: in order to speed his emancipation from his mother he had to convince Louis XIV of his reliability, since the king would withdraw his support for the regent only if he was convinced that Victor Amadeus would be as valuable a guardian of French interests as she had been. The regent meanwhile sought to delay her son's marriage and the transfer of power that would follow it. Louis XIV demanded still more concessions from her, in order to strengthen his hold on Piedmont and prepare for the war that he was about to launch against Spain. On 2 November 1683 Louvois warned the regent that she must choose either to admit a French garrison to the fortresses of Turin and Verrua, or consent to Victor Amadeus's marriage to Anne of Orleans. Each option would produce the same result – French control of Piedmont. In the face of this ultimatum the regent reluctantly consented to her son's marriage as the lesser of the two evils. On 28 January 1684 Louis XIV and the duke of Orleans signed the marriage contract. On 14 March Victor Amadeus assumed power in his own right, and his mother retired into private life. On 10 April the marriage was solemnized by proxy at Paris, and soon afterwards his bride set out to meet him. The couple were formally married on 7 May at Chambéry, and on 20 May made their ceremonial entry into Turin. Victor Amadeus's personal reign had begun.

VI
The First Years of Personal Rule and the Massacre of the Vaudois (1684–1687)

The state to which Victor Amadeus II succeeded was internally weak, riven by aristocratic faction and peasant unrest, and externally subject to the dictates of Louis XIV. During the regency the state's finances had been increasingly burdened by debt, partly because of a severe famine in 1679, which necessitated government subsidies to the overworked local charities and poorhouses, and the purchase of supplies of grain from abroad; partly by the costs of Victor Amadeus's abortive Portuguese marriage; and partly by the generous pensions paid to the regent's favourites. On his accession Victor Amadeus therefore accorded a high priority to the restoration of financial stability, an aim which he was to pursue with unremitting energy throughout his reign. In a memorandum written about this time he listed financial reform as one of his prime concerns.[1] But at this juncture he was not ready to confront the long and complex task of restructuring the fiscal system, as he would later on; for the present he sought mainly to cut back expenses. Out of parsimony (and probably also spite) he drastically reduced his mother's household and pension, relegating her to political obscurity with a modest retinue that would not outshine his own. But these economy measures did not extend to the army. He worked incessantly to strengthen his forces, modernize their equipment and improve their training, in the tradition that his dynasty had followed for a century and more. One foreign envoy noted that 'soldiers occupy all his thoughts; war, and plans for war consume almost his entire attention, together with resolute and glorious ideas'.[2] But he was seeking more than mere military glory; his ultimate purpose was to create the means to free his state from foreign domination and to establish his authority securely at home.

The problem of internal security confronted Victor Amadeus immediately upon his accession, and once more it was centred in the district of Mondovì. In the summer of 1684 the disorders spread to the region around Ceva to the south: customs officials were assaulted and the levying of tolls was interrupted. To prevent these disturbances from developing into a full-scale insurrection Victor Amadeus marched to Ceva in September with 3,000 troops. He imprisoned the ringleaders of the rebellion, proclaimed a general amnesty and then withdrew, leaving some regiments of dragoons quartered in the district to contain the unrest. But the disorders continued. Late in 1686 the country around Mondovì erupted in a new wave of rebellion provoked by the levying of an old tax on meat. At this moment Victor Amadeus was fully occupied in dealing with the Vaudois of the mountain valleys above Turin, and was in no position to suppress the rebels at Mondovì by force. All he could do was to detach Parella (who had returned from exile and was now one of his closest advisers) to pardon the insurgents and restore the settlement on the same lines as before.

Victor Amadeus followed a conciliatory policy towards the rebels at Mondovì since his authority was still insecure and he lacked the force to crush them. Not only was his army unequal to the task; he was also obliged to adjust his conduct to the demands of Louis XIV, whose tutelage remained as oppressive as during the regency. An object-lesson in the uses of French power was offered by the bombardment of Genoa in 1684 and the Doge's humiliating journey to Versailles to submit to Louis XIV's terms. Direct French intervention in Savoyard affairs went on as before. In October Louis XIV warned Victor Amadeus to stop the marriage that his uncle, the prince of Carignano, was rumoured to be contemplating with a princess of the house of Este. The marriage was solemnized in haste and secrecy early in November, to forestall Louis XIV's prohibition, whereupon the king showed his displeasure by ordering that the prince and his new bride be sent into exile.[3] In March 1685 Louis XIV abrogated the subsidy clauses of the treaty he had signed with the regent in 1682, forcing Victor Amadeus to disband the troops that he maintained with French support. Yet although this reduction in his army rendered Victor Amadeus even less capable of independent action than before, Louis XIV grew more mistrustful of him and enjoined his ambassador at Turin to watch the young duke closely. This mounting intervention led a few months later to an ultimatum from Louis XIV demanding action against the Protestant Vaudois in the mountains above Turin, and finally to an all-out military campaign aimed at the total destruction of the Vaudois, in which Victor Amadeus was compelled to accede to the pressure of his powerful neighbour.

The war of extermination against the Vaudois – for such it in fact was – must be seen mainly as an extension of Louis XIV's persecution of his own Protestant subjects, which reached its climax with the revocation of the Edict of Nantes in October 1685. Victor Amadeus II was drawn into this crusade because of the close ties that united his own Protestant subjects, the Piedmontese Vaudois, to the Huguenots just across the Alps in Dauphiné. The Vaudois were the last remnant of the medieval Waldensians, founded about 1160 by Peter Waldo of Lyon; condemned as heretical and relentlessly persecuted, they survived only as a small community in the Alpine valleys to the west of Turin. Left to himself, Victor Amadeus would probably not have persecuted them, for they were peaceable subjects who paid their taxes and posed no threat to public order. Contingents of Vaudois militiamen had taken part in the recent campaigns against the rebels of Mondovì. But in the autumn of 1685 Louis XIV's demands revived a tradition of intolerance ever present in the government's attitude towards the Vaudois, and the campaign of destruction unleashed against them soon after must also be seen as a repetition of earlier persecutions in 1487, 1561, 1655 and 1663. Hostility to the Vaudois was traditional among groups of devout nobles, lay confraternities and of course the clergy, so that when Louis XIV pressed Victor Amadeus to launch a new wave of persecution against them, his demands were strongly endorsed by Catholic opinion in the Savoyard state.

Initially Victor Amadeus resisted Louis XIV's demands, not from any belief in the virtue of toleration, but for reasons of expediency: he resented this intrusion into his domestic affairs, and he knew from previous crusades against the Vaudois that any campaign against them would be bitterly contested, for they could be formidable guerrilla fighters in their native valleys. But once his reluctance had been overcome, Victor Amadeus carried through the persecution with ruthless efficiency. He personally directed the campaign in the spring of 1686 that led to the extermination or deportation of all but a few of the Vaudois; he did nothing to ease the rigours of their subsequent imprisonment, in which thousands perished. And at the same time he sought to ingratiate himself with Pope Innocent XI (who however was not deceived), claiming the persecutions as the outcome of his own spontaneous zeal for the faith, and seeking rewards for this supposedly disinterested action.[4] The persecution might originally have been forced upon Victor Amadeus, but he soon made a virtue out of necessity. He would secure the support of devout circles at court and in the state at large; he would win glory for having finally rooted out the Protestant minority that had so long resisted his forefathers; he would obtain Louis XIV's commendation and whatever goodwill he might gain from the other Catholic states of Europe.

Louis XIV's escalating demands for action against the Vaudois in the later months of 1685 represented a new factor in their tense and troubled relationship with their sovereigns. It also underscored the fact that this relationship was more than just a matter of internal politics; it figured as an important element in the confessional hostilities that polarized all Europe. The survival of the Vaudois as a tiny Protestant minority in an overwhelmingly Catholic state was due in large part to the support of the Protestant powers abroad. Their most valuable aid came from the city of Geneva and the Protestant Cantons of Switzerland, partly by reason of their proximity, but much more because the original Vaudois Church had merged with the Reformed Churches of Switzerland in 1532–35. In 1655 when the Savoyard government launched a crusade against the Vaudois, the Protestant Cantons protested and mobilized the other Protestant powers – including Cromwell's England – in their defence.[5] But in 1655 it was French influence that had proved decisive in halting the persecutions, for at that time Mazarin was seeking closer ties with the Protestant states, particularly England, and prevailed on the Savoyard government to reach a settlement. Again in 1663, during another period of troubles, French mediation had been instrumental in restoring peace between the Vaudois and their ruler, and since that time the limited toleration under which the Vaudois lived had depended on the maintenance of French amity, or at least neutrality. But by 1685 French policy had become openly hostile, and the international balance of forces now tipped decisively against the Vaudois, placing their very existence in jeopardy. Moreover, the Protestant powers were now divided, and England was ruled by the Catholic James II. The external guarantees that formerly enabled the Vaudois to survive had largely collapsed.

They were thus left to fend for themselves, aided only by the diplomatic intercession of the Protestant Cantons. In this crisis – the most desperate in their entire history – they could trust only in their courage and skill as guerrilla fighters, and in the solidarity that held them together in the face of danger. The territory that they occupied, in the Alps west of Turin, was well suited to resistance: it consisted of the two principal valleys that converge on Pinerolo, the Val Pellice and the Val Chisone, with the quadrilateral of mountains in between, extending from the edge of the plains at San Giovanni to the crest of the Alps. This inhospitable territory could not support a large population, and in 1685 the entire Vaudois community numbered no more than about 15,000 individuals.[6] Part of this population was concentrated in little townships like La Torre or San Giovanni, but most of the Vaudois lived in hamlets and farmsteads scattered through their mountains. To a large degree they were administratively autonomous. They were grouped in about thirty parishes, each of which elected its elders, who in turn participated in the synods that met to settle communal affairs and choose the pastors. Within each parish a group of deacons dispensed charity from a common fund and saw to the day-to-day management of affairs, including the parish schools. Religious and political authority were thus indistinguishable, and leadership in the community was provided by the elected elders and pastors. The tight bonds that united mountain communities everywhere – as in the county of Nice, or in the hinterland of Mondovì – were reinforced for the Vaudois by the knowledge of being a persecuted religious minority, which conferred a sense of separateness best summed up in pastor Henri Arnaud's description of his people as 'la nation vaudoise'.[7] Preservation of the faith and preservation of the community were inseparable; after the catastrophe of 1686, as we shall see, the Vaudois refused to resign themselves to exile and dispersion, in which their uniqueness would have gradually disappeared. Even though they were free to worship as they chose in their places of exile, they preferred to fight against fearful odds to re-establish themselves in their ancestral valleys. Their faith could not be divorced from the community through which it found expression.

Yet under the pressures that bore down on them in the later months of 1685 the Vaudois began to divide: dangerous fissures appeared within the community, revealed by a growing number of conversions to Catholicism. In part this incipient disunity was the result of economic factors: the poorest villagers were tempted by the bounties and tax exemptions that the government offered to converts, while a few richer men converted out of a desire to preserve their property. But the strain within the Vaudois community was probably due far more to the long-term effects of political and religious pressure from the state. Each Vaudois parish was obliged to pay tithes to support the Catholic clergy, while it also had to contribute to the support of a hierarchy of state officials – judges, tax-collectors, a military governor and garrison at La Torre, and by now an intendant as well. All official functions – even down to that of the local notaries – were reserved to Catholics, and state officials were under orders to assist the work of the missionary fathers, who had operated in the valleys since the beginning of the century. Their activities were sponsored by the Savoyard authorities, by the Papal Nuncio at Turin and by the high clergy there, as well as by pious laymen like the old marchese di Pianezza (father to the regent's minister) who had endowed a missionary foundation at Turin, or by confraternities like the influential Compagnia di San Paolo. Under the stress of events in 1685 and early 1686 the slow pressure from prolonged missionary activity began to produce its effects, and conversion drove a wedge into the Vaudois community. Imperceptibly undermined by decades of state harassment, and faced by the fearful military might of Louis XIV, the Vaudois fell prey to despair, each village seeking its own salvation and abandoning all thought of a common front.

The news of the revocation of the Edict of Nantes in October 1685 caused alarm in the Vaudois valleys, where the population was in close touch with the Huguenots of Dauphiné across the mountains, and with the communities of Vaudois under French sovereignty in the enclave embracing the valley of Pragelato and the northern edge of the Val Chisone leading to Pinerolo. Through the summer and autumn of 1685 large numbers of Huguenots attempted to flee into exile, despite an official ban on emigration, seeking sanctuary at Geneva or in the Vaudois valleys on the Piedmontese sides of the Alps. Some of the bolder spirits among the Piedmontese Vaudois aided the escaping Huguenots, attacked the French border-patrols and even raided into French territory in support of their Protestant brethren. Most, however, held back from such actions, fearing the consequences. The rising violence along the border and the constant drift of refugees attracted Louis XIV's attention, and he demanded that Victor Amadeus curb the disorders; on 4 November the latter issued an edict forbidding the Vaudois to aid the Huguenot refugees.[8] This measure produced little effect. Louis XIV now became more insistent, and mobilized his forces at Briançon and Pinerolo for punitive action; he offered Victor Amadeus the use of these troops to pacify the region, and to convert the Vaudois in another *dragonnade*.

The disturbances in the Vaudois country gave Louis XIV a pretext to intervene yet again in Savoyard affairs, in effect dictating the conduct Victor Amadeus was to observe towards his own subjects. It was this encroachment on his already limited sovereignty that made Victor Amadeus resist the French demands and postpone action as long as he could. But in the meantime the situation was deteriorating. The clashes between bands of Vaudois and French troops roused Louis XIV to fury, and raised questions about the security of the corridor of French territory leading to Pinerolo. On 7 December 1685 Louis XIV wrote to his ambassador at Turin that 'it is the presence of the Piedmontese Vaudois on the frontiers of my state that causes the flight of my subjects, and you must inform their Prince that I am resolved not to tolerate it any longer'.[9] By now it seems that Louis XIV was convinced that the only way to restore order on the frontier, halt the exodus of refugees and secure communications with Pinerolo was by destroying or converting the Piedmontese Vaudois. Such an action would also form a fitting conclusion to his forcible conversion of the French Protestants, enhancing his stature as a devout Catholic ruler and perhaps improving his relations with the Pope, then at a particularly low point. He therefore demanded in increasingly peremptory terms that Victor Amadeus follow his own example in dealing with his Protestant subjects. On 31 January 1686, acceding finally to Louis XIV's demands, the duke signed another edict, revoking all the measures of toleration formerly granted to the Vaudois: their temples were to be razed, their pastors and schoolmasters were to go into exile, public Protestant worship was to cease, and all children were to be baptised Catholics.[10]

The edict of 31 January spread panic in the Vaudois valleys, climaxing months of rumours and alarms, and split the beleaguered community into two parties, one favouring compliance, the other resistance. The latter group – by far the smaller – began stockpiling weapons and food for guerrilla warfare in the tradition of 1561 or 1655. But the majority of the Vaudois opted for submission, or remained undecided, hoping somehow for better terms. During February tumultuous assemblies met on three different occasions to discuss the course of action to be adopted; they sent deputations to Turin, seeking delay or some softening of the edict, but Victor Amadeus refused to see them. At this the mood in the valleys turned to defiance. Public worship, suspended for a month in obedience to the edict, was now resumed. Then early in March 1686 ambassadors arrived from the Protestant Cantons to mediate. They found Victor Amadeus still unbending, and so on 24 March they appeared before yet another assembly of the Vaudois, pleading with them to submit, give up all thought of resistance, and go into exile in Switzerland or some other friendly state. The Swiss proposals completed the work of splitting the Vaudois hopelessly and irreconcilably: many accepted the offer of exile, but a few continued to urge resistance. Victor Amadeus had meanwhile agreed to the Swiss plan for exiling the Vaudois, but stipulated that they must first make an act of formal submission to him. On 2 April another assembly met in the valleys to consider this new development. Two-thirds of those present voted to submit and emigrate, but the rest – the people of Angrogna, Bobbio, San Giovanni and some from La Torre – swore to fight. At this point, with the Vaudois paralysed by their internal divisions, Victor Amadeus issued another edict, ordering an end to all military preparations and the surrender of all weapons within eight days; on this condition the Vaudois would be allowed to emigrate in peace. The Swiss envoys travelled back to the valleys, urging compliance and warning of the dangers of resistance against the overwhelming French and Savoyard forces that had by now been massed, ready to attack as soon as the spring weather permitted.

Despite the odds, however, the Vaudois resolved to fight. They had perhaps 3,000 fighting men, encumbered by 12,000 non-combatants, against a force of over 4,500 ducal troops, backed by several thousand local militiamen – including a large contingent from Mondovì – and about 4,000 French regulars commanded by Catinat. The Vaudois apparently had no unified plan of resistance; each separate village or township looked after itself, some fighting fiercely, others surrendering before a shot had been fired. On 22 April Victor Amadeus led his army from the plain at Bricherasio to attack the valleys, while the French forces under Catinat executed a flanking movement from Pinerolo up the Val Chisone. Within three days all organized resistance had ceased. Almost the entire Vaudois population was either dead or prisoners: most surrendered in return for promises of clemency and safe-conduct, which were subsequently violated. Everywhere the progress of the French and Savoyard troops was marked by hideous atrocities, as combatants and non-combatants alike were hunted down and butchered. Farms, livestock and crops were destroyed to deprive any survivors of subsistence. Altogether perhaps 2,000 Vaudois were killed in the fighting or massacred by the soldiery; the rest, apart from a small band of survivors who fought on through the summer, were taken as prisoners to Turin. Of the survivors, some 3,000 converted, many of these being children who were baptised and placed in Catholic homes. Those who remained obdurate – some 8,500 in all – were imprisoned in various fortresses. By the time of their release in March 1687 only 3,841 of them survived.[11]

Through the summer the government began resettling the Vaudois valleys, where only about 2,500 persons now remained, the part of the population that had converted before 1686. The lands of the others were confiscated and resold – often to the accompaniment of profitable speculation by the officials concerned – to Catholic colonists brought in from other parts of the state. Villages were repopulated, their elected councils reconstituted, and farming resumed under the protection of garrisons of ducal troops. The process of resettlement was impeded, however, by the raids of the small band of Vaudois guerrillas who remained in the mountains, eluding the patrols and harassing the new colonists. Suspecting that the recent converts were assisting the rebels, the government expelled many of them from the valleys, but the raids continued until November, when by agreement with the Swiss Cantons, the Vaudois 'Invincibles' went into exile, arms in hand, over the mountains to Geneva. At the same time the Swiss envoys worked to effect the release of the thousands of Vaudois in prison. Faced with the expense of maintaining them in captivity, Victor Amadeus finally agreed to let them depart to exile in Switzerland. Those who had converted while in prison – some 1,126 – were settled, by an order of 3 March 1687, in the thinly populated region around Vercelli, and expressly forbidden to return to their native valleys. Those who had survived imprisonment and remained steadfast in their faith were sent in long columns across the Alps to Geneva in the depths of winter, from the later months of 1686 into the beginning of 1687. Several hundred died on the journey. The rest were supported by charity from the Swiss Protestants until they departed again for a more distant exile in Württemberg or Brandenburg.[12] A few remained in Switzerland, however, evading the requirement that they emigrate, and planning to reconquer their homeland by force of arms.

So ended the first chapter of the Vaudois drama. In an act of intolerance that horrified all Protestant Europe Victor Amadeus had destroyed his Vaudois subjects or driven them into exile; in part he had responded to the pressure of Catholic opinion at home and fulfilled his dynasty's traditional crusading role. But above all it was Louis XIV's unrelenting will that forced Victor Amadeus to dispossess and exterminate the Vaudois. If further proof were needed of the dominance of French influence in the Savoyard state, this provided it. The campaign against the Vaudois was one more humiliating reminder that Victor Amadeus was not master in his own house, and must do Louis XIV's bidding even if it ran counter to his own intentions.

VII
Rupture with France
(1687–1690)

From the early months of 1687 Victor Amadeus II's policy began to assume a more determinedly anti-French tone. The destruction of the Vaudois did not bring an end to Louis XIV's interference in his affairs, but the diplomatic and military supremacy that allowed Louis XIV to treat Victor Amadeus as a client was being undermined by a shift in the European balance of power. The conclusion of the League of Augsburg in 1686 marked the first stage in the formation of an alliance to check Louis XIV's ascendancy. In Hungary Emperor Leopold I's armies were winning victories against the Turks, and resurgent Habsburg military power provided a rallying point for a number of German princes disgruntled with French policy. The revocation of the Edict of Nantes alarmed the Protestant powers, strengthening the hand of William III of Orange, Louis XIV's perpetual enemy. Victor Amadeus observed these changes in the international situation with close attention: any diminution of French power offered him a chance to assert his independence. Slowly, subtly, his attitude began to change. D'Arcy, the French ambassador, recorded the hints of hostility that Victor Amadeus increasingly displayed towards France, and the negotiations that he carried on with Louis XIV's enemies.

In February 1687 Victor Amadeus defied Louis XIV's orders and spent a month at Venice, ostensibly to savour the delights of the Carnival, but also to confer with his cousins the elector of Bavaria and prince Eugene of Savoy, both in the service of the Emperor, and with the *abate* Grimani, an envoy from the Habsburg court. Appearances notwithstanding, this whirlwind trip was innocent enough; such negotiations as took place behind the scenes were concerned not with a league against France but with the Savoyards' ancient dispute with Venice over the title to the kingdom of Cyprus.[1] But soon after his return to Turin in March Victor Amadeus opened discussions with the Emperor. Louis XIV soon learned of this and expressed his displeasure, for the Emperor was his avowed enemy, even though at this time the negotiations seem not to have been directed against French interests: Victor Amadeus was seeking clarification of his status as an Imperial vassal, and trying to obtain suzerainty over a number of small Imperial fiefs in the district of Le Langhe, along his southern border. His interest may well have been stimulated by the continued troubles around Mondovì, which adjoined these fiefs; many rebels sought sanctuary there, outside Savoyard jurisdiction. But his contacts with the Emperor were interpreted by Louis XIV as demonstrations of ill-will. The French king's misgivings were reinforced by other signs, such as Parella's return from exile to become one of Victor Amadeus's chief advisers (for he was well-connected at Vienna), and by the pardon granted to Pianezza, the conspirator of 1682 who had tried to unseat the regent and reduce French influence. At the same time d'Arcy reported that Victor Amadeus was now taking far more interest in matters of state, spending long hours alone in his cabinet, and devoting special care to the army. He added a grenadier company to each regiment, began to equip certain units with the new flintlock in place of the older musket, and improved the efficiency of the Ufficio del Soldo, which handled pay and provisioning. By 1690 the total strength of his forces had risen to 8,670 men: still far too little for him to contemplate any attempt at freeing himself from French domination without assistance.[2]

But the onset of war in September 1688 produced a sudden, dramatic change in the balance of power. France was forced onto the defensive by a coalition of the major European powers – the Dutch Republic, the Emperor and a number of German princes, soon England under its new sovereign William III, and then Spain. Louis XIV was caught by surprise, with his forces on a peacetime footing and below strength. To compensate for his shortage of manpower he requested the loan of three Savoyard regiments. Victor Amadeus at first delayed, not wishing to deplete his small army, but finally gave way and in February 1689 the three regiments – about 2,000 men – left to fight for Louis XIV in Flanders.[3] In the following months Victor Amadeus worked in semi-secrecy to recruit replacements for the lost regiments, arousing Louis XIV's suspicions in the process. But even though he was able to make good most of the losses in manpower, the knowledge that the three regiments were in effect hostages for his good behaviour added to the difficulties of breaking with Louis XIV and joining the coalition arrayed against France.

The spring of 1689 brought the war closer to Piedmont, as the Spanish forces in Lombardy concentrated to blockade the French garrison at Casale. In Flanders and on the Rhine the French armies gave ground slowly, devastating and burning as they withdrew, to impede the advancing allies. Victor Amadeus now intensified his contacts with the Emperor. In June prince Eugene and Grimani arrived at Turin to discuss the transfer of the Imperial fiefs in Le Langhe while at the same time opening secret negotiations for an alliance with the Emperor. Louis XIV grew concerned and on 9 September instructed d'Arcy to redouble his surveillance over the duke's actions.[4] But with his armies fully extended elsewhere, Louis XIV could do little more than protest and threaten; Victor Amadeus's chances for pursuing an independent course were increasing.

At the end of August 1689 a fresh development added to the mounting tension between Victor Amadeus and Louis XIV. On the night of 26–27 August a band of almost 1,000 Vaudois and Huguenot refugees led by pastor Henri Arnaud left Geneva on an epic march that would become known as the Glorieuse Rentrée.⁵ They traversed Savoy, crossed the Mont-Cénis, and despite the loss of many of their number during the journey, defeated a French corps blocking their path and by forced marches regained their native valleys on 6 September. There they ravaged the farms of the new colonists and ambushed patrols, spreading alarm far and wide. The Glorieuse Rentrée was in fact the conclusion of years of planning, and of earlier unsuccessful efforts by the Vaudois to return to their homeland. This time, profiting from the momentary weakness of the French forces after a summer of military setbacks, and from the relaxation of vigilance by the Savoyard border guards, Arnaud and his men succeeded. This surprise attack, even though it involved no more than a few hundred men, was profoundly disquieting to Louis XIV. A force of armed and defiant Protestants close to the border of Dauphiné might well rouse the large Huguenot population there in revolt; all through the summer of 1689 the French Protestants had been in ferment, awaiting an allied invasion and nurturing hopes of deliverance. The return of the Vaudois might well provide the spark to ignite this volatile mass, and in fact during the autumn of 1689 a few bands from the valleys crossed the mountains into Dauphiné in ill-fated attempts to foment insurrection. It was therefore essential for Louis XIV to crush the Vaudois at once, before they could endanger the security of his south-eastern frontier and his communications with Pinerolo, now of prime importance to him in view of Victor Amadeus's wavering loyalty. He accordingly demanded that the latter cooperate with him in destroying Arnaud's small band. At first Victor Amadeus seemed ready to comply; a Savoyard detachment under Parella, with some French help, cleared the Vaudois from their advanced positions in the Val Pellice and the Val di Luserna, and hemmed them into an inaccessible mountain stronghold at La Balziglia, where they entrenched themselves against the oncoming winter. With the first heavy snowfalls in late November all campaigning ceased in the valleys.

The return of the Vaudois represented a dangerous threat to Victor Amadeus's authority, and to his ability to maintain any semblance of peaceful relations with Louis XIV. The latter might exploit this opportunity to strengthen his bridgehead in Piedmontese territory at Pinerolo, to put an end to the duke's velleities of independence, and to guard against the threat from the Spanish army in Lombardy. The situation was thus full of danger for Victor Amadeus, yet it offered potential advantages too; the presence of the Vaudois gave him a plausible excuse for building up his army, and it opened up vistas of a possible accommodation with the Protestant powers. In fact the crisis caused by the Glorieuse Rentrée now became the central, decisive element in Victor Amadeus's relations with Louis XIV, and the tensions that it generated led directly to the outbreak of war in the following year. As the fighting in the valleys drew to a close in November 1689 Victor Amadeus made secret overtures to the Vaudois, offering them a safe-conduct if they would depart once more into exile. This offer, which was repeated several times, was refused. At the same time he began negotiations with the Swiss Cantons, seeking a military alliance with them in return for promises of lenient treatment for the Vaudois. Victor Amadeus must also have been aware that William III, now firmly established on the English throne, was following the fate of the returned Vaudois with close attention. For his part, Louis XIV was watching Victor Amadeus's ambiguous conduct: the new ambassador he sent to Turin, the comte de Rébenac, was instructed to be on his guard against 'the duke of Savoy's unfriendly cast of mind', and was to see that the war against the Vaudois was prosecuted with all possible dispatch, while ensuring that the duke did not use the hostilities as a pretext for increasing his army. If more troops were required to crush the Vaudois, France would supply them. Rébenac was also to induce Victor Amadeus to break off the negotiations he was believed to be carrying on with the Spanish governor of Milan, Fuensalida.[6] In sum, Rébenac's tricky – and ultimately unsuccessful – task was to keep Victor Amadeus in his appointed role as a French satellite.

Rébenac soon caught wind of Victor Amadeus's negotiations with the Emperor. On 8 February 1690 the latter invested Victor Amadeus with suzerainty over a number of fiefs in Le Langhe in return for a payment of a million lire. Rebuked by Louis XIV for subsidizing his enemy, Victor Amadeus responded that the money was earmarked for the Emperor's war against the Turks and would not be used against France. But by now Louis XIV was past accepting such flimsy assurances, and decided to secure Victor Amadeus's wavering allegiance by military means. At the beginning of March he placed Catinat in command of the forces in Dauphiné, with orders to destroy the insurgent Vaudois as soon as the spring weather arrived, and then to march through Piedmont to attack Spanish Lombardy.[7] This latter mission was to be executed with or without Victor Amadeus's permission: in effect Catinat was to secure his communications by eliminating the Vaudois, and then proceed to the military occupation of Piedmont. Louis XIV too was attempting to exploit the situation created by the Glorieuse Rentrée for his own purposes.

As the spring campaigning season approached, events moved faster. At the end of March the beleaguered Vaudois sortied from La Balziglia and ravaged the nearby villages, carrying off livestock and provisions; clearly they intended to stand and fight. On 30 March Catinat arrived at Turin to coordinate operations against them; he found Victor Amadeus unwilling to move immediately and playing for time. He was in the midst of negotiations for aid from the Emperor and the governor of Milan, and was seriously concerned by rumours of another invasion by a fresh force of Vaudois. At the same time the district of Mondovì had risen in revolt yet again, so that in May he had to go in person to pacify it. Confronted with these equivocations and delays, Louis XIV was growing impatient, when on 2 May he received proof of Victor Amadeus's plans for an alliance with Spain and the Emperor. Louvois therefore instructed Catinat to present an ultimatum: as a guarantee of his loyalty, Victor Amadeus was to hand over either 2,000 of his troops, or the citadel of Turin.[8] Meanwhile on the same day – 2 May – combined French and Savoyard forces assaulted the Vaudois entrenched at La Balziglia, to be repelled with serious losses. Catinat withdrew to regroup, but before he could resume the attack Louvois's new orders reached him on 6 May. Leaving his subordinate Feuquières in charge of the siege of La Balziglia, Catinat went to present the ultimatum to Victor Amadeus and to demand formal permission to enter Piedmontese territory with his army, to attack the Spanish forces in Lombardy.[9]

Victor Amadeus by now regarded a rupture with France as inevitable. His ambassador at Paris warned him that Louis XIV was on the point of declaring war, and the scale of French military preparations at Pinerolo and along the frontier left little doubt that this was true. But he wanted to delay the onset of hostilities as long as possible, for his army was below strength and unprepared, and his negotiations with Fuensalida at Milan and with the Imperial envoys were still not concluded. On 6 May 1690, just after the unsuccessful assault on La Balziglia, he wrote to his envoy in Switzerland announcing that he was now ready to effect the change in policy that he had been meditating for a long time. The threat from Catinat's army so close to Turin made it vital for him to secure the aid of the Vaudois, whose successful resistance showed that they were capable of giving the French 'another bone to gnaw'. He urgently needed the alliance of the Protestant Cantons as well; in return he was ready to send secret assistance to the defenders of La Balziglia and grant the Vaudois freedom of worship in their valleys, on the old conditions.[10] But for the moment he could only spin out the negotiations with Catinat, to buy time. On 9 May he granted permission for the French army to enter Piedmontese territory; Catinat took up position at Avigliana, a day's march west of Turin. Victor Amadeus meanwhile dispatched a special envoy to Versailles, with promises of submission, and declared himself ready to meet Catinat's demands for pledges of good behaviour. He withdrew his regular troops from the Vaudois valleys – partly on the pretext of the revolt at Mondovì – and recalled Parella to take command at Turin, where feverish preparations were being made for a siege. In the meantime, his secret negotiations with the Spanish and Imperial envoys were reaching a conclusion, and contacts were being made with William III.

Catinat knew well enough that Victor Amadeus was seeking to dupe him. On 20 May, acting on fresh orders, he demanded that Victor Amadeus hand over the citadel of Turin and the fort of Verrua; the duke declared that he would comply, but that he was awaiting the results of his special envoy's mission to Louis XIV. Catinat now shifted camp to Carignano, where he could control one of the principal crossings over the Po, but deferred hostile action for the time being. On 24 May Feuquières launched a new attack against the Vaudois at La Balziglia. This time the defenders were overwhelmed, only escaping under cover of a providential mist, and splitting up into several small bands hotly pursued by the French. Time was now running out for Victor Amadeus. The imminent collapse of the Vaudois would leave Catinat free to concentrate all his forces for a thrust into Piedmont, and the insistent French demands for the surrender of troops and fortresses left the duke in no doubt that he was in immediate danger. He therefore moved quickly to conclude the alliances he needed. On 28 May his envoys contacted the Vaudois fugitives and signed a truce; they were to join forces with the Savoyard troops in the valleys and prepare for a combined attack on the French.[11] On 3 June 1690 Victor Amadeus signed a treaty with Fuensalida for immediate Spanish military assistance, and on the next day concluded a similar agreement with the Imperial envoys.[12] He then formally notified Rébenac of his new alliances, performed his devotions, and announced the declaration of war to an enthusiastic throng of notables assembled at the ducal palace. He was launched irrevocably into war with Louis XIV.

VIII
The War in Piedmont
(1690–1696)

Victor Amadeus II entered the war with one overriding objective: to free himself from French domination. In consequence the treaties that he signed with Spain and the Emperor stipulated that Pinerolo and Casale should be conquered; the former fortress was to be handed over to Victor Amadeus, the latter would be at the disposition of the king of Spain.[1] The acquisition of Pinerolo and the expulsion of its French garrison from Piedmontese territory so close to Turin formed the irreducible minimum of Victor Amadeus's war-aims. The treaties went on to express a general hope for the conquest of territory in France itself; any such conquests were to be divided among the three powers signing the treaties. Victor Amadeus also took care to spell out the Savoyard claims on Monferrato, as recognized by the treaty of Cherasco in 1631. He was on delicate ground, for the Spanish Crown had interests of its own there, as sovereign of Milan, and the Emperor could claim to dispose of the marquisate of Monferrato as its ultimate suzerain. These conflicting claims would lead to endless dispute in the future, but for the moment – and as long as the Gonzaga lord of Mantua and Monferrato remained in possession – the dispute lay dormant. But Victor Amadeus had aims beyond territorial conquest. He declared war as a young prince eager to make a reputation for himself, to display his prowess and win *gloire*. By pitting himself against the monarch who had so long dominated Savoyard affairs he would show the world that he was a man to be reckoned with.

Despite this element of youthful bravado, Victor Amadeus took care to minimize the risks of the war he had just begun; he could be prudent and judicious too. Through the summer of 1690 he kept up his negotiations with the Swiss Cantons in the hope that they would guarantee the neutrality of the duchy of Savoy, and so shield at least part of his state from invasion. These hopes were soon dashed, however, for a French army overran the duchy in the first weeks of the war; only the fortress of Montmélian held out. With Savoy in his hands Louis XIV was free to concentrate his forces against Piedmont and the county of Nice, but he too hoped to restrict the scope of hostilities; he was hard pressed on other fronts and lacked the forces to mount a major campaign in northern Italy. His initial plan in the early months of 1690 had been for a diversionary effort against the Spanish forces in the Milanese, and it was only Victor

Amadeus's increasingly hostile stance that forced him to expand his scheme
of operations there. Louis XIV regarded Italy as a secondary theatre; for
him, the decisive campaigns were fought in Flanders and along the Rhine,
while the war in Piedmont was a holding action, aimed at protecting the
sensitive south-eastern frontier of France from invasion, and at procuring
local advantages.

For Victor Amadeus's allies, on the other hand, this new front presented
a number of possibilities. From the first, William III sought to use
Piedmont as the springboard for an invasion into southern France. His
support for the Vaudois was more than just a gesture of Protestant
solidarity; it was the first step in a grand design that William III pursued
throughout the war, and which the duke of Marlborough would resume
after 1702: to send a powerful army over the southern Alps, spearheaded
by Huguenot exiles and Vaudois irregulars, to light the fires of rebellion
in Dauphiné and Languedoc, destroy the great French naval base at
Toulon, and join forces with an allied fleet and army advancing from
Catalonia. Parts of this vast plan were put into effect from time to time,
in the invasion of Dauphiné in 1692, in the plans for the relief of Nice in
1693–94, then finally in the abortive attack on Toulon in 1707. William III
always devoted close attention to the war in Piedmont, for he believed,
as Heinsius wrote to Schomberg in 1692, that it was 'the real point at
which we can and must act vigorously and effectively'.[2] Such eagerness
to prosecute the war in Piedmont meant that Victor Amadeus could count
on William III's constant support through the cross-currents of allied
policy and planning, but it also entailed a considerable distortion of Victor
Amadeus's own aims. He was never enthusiastic about an invasion of
southern France, knowing the practical difficulties that beset such a plan,
while as a Catholic prince he found the prospect of leading a mixed army
of Vaudois and Huguenots to raise the French Protestants in rebellion
profoundly disquieting. So although he welcomed William III's aid, he
constantly maintained that the allies' first task must be to clear Piedmont
of the French before embarking on perilous schemes of transalpine
invasion.

If William III's support was far from disinterested, the Emperor's was
even less so. For Leopold I the Piedmontese alliance offered an opportunity
to expand his influence in northern Italy, and to establish a foothold there
in preparation for the moment when Carlos II of Spain would die and
the Spanish Succession fall vacant. The focus of Habsburg ambitions in
Italy was the Spanish viceroyalty of Milan, which entailed inevitable
conflict with Victor Amadeus, whose territorial ambitions pointed in the
same direction. He could hardly relish the prospect of weak Spanish rule
there being replaced by the more dynamic military power of the Austrian
Habsburgs. All through the war therefore Victor Amadeus remained
preoccupied by the problem of growing Habsburg influence close to his

borders, as revealed in the Emperor's designs on Milan, his renewed claims to suzerainty over the Imperial fiefs in Italy and his demands for war contributions from Imperial vassals. In the end the growing Imperial presence in Lombardy would be the chief factor that impelled Victor Amadeus to desert his allies and make peace with Louis XIV in 1696.

At the outbreak of war, however, his treaty with the Emperor – and still more that with the king of Spain – promised Victor Amadeus what he most urgently needed: manpower. His small army was no match for the much larger French forces. The Savoyard authorities worked in feverish haste to recruit the militia for local defence and to provide a reservoir for recruits. The militia was divided into two categories, to meet these separate needs: all males between the ages of twenty and forty were eligible for service, but a special unit was selected from 6 percent of the men in each community, to receive extra training and to serve alongside the regular troops when needed. The system functioned fairly well, but it placed a heavy burden on the local communities, draining them of manpower at a time when war damage and increased taxation were straining their resources to the limit. Evasion of militia service was common, and desertion frequent. But there was a distinct undercurrent of popular hostility to the French, whose ravages provoked the long-suffering peasantry to fury; everywhere Catinat's army had to fight a pitiless irregular war against the local population. The desperate need for troops led Victor Amadeus to enrol men who until recently had been arrayed in arms against him. A new regiment was formed of volunteers from the district of Mondovì, which as late as May 1690 had been in open insurrection, but which rallied to its duke on the outbreak of war. The Vaudois, now harassing the French communications in the mountains above Pinerolo, were organized into a battalion of irregulars, and later in the summer were strengthened by a fresh contingent of refugees returning from Switzerland via the Milanese. Along with the Vaudois a battalion of Huguenots and other Protestants was recruited for service, and in the following year increasing numbers of recruits allowed this force to be expanded into two new regiments. These Protestant troops were paid by Victor Amadeus's new allies, the English and Dutch governments, which hastened to conclude treaties with him as soon as the war broke out.

Victor Amadeus first began negotiations with William III through their respective envoys in Switzerland, since there were no direct links between them. For Victor Amadeus the special value of the Anglo-Dutch alliance lay in the financial support that it offered; in return he offered to restore the Vaudois to their former legal rights. The treatment of the Vaudois therefore became the central issue around which the negotiations revolved. Each side bargained hard, Victor Amadeus pressing for larger subsidies, and William III demanding full recognition of the Vaudois' rights on the basis of the various edicts of toleration since 1561. Such concessions were difficult for Victor Amadeus to make, when he had so recently proscribed the Vaudois and stripped them of all their legal rights: any restoration of their former status would arouse the opposition of devout Catholic opinion at home, and would cause tension with the Papacy and the Catholic powers not allied to him, but Victor Amadeus realized that to obtain the subsidies he so urgently needed he would have to meet William III's terms. So on 20 October 1690 his ambassador at The Hague, the president de la Tour, signed the formal treaty of alliance. The English and Dutch governments bound themselves to pay a subsidy of 30,000 écus per month (two-thirds to be paid by England), and to secure the return of Pinerolo to Victor Amadeus. No public declaration was made on the subject of the Vaudois, but a secret clause required Victor Amadeus to restore them to the status they had enjoyed before 1686. For the present, however, he deferred publishing any declaration to this effect, and merely allowed the Vaudois refugees to resettle their valleys under a régime of *de facto* toleration on the old terms.[3]

At the moment of Victor Amadeus's rupture with France, on 4 June 1690, the bulk of the French army under Catinat was still at Pinerolo, with detachments scouring the Vaudois valleys. Victor Amadeus's army was concentrated around Turin, where a Spanish army of 8,000 infantry and 2,000 cavalry soon joined him, deterring Catinat from attacking the capital. Late in June the combined allied army marched south to Carignano, to secure the crossing over the Po, while 4,000 men were detached under Parella to reinforce the hard-pressed Vaudois. Catinat had little difficulty in maintaining his communications against the ineffectual skirmishing of Victor Amadeus's men, but he was constantly harassed by the peasants of the districts where his troops were quartered. The French army reacted with unusual harshness, burning villages and towns in reprisal and levying heavy contributions. The friendly armies behaved little better, looting and inflicting widespread damage. Partisan warfare became a perpetual factor in the hostilities; as the armies criss-crossed the western and southern regions of Piedmont the luckless peasantry were reduced to beggary and flight, until by the end of the war many zones were totally ruined and deserted.

Catinat's scorched-earth tactics were more than gratuitous violence: by ravaging the countryside he intended to force Victor Amadeus to accept battle. On 2 August the French army broke camp and withdrew slowly from the area round Carignano, pillaging as it went, to lure the allies out of their position; the French took and razed the little towns of Villafranca and Cavour, massacred their inhabitants, and then retreated in a wide swathe of devastation towards Saluzzo. The threat to this important town produced the effect that Catinat hoped for. Victor Amadeus advanced in pursuit of the French and on 18 August fell into the trap that Catinat had set for him near the abbey of Staffarda. The allied army was surprised and defeated, losing about 5,000 men in casualties and prisoners, and had to retreat to Carmagnola to await reinforcements. Catinat followed up his victory by capturing Saluzzo and a number of other towns, then levied contributions over much of southern Piedmont, in territory so far untouched by the war. But this was the sole fruit of his victory. Fresh troops reached Victor Amadeus from the Milanese, and so, rather than attack him, Catinat withdrew towards Pinerolo in the middle of October, apparently to go into winter quarters. But this was a feint; in a rapid manoeuvre at the beginning of November the French army besieged and took Susa, the key to the route from Briançon into the Piedmontese plain.

The campaign of 1690 had gone badly for the allies. Savoy was lost, the western fringes of Piedmont ravaged by the French, and under Victor Amadeus's command the allied army had suffered a serious defeat. William III was disturbed by these failures and began to form a new plan for concerted action for the next campaign. Victor Amadeus's army was to be strengthened with contingents of some 4,000 Swiss, five battalions of Huguenot émigrés under Schomberg and more Vaudois exiles, together with 5,000 Imperial troops (to be paid by extra British and Dutch subsidies) and a large force of Bavarians under the elector Max Emanuel. In this way the allies intended to place 20,000 men in the field and invade France through Savoy: Victor Amadeus was to lead this army north-west to join up with a second allied thrust launched from the Rhine and passing through Franche Comté. Here in fact we have the first version of the grand design for an invasion of France from the south-east which was to become a leitmotif of Allied strategy till 1713.

The plan could not be implemented, however, since Catinat moved first. Early in March 1691 he besieged and took Nice – the citadel finally fell on 5 April – and overran the rest of the county. The extra troops earmarked to reinforce the allied army in Piedmont were slow to mobilize – most did not arrive until July or August – so that through the early months of 1691 Catinat was able to make important gains. Louis XIV urged him to concentrate his forces and besiege Turin; early in May the French seized Avigliana as the first step towards mounting the siege, but soon Catinat gave up the idea as being beyond his forces' capabilities, and advanced southwards instead. Victor Amadeus could do little to stop him: on 9 June Carmagnola fell, and from there the French moved on to besiege Cuneo, the key fortress of southern Piedmont. At the same time another French detachment penetrated into the Val d'Aosta and levied contributions, but soon withdrew. The timely arrival of the first Imperial reinforcements under prince Eugene saved Cuneo; on 28 June the French besieging force retreated in disorder. During July more allied troops arrived to join Victor Amadeus's army, and Catinat was forced onto the defensive. But the allies could not agree how to exploit their advantage;

Victor Amadeus urged an attack through the Val d'Aosta into Savoy, to relieve Montmélian – which was still holding out – and perhaps to carry out William III's original plan for an invasion of France. Delays however intervened and transport was lacking. Furthermore the commander of the Imperial troops, general Caraffa, apparently under orders not to risk his forces in any way, opposed the plan to relieve Montmélian and refused to seek out the French army and give battle. Amid these divided counsels, which underlined the fundamental divergence of interests between Victor Amadeus and his Habsburg ally, the army so painstakingly assembled dissolved in inaction. An attack on Susa failed late in October, and in December Montmélian fell to the French. Faced by the collapse of his plans, and embittered by Caraffa's obstructionism, Victor Amadeus renewed the tentative contacts he had made the year before with Louis XIV. In October 1691 a French peace-feeler was extended through the intermediary of the Pope, and in December Victor Amadeus deputed Gropello to open discussions with Tessé, the commandant of Pinerolo. But nothing came of these overtures, for Louis XIV would offer little beyond recognizing Victor Amadeus as neutral, with no territorial concessions.[4]

Through the ensuing winter William III returned to his plans for an invasion of France, and Victor Amadeus gradually fell in with the scheme, although his own preference was to capture Pinerolo and Susa, or to penetrate into Savoy and recover Montmélian. Catinat's army had been reduced and he had to remain on the defensive. In the spring of 1692 a small allied force was sent to blockade Casale, while the main body prepared to invade Dauphiné. In July the allies besieged and captured Guillestre, Embrun and Gap, spreading devastation in their path. But they advanced no further, and despite Schomberg's hopes, could not raise the Huguenots in revolt. The campaign was already losing momentum when Victor Amadeus was struck down by an attack of smallpox. The allied army remained in Dauphiné for a time, paralysed by disputes between the leaders of its different contingents, until as autumn approached it returned across the Alps, having achieved virtually nothing.

Victor Amadeus recovered slowly from his illness, which had been serious: for a time he seemed close to death, and made a will designating the young son of the prince of Carignano as his heir, since at that time he had only two daughters and no son of his own. During the winter he resumed his contacts with Tessé, but once more the discussions of possible peace terms – although more protracted this time – led nowhere. Tessé meanwhile was pursuing schemes of his own. He helped stir up a plot for an insurrection at Mondovì, to be supported by French troops, but the plan was discovered and the ringleaders executed. Trouble seems to have persisted into the spring of the following year, when another minor revolt by a local feudatory, the marchese di Monforte, had to be put down by military force, but thereafter the region became quiet once again.

Profiting from the lessons of the previous campaign, Victor Amadeus
and his allies made plans to act more effectively in 1693, mobilizing their
forces earlier and adhering strictly to a common plan. Three schemes were
considered: an attack into Savoy and then into France through the Val
d'Aosta; a thrust towards Nice and perhaps into Provence, to be supported
by the Spanish fleet; and the capture of Pinerolo.[5] This last plan was
adopted, along with a minor operation to tighten the blockade the allies
were maintaining around Casale. In June 1693 the Spanish general
Leganes captured the outlying forts that protected Casale, while Victor
Amadeus led the main force to blockade Pinerolo. Catinat withdrew most
of his army as the allies advanced, leaving Tessé in command of the
garrison at Pinerolo and the nearby fort of Santa Brigitta, and taking up a
position around Fenestrelle to command the route back to Susa. At the
same time, seeing that the allies were now fully committed to the siege of
Pinerolo, Catinat detached another force to occupy the valley of Barcelonnette and levy contributions there. Through July the allies closed their
blockade around Pinerolo, and bombarded the fort of Santa Brigitta until
it fell on 11 August. Victor Amadeus then prepared to attack Pinerolo
itself. From 20 August until 2 September he subjected the town to a heavy
bombardment, but did not move up to besiege it, and in the early days of
September there was a lull in the operations. In part this seems to have
been because the allied siege-train was short of ammunition, but it may
also have been because Victor Amadeus had resumed his contacts with
Tessé: on 22 September Gropello once more appeared, in disguise, to
negotiate with Tessé in the beleaguered town.[6]

In the meantime Louis XIV had been maturing plans of his own for a
counterstroke. Reinforcements were called up in haste from Catalonia and
the Rhine to join Catinat in the mountains above Pinerolo. The allies
remained unaware of the concentration that threatened them, and on
26 September Victor Amadeus resumed his bombardment of Pinerolo.
Catinat was now ready to move, however, and by 29 September his army
was at Avigliana, poised to cut the allied army's communications with
Turin. Victor Amadeus had to break off the bombardment of Pinerolo
and withdraw, encumbered by his siege-train. On 4 October the two
armies met at La Marsaglia, between Pinerolo and Turin. Outnumbered
and outmanoeuvred, the allies were defeated, losing some 6,000 men, and
the Piedmontese plain lay open to Catinat's attack. But once again, as in
1690, he was unable to exploit his victory. Supply problems and severe
shortages of provisions prevented the French army from besieging Turin
or Cuneo, as Louis XIV intended, and so after levying contributions as
far as Saluzzo, Catinat withdrew into winter quarters.

The defeat at La Marsaglia seems nonetheless to have made a profound
psychological impression on Victor Amadeus. The war had now dragged
on for four years with no hope of victory, Piedmont was being devastated

by the contending armies, and Nice and Savoy were suffering under French occupation. Louis XIV sensed that the time was ripe for fresh overtures to Victor Amadeus; in October the secret negotiations with Tessé were resumed. Louis XIV too had ample reason to seek peace; France was exhausted, locked in a military stalemate and facing a severe famine. He made contact with various emissaries of William III and began to explore the possibility of a settlement. From this point the French king pursued parallel but separate negotiations with William III – who acted on behalf of the allied powers together – and with Victor Amadeus. His strategy seems to have been to try to detach one member or the other from the coalition that faced him, and so cause its collapse: this strategy would succeed in 1695. Victor Amadeus tried to exploit this opportunity to resolve the critical situation in which he found himself, either by making peace if he could obtain favourable terms from Louis XIV, or by forcing his allies to redouble their efforts. He informed William III and Leopold I that he was negotiating with the enemy; to the former he pointed out that he needed larger subsidies to make up for the damage inflicted on Piedmont, while pressing the latter to carry out certain unfulfilled provisions of their alliance, notably those relating to the acquisition of Imperial fiefs, and to the proposed marriage of Victor Amadeus's elder daughter to the archduke Joseph, the Emperor's elder son. Neither of these démarches produced much effect. William III expressed concern, and arranged for some extra troops to be sent to Piedmont for the coming campaign; Leopold would make no commitments, and was severely critical of Victor Amadeus's separate negotiations with the French. Nor did the discussions with Tessé produce concrete results. Louis XIV remained reluctant to make any significant concessions, although he did grant Tessé powers to conclude a treaty (on 6 December 1693), by which the French and Savoyard armies were to make a truce and then join forces to expel the Imperial armies from Italy and make it a neutral zone. Here in fact we have the first outline of the agreement of 1696. But at this stage neither side was ready to come to terms, and Victor Amadeus merely offered 'on his word to remain inactive for the coming campaign'.[7]

Victor Amadeus kept his word; the campaign of 1694 was uneventful. But this was probably due more to the exhaustion of both armies than to the promise he had given Tessé. Louis XIV had withdrawn a large part of Catinat's army for service in Catalonia, where the French came close to taking Barcelona. This grave threat – the fall of Barcelona would knock Spain out of the war – was averted by the intervention of the allied fleet, which sailed into the Mediterranean and then wintered at Cadiz. The appearance of the allied fleet offered a chance for Victor Amadeus to recover Nice, but it was too late in the season to begin such an operation.

At this point Victor Amadeus's relations with William III entered a new and complicated phase. The treaty of 1690 included a secret clause, as we have seen, restoring the Vaudois to their former legal and religious status; Victor Amadeus, however, knowing that any concessions to the Vaudois would cause trouble at home and lead to severe friction with the Papacy, had so far evaded putting this clause into effect. But by the beginning of 1694 pressure from William III's envoys became irresistible, and the king himself spoke forcefully on the subject to la Tour, the Savoyard ambassador at The Hague. On 23 May 1694, therefore, Victor Amadeus issued an edict according the Vaudois the limited toleration they had enjoyed before 1686.[8] The result was an immediate condemnation, from Pope Innocent XII, which the Senate of Turin refused to allow to be published in Victor Amadeus's states. The dispute gradually escalated into a major conflict, which would last until the end of the reign, as questions of jurisdiction and clerical immunities were added to the original issue. But the edict regularized the position that the Vaudois had conquered for themselves in 1689–90, and defined their legal status within the Savoyard state for the next century. The interpretation of the edict, however, gave rise to endless disputes, providing fertile ground for clerical and bureaucratic chicanery, and also for intervention by successive English and Dutch envoys. The edict of 1694 became an instrument that the Protestant powers could use to interfere in Savoyard affairs. Victor Amadeus had originally played upon Anglo-Dutch sympathy for the Vaudois to facilitate concluding an alliance, and had probably not expected that his new allies would seek to exercise an informal protectorate on their behalf. But even so the situation contained advantages for him. Anglo-Dutch solicitude for the 'poor Vaudois' was a potent factor cementing an alliance that formed the essential counterpoise against France, and any interference by the distant Protestant powers was a far less serious threat to his sovereignty than was Louis XIV's imperious influence close at hand.

At this juncture William III also pressed Victor Amadeus to modify his commercial policies for the benefit of the allies. Here the British government had a number of related aims in view. In the first place it wanted to increase the supply of raw and spun silk for the burgeoning English silk-weaving industry, whose usual sources of supply had been disrupted by the war. Much of the industry's raw material came from Italy, and Piedmont produced some of the best raw and spun silk. William III's ministers also hoped to enlist Victor Amadeus in their embargo on French goods, while at the same time they were looking for new markets for English woollen cloth. In December 1694 Van Der Meer, the Dutch envoy at Turin, presented a memorandum urging Victor Amadeus to ban the import of French cloth; such a ban would be particularly effective at this moment, since French trade in the Mediterranean was paralysed by the allied fleet.[9] Van Der Meer argued that Victor Amadeus could substitute English and Dutch cloth for the French cloth that his dominions were believed to import in large quantities. A month later lord Galway, the English envoy at Turin, in his turn proposed supplying English cloth to Piedmont, notably for uniforms. Galway's proposal actually went further than this, for it was based on a scheme put forward by the Lutestring Company in London, which specialized in the production of high-grade silk textiles, and which was seeking to import spun silk and export woollen textiles to Piedmont in return.[10] For the moment nothing came of the proposal. Victor Amadeus did not join the embargo on French goods, for in fact since the outbreak of war the amounts imported had fallen significantly. Nor did he agree to import cloth from his allies; only a trial shipment of English cloth seems to have reached Piedmont before the end of the war. But this first attempt at commercial cooperation fore-shadowed a more successful effort by the British government to penetrate the Piedmontese market during the next war, when the two states were once again allies.

Military operations in 1694 had been severely restricted by the growing shortage of supplies and provisions in the impoverished countryside. To the devastation caused by the war were now added the effects of a grave subsistence crisis which struck Piedmont and northern Italy in 1694 and reached its peak in the following year. Already in January 1694 all export of grain from the Savoyard states had been forbidden and the markets closed until the harvest in July. But the harvest failed, climaxing several bad years, and famine became imminent. The government ordered all stocks of grain within the state to be declared, and renewed the customary bans on export and hoarding. Early in 1695 a special commission was set up to deal with the problem of rapidly rising prices. The situation soon became critical, for the harvest of 1695 failed too. At the beginning of September 1695, as the full extent of the disaster became apparent, Victor Amadeus established a special fund to buy grain abroad: the wealthy were ordered to buy shares in the fund, which would yield a return of 7 percent (considerably more than shares in the government debt).[11] Over 300,000 lire were raised in this way and some grain was imported, but the government's efforts could bring only a small measure of relief. In the countryside there was starvation, and thousands of beggars flocked to the hospitals in the towns. Piedmont was experiencing what was probably its most severe subsistence crisis in the entire seventeenth century, and the resultant economic distress undoubtedly increased Victor Amadeus's desire to conclude peace as soon as possible.

Yet the war continued. In the closing months of 1694 the Imperial envoys proposed that Casale be made the principal objective of the allied armies for the next campaign. Coming from this quarter, the suggestion was disquieting for Victor Amadeus; though he was eager to eliminate the French garrison at Casale, he had no wish to see a Habsburg force take its place. He was also concerned by the French peace proposals that William III communicated to the allies in November 1694, for they contained no mention of Pinerolo, and when la Tour questioned the king on this point, he was told that there was little hope of obtaining it.[12] Victor Amadeus was thus faced with the imminent possibility of the Emperor's seizing Casale, while Pinerolo remained in French hands. This led him to intensify his negotiations with Tessé. On 15 March 1695 Gropello warned Tessé that the siege of Casale was imminent: rather than letting the Emperor conquer it, Victor Amadeus proposed that the French garrison surrender after a brief siege, on condition that the place be dismantled and handed back to its rightful owner, the duke of Mantua. On 29 April Louis XIV agreed to these terms: for his part, Victor Amadeus agreed to prevent his allies from attacking any other French positions for the duration of the campaign. Tentative negotiations were begun for the betrothal of Victor Amadeus's elder daughter to the duke of Burgundy.[13] The elements of the separate peace treaty of 1696 were now taking shape, under the threat of Imperial expansion in Lombardy. As a further indication of the seriousness with which he viewed the growth of Habsburg influence in the Milanese, in May 1695 Victor Amadeus dispatched an envoy to Madrid with secret instructions to obtain the governorship of Milan.[14] The proposal leaked out before the mission could take place, but the episode clearly reveals Victor Amadeus's concern with the advance of Habsburg power in northern Italy.

On 25 June 1695 the siege of Casale began, and after token resistance the French garrison surrendered on 9 July. The unseemly rapidity of the siege increased the suspicions of Victor Amadeus's allies, but he was able to explain – plausibly enough – in response to Galway's enquiries that his only desire was to see the place demolished, adding ironically that 'he had some suspicion that not all his allies were of the same sentiment'.[15] The rest of the campaign passed in demolishing the fortifications at Casale, and the work was not completed until well into September – long past the time for starting further operations. The tempo of the secret Franco-Savoyard negotiations meanwhile accelerated. On 23 November Gropello visited Tessé at Pinerolo with fresh proposals: Victor Amadeus was willing to abandon his allies in return for the cession of Pinerolo. Louis XIV at first refused to consider the proposal, but gradually became more amenable, since by making separate terms with Victor Amadeus he would be able to split the allies and bring an end to the war. Viewed in this light, the cession of Pinerolo became more acceptable, and in February 1696 Louis XIV authorized Tessé to conclude an agreement on this basis. Meanwhile Victor Amadeus was preparing for the next season's campaign with his allies, in which the objective would be Pinerolo. Victor Amadeus was determined to secure the place, either by treaty from his foe or by conquest with the aid of his friends, and Louis XIV's offer came first. On 30 May 1696 Tessé and Gropello signed the draft treaty; on 29 June, after some last-minute tergiversations by Victor Amadeus, the final version was signed, and on 6 July Louis XIV ratified it. Besides ceding Pinerolo with its dependent corridor of territory, but shorn of its fortifications, Louis XIV agreed to restore all Savoyard territory conquered during the war, as soon as the allied armies had left Italy. The French and Savoyard armies were to join forces to make the allies accept the neutralization of the Italian theatre of war. To give Victor Amadeus's allies time to agree to this, a truce was to be declared. In addition, the Savoyard ambassadors were to receive royal honours at the French court, in recognition of their master's claims to a regal title, and Victor Amadeus's daughter Marie Adelaide was to marry the duke of Burgundy.[16]

A polite fiction was worked out to cover Victor Amadeus's defection from his allies. On 12 July Catinat's army, reinforced for the occasion, advanced on Turin as if to besiege it, offering Victor Amadeus a pretext to sue for a truce, and he now dropped out of the alliance. For the allies this was a grave blow; as Shrewsbury wrote to William III, 'the war cannot be carried on with advantage in other theatres . . . in all appearances this campaign will end in a very discouraging manner for the Allys'.[17] The allied generals and envoys at Turin worked desperately to prevent Victor Amadeus's defection, but he refused to be deflected from his course. At the beginning of August the allied forces evacuated Turin and withdrew towards Lombardy. When the truce expired Victor Amadeus joined his army to Catinat's, and their combined forces, now superior to the remnants of the allied army, moved up to besiege Valenza as the first step to an invasion of the Milanese. The allies were forced to sue for peace: on 7 October a truce was proclaimed at Vigevano, Italy was declared a neutral zone, and in the next two months the allied armies departed.[18]

Victor Amadeus had secured peace for his exhausted state, and had obtained possession of Pinerolo and the neutralization of Casale. But these advantages were bought at a considerable price. By deserting his allies he acquired a reputation for devious *Realpolitik* and cynical self-interest that he would never shake off, and while he had earned the enmity of his former allies, he had not won the friendship of Louis XIV. He was isolated, and this isolation would effectively exclude him from the negotiations over the Spanish Succession in the following years. The cost of the war had been heavy for Victor Amadeus's subjects too. Peace offered an opportunity to repair the widespread damage, to restore the battered economy and to stabilize the state's overstrained finances. The war had revealed serious weaknesses in the administrative and fiscal structure of the state, calling for sweeping reorganization and reform. Freed from the burden of waging war, Victor Amadeus set about these tasks with characteristic energy and thoroughness.

IX
The First Period of Reform
(1696–1703)

War and famine had sorely tried the Savoyard state, stretching its resources almost to breaking-point. On his way through Piedmont in 1702 Joseph Addison could still follow the swathes of destruction carved by the French armies during the late war.[1] Towns had been sacked, agriculture disrupted, commerce impeded; poverty and vagrancy had reached dangerous levels.[2] The financial reserves of many communities were exhausted, their debts swelled by war contributions, pillage and the cost of emergency stocks of grain. The state's finances too had been severely strained, despite the Anglo-Dutch subsidies and the pitiless exaction of war taxes. The state debt had risen from 16,211,605 lire to 26,035,782 lire in the course of the war – an increase of 61 percent – and interest payments on it now accounted for one-fifth of government expenditure.[3] The restoration of financial stability would require not merely the imposition of new taxes or minor tinkering with the fiscal mechanism, but a thorough overhaul of the entire structure, for only in this way could real revenues be increased without aggravating the burden on the overtaxed communities.

The successful conclusion of the war, the withdrawal of the French armies and the recovery of Pinerolo, greatly enhanced Victor Amadeus II's prestige at home, making it easier to overcome opposition to the reforms that he now initiated. Some of the impetus behind these reforms came from the need to expand the state's military capability. Financial stability was essential to place the army on a sound footing and follow up the military and diplomatic success already achieved. As a member of the coalition leagued against Louis XIV Victor Amadeus had begun to map out a new role for the Savoyard state in European affairs, initiating a process of expansion that would continue until 1748. To pursue this course he needed to mobilize all the resources the state could muster; efficient management would help make up for the small size of the Savoyard state and for the poverty and backwardness of many of the regions that comprised it. But we should not attribute the entire thrust of reform to the need for recovery after a damaging war, or for expanded military power. Victor Amadeus was also seeking to extend the central government's authority in every corner of the state, curbing local autonomy and bringing the nobles and clergy to heel. He set out to create a system of institutions that would focus power at the centre of government, in his own person, and that would transmit his orders rapidly and unquestioningly to every corner of the state. Many of the changes he now began to effect can be traced back in origin to the early years of his reign or still further; they form part of a continuing process of innovation that had been going on for a century. This underlying dynamic was given special urgency by the pressures of war in the 1690s, as it had been during the long-drawn hostilities of the early part of the century, but there was also a strong element of continuity, exemplified as we shall see in the establishment of the intendants, or in the measures to standardize tax assessment.

By 1696 Victor Amadeus had found the collaborator who would provide much of the technical skill and driving force behind the programme of fiscal reform: Giovanni Battista Gropello.[4] Apart from the duke himself, Gropello was the principal architect of the new fiscal structure. Of humble origins, Gropello began his career as a minor official of the gabelles, and in 1692 became *referendario* of the province of Susa. Soon afterwards he acted as the trusted intermediary in Victor Amadeus's secret negotiations with Tessé. In 1695 he attained the rank of *mastro auditore* in the Camera dei Conti, and on 5 March 1697 he was made Generale delle Finanze, with overall direction in fiscal and economic matters. His duties ranged over the whole spectrum of state affairs, and in the following years we find him wherever ruthless pressure was needed to carry out his sovereign's orders: directing the repression of the revolt at Mondovì in the summer of 1699, haranguing the Estates of the duchy of Aosta, acting as intendant-general and president of the Chambre des Comptes in Savoy. His rise was celebrated in the customary manner, by the acquisition of a noble title: in 1699 he was named conte di Borgone.

Along with Gropello we should note the appearance of another of Victor Amadeus's closest collaborators, who would attain ministerial rank later in the reign: Pierre Mellarède, born about 1659 into a bourgeois family from Montmélian, trained in the law, and beginning his government career as *avocat des pauvres* in the Senate at Chambéry.[5] In 1699 he was appointed intendant of Nice and Oneglia, a key position for the implementation of the fiscal and administrative changes initiated by Victor Amadeus and Gropello. Mellarède served subsequently on a number of important diplomatic missions, produced legal treatises in support of his master's political rights and territorial claims, and in 1717 became secretary of state for internal affairs. He too attained noble rank, assuming the title of comte de Bettonet in 1717. Devoted and energetic subordinates like Mellarède and Gropello provided the technical expertise for carrying through the reforms, but the direction of policy was determined by Victor Amadeus himself. None of his advisers, however important, ever attained the status of first minister.

An essential prerequisite for the successful implementation of the reforms that Victor Amadeus contemplated was the consolidation of all the different local officials into a uniform bureaucratic echelon. The nucleus of this new system was provided by the *referendarii* established in the Piedmontese provinces since the early seventeenth century. Victor Amadeus and Gropello now standardized the duties and procedures of the *referendarii* and extended them into Nice and Savoy; about this time they began to be known by the title of 'intendants', in evident imitation of French administrative practice, although there were fundamental differences between the French and Savoyard intendants. The latter were, in origin at least, venal officers, whereas the French were not. Moreover, the Savoyard intendants administered a much smaller territory than their French counterparts; the provinces of the Savoyard state were a fraction of the size of a French généralité, and correspondingly easier to govern. The Savoyard intendants also enjoyed far less initiative than the French; they were merely the executants of orders emanating from the capital. Victor Amadeus II and his successors kept their intendants under tight control, and shifted them frequently, to prevent their building up local ties, as so often happened in France. The intendant system became the most critical administrative structure holding the Savoyard state together. From 1679 we find references to an intendant in the Vaudois valleys, a sensitive area where the government maintained particularly careful control. In 1686 the first intendant appears in the duchy of Savoy. Two years later the county of Nice received its first intendant; his instructions are dated 8 January 1689. His prime duty was to see to the exaction of taxes, but he was also to supervise public works, maintain stockpiles of grain for emergencies, and manage the ducal demesne lands. He was enjoined characteristically 'to take special care not to burden the state finances with superfluous expenses'. He was to report regularly to the Generale delle Finanze and receive all his orders from him.[6]

It seems evident from the interchangeability of their titles, and from the piecemeal way in which they superseded the existing provincial *direttori* and *referendarii*, that Victor Amadeus II's intendants grew out of this older network of officials. They were not created by the edict of 1696, as Quazza and others have suggested; they existed long before, both in name and in substance.[7] Victor Amadeus merely extended to the rest of the state what had been until this time a purely Piedmontese institution, and then standardized its functions. In Nice and Savoy the French occupation interrupted the development of the system, and intendants reappeared there only after the war. The first systematic regulation for the intendant of the duchy of Savoy (or intendant-general as he was now styled) dates from 1700. In Piedmont on the other hand the war seems to have stimulated the development of the provincial intendancies. An indication of their growing importance is provided by the instructions issued for them on 17 July 1693. As in the earlier instructions for the intendant of Nice, the primary emphasis was on the need to see that all taxes were paid punctually and in full. But the intendants were also to enquire into the reasons for non-payment, to revise the local tax-registers, and to check the malversations and mismanagement of the communal councils and their tax-collectors. Stabilizing the finances of the local communities now became a central part of the intendants' duties, pointing the way to other reforms initiated after 1696. As soon as the war was over a new comprehensive regulation was issued for the intendants, placing still further emphasis on the financial plight of the local communities, which had become one of the government's most urgent concerns. The intendants' original tax-collecting function had expanded; they were now the instruments through which the central government implemented fiscal and administrative reforms and gathered greater authority into its own hands.[8]

The intendants' strategic role as the spearhead of centralization and reform is best exemplified by their activities in Savoy or the county of Nice, where governmental authority was less assured than in Piedmont. In October 1698 Victor Amadeus and his ministers clashed with the syndics of Nice, ordering them to disavow a recent tract claiming fiscal immunity for the city. Mellarède was commissioned to refute the pamphlet, and his *Traité des droits des ducs de Savoie* set out to prove the sovereign's right to tax at will. Soon afterwards Mellarède was appointed intendant of the county of Nice and Oneglia, where he continued the assault on local privileges. In April 1700, on the occasion of Victor Amadeus's visit to Nice, the central government took over the city's gabelles on wine and fish, its chief sources of revenue. Some time later the tobacco tax, hitherto levied only in Piedmont, was extended to the county. Mellarède ignored the city council's protests, and went on to impose another new tax, the levy of official stamped paper. During this period he also conducted a complete revision of the county's tax-registers and surveyed its economic resources.

In Savoy the attack on local privilege was led by Gropello, appointed intendant-general of the duchy in 1696, and by his successors, who became locked in continual disputes with the sovereign courts at Chambéry. The re-establishment of the intendancy in Savoy was motivated in part by Victor Amadeus's desire to reassert his authority there and to stamp out disloyalty after six years of French occupation. He appointed a special tribunal, headed by Gropello, to try crimes committed during the war years, and purged all French nominees from among the magistrates of the Senate. But he was concerned above all to increase the revenues from the duchy and to standardize the assessment of taxation; here the appointment of the fiscal expert Gropello as intendant-general was crucial. Just after the end of the war Victor Amadeus ordered the introduction to Savoy of the *tabellion*, or compulsory registration of deeds by official notaries, as in Piedmont: the number of notarial posts was restricted, and they were made hereditary in return for a fee. The Senate of Chambéry protested, refused to register the edict until 1702, and did so only after receiving a withering lesson in Victor Amadeus's principles of government: 'as for laws and edicts, the sovereign alone determines them, either of his own will or through the ministers of state . . . Once he has heard their opinions, he orders as master that which he sees fit.'[9] Even then, however, the Senate registered the edict with major modifications, so that the issue remained unresolved when Savoy was reoccupied by the French a year later.

The Chambre des Comptes proved more contentious still. In December 1698 it refused to approve the introduction of the *dogana*, a tax on goods entering the state levied in Piedmont since 1563, claiming (perhaps with some reason) that the new import duties would adversely affect the duchy's economy. To counter this opposition Victor Amadeus named Gropello president of the Chambre des Comptes and transferred many of its fiscal and economic functions to him in his new office of intendant-general. The magistrates retorted by blocking the revision of the local tax-registers, which Gropello was just then initiating. He despatched comte Anselme de Montjoye on a tour of inspection of the duchy of Savoy with orders to enquire into the reasons for the communities' poverty and indebtedness, and to revise the local tax-registers.[10] Montjoye's inquest revealed that up to 40 percent of the *taille* was not being paid because of the immunities enjoyed by the privileged, which shifted the tax burden onto the poor and weighed down the communities' finances. Accordingly on 21 July 1701 an edict ordered those with fiscal immunities to compensate the communities in which they lived for the taxes due from their lands. The Chambre des Comptes sprang to the defence of the privileged orders, refusing to register the edict until forced to do so the following year, and then only with amendments that deprived it of any effectiveness.

Conflict with the sovereign courts stemmed largely from the government's efforts to increase taxes, for Victor Amadeus and Gropello were trying to squeeze as much as possible out of the existing tax structure, while preparing to overhaul it completely and thus render it more efficient and equitable. The result of their efforts was to raise state revenue by about 31 percent between 1689 and 1700, from 7,534,841 lire to 10,917,442 lire per annum.[11] In part this was done by imposing new taxes like the levy of stamped paper, first introduced in 1696 and maintained after the peace, or by converting the *sussidio militare* in 1700 from a wartime levy into a perpetual tax. Revenues from the county of Nice rose, as Mellarède introduced new taxes; the Estates of Aosta were also made to increase their contribution. In June 1697 Gropello informed the Conseil des Commis that Victor Amadeus was planning to do away with their privileges and make them pay the same taxes as the other regions of the state, 'in order to render the Val d'Aosta uniform with his other dominions'.[12] Met by a refusal, Gropello switched tactics and tried blackmail, demanding a special *donativo* in return for confirmation of the Valley's traditional fiscal immunities. When the Estates met in August 1699 they voted twice their previous quota of taxes, plus a special *donativo* of 50,000 lire; their privileges were duly confirmed.

The government also continued the creation and sale of offices; 840,000 lire had been raised in this way between 1690 and 1696. In May 1696 the intendants were ordered to pay a *finanza* in return for confirmation in their posts. Another edict created positions of treasurer for each town or community and offered them for sale, and in 1698 twelve provincial treasurerships were created and sold. Apothecaries were licensed by the state and allowed to dispose of their posts at will in return for a fee, while the system of licensed notaries or *tabellion* was extended to the duchy of Aosta, the newly-recovered district of Pinerolo and the duchy of Savoy (with repercussions in Savoy that we have already noted). But these measures were actually the last creations of venal office. Apart from an isolated edict in 1704 making the positions of syndic in each community venal and hereditary, from this time the government seems to have preferred not to raise money by the sale of offices. Possibly Victor Amadeus and his advisers were unwilling to pay the penalty of bureaucratic rigidity that would have resulted from the widespread extension of venality. By restricting its scope they ensured that Savoyard officialdom would remain relatively responsive, unencumbered by a welter of positions created only for fiscal ends.

While they worked hard to increase revenue by means of these different expedients, Victor Amadeus and Gropello were also laying the foundations for a thorough reconstruction of the entire fiscal apparatus. At this stage they did little to streamline the cumbrous machinery that levied taxes; in the years after 1696 they concentrated on measures to redistribute the burden of taxation, for one of the fundamental weaknesses of the Savoyard fiscal system – like every other at this time – lay in inequitable assessment and distribution, which shifted the weight of taxation away from the more prosperous classes. If Victor Amadeus wished to create a more equitable and therefore more productive tax-system he would have to attack the whole concept of fiscal privilege. But a frontal assault on privilege was too dangerous. Instead he sought to minimize the adverse effects of privilege by rooting out the unjustified tax exemptions enjoyed by the clergy and nobility, thus reducing their immunities to the strict letter of the law, and removing the chief obstacle that prevented the existing fiscal system from yielding its full potential.

A great many exemptions had been created by the government itself, through infeudations or by alienating the right to collect the *tasso* in return for ready cash. During the past war the state had raised 6,170,000 lire through grants of infeudation; calculated at an average return of 5 percent, this represented 308,000 lire a year in tax revenue lost to the fisc. So on 24 March 1698 a new tax was imposed, equal to this sum, to pay off the capital over twenty years and so redeem the lost revenue. Two years later this scheme was abandoned; the new tax was turned into a permanent levy and merged with the *sussidio militare*. Just how many infeudations were redeemed by this tax is not clear, but from this time the government seems to have abandoned them as a way of raising emergency funds. It continued, however, to alienate the right to collect the *tasso*, which amounted to much the same thing – the granting away of state revenues in return for a lump-sum payment, but without the connotations of political jurisdiction that were associated with infeudation. By 1700, 648,145 lire a year in revenues from the *tasso* had been alienated to private persons or institutions, 38 percent of this between 1690 and 1696. But the loss of revenue was even higher than this estimate would suggest. In 1702 an investigation ordered by Gropello revealed that the *tasso* in Piedmont brought in only 638,281 lire a year out of a nominal total of 1,648,858 lire. The state was thus realizing only about 39 percent of the revenue that it was supposed to obtain from the principal direct tax levied in Piedmont; this compares with the estimate by Montjoye in the same year that only about 40 percent of the *taille* in Savoy actually reached the government's coffers. The main reason for this alarming fiscal haemorrhage lay in the extensive immunities claimed by many taxpayers. The inquest suggested that a considerable proportion of these – perhaps one-fifth – were invalid, or of dubious legality.[13] The leading beneficiaries were naturally the clergy and the nobility. The primary goal of Victor Amadeus's programme of fiscal reform thus became the elimination of those exemptions that were fraudulent and the minimization of those that were legal. Following the enquiry of 1702 Gropello apparently planned to deal with the frauds and evasions that it had revealed, but the onset of war next year meant that his plans had to be shelved for another decade. And in the interim its desperate need for money forced the government to embark on another series of alienations of the *tasso* from 1704 to 1709, although on a smaller scale than in the 1690s. This practice of mortgaging the state's revenues would cease only with the end of the war.

The vast range of exemptions, whether deriving from ancient feudal privilege, recent grant, or outright usurpation, cast a disproportionate weight of taxation onto the overburdened local communities. Since the sixteenth century the communities had formed the basic units through which taxation was collected; if their finances broke down, the state's entire fiscal machinery would collapse too. Victor Amadeus and Gropello therefore worked hard to stabilize the local communities' budgets, in order to create a solid and resilient tax-base. The history of the Savoyard state in the seventeenth century is punctuated by similar initiatives – almost entirely abortive, however – prompted by the faltering condition of the communities' finances. By the end of the century many communities had sunk irretrievably into debt even though they had sold off most of their common lands and other assets. War and famine in the 1690s completed the ruin of many communities' finances, and focused the government's attention on the problem: hence the injunction to the intendants in 1693 to remedy the ills afflicting communal finances. The instructions issued in 1697 were even more explicit: the intendants were to ensure that the communities paid their taxes to the government before meeting any other financial obligations. Debts to private parties were only to be paid after the state had received its share, and private creditors were not to press the communities for payment. These creditors were generally local feudatories or religious foundations; the state in fact had to compete with them for the revenues from the communities. By intervening to protect the local communities from their powerful creditors the intendants took their place in the front line of the government's struggle against the privileged orders. But the problem was vast and intractable. Early in 1703 the government ordered yet another enquiry into the finances of the local communities of Piedmont, indicating that the situation was still unresolved. But the war supervened and all projects for financial reform at the local level had to be abandoned; they were resumed only after 1713.

Inquests into communal debts and efforts to balance local budgets were only part of the government's programme to revitalize the tax system. A more promising approach lay in creating an accurate, up-to-date tax-register for each community, which would minimize the possibility of fraud and evasion, and provide a clear statement of all assets and revenues. This line of policy would lead finally to the reform that Victor Amadeus II regarded as his greatest achievement – the great *perequazione* ('equalization') of the later years of his reign, a massive land-survey and revision of all the local *catasti* of Piedmont and Savoy. Again we should point out that there was nothing especially new about such an initiative; projects of cadastral revision had been put forward frequently over the past century. On each occasion however the government's orders had been ignored, and by Victor Amadeus's reign most local *catasti* were generations out of date, serving merely to perpetuate ancient inequities in the distribution of taxation. What was new about Victor Amadeus II's plan for cadastral reform was first that it was carried through to a successful conclusion, and second that it was conducted with a new, radical thoroughness in accordance with a method gradually elaborated in the course of the operation, constantly tested and improved against the requirements of actual practice.

Victor Amadeus's plans for revising the communal land-registers follow directly from similar measures taken during the regency. In October 1688 he had ordered that the syndics of each community conduct a new land-survey, but the project vanished without trace during the subsequent war. In April 1697 he issued new instructions for the compilation of a land-register for the Piedmontese provinces. This time the responsibility was not entrusted to the local authorities; instead a special committee was set up in June of that year to execute the new survey, and to examine the related problem of communal finances.[14] The committee required the keepers of the local *catasti* to report their present condition and to list all properties that enjoyed immunity, particularly those belonging to the Church. The new *catasti* were to be based upon a measurement of all the parcels of land in each community, together with an estimate of their value. Here we encounter the origins of the *perequazione*, which was to be conducted by skilled surveyors and valuers under the direction of the intendants, and not by the often inexpert and partial officials of the local communities. The first experiment in drawing up local *catasti* along these lines seems to have begun in the province of Cuneo early in 1698, and the survey was gradually extended to other provinces, with the government issuing constant orders for improvements in the methods by which it was carried out. The onset of war interrupted the operation, but once the invading French armies had been expelled from Piedmont the survey was resumed even more systematically and painstakingly than before.

The first part of the great land-survey to be completed was the segment covering the county of Nice, which was supervised by the intendant Mellarède.[15] Preliminary work apparently started in 1698, and on 4 February 1702 Mellarède issued detailed instructions to the local communities on the revision of their *catasti*. It seems that the county served as a kind of laboratory in which methods could be tested before the procedure was extended to the entire state. The survey was carried out in the old manner, relying on declarations by each property-owner of the extent and value of his lands, and of any exemptions he claimed. Measurement and valuation by skilled surveyors were used only in cases where no prior record existed of the size and worth of a parcel of property. It may well be that the inaccuracy of this method, and the ample possibilities of fraud that it entailed, determined Victor Amadeus and Gropello to conduct the rest of the *perequazione* by means of the slower, costlier but far more reliable methods of expert surveyors. Mellarède reported regularly to Gropello on the opposition he encountered from the local notables, who feared that they would lose their exemptions, and from the city of Nice, which claimed that any attempt to change the tax-register violated its privileges. Mellarède gave way on this point, and Nice remained one of the seven communities in the county that failed to draw up a new *catasto*. Along with his instructions on the revision of the *catasti*, Mellarède ordered that a record be kept of all changes in the ownership of land within each community, and of all grants of exemption that withdrew lands from the tax-register, so that the *catasti* would remain up to date. He also issued instructions on how the communal accounts were to be kept; a standard form was to be followed in every community, with careful precautions to eliminate fraud. The whole programme was rounded off by Mellarède's inquest into the local communities' debts and resources, conducted in 1701, which revealed a wide inequity in the distribution of the tax-burden between communities. The revision of the *catasti* seems to have removed some of the most glaring of these inequalities. We may note too that by drawing up the new *catasti* the government completed the process of assimilating the county of Nice to the tax-system prevailing in Piedmont. The Estates of the county had ceased to meet, and the tax-registers now served to levy a land tax like the *tasso* rather than the old *donativo* voted by the Estates.

In drawing up his plans for fiscal reform, Victor Amadeus was particularly concerned with the privileges claimed by the clergy. Mellarède's instructions to the local communities devoted special attention to clerical immunities, and in fact formed part of a general offensive against the clergy that was being conducted throughout the state. Victor Amadeus had become embroiled in a bitter dispute with the Papacy, and in order to force the Pope to make concessions he brought heavy pressure to bear on the clergy within his domains. The origin of the dispute goes back to the edict of 1694 granting toleration to the Vaudois, but other questions soon complicated the issue, many of them perpetual sources of discord between the Savoyard rulers and the Church: clerical tax exemptions, the power of the Papal Nuncio and the Inquisition, rights of preferment to abbeys and bishoprics, and regalian rights over the revenues of vacant benefices. These latter issues had been settled by an Indult in 1451, but the situation had changed a great deal since that time. The Papacy claimed that the agreement applied only to lands actually under Savoyard rule in 1451, while Victor Amadeus II – like his predecessors – naturally sought to extend it to territories acquired since then. The question was complicated by the fact that in the past when Savoyard rulers had been unable to assert their rights of preferment, successive Popes had made appointments by themselves, and so could now claim that the agreement had lapsed. For Victor Amadeus II the central issue at stake was that of state power, or the incursion of the Church into matters that he felt belonged to secular jurisdiction. He believed that his right to appoint suitable abbots and bishops was essential for the maintenance of good government in his domains: as he remarked to the Papal envoy in 1703, 'he was only thinking of the interests of his sovereignty, which his predecessors had neglected'.[16]

The Catholic Church was in fact an extremely powerful presence in the Savoyard state. Since 1560 a Papal Nuncio had resided at Turin, often intervening to support the jurisdiction of the Church courts and the Inquisition, and seeking to harden the government's policy against the Jews and the Vaudois. Pressure from the Papal Nuncio had certainly contributed to the persecutions of the Vaudois in 1655 and 1686, and was probably one of the reasons behind the decision to establish a closed ghetto for the Jews of Turin in 1679, a measure gradually extended to the Jewish communities in other cities. The activities of the Nuncio and the Papal

Inquisitors were constantly opposed by the Senates of Turin and Chambéry, which upheld the secular courts against them and prevented the publication of Papal documents without the government's approval. The Senates were zealous propounders of state supremacy and ardent forwarders of jurisdictional disputes; the magistrates of Chambéry in particular were profoundly influenced by Gallican doctrines, which they codified in 1728 as the *Recueil de la pratique de Savoie dans les matières ecclésiastiques*.[17] The Senates' vigilant and aggressive attitude in the endless wrangling with the Church courts and the Inquisition set the tone of Savoyard policy in Church-state relations; other state officials followed the sovereign courts' lead, and Victor Amadeus could rely on their full support in his efforts to reduce clerical and Papal influence.

The Church made its influence felt particularly through its control of education. Most towns and villages had a school, where the local children received some instruction in the catechism, and less frequently in the rudiments of literacy and arithmetic. When the community hired a master to run its school, he would usually be a cleric; in other cases the children would be taught by the parish priest. All this added up to a virtual clerical monopoly of elementary education. The same held true for the colleges and institutions of higher education. Since the later sixteenth century the Jesuits had established a commanding position, setting up colleges of their own or staffing many that had been founded earlier. At the university of Turin they shared teaching duties with other Orders, notably the Dominicans, also well represented in the field of education. Along with the Jesuits a number of other new Orders had appeared in the Savoyard states since the sixteenth century: congregations of Oratorians, Theatines, Capuchins and Carmelites had been established at Turin and in other cities. In Savoy we have already noted the upsurge of piety at this time, associated particularly with Saint François de Sales and the Order that he founded. The Theatines at Turin enjoyed the protection of successive Savoyard dukes and received generous financial support in the building of their monastery and its church, designed by the great Guarini, himself a Theatine, next door to the ducal palace. The Carmelites were especially favoured by the regent Christine, mother of duke Charles Emanuel II, in the middle of the seventeenth century; she aided them in building their convent, attended regular retreats there, and was finally buried in their church in 1663. With the support of the dynasty and the nobility the regular clergy thus held a commanding position in society, dominating education and playing a very significant role in the dispensation of charity as well. The Savoyards always conceived of themselves as Counter-Reformation princes, ardent defenders of the faith against the nest of Protestants in their states, keepers of the Holy Shroud, and obedient sons of the Church. Victor Amadeus followed this tradition of public piety and veneration for the Church. But he also carried on

another, contradictory tradition equally evident in his forebears' relations
with the Church: a jealous, vigilant defence of the interests of the secular
power against the encroachments of the clergy and the Papacy. This was
the tradition embodied by the magistrates of the Senates of Turin and
Chambéry, pious Catholics to a man, but always ready to draw a firm line
between Church and state.

Victor Amadeus II therefore, despite his ostentatious public attachment
to the Catholic Church, and his persecution of the Vaudois, was deeply
concerned at the vast influence wielded by the clergy. We might note that
this clash of jurisdictions was by no means restricted to the Savoyard state:
every Catholic ruler from the Venetian Senate to Louis XIV confronted
the same problem. In 1703 Victor Amadeus summed up his position in
the following terms:

> The ecclesiastical and the secular powers derive equally from the
> authority of God; that is to say, the Church is given power in spiritual
> affairs, and the other power, which is the state, is given power in tem-
> poral matters; the latter is subordinate to the former only in purely
> spiritual questions.[18]

This view of Church-state relations recalls that of Louis XIV, and the
points at issue between Victor Amadeus and the Pope were very similar
to those that caused prolonged conflict between the French king and the
Papacy. Like Louis XIV, Victor Amadeus II was a conventionally religious
man with rather simple ideas of theology and ecclesiology. For him the
political power and social influence of the clergy were a form of usurpation, to be reclaimed by the state. He did not question the Church's
authority; it was a matter of divine ordination, like monarchy itself. He
was merely concerned to contain it within what he regarded as its proper
limits.

Pope Innocent XII's denunciation of the edict of toleration for the
Vaudois in 1694 offered an example of what Victor Amadeus held to be
unjustified meddling in state affairs. Although a few years before he had
tried to enlist Papal support for his crusade against the Vaudois, he now
chose to define his dealings with the Vaudois as domestic politics, or at
most as the fulfilment of his treaty obligations to his Protestant allies.
Papal interference was not welcome, particularly since Victor Amadeus
knew that Innocent XII's opposition was largely due to pressure from the
French ambassador at Rome. From this point relations with the Papacy
deteriorated rapidly and latent tensions burst into the open. In retaliation
for the Pope's action, Victor Amadeus renewed the often repeated demand
for the abolition of the Inquisition in the Savoyard states. The Pope
naturally refused, so Victor Amadeus in his turn ordered that a lay
observer be present at all proceedings conducted by the Inquisition, and
that all its sentences be reviewed by the Senates. At the same time he

expelled all foreign clerics who formed part of the Inquisition within the Savoyard lands. These restrictions effectively hamstrung the Inquisition, as they were intended to, and gratified the traditional animosity of the sovereign courts against it.

The dispute now escalated. In 1697 Victor Amadeus reasserted his claim to appoint the heads of three important abbeys and to enjoy their revenues during vacancies; the Pope disagreed, and in January 1698 the Senate of Chambéry formally upheld the duke's claims. Meanwhile the government began to take steps to rectify the anomalous situation in border regions that fell under the jurisdiction of bishops not subject to Savoyard authority – parts of the county of Nice, which came under the jurisdiction of the bishop of Ventimiglia, and parts of Monferrato which were dependent on the bishops of Acqui and Casale. The Savoyard authorities requested these foreign prelates to appoint special vicars to administer the parts of their sees under Savoyard rule. The bishop of Ventimiglia refused, so Savoyard officials sequestrated the lands he held in their territory; when he in turn excommunicated these officials, the Senate of Nice ordered the local population, clergy and laity alike, to ignore his sanctions. The dispute with the Church had now become so envenomed that the Pope refused to approve the candidates nominated by Victor Amadeus to vacant bishoprics. From 1697 a growing number of sees was left without bishops, creating a problem for the government, which relied heavily on their services in local administration.

Victor Amadeus meanwhile broadened his attack by launching an investigation into the clergy's landed wealth and fiscal exemptions: his dispute with the Church now merged with his programme of fiscal reform. This line of policy posed a severe threat to the power of the clergy, which derived from their landed wealth. In Piedmont, as in the other Italian states, Church lands and endowments had grown steadily in the century or so since the Counter-Reformation, as resurgent piety brought a wave of benefactions and legacies. Like his predecessors, Victor Amadeus was worried by the extent of the Church's landed wealth and by the immunities that it had imperceptibly acquired. This had shifted a growing share of taxation onto the local communities, jeopardizing the stability of the entire fiscal system. Even if he had not become involved in his burgeoning jurisdictional dispute with the Pope, Victor Amadeus would have had to confront the problem of clerical immunities as part of his programme of fiscal reform; as things stood, the other elements in the dispute gave a special edge to the measures that he now undertook to curtail clerical immunities. But he never questioned the Church's right to tax exemptions; he aimed merely to do away with unjustified immunities and to recover revenues he believed were legitimately due to the state.

Victor Amadeus's first measures to limit clerical tax exemptions go back to the period before the Nine Years War, and even during the fighting he had devoted some attention to the question, ordering investigations of clerical landholding in certain provinces. In 1697 he issued an edict to restrict the transfer of lands to the Church: local magistrates were to limit the number of candidates for ordination when there were already enough priests in their district, and were to examine the transfer to the Church of any lands belonging to them, to ensure that the local tax-registers would not be deprived of the share of the *tasso* paid by their lands. In April 1697 a special committee was established to examine the whole question of fiscal exemptions, and in September it ordered the local communities to report on the extent of clerical landholdings in their districts. This order was repeated in December 1699, and stirred up a vigorous protest from archbishop Vibò of Turin; apparently under pressure from Rome, on 20 March 1700 the archbishop denounced the committee's inquiry in a public broadsheet, and cited its members before his tribunal. The government naturally declared his protest null and void, but on 17 July he ordered all the clergy under his jurisdiction to cease paying taxes. Predictably at this point the Senate of Turin intervened, declaring all his pronouncements illegal.[19]

In November 1700 Clement XI was elected Pope and tried to open fresh negotiations with the Savoyard ambassador at Rome, but these overtures foundered on issues of protocol and Victor Amadeus soon recalled his ambassador. Within a short time the Nuncio at Turin died, and Victor Amadeus refused to receive his successor. Meanwhile the attack on clerical immunities went on: in May 1702 Victor Amadeus re-enacted an old law limiting the acquisition of landed property by the clergy in the duchy of Savoy, and contemplated extending this to Piedmont as well. A new source of discord then developed as a result of the renewal of hostilities in northern Italy in 1701. At the end of the year some Savoyard troops were quartered in territories under Papal suzerainty near Asti, over which the Savoyards also claimed overlordship. The local feudatories protested, and the Papal court ordered them not to recognize Savoyard authority. The Camera dei Conti at Turin quashed this order, and the Papal authorities retaliated with threats of excommunication. Clement XI, however, was chary of taking such extreme steps, and despatched an envoy to attempt negotiation on all the matters in dispute – preferments and regalian rights, jurisdictional questions, clerical immunities and suzerainty over the Papal fiefs. Discussions continued through the summer of 1703, but ceased after Victor Amadeus became involved in war with France towards the end of the year. All these issues remained unresolved for the duration of the war, and would be exacerbated by the Savoyard acquisition of Sicily in 1713. The dispute with the Papacy continued to the end of Victor Amadeus's reign, and beyond.

One critical issue of state policy, however, was resolved during the period between the wars with France: this was the problem of disorder in the district of Mondovì. The central issue at stake here had always been the refusal of the city and its territory to pay the salt tax, and in the climate of fiscal reform propagated by the government after 1696 conflict was inevitable. The inquests into feudal immunities, the assault on clerical exemptions and the suppression of the privileges of Mondovì thus form part of the same general pattern. But Victor Amadeus seems to have had other reasons for wishing to suppress this perpetual hotbed of insurrection; it also threatened the internal security of the state, as Tessé's intrigues with disgruntled elements there in 1691 and 1692 had shown. Moreover, the state now possessed a war-hardened army capable of crushing the rebels once and for all, and Victor Amadeus was prepared to use it.

On 29 June 1697 an edict ordered the levying of the salt gabelle in the district of Mondovì.[20] The city and the lowland villages complied without serious trouble and only the mountain communities resisted; bands of armed men roamed the countryside, threatening the villagers of the lowlands and the agents of the tax-farmers. To deal with the mounting disorder Victor Amadeus led a body of troops to Mondovì in July 1698, and with this backing supervised the levying of the salt tax. The tax-registers of all the communities were now divided, the city of Mondovì was separated from the rest of the district and its municipal government purged of potentially dissident elements. The ban on the carrying of weapons was re-enacted and new measures were promulgated against banditry. Victor Amadeus then departed, leaving the marquis des Hayes in command of the troops. During the next months the disorders continued, for the discontent was exacerbated by a poor harvest. In November 1698 the rebels sacked Vico and killed or molested the officials of the salt gabelle there. More troops were now sent to reinforce des Hayes's men, so that by the beginning of 1699 he commanded a total of about 8,000 infantry and 2,000 cavalry, together with the local militias from Cuneo, Fossano, Pinerolo and Saluzzo. In January 1699 the rebels attacked Mondovì itself, but were repulsed. Des Hayes now prepared to crush them, concentrating his forces and making secret agreements with many leaders of rebel bands to betray their followers in return for money or pardons.

Conditions in the rebellious district had changed radically since the revolts of 1680–81. Mistrust and hostility divided village from village, city from countryside, family from family. The incipient divisions apparent earlier had now become deep and unbridgeable, so that it was easy for des Hayes to play off one faction against another and to persuade some rebel chiefs to desert their followers. At the same time the balance of forces had shifted in the government's favour. The insurrection no longer confronted a weak and unstable regency, but an undisputed sovereign whose authority was enhanced by success in war, and who was determined to admit no challenge to his absolutist principles. The ruthless des Hayes was given overwhelming military forces and ordered to destroy the rebels. He rejected offers of negotiation that the rebels put forward through the bishop of Mondovì, and moved systematically to secure the lowland districts, hemming the rebels into the mountains. On 26 May 1699 the ducal army attacked the far less numerous rebels at their stronghold close to Vico and routed them; some rebels fought desperately, but others defected and joined des Hayes's forces. This battle finally broke the revolt. Des Hayes advanced into the mountainous hinterland to reduce the last centres of resistance, while Gropello arrived from Turin to aid in the repression. Only the village of Montaldo remained defiant, but within a few days it was occupied and severely punished as an example. Forty-nine rebels were hanged on the spot, and eight of the nine hamlets that comprised the village were destroyed; their inhabitants – 564 families or 2,578 people altogether – were banished to the marshlands of Vercelli.[21] The last rebels were hunted down, Gropello making sure that the seigneurs of the nearby Imperial fiefs of Le Langhe denied them sanctuary. A draconian edict on 8 July forbade the bearing of arms by the people of the district on pain of death, banned assemblies of more than five persons and the use of rebel slogans, ordered the removal of gunports and other fortified elements from all buildings, and decreed the cutting down of the chestnut plantations around Montaldo to deny any remaining rebels both food and cover.

From this time the district of Mondovì remained tranquil. The state had finally overcome the revolts that had challenged it for so long, putting an end to a cycle of peasant insurrection that had lasted for half a century. The repression of Montaldo is a critical moment in the affirmation of state power by Victor Amadeus II; the government's ability to override ancient fiscal privilege and local autonomy had been strikingly demonstrated, and internal disorder no longer troubled the state. The district of Mondovì was now integrated into the system of local administration, its privileges submerged by the uniform laws of the state. An intendant held sway over the municipality of Mondovì and the surrounding villages. The salt tax was levied in the same way as in the rest of Piedmont: the 'Salt War' was over, and the state had won.

X
The Spanish Succession
and the Approach of War

Victor Amadeus II had inherited a claim to the Spanish throne through his great-grandmother the Infanta Caterina, daughter of Philip II and consort of duke Charles Emanuel I, and he therefore expected some territorial compensation in the projects for dividing up the Spanish empire prior to Carlos II's death in November 1700. His ambitions centred on the state of Milan, and in fact the peace treaty he concluded with Louis XIV in 1696 had promised him French support in conquering it, as his share of the Spanish inheritance. But with the conclusion of the treaty of Vigevano and the general pacification of Italy in October 1696 this commitment lapsed, and Louis XIV took care not to renew it. By making a separate peace with France Victor Amadeus had outraged his former allies, and he was now diplomatically isolated, dependent largely upon the fleeting and self-interested assistance of Louis XIV in the negotiations that the French king was conducting with William III to achieve a settlement that would satisfy the contenders for the Spanish Succession, and so avert the war which seemed likely to break out as soon as Carlos II died. During the negotiations leading up to the First Partition Treaty (October 1698) William III rejected Louis XIV's suggestions that some recognition be given to Victor Amadeus's claims. To grant Milan to the ally who had so recently left him in the lurch was (he said) no more than 'a joke'.[1] The First Partition Treaty therefore made no mention of Victor Amadeus's rights and gave him no territorial compensation.

Exclusion from the treaty led Victor Amadeus for a time to seek an accommodation with the Emperor, who had refused to ratify the treaty even though it assigned Milan to his son, and thus gratified an ancient ambition of the Austrian Habsburgs. But this brief flirtation with the Emperor, based on little beyond a shared dissatisfaction with the Partition Treaty, could not last; the fundamental rivalry over Milan, which would dominate Victor Amadeus's relations with the Emperor in the coming war, inevitably eclipsed any temporary entente. Victor Amadeus was faced by an insoluble dilemma, as the English envoy Hill observed in 1699:

He is afraid that either the French or the Emperor should come to be the duke of Milan, and I could scarce perceive for which he has the greater aversion. The French, at present, are more terrible, because they are more powerful; but the Emperor has so great pretensions upon almost all of the dominions of His Royal Highness [Victor Amadeus], which are certainly fiefs of the Empire, that he would be the more dangerous neighbour . . . I believe the Duke of Savoy would as willingly have the French at Milan as the Imperialists; but he would rather see the Turk than either of them. His Highness cannot conceal how much he is tempted himself to endeavour to seize on the State of Milan, if the death of the King of Spain causes a scramble.[2]

Hill perhaps overestimated the force of the Emperor's claims on the Savoyard state as a fief; only certain parts of the state actually formed part of the Empire, and no Savoyard ruler had accepted Imperial investiture since 1632. But the events of the last war had shown that the Emperor intended to exploit to the full his claims to feudal overlordship in Italy, and Victor Amadeus was on his guard against any extension of Habsburg influence. For the duke to seize Milan by himself was out of the question. He could not count on much support among the population, and in any case he could never hope to hold onto Milan against the will of either Louis XIV or the Emperor. He could only act as the ally of one or the other, in the hopes of securing some Lombard territory as his reward. Both Louis XIV and the Emperor were ready to use him in this way, but neither would help him make good his own ambitions.

Nor could Victor Amadeus look for support to the other Italian states. He was divided from the Pope by a deepening jurisdictional wrangle. The republic of Genoa traditionally suspected Savoyard designs to secure a foothold on the coast, and still remembered the war of 1672. The minor states of the Lombard plain – Parma, Modena, Mantua – feared Savoyard expansionism; the duke of Mantua in particular, as lord of Monferrato, had reason to fear Victor Amadeus's territorial appetite. Cosimo III, grand duke of Tuscany, clung to an abject policy of neutrality, and resented Victor Amadeus's claims to royal honours, which he sought for himself. So despite their alarm and foreboding at the Emperor's revived pretensions in Italy the lesser states could not combine; least of all would they do so under Savoyard leadership. The only possible exception was Venice, threatened with encirclement if the Habsburgs – whose lands already bordered those of the republic in the Alps – were to become masters of Milan. In 1697 Victor Amadeus broached the possibility of a joint attack to partition Milan with the Venetians, and in March 1698 news of this proposal leaked out through the republic's ambassador in Paris. Nothing more was heard of the plan: given the extreme military weakness of Venice and the mistrust that divided the two states, it would have had no chance of success.

The closed circle of Italian diplomacy thus offered Victor Amadeus no possibilities for improving his position, and he remained dependent on the decisions of the major powers. All the time, however, he remained alert for any minor advantages that might come his way. Slowly and patiently he pursued negotiations to purchase the Imperial fiefs adjoining his dominions, in accordance with his treaty with the Emperor in 1690. This policy yielded few dividends, however, for the local lords were unwilling to exchange the distant and innocuous suzerainty of the Emperor for the invasive overlordship of the duke of Savoy. But Victor Amadeus managed to purchase a few fiefs in Le Langhe and the Ligurian mountains, and in 1699 he acquired the fief of Desana, near Vercelli, whose ruling family had died out. In the same year a revolt by the subjects of the prince of Masserano, a Papal fief close to Biella, seemed to offer the long-awaited chance for Victor Amadeus to establish his rule there, but the onset of war in 1701 upset his plans; the principality was quickly occupied by French troops. These limited acquisitions, accumulated over a long period of time, were hardly spectacular. But they increased the solidity of the state by rounding out its frontiers and removing enclaves of alien jurisdiction.

Early in 1699 the First Partition Treaty fell into abeyance because of the death of the Electoral Prince of Bavaria, the compromise candidate who had been its chief beneficiary. Louis XIV and William III resumed their negotiations, this time giving greater consideration to Victor Amadeus's claims. Louis XIV was determined to prevent the Emperor from obtaining Milan, and therefore put forward a complex scheme of exchanges in which the duke of Lorraine would receive Milan in exchange for his duchy, while Victor Amadeus would cede his lands to France in return for the kingdoms of Naples and Sicily. Such a plan did not suit Victor Amadeus's purposes; he preferred to retain his hereditary lands in Piedmont (although he was ready to sacrifice Savoy and Nice) and extend them by acquiring territory in Lombardy. But the scheme at least offered recognition of his rights to part of the Spanish inheritance. Nor were his hopes for Milan entirely forgotten, and by March 1699 Louis XIV contemplated offering Milan to Victor Amadeus as a compromise candidate if the duke of Lorraine refused it, to prevent it from passing to the Habsburgs; in October of that year, when the Savoyard ambassador once more raised the question of Milan, the French government did not dismiss Victor Amadeus's claim out of hand. But the final version of the Second Partition Treaty, signed in March 1700, assigned Milan to the duke of Lorraine, with Victor Amadeus to receive it only if he refused.

Victor Amadeus was disappointed at his exclusion from the treaty: by the beginning of June 1700 the duke of Lorraine had accepted Milan, dashing any hopes that Victor Amadeus might still have cherished. But there were many signs that the treaty could not be made to work and would have to be modified. The first and gravest obstacle lay in the Emperor's refusal to countenance it. Once again dislike of the terms of partition drew Victor Amadeus and the Emperor briefly together. On learning the treaty's provisions, Leopold proposed that Victor Amadeus aid him in seizing Milan, in return for the remainder of Monferrato, which would be confiscated from the pro-French duke of Mantua. The adroit marchese di Priè, then serving as Savoyard ambassador at Vienna, worked hard to develop this project into a firm alliance, cemented by the marriage of the newly-born prince of Piedmont to a Habsburg princess. These proposals prefigured the alliance between Victor Amadeus and the Emperor that was eventually concluded in 1703, but the terms offered only partial satisfaction to Victor Amadeus's ambitions. So although he continued his negotiations with the Imperial court he turned increasingly to consider the more tempting offers emanating from Versailles.

Louis XIV deliberately extended hints of a possible revision of the treaty in order to keep Victor Amadeus from allying with the Emperor, but he seems also to have been genuinely interested in modifying it if some more advantageous arrangement could be worked out. Early in July Victor Amadeus therefore despatched the *abate* de la Tour (related to his envoy to William III in the 1690s) to lay fresh proposals before Louis XIV and William III, for he now believed that the treaty was not so much a hard-and-fast settlement as a 'project' to be altered by negotiation.[3] La Tour was to suggest that the duke of Lorraine be given the kingdoms of Naples and Sicily instead of Milan, which could then be transferred to Victor Amadeus. In return he would cede 'part of our states' – unspecified, but presumably Savoy or Nice, or both – to France. This plan presented advantages for all the parties concerned. The duke of Lorraine would receive a larger and more prestigious kingdom; Victor Amadeus would receive Milan, fulfilling his ancient ambition and at the same time excluding the Habsburg claimant; Louis XIV would exchange the more distant Italian possessions of the Spanish monarchy, which would have fallen to the Bourbon claimant, for the contiguous territories of Lorraine and Savoy. From Victor Amadeus's point of view, Milan was far more desirable than his transalpine dominions: richer, more populous, geographically and linguistically easier to integrate with Piedmont. If the plan had been implemented the entire character of the Savoyard state would have changed; from being a multi-lingual assortment of territories straddling the Alps it would have become an exclusively Italian state, the most powerful in the north of the peninsula, with vastly enhanced possibilities of expansion. La Tour was first to sound out Louis XIV's reaction to this proposal, and then to seek William III's approval, judged to be more problematical.

In the course of la Tour's mission another plan surfaced, or rather an old scheme was revived, probably on French initiative: this was the possibility that Victor Amadeus might exchange his domains for the kingdoms of Naples and Sicily. By the beginning of September William III was coming round to the idea, and as time went on he became more enthusiastic, seeing it as the best guarantee for English and Dutch trade in the Mediterranean. Victor Amadeus's real objective however was still Milan; the greater wealth of the southern kingdoms and the prestige of their crowns would be more than cancelled out by their lack of hereditary attachment to his dynasty. By mid-October he had reached preliminary agreement with Louis XIV to cede Nice, Savoy and the valley of Barcelonnette in return for Milan, the rest of Monferrato (which the French would obtain from the duke of Mantua) and the tiny principality of Finale on the Ligurian coast, traditionally included among the Spanish dominions in Lombardy. But by now Louis XIV was pursuing the negotiation merely to keep Victor Amadeus from seeking alliances elsewhere, for he had hopes that Carlos II's new will bequeathed the entire Spanish empire to the Bourbon candidate: if he refused it would pass to the Habsburgs, and after that it would revert to Victor Amadeus and his descendants. Carlos II died on 1 November and as soon as his will was made public the threads of these negotiations abruptly snapped. Louis XIV's grandson the duke of Anjou inherited the Spanish throne as Philip V, and the offers to Victor Amadeus fell into oblivion.

The Bourbon candidate's accession in Spain placed Victor Amadeus in a dangerous strategic position, with little room for manoeuvre. The Spanish governor of Milan declared at once for Philip V, sandwiching Victor Amadeus between two blocs of Bourbon territory and cutting him off from potential allies. Louis XIV no longer needed to entertain him with negotiations; instead, in December 1700 Tessé reappeared at Turin to press for permission for the French troops being sent to reinforce the Spaniards in the Milanese to pass through Piedmont. On learning of Philip V's accession Victor Amadeus had urged the Emperor to attack Milan at once, before the French could secure it. Leopold was already planning just such a move, but winter delayed the march of the Imperial army under prince Eugene, and it did not enter northern Italy until late May 1701. By then the Bourbons were firmly in control of Lombardy. Victor Amadeus had at first resisted the French requests for transit, evidently hoping to win time for an Imperial invasion of Milan, and incurring Louis XIV's displeasure. His delaying tactics proved fruitless in any case, for the French forces were despatched by sea instead, landing at Vado and Finale and reaching Milan in January 1701. Faced by encirclement, with no sign of aid from the Habsburg side, Victor Amadeus finally gave way and allowed the French troops to cross his territories towards Milan. Tessé meanwhile broached the subject of a formal military alliance, as part of Louis XIV's efforts to build up a league of Italian states to strengthen the Bourbons' hold on Lombardy: first to join was the duke of Mantua, by a secret convention on 22 February 1701. Venice and the Papacy rejected the French overtures; Parma declared its neutrality under Papal protection; the duke of Modena agreed to bar Imperial forces from his state. No Italian league was formed, but a loose grouping of states – the Savoyard included – began to gravitate around the Bourbons.

Tessé's proposals contained no offers of territory; Victor Amadeus was merely to receive the title of supreme commander of the combined Savoyard and Bourbon armies in Italy and a subsidy to expand his forces. The alliance would be sealed by the marriage of his younger daughter Marie Louise to Philip V; in this way Louis XIV sought to bind him more closely to the Bourbon cause. A treaty was signed on these terms on 6 April 1701, giving Louis XIV unimpeded access to Lombardy via the Alpine passes and securing the support of the Savoyard army in excluding the Habsburgs from Milan.[4] These terms were far from alluring to Victor Amadeus. He was in fact being forced to help consolidate Philip V's hold on northern Italy, acting against his own interests and helping a formidable rival to establish his power. The Bourbon alliance offered no chance of territorial expansion and reduced him to the status of a satellite as in the days before 1690, or of a mercenary captain with an army for hire. But he had no choice; if he refused, Philip V would still hold Lombardy, and the Savoyard state would be open to pressure from all sides. Victor Amadeus therefore chose the only course that would preserve whatever minimal freedom of action was left to him, hoping that circumstances would change. At the same time he kept up his contacts with the Emperor through the marchese di Priè (who was not recalled from Vienna until the end of 1701), explaining that he had only joined the Bourbon alliance under duress – which was in fact the case – and that he would have preferred to ally with the Habsburgs.[5] This too was true, for as the weaker party Leopold would have been forced to offer concessions in return for Victor Amadeus's support.

At first all went well for the Bourbons. They secured the Spanish territories in Lombardy without opposition and then occupied the strategic fortress of Mantua at the beginning of April 1701, with the secret agreement of its duke. At the end of May, however, prince Eugene crossed the Alps at the head of an Imperial army of close to 30,000 men; the Bourbon forces in northern Italy, commanded by Catinat, numbered about 39,000 at this time. Eugene soon forced the Bourbon army back in a series of skilful turning movements, and on 1 September he scored a victory at Chiari, forcing Catinat to retreat almost to Milan. Victor Amadeus fought bravely in this battle at the head of the Bourbon army, but this did not save him from the accusations of double-dealing that were already gathering around him. Both Catinat and Tessé, who knew him of old, believed he was in touch with his cousin prince Eugene. Such fears were not groundless, for Victor Amadeus was still maintaining his diplomatic contacts with the Emperor, and was making approaches to William III. He was also exploring possible avenues of cooperation with Venice and the other Italian states. But his contacts with the Emperor did not lead to any tangible advantage, since Eugene's victories persuaded Leopold that he could conquer Lombardy unaided, and so would not need to buy Victor Amadeus's aid with territorial concessions. The Imperial successes continued throughout the winter, further hardening Leopold's attitude; the Bourbon forces were expelled from the Modenese, whose duke now declared for the Emperor, and on 1 February 1702 Eugene captured the French headquarters at Cremona in a surprise attack, although he was later forced to withdraw. In the meantime the Imperial forces had blockaded the French garrison in Mantua and taken up winter quarters in the surrounding countryside.

The reversal of Bourbon fortunes induced Louis XIV to renew his discussions with Victor Amadeus over the terms of their alliance, holding out hopes of the cession of territory in Monferrato. But this was merely to gain time while the Bourbon army was reinforced and placed under a more dynamic general, Vendôme; to hearten the troops still more, Philip V appeared in the spring of 1702 to take supreme command of all the Bourbon armies in Italy, in effect superseding Victor Amadeus as generalissimo. On his way to the front Philip V had a formal meeting with his new father-in-law at Acqui, from which Victor Amadeus emerged profoundly displeased, for Philip refused him royal honours and the right to dine at his table. Victor Amadeus retired in dudgeon to Turin and took no part in the ensuing campaign. During the summer of 1702 the Bourbon army recovered most of the territory it had lost and in August defeated prince Eugene's troops at Luzzara. The pendulum now swung back. The Imperial forces in Italy were hard pressed, while in Hungary a revolt was rapidly gaining momentum and the elector of Bavaria was threatening Austria from the west. By the later months of 1702 Leopold faced the possibility that his army in Italy would be overwhelmed, allowing the Bourbon forces there to advance north through the Tyrol and join up with the Bavarians in a march on Vienna, while the Hungarian insurgents attacked from the east. As his strategic position deteriorated the Emperor became convinced that he must detach Victor Amadeus from the Bourbon alliance, to relieve the pressure on his outnumbered army in Italy.

Already in February 1702 Leopold had sent a secret envoy to Turin to sound out Victor Amadeus's willingness to change sides. At this time the Emperor would make no offers of territory and the talks did not progress. But as the position of the Imperial forces became worse, Leopold became more accommodating. He was furthermore being pressed by his allies the Maritime Powers to offer the concessions needed to secure Victor Amadeus as an ally. Both William III and then Marlborough, who took over the direction of the war on the king's death, regarded the Savoyard alliance as the key to victory in Italy, and as the hinge of a grand Mediterranean strategy embracing Spain and southern France as well, supported by English and Dutch naval power. By July 1702 the Emperor was offering concrete territorial concessions: Monferrato, to be confiscated from the duke of Mantua in punishment for his alliance with France, and certain districts in western Lombardy as well. These terms made the Imperial alliance increasingly attractive. In any case Victor Amadeus was looking for a way out of the imprisonment imposed on him by the Bourbon alliance, and was perhaps influenced by the pro-Habsburg sentiments of Priè, who had now eclipsed Saint-Thomas to become his chief adviser for foreign affairs. But any decision to forsake the Bourbons and side with the Emperor was fraught with terrible risks, far graver than in the previous war, since Piedmont was now flanked by potentially hostile armies on the French frontier and in Lombardy, and was open to attack from both directions.

In November 1702 the Emperor increased his offers, adding the Val Sesia and Novarese to the districts in Lombardy he was ready to cede in return for Victor Amadeus's alliance. Further reverses inflicted on the Imperial armies during the campaign of 1703 made him still more eager to detach Victor Amadeus from his Bourbon allies as the only means for preventing total defeat in Lombardy. Victor Amadeus for his part was equally alarmed at the success of the Bourbon armies; if they achieved complete domination in northern Italy his own position would become extremely precarious. In July 1703 a secret Imperial envoy, count Auersperg, arrived in Turin to begin negotiations for a treaty of alliance.[6]

Louis XIV had long been aware of Victor Amadeus's contacts with the Imperial court, and soon learned of Auersperg's mission. But he still hoped to avoid pushing Victor Amadeus to extremes and so merely warned the Savoyard ambassador in Paris that he knew of his master's dealings with the Emperor. Through the months of negotiation in the summer of 1703 Victor Amadeus betrayed serious symptoms of anxiety, and in his discussions with Auersperg constantly pressed for firmer guarantees of support from the Emperor and his allies. By now the English and Dutch governments were becoming involved in the negotiations, urging the Emperor to make the concessions that Victor Amadeus required. Since the outbreak of war he had been in indirect communication with them through his envoys in Switzerland and at Vienna, and for a time directly through his ambassador in London, Maffei, until the latter was recalled in mid-1701. He was especially eager to make the Maritime Powers guarantee any agreement he reached with the Emperor, for he remained unsure of the latter's sincerity. By July 1703 the British government was convinced that Victor Amadeus was ready to break with France at any moment, and accredited an envoy, Richard Hill, to his court on 6 August.[7]

Louis XIV was now convinced, through reports from his well-informed ambassador at Turin, that a rupture was inevitable. The Bourbon forces in Italy were poised to cross the Alps and join the elector of Bavaria, but early in September Louis XIV instructed their commander Vendôme to be ready to deal with Victor Amadeus's coming defection. On 29 September Vendôme carried out his orders, capturing and disarming the bulk of the Savoyard forces at San Benedetto on the river Po in Lombardy: here Victor Amadeus lost about 4,500 of his best troops.[8] The seizure of his regiments cut short any remaining hesitations in Victor Amadeus's mind. He hurried to put Turin into a state of defence, arrested ambassador Phélipeaux and all the French subjects in his dominions, and on 6 October issued a disingenuous manifesto explaining that Louis XIV had forced him into war. On the same day he secretly signed a draft treaty of alliance with the Emperor, but as yet he did not make a formal declaration of war against Louis XIV; he was still playing for time, trying to delay Vendôme's advance and putting the finishing touches to the treaty in continued negotiations with Auersperg. On 20 October Vendôme reached Casale and demanded that Victor Amadeus disarm his remaining troops and hand over the fortresses of Cuneo and Verrua as pledges of his continued adherence to France. Victor Amadeus could now delay no longer. On 24 October he declared war on France, and two days later Auersperg made a public entry to Turin, as if he had just arrived hot-foot from Vienna to sign the treaty of alliance. A treaty was formally signed on 8 November, as French armies moved up to invade Savoy and advanced into Piedmont from the east.

The Habsburg alliance, although offering Victor Amadeus the only possible escape from the stranglehold in which the Bourbon powers held him, was nonetheless beset with hazards. Leopold regarded Victor Amadeus not only as an ally, but as a rival for Milan, and therefore sought to minimize the cession of territory needed to obtain his alliance for fear of making him dangerous in the future. Much hard bargaining therefore went into the treaty, and the final document – only signed in June 1704 after prolonged discussions at Vienna – was full of unresolved ambiguities.[9] Leopold recognized the Savoyard claim on the Spanish inheritance, and in compensation agreed to give up the rest of Monferrato (to be conquered from the duke of Mantua); the region of Lombardy between Alessandria and Valenza; the district of the Lomellina; the Val Sesia, and various enclaves to permit communication between these territories. An army of 20,000 Imperial troops was to help Victor Amadeus defend his states, and then aid him in conquering a barrier composed of Alpine territory along his frontier with Dauphiné. The Emperor bound himself to obtain subsidies for Victor Amadeus from the Maritime Powers, who would also guarantee the agreement. In November 1703, when the first version of the treaty was signed, Victor Amadeus had added a secret clause to it, requiring that the district of Vigevano be ceded to him as compensation for the loss of his troops at San Benedetto and for the perils that he faced. This went beyond Auersperg's instructions and he objected to it; the Emperor refused to ratify it, and so in the final version of the treaty signed in the following year the matter was left open, Victor Amadeus stipulating that he would accept some 'equivalent' for the Vigevanasco which the Emperor's 'generosity and benevolence' would determine. This clause was to remain a source of discord for decades to come. Further discord would soon arise from another secret clause which bound the Emperor to cooperate in an invasion of France. This stipulation was inserted largely to satisfy the British government, and never secured more than lukewarm adherence from the Emperor, since it represented a diversion of his war aims, as would become clear during the abortive attack on Toulon in 1707.

There was acrimony and latent tension in Victor Amadeus's relations with the Emperor from the moment their alliance was concluded, but at this critical moment the pact offered assistance when the duke badly needed it. By November 1703 Vendôme had occupied the frontier region in the east of Piedmont and Monferrato, but he delayed advancing further, apparently since Louis XIV wished to make a final attempt to patch up some form of agreement with Victor Amadeus.[10] In this interval a corps of Imperial troops under count Guido Staremberg was able to reach Piedmont by forced marches. Setting out from Mirandola on the night of 24 December, Staremberg swung far to the south in order to avoid Vendôme, who moved to intercept him. Staremberg's troops made contact with a Savoyard force under Parella near Canelli on 12 January 1704; although their original strength of about 14,000 men had been somewhat depleted by the rigours of the march and by combat, they represented a vital reinforcement for Victor Amadeus, whose own army was being feverishly brought back up to strength. Their arrival doubled the forces at his disposal and stiffened his capacity to resist. But even with this addition to his army Victor Amadeus faced a desperate struggle against overwhelming odds.

XI
The War of the Spanish Succession in Piedmont

By changing sides in the autumn of 1703 Victor Amadeus embarked on a prodigious gamble: at stake was nothing less than the future of his state and his dynasty. This war would be very different from the previous one. Louis XIV now aimed at the total domination of Piedmont, as the essential condition for maintaining the Bourbon hold on Lombardy. In the 1690s the French armies had periodically invaded and withdrawn; this time they came to stay. Louis XIV was no longer fighting a diversionary campaign in a secondary theatre, for Italy was now vitally important to him; he could not let Milan fall to the Habsburgs. So he aimed to isolate Victor Amadeus from the Habsburg forces in eastern Lombardy, destroy his army and occupy his entire state, to guarantee communication between France and Milan.

The French commanders worked systematically towards these strategic goals and came very close to achieving them. By the summer of 1706 only Turin and southern Piedmont were left to Victor Amadeus; if the French armies had overrun this last remnant of his territory he might well have become a dispossessed wanderer like the duke of Lorraine, his state permanently occupied and facing gradual absorption by France. The French defeat at Turin in September 1706 was thus a critical moment in the history of the Savoyard state, and of Europe as a whole; it saved Victor Amadeus from French domination and ensured that the Habsburgs, not the Bourbons, would succeed to the former Spanish territory of Milan and would dominate northern Italy. But the cost of victory was enormous. The devastation inflicted on Piedmont was far more serious than in the 1690s, for the French armies occupied more territory for a longer period of time and systematically raided the areas that they did not directly control; the unoccupied regions were also subjected to the marauding of the Imperial troops, who were hardly ever paid and were compelled to live off the countryside.

Staremberg's troops had arrived in the nick of time to ward off an immediate French thrust into Piedmont, but they were cut off from the rest of the Habsburg army in Lombardy, receiving neither pay nor reinforcements, and depending on Victor Amadeus's overstrained finances for support. But at this point the duke urgently needed soldiers. Five of his ten regular regiments had been captured at San Benedetto, together with some elements of cavalry. Most of the lost regiments were quickly reconstituted with recruits from the militia, so that in 1704 his army attained a strength of 26,547 men.[1] A series of reforms over the past decade had greatly improved the efficiency of the Savoyard forces. After 1690 the cream of the local militias was formed into a special corps from which the line regiments were replenished, while the rest of the militiamen were used for local defence. As in the previous war, companies of Vaudois irregulars were recruited, and Victor Amadeus had two regiments of Protestant troops (mainly exiled Huguenots) and two more of Swiss and German mercenaries. Since 1697 the artillery and engineers had formed a special arm of the service, under direct military command instead of forming independent units as they had until then. The Ufficio del Soldo had been formally separated from the Segreteria di Guerra, so that the logistical and financial services of the army were no longer intermingled with its overall strategic direction. On the outbreak of his second war with France Victor Amadeus therefore commanded a reasonably efficient army which, with Staremberg's corps, totalled roughly 35,000 men. This was enough to deter Vendôme from invading Piedmont at once, and it forced him to advance slowly, fortress by fortress, towards Turin. But the campaign of 1704 would reveal some grave deficiencies in the Savoyard army, stemming chiefly from the haste with which it had been brought up to strength by drafting raw militiamen to replace regular troops.

Victor Amadeus's finances could not support an army of this size for long: if he was to survive he required large subsidies from his allies. His treaty with the Emperor stipulated that the Maritime Powers would give him financial help, and in fact they began forwarding money to him at the end of 1703, even before a treaty had been signed.[2] At the end of October 1703 Victor Amadeus set out to establish formal diplomatic relations with the Maritime Powers by sending conte Maffei back as ambassador to London; in January 1704 Hill and the Dutch ambassador Van Der Meer reached Turin, and proceeded at once to negotiations for a treaty, which was finally signed in August 1704.[3] The alliance with the Maritime Powers was crucial not only because of the subsidies and the possibilities of naval support that it offered: Victor Amadeus also required his new allies to recognize his rights to the Spanish throne and to guarantee that the Emperor would carry out the terms of the treaty he had signed, which were already in dispute, and which after the victory of 1706 would lead to endless wrangling. But the Maritime Powers, especially Britain, had aims of their own; they were not content to remain merely bankers to their new ally, as Hill's instructions and the terms of the treaty plainly reveal. British strategy formed a continuation of the plans pursued during the 1690s for an invasion of southern France, backed by a rising of the French Protestants. The revolt of the Camisards in the Cévennes mountains of Languedoc in 1703 gave new impetus to these projects, and aroused hopes that Victor Amadeus would join forces with them to attack Toulon, to cut at the roots of French naval power in the Mediterranean. The British government also sought to enlist the support of the Vaudois in this design. Hill was to persuade Victor Amadeus to restore all their privileges and 'to put them into arms, and encourage and assist them to march into Dauphiny to the assistance of the Cevennois [Camisards], sending with them some regular troops'.[4] The project for an invasion of France was central to British strategy and was pursued with single-minded energy until 1707. Victor Amadeus thus became the linchpin in Britain's design for the war against Louis XIV. His adherence to the Grand Alliance offered more than just a diversion; the British government believed that a successful attack from Piedmont into the south of France would bring Louis XIV to his knees. In its potential for penetrating a weak spot in the French defences and sparking a Huguenot insurrection the war in Piedmont promised strategic advantages that no other theatre could offer. The Maritime Powers were therefore ready to pay handsome subsidies to support Victor Amadeus: 100,000 écus as an initial payment to recruit his depleted forces, and 80,000 écus a month thereafter. As in the previous war, two-thirds of the subsidies were paid by Britain, the other third by the States-General.

Trouble arose, however, over the issues of trade and of religious toleration for the Vaudois. The British government believed – incorrectly – that a large volume of French trade still flowed into the Savoyard state, mainly in the form of woollen textiles. Hill was ordered to halt the import of French cloth and persuade Victor Amadeus to buy English woollens instead, to make uniforms for his troops. 'It is to be hoped, that he will make no difficulty of choosing to be supplied at cheap rates from his friends, rather than at dear rates from his enemies.'[5] (Price-lists and samples would be forwarded to him on request.) Hill was also to try to draw Victor Amadeus into the plan for an allied embargo on French trade, but this proved unnecessary since the volume of French goods entering the Savoyard state had fallen dramatically with the onset of war, and the matter was soon quietly dropped, although it would recur later in the war. British policy aimed to develop the commercial contacts essayed in the previous war, using the leverage provided by the military alliance to gain a foothold in the Savoyard state and replace France as its dominant trading partner.

Hill also pressed for renewed guarantees of toleration for the Vaudois and any other Protestants in areas which Victor Amadeus might conquer along the Alpine barrier projected in his treaty with the Emperor. These stipulations were incorporated into a secret clause appended to the treaty. The fate of the Protestant Vaudois was, as ever, a matter of concern to the British and Dutch governments. In 1698 Victor Amadeus had been forced, under pressure from Louis XIV, to expel all recent Protestant immigrants from the Vaudois valleys, in accordance with a clause in their treaty of 1696.[6] Most were Huguenot refugees, many of whom had fought for Victor Amadeus in the last war, including Henri Arnaud, the hero of the Glorieuse Rentrée, born a French subject in 1641. As we have already seen, the Maritime Powers were particularly concerned to enlist the Vaudois in support of their co-religionists in the Cévennes. In any case Victor Amadeus had already issued a proclamation appealing for aid from his Protestant subjects on 5 October 1703; in response they raised a total of thirty-four companies of troops for him during the war. A large proportion of these troops, plus a number of other Protestant auxiliaries, were paid directly by the States-General or the British government, and even though the planned invasion in support of the Camisards never took place, the Vaudois performed valuable service, bearing the brunt of the fighting in their region after the French invaded it in the summer of 1704.

At the time he was concluding his treaty with the Emperor and establishing contact with the Maritime Powers Victor Amadeus was also engaged in a critical negotiation with the Swiss Cantons. On 25 October 1703 he sent Mellarède post-haste to Berne, to enlist the Confederation's support for a number of proposals.[7] His primary aim was to obtain a Swiss guarantee to preserve the neutrality of Savoy, arguing that the Protestant Cantons and Geneva would be menaced if Louis XIV were to occupy the duchy. Mellarède found the Protestant Cantons receptive to this project, but the swift French invasion of Savoy forestalled any action to preserve the duchy. For a time the talks seemed to open up the possibility of a formal alliance between Victor Amadeus and the Protestant Cantons, but in the end the latter preferred to maintain their traditional neutrality. Mellarède was nonetheless able to recruit considerable numbers of Swiss mercenaries to swell the depleted ranks of the Savoyard army, thus fulfilling another objective of his mission. Victor Amadeus had hoped that by neutralizing Savoy and denying it to Louis XIV he could cut off direct communication between France and the Bourbon army in Lombardy; now that he had closed the Mont-Cénis to them, French supplies and reinforcements could reach northern Italy only through Savoy and the southern Canton of Valais, then over the Simplon pass into the Lombard plain. The Catholic inhabitants of the Valais refused to close their territory to French forces, but despite their hostile attitude Victor Amadeus was able to maintain contact with his allies through Swiss territory, receiving the Maritime Powers' subsidies with the help of the bankers of Geneva, exchanging ambassadors and diplomatic correspondence, and also keeping in touch with the leaders of the Camisards and other Protestants plotting against Louis XIV.

The lifeline to the outside world provided by the Swiss Cantons became ever more vital as Louis XIV's armies tightened their encirclement. Early in November a French army commanded by Tessé invaded Savoy, entering Chambéry unopposed and going on to occupy the remainder of the duchy by the beginning of 1704. Only the fortress of Montmélian held out; its garrison did not capitulate until the beginning of 1706. Meanwhile Vendôme bore in from Lombardy along the line of the Po, aiming for Turin. In the summer of 1704 he captured Vercelli, whose garrison (composed in part of new recruits) capitulated after a siege of about one month, on 21 July. The loss of this strong place after an unexpectedly brief resistance was a severe moral and strategic blow; as Hill reported from Turin, 'everybody is dejected'.[8] This despondency was increased by the threat of another French attack over the Mont-Cénis. The French forces in Savoy, now under the command of the duc de la Feuillade, crossed the Alps and took Susa on 12 June, then fanned out to occupy the surrounding valleys. Pinerolo offered to surrender and the Vaudois of the Val San Martino constituted themselves a tiny separate republic under French protection, but the other Vaudois resisted, harassing la Feuillade's communications over the Alps. Vendôme now moved to occupy northern Piedmont. On 30 September he took Ivrea and then advanced into the Val d'Aosta to meet another French force invading over the Little Saint Bernard pass. Within a few days the Valley had been overrun and Victor Amadeus's communications with the Swiss Cantons were severed for a time. Finally as winter came on Vendôme settled down to besiege the fortress of Verrua, overlooking the Po on the route to Turin, but here he met stiff opposition; the place did not fall until 8 April 1705, and the besiegers suffered heavy losses. All through the winter French raiding parties scoured the country as far as Turin and south into Monferrato. As Hill observed, 'Piedmont is in a manner besieged at present, and His Royal Highness has need of all his courage and resolution in the condition he is now'.[9]

Under these circumstances there was no possibility that Victor Amadeus would be able to cooperate in the various schemes put forward by the British government for aiding the Camisards or for a combined assault on Toulon. By the end of the campaign the Savoyard army was severely depleted, for the French deliberately refused to exchange any of the prisoners they took. Staremberg's corps was reduced to about half its original strength and was not receiving reinforcements. Fresh troops were desperately needed to stem the French advance, and Victor Amadeus therefore pressed his allies for aid. In the summer of 1704 the States-General hired a force of Württembergers to serve in Italy, and on 28 November Marlborough signed a treaty for a contingent of 8,000 Prussians, to be paid by the Maritime Powers over and above the subsidies they were already paying to Victor Amadeus. Subsequently more troops were hired: Swiss, Hessians and a contingent from the Palatinate. But none, apart from a few Huguenot refugees, could reach Piedmont directly, for the French encirclement was complete after the occupation of the Val d'Aosta.

Instead they joined prince Eugene's army in Lombardy, where their presence helped ease some of the pressure on Victor Amadeus, forcing Vendôme to keep a large force east of Milan to block Eugene's path and preventing him from concentrating all his army for the war in Piedmont. The indirect pressure of other allied forces also helped to distract la Feuillade; through the summer of 1704 he had to keep an eye on the Anglo-Dutch fleet cruising off the French Mediterranean coast, threatening a descent in support of the Camisards, so that he was unable to advance from Susa to meet Vendôme and besiege Turin. But the allied victory at Blenheim in August 1704 had little impact on the campaign in Piedmont, and did not open the way for aid to reach Victor Amadeus's hard-pressed army. Allied operations in other theatres thus slowed down the French timetable for the conquest of Piedmont but did not bring it to a halt.

In March 1705 la Feuillade occupied the county of Nice, capturing Villefranche and then the town of Nice itself; only the citadel held out. Victor Amadeus had lost another part of his state, and southern Piedmont was now open to invasion over the pass of Tenda. At the beginning of April Verrua fell, and for a time it seemed as if Vendôme would march on Turin; feverish preparations were made in the capital to withstand a siege. But the French plan called for the systematic occupation of all the surrounding territory first. Nor was la Feuillade ready to join in forming the siege, for he was still preoccupied by the possibility of an allied landing in southern France. Vendôme therefore spent the summer eliminating the last centres of resistance at Crescentino and Chivasso, two minor fortresses which fell in July after lengthy resistance. By then Vendôme was preoccupied by the advance of Eugene's army towards Milan, and moved eastwards with a large detachment of his army to meet this threat, halting his advance in Piedmont. On 16 August he defeated Eugene's army at Cassano d'Adda and forced him to retreat. With his rear thus secure, Vendôme returned to Piedmont, intending to begin the siege of Turin with the help of la Feuillade's army, which had moved in from the west and was already blockading the city. But the French commanders judged the season too far advanced to commence a formal siege against so strong a place, and in October they pulled back from Turin, planning to return and deliver the final blow in the next campaign. The protracted resistance of Verrua and Chivasso, and the diversionary effects of prince Eugene's army in Lombardy had prevented Louis XIV from completing the conquest of Piedmont that year. Nevertheless Victor Amadeus's situation was desperate. In December 1705 the citadel of Nice capitulated to the French, and Montmélian in Savoy fell soon after. Victor Amadeus had lost his last foothold on the other side of the Alps and his last link with any help that the allied fleet might bring.

At this critical juncture Victor Amadeus renewed his appeals for immediate aid from his allies, especially Britain; in January 1706 he despatched Maffei on another mission to London to request troops and money.[10] Maffei found Queen Anne and her ministers eager to help. Shortly before, in November 1705, Marlborough had made a special journey to Vienna, where he arranged an extraordinary loan of 300,000 talers guaranteed by the governments of the Maritime Powers, mainly to pay for more contingents of German mercenaries to reinforce Eugene's army. He found the new Emperor Joseph I (who had succeeded Leopold in May 1705) determined to prosecute the war in Italy more vigorously. On his return to England Marlborough was instrumental in negotiating a further loan of £250,000 sterling from private sources for the same purpose. These loans ensured that the Habsburg forces in Lombardy would be able to assume the initiative in the coming year. But in the meantime Victor Amadeus was pressing for troops to be sent directly to him; by now his army had dwindled to less than 12,000 men.[11] For a time Marlborough contemplated leading a corps of 20,000 picked troops from Flanders to northern Italy, in an even more ambitious version of his strategy in the Blenheim campaign, to join forces with Eugene, succour Victor Amadeus and invade southern France. But the situation in Flanders made it impossible for him to leave, while the reverse inflicted on Eugene's army at Calcinato (19 April 1706) raised doubts about the possibilities of decisive action in the Italian theatre. Marlborough remained in the north, winning a victory at Ramillies on 23 May, while Eugene was left to relieve Turin on his own, if Victor Amadeus could hold out long enough.

At the beginning of 1706 la Feuillade's army in Piedmont consisted of about 45,000 men, while Vendôme had roughly 48,000 in Lombardy, facing the Habsburg army under prince Eugene, which by mid-May totalled close to 50,000 men.[12] But the Imperial forces were as usual slow to concentrate, allowing Vendôme to defeat them at Calcinato, while la Feuillade closed in on Turin. Victor Amadeus's army was too small to dispute the French advance, but the city was well fortified – work had gone on all winter to build additional outworks – and amply provided with provisions and ammunition. On 23 May la Feuillade began the formal siege, but at first could not draw a complete perimeter around the city, so that until mid-June communication was possible to the east, across the Po. The siege would be arduous and fierce.

After Ramillies Louis XIV had been forced to withdraw some of his troops from Italy, with their commander Vendôme, to shore up the front in Flanders. Eugene's army was now strong enough for him to take the offensive; urged on by news of the tightening siege round Turin, he evaded the French army blocking his path and slipped south of the Po near Ferrara on 16 July. With the river between him and his enemy Eugene consolidated a base area around Reggio Emilia in preparation for a march to the west. On 15 August he set out by forced marches for Piedmont, while the French army (now commanded by the duke of Orleans) followed on a parallel route north of the Po without intercepting him. On 29 August Eugene's army made contact with Victor Amadeus's troops and secured the crossing over the Po at Carmagnola. Victor Amadeus had left Turin as the French siege-lines closed around the city in the middle of June. With only a small escort of cavalry he had eluded la Feuillade's attempts to capture him and harassed the French supply lines as he waited for the Imperial army to come up. While Victor Amadeus and Eugene concentrated their forces south of Turin, the French army from Lombardy joined la Feuillade in the lines around the city, and pressed the siege in a series of desperate assaults, as they strove to reduce the defenders before relief could reach them. But the defence held firm and the besiegers lost heavily; the total French army, including Orleans's force, was now only about 41,000 men all told – half what it had been at the outset of the campaign.

The combined Savoyard and Imperial field army totalled about 30,000 men. Yet despite this inferiority in numbers Victor Amadeus and Eugene had to move at once to relieve Turin, for the city was close to capitulating after more than three months of siege and bombardment. On 2 September the two commanders climbed the high hill of Superga east of the city to reconnoitre the besiegers' positions. Two days later they led the army from Carmagnola towards the French lines, skirting them to the west and taking up a new position between the little townships of Venaria Reale and Collegno. By an inexplicable error the French failed to attack them and let them concentrate opposite the weakest point in the besieging lines, where the rivers Dora and Stura flow towards the Po north-west of Turin. Here on 7 September the Prussian corps and Eugene's Imperial infantry advanced to the assault, and after several hours of bitter fighting gained a footing in the French entrenchments. Victor Amadeus in person then led a cavalry charge that broke through the French lines, and at the same moment the garrison of Turin sortied. The French lines began to roll up, panic spread among the many units not yet engaged and the besieging army broke, streaming westwards in retreat towards home. Late in the afternoon Victor Amadeus and his cousin rode into Turin, heard a Te Deum in the cathedral and enjoyed what meagre festivities the starved city could afford. Two days later Victor Amadeus wrote to all the bishops of Piedmont, ordering Te Deums to be sung in gratitude for the victory that had preserved his state. He then set about the urgent tasks of re-establishing the foundations of government (for much of the judicial and fiscal administration had been evacuated from Turin during the siege) and reorganizing his forces, in preparation for a campaign to reduce the places in Lombardy still under Bourbon control. Victor Amadeus and Eugene decided to ignore the vanquished French army which was still occupying Pinerolo and the Val di Susa, even though it represented a significant force and could have taken them in the rear. This calculated risk paid off, for Louis

XIV had decided to abandon the Italian theatre and did not order his army in the Alps to make a diversion in support of the garrisons in Lombardy.

The consequences of the battle of Turin were immediate and momentous. Piedmont was freed from the invader and the survival of the Savoyard state was assured. The state of Milan and the duchy of Mantua soon passed to the Habsburgs, whose dominion was to last a century and a half. But victory brought out the latent divisions between Victor Amadeus and the Emperor. At issue was the fulfilment of the treaty of 1703 which had ceded Monferrato and certain Lombard territories to the duke of Savoy; the equivocations in the text of the treaty would lead to years of dispute. And behind this loomed the wider issue of Victor Amadeus's long-standing designs on Milan, which he had not abandoned even in the darkest days of the French invasion. Habsburg rule in Milan blocked his chosen avenue of expansion, while the Emperor naturally regarded Savoyard ambitions as the chief threat to his new possessions. Dissension now appeared between the allies, transformed by victory into bickering and mutually suspicious neighbours.

First, however, they had to deal with the French forces still in northern Italy. By the end of September nearly all Piedmont and the Val d'Aosta had been liberated, either by Victor Amadeus's troops or by risings of the local population. Savoy and Nice would remain occupied until 1713, but the vital nucleus of the Savoyard state was now free of the invaders who devastated it for so long; orderly administration could be restored, reconstruction could begin. Victor Amadeus now advanced to support Eugene in expelling the French troops from Lombardy. Early in March 1707 resistance ended with the capitulation of the citadel of Milan, and by a convention signed on 13 March Eugene allowed the French army to withdraw under safe-conduct, thus creating the conditions for the next phase of his operations in Italy – the conquest of Naples.

But while Victor Amadeus was cooperating with the Emperor in Lombardy, their dispute over the execution of the 1703 treaty was intensifying. All through the war Victor Amadeus had complained of the sluggishness with which promised Habsburg assistance reached him, while he and his subjects bore the brunt of the fighting that was to establish Habsburg rule in Lombardy. To his mind the Emperor's failure to assist him and the sufferings inflicted on his people by the common foe justified him in demanding that the treaty be fulfilled to the letter, and in requiring further compensation for the trail of unpaid bills left by the Imperial troops in Piedmont. Soon after the victory at Turin Victor Amadeus requested that he be given immediate possession of the lands due to him under the terms of the treaty.[13] The Emperor demurred, claiming that the territories were to be ceded only at the end of the war. So Victor Amadeus turned for help to the British government, itself long dissatisfied with the inertia of its Habsburg ally and eager to gratify the duke of Savoy for his constancy and military value. Joseph's reluctance to hand over the promised territories did not stem solely from a natural desire to enjoy them for as long as he could, but also from an earlier secret agreement forced on his brother, the Archduke Charles, titular king of Spain, separating Milan from the Spanish inheritance and joining it to the Austrian Habsburg domains. Joseph naturally did not want word of this agreement to leak out for fear of its effect on public opinion in Spain.[14] The matter was further complicated by the fact that the duke of Mantua had not yet been formally judged a contumacious vassal of the Empire, so that he could not be legally dispossessed of his lands in Monferrato, which were to be ceded to Victor Amadeus. But under pressure from his allies Joseph I agreed in January 1707 to cede the Lombard territories, and the mechanics of the transfer were worked out over the next two months. In March 1707 Victor Amadeus was invested with Alessandria, the Lomellina and Val Sesia, and took possession of Monferrato pending condemnation of the duke of Mantua, after which he would receive formal investiture.[15] But the Emperor refused to give up the Vigevanasco or its equivalent, as required by the treaty, and turned a deaf ear to requests for payment for the upkeep of the Imperial troops who had campaigned in Piedmont. These questions remained to envenom relations between Victor Amadeus and the Imperial court for years.

Victor Amadeus was determined to obtain possession of all the territories stipulated in the treaty of 1703, as the reward for his sacrifices on behalf of his allies, and because he desperately needed the revenues that they would provide. With Nice and Savoy still occupied, and much of Piedmont devastated, the new territories in Lombardy and Monferrato represented a crucial addition to the resources of the overtaxed Savoyard state: an area of roughly 4,000 square kilometres, a population of perhaps a quarter-million souls at this time, and annual revenues of 1,200,000 lire a year or so in peacetime.[16] The new provinces were equal to about one-eighth of the total area of the Savoyard state in 1700, and added the equivalent of around one-fifth of its population in that year. By 1710 the government estimated that the newly acquired territories provided one-tenth of the state's revenues. The administrative assimilation of the new provinces began at once. An intendant was appointed, and the Senate of Casale was transformed into a sovereign court dependent on the Senate of Turin. But local privileges and customary law were respected – particularly in the isolated Val Sesia with its long tradition of separatism. The new provinces retained their former tax structure, which was riddled with frauds and inequities, but with the advent of the intendants Savoyard reformism was making its first inroads at the expense of local autonomy.

With the extra revenues from the Lombard provinces and Monferrato, and the whole of Piedmont once more paying taxes, Victor Amadeus was able to increase the strength of his army. The victory at Turin opened up the possibility of offensive operations against France, and though his own views at this time centred on extending his frontier to a more defensible line along the crest of the Alps, his allies had more ambitious plans: the British government now grasped the opportunity to carry out its long contemplated strike against Toulon. To this project Victor Amadeus readily assented, particularly since an invasion of southern France might well allow him to recover the county of Nice or strengthen his Alpine barrier. Planning for the expedition was already under way before the end of 1706, but in the meantime the Emperor was devising a plan of his own for the conquest of Naples, which clashed with the British project. Joseph I insisted that the invasion of Naples should precede the attack on Toulon, for he naturally wanted to secure the rest of the Spanish inheritance in Italy before participating in a scheme whose utility seemed to him at best dubious. The armistice that prince Eugene had concluded in Lombardy in March 1707 cleared the way for the Imperial army to march south, but displeased the Maritime Powers, since it freed a French army to fight on other fronts. The prospect of further Habsburg conquests in the Italian peninsula also disturbed Victor Amadeus, who in any case (as we have just noted) had his own reasons for favouring the planned invasion of France, so that the split over strategy left him in closer alignment with his British allies and widened the gulf that already separated him from the Emperor.

The division in the allies' councils augured ill for the proposed thrust against Toulon. In April 1707 an allied army of 35,000 men concentrated in northern Italy, ready to march into France, while the allied fleet sailed from its base at Lisbon to provide support. But at this point 10,000 Imperial troops were detached from Lombardy to conquer Naples. They achieved their objective in a swift campaign – although since they had no fleet they could not invade Sicily – and by early July had secured the entire southern kingdom apart from a few isolated garrisons. But to the British government the operation represented a dangerous diversion of the allies' forces, and a source of delays that contributed to the fiasco that soon ensued at Toulon. The combined force of Savoyard, Imperial and hired contingents gathered at bases in Piedmont during June, and crossed the Alps at the end of the month under the command of Victor Amadeus and prince Eugene. On 10 July the allied army entered Nice, while the fleet cruised offshore, and by the end of the month the combined forces were besieging Toulon. But the defenders had had time to prepare and the siege ran into trouble at once. Furthermore, the hoped-for rising of the Camisards in the Cévennes failed to materialize and the besiegers soon found themselves hemmed into their lines around Toulon by a French relieving force. On 22 August the allied army abandoned the siege and withdrew as best it could, harried in its retreat by the local population and plagued by desertion. But the expedition was not a total failure. The defenders of Toulon had been forced to scuttle the warships in the harbour to protect them from bombardment, and the ships were never raised; the French Mediterranean fleet had ceased to exist.

By mid-September the allied army had returned to Piedmont and was regrouping around Pinerolo for a quick thrust to expel the French forces still occupying the mountains west of Turin. Early in October Susa was recovered, clearing the way for an attack into the mountains of Dauphiné the following year, in a twofold strategy aimed at reinforcing Victor Amadeus's frontier and diverting French strength from other fronts, particularly Spain, where the allied cause was now sinking. In 1708 Victor Amadeus resumed the attack, capturing the important fortresses of Exilles and Fenestrelle, and expelling the French from the Vaudois valleys. This strategy was to be followed for the rest of the war. Each year the Savoyard army and a contingent of Imperial troops would invade southern France, through Dauphiné, Savoy or the Barcelonnette valley, stretching the French defences thin. In this way Victor Amadeus performed a vital function within the general scheme of the allies' strategy. But after the conquests in 1708 his efforts slackened. He had attained his immediate, limited objective by conquering the French enclaves east of the Alps and making his frontier more easily defensible, but to recover the lost provinces of Nice and Savoy was beyond his means. He could not overcome the difficulties inherent in mounting a full-scale invasion across the Alpine passes, particularly since the economic basis of his military power was being undercut by the severe winter of 1708–9 and the bad harvests that followed it for several years. The resultant agrarian crisis reduced revenue and increased the difficulties of provisioning the army. Political factors also intervened to discourage him from pursuing the war with all his energy. After 1708 his dispute with the Emperor became acute; relations became so bad that for two years Victor Amadeus refused to lead the allied army in person on its annual raids into France, as a protest against what he regarded as the bad faith of his ally. For his part the Emperor was not eager to press the war in the Alps, which offered him no reward beyond its diversionary effects, so that the Imperial forces were late each year in arriving for the summer campaigns and their commanders were unenthusiastic about any effort to liberate Victor Amadeus's transalpine domains.

The Savoyard conquests in the French Alps in 1708 included the high valley of Pragelato, which was inhabited by a community of Vaudois. Possession of this territory, though desirable for strategic reasons, raised the question of how this additional group of Protestant subjects was to be treated, especially since the British government soon declared its concern for their welfare. Victor Amadeus was reluctant to accord them the same degree of toleration as the other Vaudois in his states, apparently for fear of encouraging an influx of returned exiles, and many former inhabitants in fact returned to Pragelato after the Savoyard conquest, laying claim to lands forfeited during the persecutions and wars since 1685. But Victor Amadeus could not afford to antagonize the British government, his most potent ally, by refusing freedom of worship to the Vaudois of his newly conquered territory. He therefore allowed them *de facto* toleration but refused to announce this concession publicly, excusing himself on the grounds that such a step would further prejudice his tenuous relations with the Papacy. In this way he avoided conflict with his Protestant allies during the peace negotiations after 1709. In reality, however, he had no intention of tolerating his new Vaudois subjects' religion. Writing to his ambassador at The Hague in March 1710, Victor Amadeus ordered him to evade any demands by the Protestant allies that a guarantee of freedom of worship for the Vaudois of Pragelato be written into the peace treaty.[17] The consequences of this devious policy would gradually reveal themselves after the peace of Utrecht in 1713, which formally transferred Pragelato and the other former French Alpine territories to Savoyard rule, while not embodying any clause requiring that their Protestant inhabitants enjoy religious toleration. For the present, however, Victor Amadeus was still preoccupied by the need to continue the war with Louis XIV, and by his rapidly deteriorating relationship with the Emperor, which now threatened his hold on the newly acquired territories in Lombardy and Monferrato. To settle his differences with Vienna, to confirm his conquests and win back Nice and Savoy, still occupied by the French, and to secure compensation for the sacrifices his state had endured, he pinned his hopes on the peace negotiations that opened in the spring of 1709, in which his trump card was to be the support of the British government.

XII
Negotiations for the Peace of Utrecht

After 1706 the central preoccupation determining Victor Amadeus's foreign policy, apart from the actual prosecution of the war against France, was the growth of Habsburg power in Italy, which forced him into ever-closer reliance on the Maritime Powers as the only counterpoise to Imperial influence. Joseph I's conquest of Milan and Naples made him by far the strongest ruler in the Italian peninsula. Meanwhile Habsburg forces occupied Mantua and the lesser states of Mirandola and Castiglione, whose rulers had sided with the Bourbons, and in 1708 a decree reasserted the Emperor's claim to suzerainty over the north Italian states and Tuscany. Throughout this region the Imperial war-commissioners levied contributions and quartered troops. Even Victor Amadeus, fighting as the Emperor's ally, was assessed for a contribution. He ignored the demand, but its intention was clear: Joseph I was implying that Victor Amadeus was his vassal. Some (but not all) of the Savoyard domains were subject to Imperial overlordship, but the practice of actual investiture had lapsed in the previous century. The Emperor was trying to revive these languishing ties of dependency.

The establishment of Habsburg hegemony aroused apprehension not merely at the Savoyard court but all over Italy, so much so that in August 1708 Louis XIV thought it worthwhile to send Tessé on a mission to the Pope and the Italian princes in the hope of forming a league, ostensibly neutral but in fact to oppose the Emperor's growing power. Part of Tessé's purpose was to detach Victor Amadeus from his allies by playing on his fears of Habsburg encroachment, but the duke refused to be drawn, preferring to rely on the good offices of the Maritime Powers – particularly Britain – to smooth out his disagreements with the Emperor. This growing community of interest between Britain and the duke of Savoy was to be a determining factor in the negotiations that ended the war.

The Maritime Powers had already interceded on Victor Amadeus's behalf soon after the battle of Turin, when it seemed for a moment that Joseph I would refuse to hand over the territories stipulated in the treaty of alliance of 1703. Special British and Dutch envoys were despatched to Vienna, but even before they arrived the Emperor agreed, in January 1707, to yield the disputed lands. Nonetheless a great many issues still remained unresolved. Joseph refused to cede the Vigevanasco, subject of so much hard bargaining in the treaty negotiations, and would not offer an equivalent for it. Nor would he discuss the Savoyard right to acquire suzerainty over the Imperial fiefs of Le Langhe, even though it had figured in the treaties of 1690 and 1703. Joseph also refused to invest Victor Amadeus formally with the lands in Monferrato conquered from the duke of Mantua, even though he already enjoyed *de facto* possession of them. In November 1707 the duke renewed his request for investiture of all the lands ceded to him under the 1703 treaty (while carefully excluding the hereditary domains of his house, for which he claimed no investiture was needed), but once more he was rebuffed. Meanwhile yet another dispute had arisen over the possession of four villages in the Lomellina occupied by Victor Amadeus, which the Imperial authorities in Milan held were not included in the terms of the 1703 treaty.

By now Victor Amadeus was so exasperated that he refused to lead the allied army on campaign in 1708 until his demands had been met. This stirred the Maritime Powers to renewed action. This time their envoys found the Emperor more conciliatory, for he had become embroiled in a dispute with the Pope, occasioned initially by the Imperial war-commissioners' levying contributions in the duchy of Parma, which Joseph claimed was an Imperial fief. The Pope however contended that Parma was a fief of the Church, and in retaliation he refused to invest the Habsburg claimant with the kingdom of Naples after its conquest in 1707. In May of the following year Imperial troops seized Comacchio, a town in the northern Papal States claimed by the Emperor's ally the duke of Modena, and in September open war broke out between the Imperial troops and the hastily-assembled Papal levies, leading to a comic-opera invasion of the Papal States and Clement XI's forced capitulation in January 1709. This conflict forced the Emperor to look for support among the other Italian states; Victor Amadeus, whose relations with the Papacy were extremely bad, seemed to him a natural ally who should be conciliated. So in July 1708 the Emperor formally invested him with the duchy of Monferrato, finally confiscated from the duke of Mantua by a decision of the Imperial Aulic Council a month before. Joseph also confirmed the Savoyard right to acquire suzerainty over the fiefs of Le Langhe, but turned down Victor Amadeus's request that his hereditary title of Imperial Vicar be extended to cover the disputed lands of the Vigevanasco, since this would have amounted to a disguised form of cession. The duke now tried to make the most of these concessions by demanding oaths of fealty from all the Imperial vassals of Le Langhe, in fact overstepping the terms of the Emperor's grant. This move continued the Savoyards' traditional policy of piecemeal acquisition of the enclaves in this region, and would have brought a useful area of strategic territory along the Ligurian frontier under Victor Amadeus's direct rule. But three fiefholders protested to

Vienna, and in July 1709 the Emperor issued a declaration in their favour, denying the Savoyard claims to suzerainty.

Relations with Vienna had now plainly reached an impasse. As the allied campaign opened in the spring of 1709 Victor Amadeus once more refused to assume command of the army and appealed to the Maritime Powers for formal arbitration in the dispute. A British envoy, Brigadier Palmes, was sent to Vienna, but negotiations there proceeded at a glacial pace. Joseph I refused to accept his allies' binding arbitration and would agree only to non-binding mediation. In April 1710 Palmes and his Dutch colleague suggested a compromise settlement – the extension of the Imperial Vicariate to the disputed territories – but without success. Later in the year Palmes was joined by the earl of Peterborough, sent to give new impetus to the negotiations by the Tory administration that had recently come to power in Britain. Victor Amadeus meanwhile had ordered Mellarède to Vienna to reopen discussions about the fiefs of Le Langhe. These negotiations were just beginning to show some sign of success when they were interrupted by Joseph's death in April 1711 and the accession of his brother Charles, recognized by the allies as claimant to the Spanish throne. Finally in June 1712 the mediators delivered their decision, which was wholly favourable to Victor Amadeus. The Emperor was to cede territory equivalent to the Vigevanasco, and all boundaries and definitions of the extent of territory – for instance the disputed villages of the Lomellina – were determined in a liberal sense, against the restrictive interpretations proposed by Vienna.[1] The mediators' decision, however, produced no practical result, for the new Emperor Charles VI disregarded it, and instead seemed bent on prosecuting the quarrel with Victor Amadeus by force. He rejected a compromise that the latter put forward, by which his son would marry one of Joseph I's daughters, with the duchy of Milan as dowry. To safeguard Victor Amadeus in possession of his new lands therefore became a cardinal aim of British policy, to be carried through at the peace talks which had recently opened at Utrecht; the Habsburg–Savoyard conflict over the implementation of the 1703 treaty thus merged with the negotiations to end the war. The new Tory administration, which was even better disposed to Victor Amadeus than the Whigs had been, now worked to incorporate a guarantee of Victor Amadeus's gains into the final peace treaty, and to declare Italy a neutral zone in order to prevent the Emperor from attempting to take back the disputed lands by military force.

British support for Victor Amadeus, however, came with strings attached. Britain's trade to Italy had grown spectacularly in the last quarter of the seventeenth century, and after 1706 the focal points of this valuable commerce seemed to be threatened by the extension of Habsburg power.[2] The Emperor had seized the kingdom of Naples, a vital source of raw silk, and seemed on the point of rounding off his conquest by annexing Sicily, where British merchants had long been established (even though he was in fact unable to do so). The spread of Habsburg influence in northern Italy aroused fears for the chief trading ports there. After the occupation of Mantua, Venice was encircled on three sides by Habsburg territory, while the conquest of Lombardy brought the Habsburgs within striking distance of Genoa. The imminent demise of the Medici grand dukes and the Emperor's claims on Tuscany as an Imperial fief constituted a particular menace to Livorno, the real hub of British commercial interests. All this called for the establishment of a countervailing force to offset Habsburg power, and the Savoyard state was the natural choice for this role because of its proven military strength and its strategic position. British partisanship on behalf of Victor Amadeus II was thus grounded in a clear-sighted appreciation of the interplay of commercial and political interests in Italy and the western Mediterranean, and can be seen as part of a wider strategy opened up by the conquest of the naval bases at Gibraltar and Port Mahon, and the commercial and military entente with Portugal. And as in the case of Portugal, the British government expected its Savoyard ally to make direct commercial concessions; earlier attempts to develop the commercial side of the alliance in the 1690s and Hill's orders in 1703 plainly indicate the drift of British policy. Soon after the battle of Turin, as commercial relations with Piedmont became feasible once more, English merchants began to appear at Turin, buying up silk and offering woollen cloth for sale. Their initiative benefited from the virtual stoppage of trade between France and Piedmont caused by the war, crowned in 1706 by a French embargo on trade across the Alps. Imports of French cloth now ceased, so that the objective sought by the British government since the outset of the wars had been achieved: with French goods now excluded from Victor Amadeus's domains, English goods could move in to take their place. Late in 1708 the first shipment of English cloth – for army uniforms – was sent to Piedmont aboard the Mediterranean fleet, inaugurating what was to become a regular traffic, until by the 1720s English woollens were being exported to Piedmont in considerable volume. British goods had penetrated a market hitherto closed to them and would pose a serious problem for the Savoyard government as it sought to develop its own textile industry.

But this was the price that Victor Amadeus had to pay for British support during the peace negotiations. Commercial considerations were fundamental to the settlement that Britain sought to achieve in Italy: equilibrium in the peninsula would prevent the Habsburgs from establishing unchallenged political – and therefore commercial – sway. Because of his value in assuring this balance of forces, and in recognition of his past services in preventing the consolidation of an equally perilous Bourbon hegemony, Victor Amadeus figured as Britain's most favoured ally at the Utrecht conference. It is no exaggeration to say that the terms he received

– notably the acquisition of Sicily, which went beyond and even contrary to his wishes – were more of Britain's making than his own.

From the start of serious peace negotiations in the spring of 1709 the British government – still then dominated by the Whigs – adopted a very protective attitude to its Savoyard ally. The British plenipotentiaries were instructed that 'Her Majesty is likewise very intent that the duke of Savoy should have full satisfaction at the ensuing peace, and will expect that for the sake of his allies, as well as his own security, the Barrier . . . be made good for him'.³ This was the Alpine barrier promised in the treaties of alliance, to be made up of the territory in Dauphiné conquered in 1708. (The demand for this barrier would be included in the peace preliminaries of 1709, which Louis XIV rejected, and was to become one of the allies' regular demands in the years to come.) Victor Amadeus's own aims were rather more ambitious. His instructions for the Savoyard plenipotentiaries in 1709 reveal that his central preoccupation was, as ever, Milan, 'the great object of our intentions for the solid expansion of our House'.⁴ Realist that he was, Victor Amadeus understood that this aim could not be achieved by a direct demand; rather, the chance to acquire Milan would arise – if it arose at all – out of the schemes for territorial exchange that would be mooted during the conference. Failing Milan, as second best – and a poor second too – he was willing to consider the acquisition of Naples and Sicily. This idea had been first put forward during the Partition Treaty negotiations, and would gratify his claim for some part of the Spanish inheritance. When talks resumed early in 1710 at Geertruydenberg both these schemes were actually suggested, by the Dutch pensionary Heinsius and the Imperial envoy Zinzendorf. The Savoyard envoy del Borgo was encouraged by this to embroider a plan of his own, partly on the basis of Victor Amadeus's earlier directive: the duke would obtain Naples and Sicily, together with the former Spanish enclaves on the coast of Tuscany known as the State of the Presidi; the Savoyard lands would then be partitioned between the Bourbon and Habsburg contenders to the Spanish throne. Victor Amadeus judged del Borgo's scheme 'grandiose and feasible', but reiterated his earlier doubts about the desirability of 'transplanting' his dynasty in this way.⁵

It was characteristic of Victor Amadeus's methods in diplomacy that although he recognized that his best chance of political gain was through British support during the peace negotiations, he remained ready to explore all other avenues. While the Geertruydenberg talks were going on in March 1710 he was receiving private overtures from Louis XIV, centring once more on the possibility of exchanging the duchy of Savoy for Milan. Louis XIV was well aware of Victor Amadeus's strained relations with the Emperor and evidently hoped to detach him from his allies as he had in 1696 under similar circumstances. Victor Amadeus knew that the French king could not deliver what he was proposing and refused to be tempted. But as the campaign of 1710 drew to a close he renewed the secret negotiations by approaching the duke of Berwick, then commanding the French army in the Alps. The timing of this offer suggests that Victor Amadeus was worried by the recent change of ministry in Britain, fearing that the fall of the Whigs would undercut British support for him, and that he was exploring an alternative diplomatic strategy. These secret contacts continued into the summer of 1711, by which time it was evident that the Tory administration was even more dedicated to upholding Savoyard interests and more hostile to the Habsburgs than its predecessor had been.

The anti-Habsburg trend of British policy gathered momentum after Joseph I's death and the accession of Charles VI in April 1711. As titular king of Spain and its empire, and lord of the Habsburg hereditary lands, the new Emperor could command a formidable group of territories that threatened to upset the balance of forces in Europe. Britain had entered the war to prevent the Bourbons from amassing just such a bloc of states and could not permit the Habsburgs to achieve the same result. The new threat of a vast Habsburg empire dominating central Europe and the Mediterranean made the Savoyard state more valuable than ever as a strategically placed counterweight. Some of the British government's views on these developments were articulated by lord Peterborough when he visited Turin for discussions in May 1711.[6] Peterborough suggested the possibility of granting Sicily to Victor Amadeus as a means of checking Habsburg expansion in Italy – an idea destined to reappear in the later stages of the Utrecht negotiations. He went on to ventilate (perhaps on his own initiative) the possibility of giving Victor Amadeus the Spanish throne in order to deny it to both Bourbon and Habsburg claimants, for the Dauphin had just died and Philip V of Spain now stood in the direct line to the French throne. Victor Amadeus dismissed this notion as 'an agreeable chimera'. In a more practical vein, Peterborough went on to suggest that the duke might reach some accommodation with the Emperor by marrying the prince of Piedmont to a Habsburg princess – a project which Victor Amadeus was to pursue in his negotiations with Vienna for the next two years. In fact much of the later direction of the negotiations between Victor Amadeus and the British government was foreshadowed in these discussions.

The Tories meanwhile had entered into secret talks with the French and by the end of July 1711 had reached the basis of an agreement. This private understanding made it possible to summon a general peace conference, at Utrecht in January 1712, at which all the belligerents were represented. The British plenipotentiaries went armed with instructions to look after Victor Amadeus's interests: he was to be restored to all his domains and granted the Alpine barrier. They were to enlist the aid of the Dutch to prevent the Emperor from taking back 'those towns and places, which have been yielded to [Victor Amadeus] by virtue of the treaty of 1703' in Lombardy and Monferrato. This end would best be achieved, their instructions went on, by neutralizing Italy and evacuating all foreign military forces from the peninsula, and through a general guarantee of the territorial *status quo* there.[7]

On 2 January 1712 Victor Amadeus drafted instructions for his own plenipotentiaries at Utrecht, Mellarède, del Borgo and Maffei. His plans went far beyond those of his British allies. Above all he wanted Milan:

> Nothing must be neglected to obtain the state of Milan, or (in descending order) that part of it beyond the river Adda, or at least the part beyond the Ticino and Lake Maggiore, with the province of Tortona and the marquisate of Finale, for the general reason of making it possible for us to create an equilibrium in Italy against the preponderance of the House of Austria.[8]

Here we might note that Victor Amadeus seems to be echoing his British ally's preoccupation with achieving a balance of power as the basis of the peace treaty, in terms that seem deliberately framed to harmonize with British policy. But Milan was an unrealizable objective, for no amount of British support could pry it loose from Habsburg control; Charles VI saw it as his most valuable conquest of the entire war. The Savoyard representatives were also ordered to secure compensation for their master's rights to the Spanish throne, as set out in Carlos II's will and recognized by both the Emperor and the Maritime Powers in their treaties with him. Victor Amadeus was clearly setting his sights high, and we should probably see his intentions here against the background of his other diplomatic moves at the time, which might provide the leverage necessary to achieve these broader aims. Late in 1711 Louis XIV had again broached the idea of recognizing him as ruler of Milan, opening another round of secret talks. Victor Amadeus was also making fresh approaches to the Emperor, renewing his proposals for a dynastic marriage with Milan as dowry. In fact he cherished great hopes of what would accrue to him from the Utrecht conference. On 5 March 1712 his plenipotentiaries presented their demands. They did not mention Milan, for Victor Amadeus had told them to wait for one of the other powers to raise that issue. After setting out the Savoyard claim on the Spanish inheritance they asked for an expanded Alpine barrier which would include the fortresses of Briançon and Montdauphin in Dauphiné, Fort Barraux in Savoy, plus a strip of territory along the Rhône bordering France. They asserted suzerainty over the principality of Monaco, in accordance with a long-standing Savoyard claim. Finally they requested that trade between France and Piedmont be obliged to resume its traditional route over the Mont-Cénis, as it had before 1690 under treaty arrangements dating back to the early sixteenth century.[9] The wars had deflected traffic northwards to the Simplon and other passes, and the Savoyard fisc stood to lose customs revenue if the old pattern of transalpine trade were not restored.

At this juncture the Utrecht negotiations took an unexpected turn on the news that the duke of Burgundy, heir to the French throne, and his eldest son had died of smallpox. Now only two sickly infants, Burgundy's surviving sons, stood between Philip V and the French crown once the aged Louis XIV died. The spectre of a union of the French and Spanish crowns – which had led the allies into the war – was thus resurrected. To meet this new contingency, in April 1712 the British government proposed a daring scheme of territorial exchanges in which Victor Amadeus figured as the *deus ex machina* through whom balance would be achieved. To avert the merging of the two crowns he would be given the Spanish monarchy while Philip V would be compensated with Naples and Sicily, together with the Savoyard domains and Mantua.[10] Louis XIV assented to this plan on 18 May and wrote to Philip V urging him to accept; if he refused, he would have to accede to Britain's requirement that he renounce his rights to the French throne. Philip, however, rejected the proposal, preferring the security of the Spanish throne (where he was now solidly established) to such an uncertain future. On 8 June Torcy, the French secretary for foreign affairs, communicated this decision to his British counterpart St John.

The British ministers were taken aback by this refusal. They had summoned Maffei to London, expecting to announce to him that his master would be the new king of Spain, but now they put forward another proposal which had evidently been kept in reserve. On 23 June Queen Anne informed Maffei that her government intended to obtain the kingdom of Sicily for Victor Amadeus.[11] Sicily still formed part of Philip V's domains, since the Habsburg army in the kingdom of Naples had never managed to conquer it, for lack of a fleet. But in practical terms Philip did not control the island; it was at the disposition of the British government, whose fleet dominated the Mediterranean. Writing to Torcy on 23 July St John explained: 'of all the Allies there is none whose interest the Queen has more at heart than the duke of Savoy . . . it is neither for the interest of Great Britain nor France that the kingdom of Sicily should be given to the House of Austria, and therefore she demands it for the duke of Savoy.'[12] As the Tuscan envoy at Utrecht correctly noted, this demand was based on concern for British trade at Messina and for the shipping lanes to the Levant which passed close by the Sicilian coast. But there also seems to have been a desire on Queen Anne's part to procure a crown for her Savoyard cousin, whose rights to the throne of Great Britain had been set aside by the Act of Succession in 1701 because he was a Catholic.[13] The Queen seems to have had a particular fondness for Victor Amadeus, and perhaps this chance to obtain for him the royal title that went with the kingdom of Sicily assuaged her guilt at his exclusion from the English succession. Still another consideration weighed in this decision, however: the grant of Sicily would also satisfy the Savoyard claims on the Spanish inheritance. And finally it would neatly counterbalance the Habsburg possession of Naples and deny Imperial hegemony over the Italian peninsula. In August 1712 St John – recently created lord Bolingbroke – went to Versailles and secured Louis XIV's consent to this arrangement. On 4 September Philip V agreed to cede Sicily, and the basis of the peace treaty, as it would affect Victor Amadeus, was now decided.

The initiative for the transfer of Sicily thus came from the British government: Victor Amadeus was not asked beforehand whether he wanted the island, and the decision was communicated to him as a *fait accompli*. He was not happy with this turn of events; as Peterborough reported, 'nothing can express the Uneasiness of Mind of the Duke of Savoy, after these offers had been made to him'.[14] He would far rather have received Milan, or some part of Lombardy. Sicily's crown and revenues were highly desirable, and the island might serve as a springboard for later aggrandizement in Italy. But Victor Amadeus knew that it was an apple of discord intended to keep him perpetually at odds with the Habsburgs, and that it had been given to him as much to serve his British ally's purposes as his own. He would be bound by the Anglo-French agreement not to dispose of the island or exchange it for other territory, which showed that he had been installed there not in full sovereignty but as guardian of British interests, at Britain's pleasure. In the months before this prohibition was formalized in the peace treaty he made some tentative efforts to exchange the island for territory closer to home. He was immediately made to feel the weight of British protection: garrisons of British troops were offered to help defend the island – assistance which he prudently turned aside – and he was pressed to conclude a trade agreement favouring the British merchants in Sicily. He managed to evade this demand too, and when on 8 March 1713 a treaty was signed to regulate commerce in his new realm, British merchants received no more than the conditions they had enjoyed under Spanish rule.[15]

As Victor Amadeus had foreseen, news of the projected cession of Sicily further envenomed his relations with the Emperor. The island had traditionally formed part of a joint kingdom with Naples, and to amputate it from the mainland in this way was plainly detrimental to Habsburg interests. Charles VI's resentment against Britain for this affront, and for concluding a separate truce with France in July 1712 – an ironic echo of Victor Amadeus's separate peace in 1696, so roundly condemned at that time by the British government – was now visited on Victor Amadeus. Rumours began to circulate that the Imperial forces in Italy, backed by others soon to return from Catalonia, would invade the Savoyard domains and reconquer the territory ceded to Victor Amadeus in Monferrato and Lombardy. Charles VI was in fact accusing his ally of joining

Britain in a separate peace with France, contrary to the treaty of 1703, and argued that if he did so the alliance between them would lapse, nullifying the clauses in it that had ceded Monferrato and Lombardy.

To parry this threat the duke sought to hasten the conclusion of a general pacification which would include the neutralization of Italy, while casting about for support in other quarters. Since the start of the Utrecht conference the Savoyard representatives had been sounding out other Italian diplomats – especially the Venetians, also directly threatened by the Emperor – about the chances of forming a league to preserve the peninsula's neutrality. In the autumn of 1712 these approaches were renewed, more urgently, but in vain: the other Italian princes were as alarmed by the growing power of the house of Savoy as they were by the prospect of Habsburg domination, and the planned transfer of Sicily redoubled their fears of Savoyard expansionism. An attempt to enlist support from the Protestant Swiss Cantons also failed. The Bourbon powers, however, readily agreed to recognize the neutralization of Italy – as their interests of course dictated – and the British government refused to ferry Charles VI's army (and his consort) back from Catalonia unless he agreed not to disturb the peace of the peninsula. This provided the immediate guarantee of security that Victor Amadeus required, but the outlook remained uncertain: the Emperor would probably seek revenge as soon as an opportunity presented itself.

By the beginning of 1713 the main lines of the settlement between Britain, France and the Savoyard state had been worked out, and only one problem remained: the question of Victor Amadeus's Alpine barrier. It was clearly in his interest to speed the conclusion of a general peace treaty to forestall any offensive action by the Emperor, and he therefore gave up his demands for Briançon, Montdauphin and the corridor of land along the Rhône frontier, all of which Louis XIV had persistently refused. Victor Amadeus let the British negotiators handle the question, and a solution was quickly found: the new frontier line would follow the crest of the Alps, leaving Briançon and Montdauphin in French hands, but giving Victor Amadeus the district of Pragelato, which included the fortresses of Exilles and Fenestrelle that he had conquered in 1708. To compensate Louis XIV for this lost territory, Victor Amadeus was to cede the valley of Barcelonnette, which was in any case geographically and economically closer to France than to the rest of the Savoyard state. Victor Amadeus quickly accepted this rearrangement of his Alpine frontier, which gave him a more defensible boundary backed by two redoubtable fortresses.

The last obstacle to peace with Louis XIV had now been removed, and Victor Amadeus's envoys signed the treaty with France on 11 April 1713 at Utrecht.[16] It restored him to possession of Nice and Savoy, defined the new Alpine border, guaranteed the Emperor's cession of Monferrato and parts of Lombardy, and recognized Philip V's transfer of Sicily. The treaty further gave formal recognition to the Savoyard right of succession to the Spanish crown after the death of Philip V, excluding the lines descended from the dukes of Berry and Orleans, and thus confirming the separation of the French and Spanish thrones. Trade between France and the Savoyard state was to be restored, with traffic passing through the Mont-Cénis and Susa as before the wars. A few minor adjustments to the Alpine boundary and the Savoyard claim to suzerainty over Monaco were left for settlement later. On 10 June Philip V formally ceded Sicily to Victor Amadeus, and on 13 July a general peace treaty was signed between the two sovereigns.

In the Savoyard states the conclusion of peace was greeted with public jubilation. For three days the streets of Turin were illuminated; processions and parades celebrated the end of the war and Victor Amadeus's elevation to the dignity of king. On 3 August these festivities culminated in a great Te Deum, salvos of cannon and musketry, music, dancing in the streets, bonfires and fireworks.[17] There was ample cause to rejoice, for the war had been long and cruel. Most of the Savoyard domains had been occupied, Piedmont had been ravaged and a large proportion of its population reduced to misery by war taxation, the quartering of troops and the famine that followed the 'great winter' of 1708–9. The demonstrations of joy were increased by Victor Amadeus's immediate remission of a number of special war taxes and a proportion of the debts incurred by the local communities during the war years.

The cost of the war had indeed been heavy. In 1710 the government had drawn up a provisional balance-sheet of its losses in order to bolster the claims it was making for compensation at the peace conferences.[18] This is how it estimated the damage due to the war:

War contributions, ravaging by enemy and allied troops in Piedmont, thefts, burning	38,038,403 lire
Ravaging by allied troops in the newly acquired provinces	296,573
Destruction of artillery and fortifications	9,001,781
Direct taxation uncollected due to enemy occupation	22,600,192
Gabelles uncollected because of war	3,059,288
Extra expenses for the army, minus allied subsidies	8,798,360
Total	81,895,391 lire

A revised computation for the damage sustained by buildings and fortifications, compiled a few months later, raised the total estimate of war-damage to 94,675,273 lire, roughly equal to the state's entire revenues for a decade. A breakdown of the damage, province by province, reveals that the impact of the war had been most brutal in the provinces of Turin, Vercelli, Asti and Ivrea, while the southerly provinces, never occupied by the French, were relatively unscathed. But everywhere the war had caused devastation and had disrupted trade and agriculture. The deliberations of the communal councils reveal day by day the enormous sacrifices that the population had been called upon to bear: at Alba, or at Saorge in the county of Nice, the local syndics were beset by endless demands for recruits – who were frequently taken by force – for food and forage, for transport, for the billeting of troops, over and above the drain of war taxation. We find for instance that in October 1709, after the disastrous harvest of that year, the syndics of Alba protested that they could no longer pay their taxes or meet the interest payments on the municipal debt. But the government was unmoved: the town was forced to pay its taxes and find money to service its debt without any remission.

Victor Amadeus's kingly title, the enlargement of the state's boundaries and the increase in its prestige thus cost a terrible price in hardship and suffering. Victory was due first and foremost to the sacrifices of the population, who bore the costs and privations of the war. We should not repeat, uncritically, the patriotic myths fostered by historians of the last century, who pictured the Piedmontese people united in devotion to their ruler and unstinting in their self-sacrifice. The glorification of Pietro Micca, the sapper who repelled an incursion during the siege of Turin by blowing up a powder-magazine, entombing himself and the French attackers together, has to be balanced by incidents of disaffection, among the Vaudois of the Valle di San Martino, or at Mondovì, that ancient hotbed of sedition, in the summer of 1706.[19] But the people held firm, even though they grumbled at the crushing taxes and evaded service in the army; in places they would band together spontaneously to fight the invaders, and in the end their dogged resistance kept the state going.

It might be argued that such sacrifices were a cruel and unnecessary burden imposed on the population of the Savoyard state by the selfish ambition of its ruler. Certainly Victor Amadeus's passion for military glory and prestige helped draw his people into two bitter wars between 1690 and 1713. Given their choice his subjects would have preferred to have been left in peace, but this alternative did not really exist for them. If Victor Amadeus had remained neutral his subjects would still have suffered grievously from a war fought across their land by the great powers on either side of it: the fate of the other Italian states which tried to stay neutral sufficiently demonstrates this. In this sense, therefore, Victor Amadeus and his subjects had no choice: had he not elected to fight, war would have been thrust upon him. Instead he followed his dynasty's tradition of accepting war as inevitable and wringing from it whatever advantage he could.

Two decades of warfare effected fundamental changes in the organization of the Savoyard state and produced a striking increase in its military strength. The size of the army rose from 8,760 men in 1690 to 22,412 in

1710; after the peace of Utrecht it remained at about this level, and in 1730 (a peacetime year) the army numbered over 24,000 men.[20] This leap in scale was due in considerable measure to the subsidies that Victor Amadeus had received from his allies in both wars, for the extra money enabled him to maintain a larger army than the state's resources could support unaided. Enhanced military capacity in turn made possible the conquest of additional territory, which then augmented the revenues and so allowed for the upkeep of a larger military establishment. The two decades of war against Louis XIV thus magnified a tendency already apparent in the evolution of the Savoyard state for the past century – the militarization of government and society to a degree unequalled in any other Italian state and almost unsurpassed in the rest of Europe. Only Prussia had an army that was larger in proportion to its population. In 1689 the Savoyard army accounted for about one-third of total expenditure: by 1731, in a budget twice as big, it accounted for close to one half.[21] The priority accorded to the army was underlined by the difference between civilian and military pay scales: civil functionaries were paid far less than army officers of comparable seniority.

The allies' subsidies also produced a more obvious and dramatic result: without this steady influx of cash Victor Amadeus would have been defeated in the critical years after the French attacked him in October 1703. Between early 1704, when the first funds began to arrive, and their termination in March 1713, the Maritime Powers contributed 37,284,925 lire to the Savoyard budget, or about 20 percent of the total on paper.[22] If we compare the amount received in subsidies with the revenues that the government actually collected (approximately 85 percent of the budgeted figure) the allied contribution becomes even more impressive, rising to about 23 percent of real revenues. This proportion was higher still in the desperate years up to the battle of Turin, as Victor Amadeus's tax-base was eaten away by the invader: in 1706 roughly 40 percent of the state's real income was provided by the Maritime Powers. Without this financial support the Savoyard army would have disintegrated for lack of pay. Nor should we overlook the indirect effects of the subsidies on Savoyard war finance. The regular payments from abroad were a dependable source of income that allowed Victor Amadeus and Gropello to borrow on a large scale and make punctual interest payments on their extensive war-loans. If finally we add the other moneys paid by the Maritime Powers – special loans to expand the Emperor's army and speed it to the relief of Turin, or the cost of numerous regiments of mercenary and Protestant troops fighting in northern Italy – the full significance of the allied contribution to the Savoyard war effort becomes apparent. Without it Victor Amadeus and his state could not have survived.

Alliance with the Maritime Powers also signalled the opening of a new era in Savoyard diplomacy, raising Victor Amadeus's stature among the princes of Europe. By the time of the Utrecht conference the Savoyard state had established itself as a significant element in the power-game of European diplomacy. Although Victor Amadeus might not treat on equal terms with the great powers, he had proved his worth as an ally: his tenacious fight against heavy odds, culminating in the victory at Turin, had formed a vital part of the allies' strategy against France. At Utrecht the Savoyard diplomats reaped their reward and secured a place in the charmed circle where the real decisions were made, working in close collaboration with the great powers, rather than observing impotently from the outside like the envoys of other Italian states. Victor Amadeus's royal title was one sign of the new international standing that his state had achieved; another was the new scale that the Savoyard diplomatic service had attained by 1713. At his accession there had been Savoyard envoys to the various Italian courts and at some minor capitals outside Italy, but the only permanent representation to a major power (if we exclude the Holy See) was the Savoyard embassy in Paris. After 1690 the search for allies opened up new horizons and led to the development of permanent contacts with the other major capitals – London, The Hague, Vienna, Madrid – and stimulated a swift increase in diplomatic expertise, so that by 1713 Savoyard diplomats enjoyed a reputation for finesse that matched and complemented their state's heightened military potential.

The Utrecht settlement also marks a new stage in the geopolitical evolution of the Savoyard state. The acquisition of the new provinces in Monferrato and Lombardy enhanced the predominance of the Italian territories over the transalpine regions; strategically, politically and economically the latter were now more than ever peripheral, a fringe flanking the state's real centre of gravity. Two lengthy French occupations had demonstrated that the duchy of Savoy and the county of Nice were vulnerable and ultimately expendable; the state had survived without them. Victor Amadeus's readiness to barter them for Milan suggests that he recognized this fact, and that he would have liked to have consolidated the Piedmontese nucleus of his state by sacrificing the western provinces. The new boundary along the watershed of the Alps indirectly reflects a growing consciousness of the separation between the two main regions of the state. And while the Alpine frontier was now conceived as a static defensive zone to block invasion, the eastern frontier towards Lombardy was fluid and open, the point of departure for future conquests. The treaties of Utrecht thus confirmed the eastward movement of the Savoyard state's vital centre, in a centuries-old process. But they added a new factor that would radically alter this time-honoured tradition of territorial development. The acquisition of Sicily – soon to be exchanged for a more durable dominion in Sardinia – launched Savoyard expansion into another direction, confronting Victor Amadeus's government with a vast new range of tasks, but also with new potentialities for future growth.

XIII
Sicily, Sardinia and Foreign Relations to 1730

In October 1713 Victor Amadeus and his queen embarked aboard a British squadron at Nice and sailed to take possession of Sicily. The Spanish viceroy evacuated his troops and formally handed over the island to its new sovereigns, who were crowned in the cathedral of Palermo on 24 December.[1] Nobility and commons hailed their new king, whom they hoped would restore the prestige and prosperity of bygone times when Sicily had been ruled by its own monarchs and not by the viceroys of distant sovereigns. The presence of the court and government at Palermo seemed to promise offices and honours for the privileged classes, lucrative orders for the merchants and artisans, pomp and show for the masses. But these expectations were soon disappointed. Victor Amadeus stayed less than a year in Palermo before he returned to Piedmont, the real centre of his power. His court was drab and parsimonious, affording little profit or delight to the people of Palermo. The key positions in the government went to natives of his mainland domains, so that the Sicilian nobles felt slighted and soon looked back nostalgically to the days of Spanish rule. When Philip V's forces launched their invasion in 1718 few Sicilians resisted them in the name of Victor Amadeus II. Savoyard rule had not been granted sufficient time to overcome the initial mistrust and indifference of the population, and Victor Amadeus's short reign left few marks on government and society.

Even before he went to Sicily Victor Amadeus had been gathering information about his new kingdom, and during the five years or so of his reign there he worked with characteristic thoroughness to acquaint himself with its customs, economic conditions, administration and military capabilities. Above all he sought to strengthen the island's defences against the ever-present threat of attack from Habsburg Naples. He examined the problems of trade, manufacturing and agriculture, and in September 1714 ordered a census of the population, both human and animal, and of landed revenues: the total population was found to be 1,135,120 souls.[2] Despite centuries of misgovernment and exploitation, Sicily was a rich prize, and a notable addition to the Savoyard domains. It produced a surplus of grain, olive oil and raw silk for export. Palermo was a valuable port and a centre of manufacturing, with thriving guilds. Messina, the centre of the silk trade, was slowly recovering from the depression that had followed its revolt against Spanish rule in 1674–79 and the subsequent loss of its privileges. The island as a whole yielded substantial revenues – although throughout Victor Amadeus's brief reign its budget had to be supplemented by funds from the mainland – and could be made to yield more by judicious economic measures and the elimination of corruption. An energetic Piedmontese, the *contadore* Fontana, was appointed to run the Sicilian finances, and set about reforming the tax system, particularly the notoriously corrupt customs office at Palermo, where the government dismissed the chief officials and assumed direct responsibility for collecting customs duties. Revenue rose, but the privileged classes of Palermo resented this affront and the Savoyard authorities' popularity suffered. Nor did Victor Amadeus win popular support by lowering taxes, since he urgently needed revenue; all the old gabelles, export duties and direct taxes remained at their former level.

Taxation was levied through the Sicilian Parliament, which assembled late in February 1714 to swear fealty to its new sovereign and to vote a series of *donativi* to cover the costs of government. Parliament then put forward suggestions of its own for reform: more rigorous sumptuary laws to curb luxury, improvements in the judicial system, the recruitment of local Sicilian troops, the establishment of a free port at Messina. Some of these projects fitted in with plans that Victor Amadeus was already contemplating: during the following months he set up two regiments and an elite bodyguard of Sicilian volunteers, and in June he travelled to Messina where he restored the city's privileges, established a free port and instituted a state trading company to handle the export of grain, silk and other commodities. He also began to build a small navy for coastal defence and communication with his mainland states. Within a year of his arrival the Sicilian fleet had grown from a single seaworthy galley to four, and in the next couple of years he added four sailing warships to this total – two of them built in Sicily itself. The development of an effective naval force took on new urgency in the summer of 1714, for after the death of Queen Anne and the accession of the more pro-Habsburg George I Victor Amadeus could no longer count on the support of the British Mediterranean squadron.

His hold on Sicily was far from secure: even with his own troops manning the island's fortresses – by 1718 close to 10,000 Piedmontese soldiers were stationed in Sicily – an invasion would be hard to withstand. Charles VI would not recognize him as king of Sicily, and in the treaty of Rastatt (signed early in 1714 to end the hostilities between France and the Empire which had continued after the peace of Utrecht) he pointedly refused to guarantee the integrity of the Savoyard domains. It was evident that he would try to reunite Sicily to the kingdom of Naples, and might use his army in Lombardy to attack Victor Amadeus's mainland possessions, now that he was no longer at war with France. Philip V also cher-

ished ambitions to recover Sicily and the other erstwhile Spanish dominions in Italy. He had relinquished the island to Victor Amadeus only with
great reluctance, and by the treaty of cession in June 1713 he retained a
number of fiefs – notably the county of Modica – confiscated during the
last war from adherents of the Habsburg cause. These estates were
administered by Philip V's agents as a 'second sovereignty' apart from the
rest of Sicily, and acted as centres of propaganda to foment discord among
the population, which was still strongly pro-Spanish.[3]

The deteriorating international situation impelled Victor Amadeus to
return to his mainland possessions, to observe developments more closely
and marshal his forces more effectively. On 8 September 1714 he sailed
from Palermo to Villefranche, leaving the trusted Maffei as viceroy, and
dashing Sicilian hopes of becoming the new centre of the expanded
Savoyard monarchy. Maffei governed the island conscientiously, pursuing his master's plans for reform, and mounted campaigns to repress the
brigandage that was rampant in many regions of the interior. But he faced
a very difficult task. Besides being menaced from abroad, Sicily was
internally divided by a bitter dispute between the secular authorities and
the Church. As king of Sicily, Victor Amadeus had stepped into a
centuries-long quarrel that had bedevilled relations between its successive
rulers and the Papacy. His acquisition of Sicily exacerbated his own
already bitter dispute with the Pope. Clement XI refused to recognize
him as king of Sicily and sought to exploit the opportunity afforded by
the change of government to do away with the Sicilian crown's special
prerogatives in ecclesiastical matters. Since the Norman conquest the
kings of Sicily had enjoyed broad control over episcopal appointments
and Church affairs, which they exercised through the Tribunal of the
Monarchy: when he inherited the Sicilian crown, Victor Amadeus also
inherited the Tribunal and its traditional anti-Papalism. He found it locked
in a dispute with the Sicilian episcopate over a question of fiscal immunity
claimed by the bishop of Lipari. In 1711 the bishop had excommunicated
some customs officials for levying duty on a couple of pounds of chick-
peas belonging to his household. The Tribunal nullified the excommuni-
cations, whereupon the bishop imposed an interdict on his diocese and
left to seek help at Rome. The Papal curia issued a declaration denying
the Tribunal's power to lift ecclesiastical sanctions, which was published
early in 1712 by several Sicilian bishops. Counter-measures duly followed
from the Spanish viceroy and the Tribunal, so that by the time Victor
Amadeus reached Sicily the archbishop of Messina and the bishops of
Agrigento and Catania had followed their colleague into exile, the last
two leaving their sees under interdict.

With his control of the island still far from sure Victor Amadeus could
not risk a rupture with the Church, and from December 1713 he sent a
series of envoys to Rome to seek a settlement, while working to minimize

the effects of the interdicts in Sicily itself. In this he was supported by a large body of public opinion; Parliament in March 1714 had exhorted him specifically to uphold the Tribunal's powers. Clement XI, however, was determined to make the most of his opportunity and abrogate the Tribunal, so he aggravated the dispute by refusing to allow collection of the *crociata* (the tax paid by the Sicilian clergy) and by demanding that Victor Amadeus accept investiture of Sicily as a Papal fief. In August and again in November 1714 the Pope warned the Sicilian clergy and laity to observe the episcopal interdicts, and finally on 20 January 1715 he took the long-meditated step of publishing a Bull abolishing the Tribunal. Papal hostility thus threatened Savoyard rule in Sicily from its inception. The diocese of Agrigento in particular was a focus of opposition, for the clergy there were more ardently Papalist than in the rest of the island. Nonetheless Victor Amadeus held firm: the most recalcitrant clergy were imprisoned or exiled, swelling the ranks of the dissidents in Rome who urged the Pope to take ever more stringent measures and exaggerated the degree of support that their cause enjoyed. Many of the clergy, however, sympathized with the secular authorities. In 1715 the government published a defence of its position by two Sicilian clerics, and in the pamphlet war that raged during these years the Sicilian Church was evenly divided on the issue.[4] Nor did the arguments of the pro-Papal faction seem to have swayed lay opinion, which either remained indifferent or supported the government. Victor Amadeus was also able to count on a measure of support from the French and Spanish governments, both of which were alarmed by the implications of the Papal claims for their own often tense relations with the Church. Clement XI gradually came to realize that he had overplayed his hand, and in June 1716 offered to rescind his measures against the Tribunal on condition that he be allowed to choose its head. Victor Amadeus refused this compromise, since the Pope still would not recognize him as king of Sicily, but this conciliatory overture indicated that a shift was taking place in Papal policy. Negotiations went on, but without decisive result, until the Spanish attack on Sicily in the summer of 1718.

If Victor Amadeus had retained control of Sicily the Church would probably not have constituted a serious obstacle to his authority, for by 1718 clerical opposition had been largely overcome. The aristocracy, however, posed a far more dangerous threat. Any attempt at reform such as Victor Amadeus was carrying out in his mainland possessions would have aroused the ire of the feudal baronage that owned much of the land and dominated the Parliament and local government. Victor Amadeus may have planned a programme of fiscal and administrative reforms in Sicily, although little was done once he had left the island at the end of 1714: Maffei as viceroy had no power to institute changes. In 1717, when Victor Amadeus reorganized the central government, he took an initial step towards integrating the Sicilian financial administration with the mainland by placing the Direttore delle Finanze at Palermo under the direct control of the Generale delle Finanze at Turin, and ordering the former to adopt Piedmontese administrative procedures. But these tentative essays were cut short by the loss of the island in 1718. By then Savoyard rule had not won the allegiance of any significant elements in society. The privileged classes in particular were alarmed at the threat to their position represented by even these first modest changes in the island's administration. They were still more concerned by the possibility that Victor Amadeus would institute an enquiry into their usurpation of royal lands, similar to the *perequazione* then under way in Piedmont; the census of 1714 may well have looked to them like the first move in that direction.

Anti-aristocratic reforms like those pursued in Piedmont and Savoy would have led Victor Amadeus into frontal collision with the Sicilian barons, who were impatient of any policy that strengthened the central government and so curbed their own power. The structure of Sicilian society was completely different from that of his mainland domains: a few score aristocratic families – one estimate later in the century counted seventy or eighty in all – divided the island between them. They owned vast estates cultivated by a subservient peasantry, and dominated the governments of the towns as well. This latifundist baronage enjoyed a degree of wealth and power that few, if any, families in the original Savoyard lands could equal. Their dominance kept the Sicilian administration weak, and severely limited its capacity to raise revenue, whereas the Piedmontese aristocracy by contrast was fast becoming a service nobility integrated into the state mechanism. Furthermore the Sicilian aristocracy, because it dominated Parliament, was in a position to block the government's efforts to prosecute reform or to increase taxation. Parliament in essence institutionalized the aristocracy's social and political ascendancy and could have become a formidable instrument of opposition in any clash with the central power.

Such a trial of strength never came, however, because international power politics, which had given Sicily to Victor Amadeus, combined to take it away from him within a few years. In the spring of 1714, after the treaty of Rastatt had ended the war between the Emperor and Louis XIV, liberating the Habsburg armies for a possible campaign in Italy, Victor Amadeus began seeking more effective international guarantees of his newly acquired territories. There was renewed talk of a league of Italian princes to counter Imperial influence. Envoys from Parma and Tuscany – both states imminently threatened by Habsburg claims of overlordship – joined the Savoyard ambassador in pressing the British government to action. Britain's good offices, however, failed to persuade the French to insert a clause explicitly guaranteeing Victor Amadeus's new possessions into the treaty of Rastatt, and so by July 1714 Bolingbroke was preparing to form an alliance with France and Spain for this purpose, and to use the British squadron in the Mediterranean to protect Sicily against the Emperor. Queen Anne's death on 12 August and the fall of the Tory ministry put a stop to these negotiations, and from this moment British support for Victor Amadeus – the vital guarantee of his gains at Utrecht – began to wane. George I and his new ministry set out to heal the breach with the Habsburgs, whom they regarded as Britain's traditional ally, unjustly thrown over by the Tories in 1712–14. It gradually became clear that in order to cement their rapprochement with the Emperor they were willing to sacrifice Victor Amadeus. For the present the latter felt secure enough, since the Emperor was not yet ready to attack him. But the long-term prospects confronting him were decisively altered by the change in British policy, and in the autumn of 1714, as George I's new ministry took over, Victor Amadeus sailed back from Sicily to his mainland domains to be ready to deal with the new diplomatic situation.

The shift in British policy requires some explanation. As elector of Hanover, George I needed the Emperor's backing for the territorial acquisitions he was then pursuing in northern Germany – a factor that had been of no concern to the previous ministry. At the same time the Whigs were reassessing British policy in the Mediterranean, where the Utrecht treaties had failed to resolve a number of crucial issues. Charles VI and Philip V had not signed a formal peace treaty. The former had not renounced his claims on the Spanish throne, while the latter still cherished ambitions to recover the lost Spanish dominions in Italy – ambitions which the British government had partially endorsed in a secret clause appended to the treaty of Utrecht.[5] In August 1714 Philip V (whose consort, Victor Amadeus's younger daughter, had died early in the year) announced his intention of marrying Elizabeth Farnese, heiress to the duchy of Parma and (by a distant claim) to Tuscany as well. The ruling dynasties of both these states were now close to extinction, and Philip V was staking out a hereditary claim on them against the Emperor's claims to feudal over-lordship. Conflict between the two sovereigns could therefore be expected as soon as either Parma or Tuscany fell vacant.

The Whigs were also determined to protect Britain's commercial interests in the Mediterranean. But they perceived the chief threat to trade as coming not from the Habsburgs but from the reviving naval power of Spain. A balance of power in the Mediterranean was, as ever, the frame-work in which British trading interests were to be pursued, but Philip V was now regarded as the potential disturber of the peace – an assumption soon proved correct by the Spanish attacks on Sardinia and Sicily in 1717–18. The crucial flaw in the treaty of Utrecht had been its failure to integrate Spain into the concert of Mediterranean powers. The Whigs therefore aimed to replace the original bipolar scheme there – from which Philip V had been excluded and in which Victor Amadeus served to

counter the Habsburgs – with a tripartite scheme in which Spanish and
Habsburg interests would be poised against each other, with the Savoyard
state as a lesser force between them. The chief threat to peace came from
the enmity between Charles VI and Philip V, so that British policy had to
build a settlement between these two leading powers; if territorial adjustments were needed to facilitate the settlement, Victor Amadeus would
have to foot the bill. Sicily was the natural focus of any such arrangement,
for Charles VI wanted to reunite it with Naples, Philip V still coveted it,
and Victor Amadeus's control depended upon command of the sea, which
rested with the British fleet. The Whigs could exploit this fluid situation
to achieve a settlement. They were ready to gratify both Philip V's and
Charles VI's ambitions for more territory in Italy, but since they feared
the resurgent Spanish fleet they intended to keep the strategic naval bases
of Sicily (and Sardinia too) out of Philip V's hands, and to reward him
instead with compensation in Parma or Tuscany. The Emperor's claims
on these territories would be compensated by the grant of Sicily, while
Victor Amadeus would receive Sardinia in exchange. Out of these underlying conditions came the final settlement of 1718–20.

The realignment of the major powers thus created a situation fundamentally unfavourable to Victor Amadeus II, emphasizing the fact that
even though the Savoyard state might have grown in power and prestige,
it was still not strong enough to pursue an independent diplomatic course
or to defy the great powers. Victor Amadeus's success at Utrecht had been
achieved as a result of the divisions between the major states: the rapprochement between Britain and the Emperor now altered the rules of
the diplomatic game to his disadvantage. He could try to exploit any
momentary advantage that might come his way as a consequence of the
tension between Charles VI and Philip V, but in the long run there was
little he could do. In 1713 he had lost an opportunity to acquire the port
of Finale on the Ligurian coast, part of the former Spanish dominions
conquered by the Emperor, who had sold this small enclave, despite an
urgent Savoyard counter-bid, to the republic of Genoa.[6] The ensuing
dispute over Finale heightened the old tensions between the republic and
Victor Amadeus, as the Emperor had intended. The Genoese sought to
prevent Victor Amadeus from acquiring any more Imperial fiefs in Le
Langhe, on the border between their respective territories, and in 1720
offered to admit many of the local feudatories to the Genoese patriciate in
order to block the advance of Savoyard influence there. Victor Amadeus
nevertheless kept up his efforts to buy the overlordship to these fiefs
whenever he could, seeking to extend his border south-eastwards in the
direction of the disputed duchy of Parma. He maintained a discreet watch
over developments there and in Tuscany, but his suggestions for some
form of concerted action evoked no response from their rulers: the duke
of Parma preferred to rely on Philip V, his new relation by marriage, while

the grand duke of Tuscany sedulously avoided any diplomatic action that might offend the Emperor. The other Italian principalities likewise refused to enter into any arrangement to combat the mounting threat of Habsburg influence. Early in 1716 10,000 Imperial troops marched into Genoese territory to prosecute a border dispute; this incursion brought them perilously close to the Savoyard frontier, prompting Victor Amadeus to renew his search for international guarantees of his state's territorial integrity.[7] The outbreak of war a few months later between the Emperor and the Turks removed the immediate threat of an attack on the Savoyard lands, but the danger had only been postponed, and not laid to rest.

No guarantees were forthcoming, however, even from Philip V. Nor could help be expected from the Pope, the other natural antagonist of Habsburg power in the Italian peninsula, because of his dispute with Victor Amadeus over the Sicilian Church. In the meantime the British government was establishing closer ties with Charles VI and beginning to formulate plans for settling the tensions in the Mediterranean. The point of departure for this 'southern peace plan' was a series of conversations between the Whig minister Stanhope and the Savoyard ambassador Trivié, in February 1716. Stanhope later claimed that he had been told that Victor Amadeus was willing to cede Sicily to the Emperor, in exchange for Sardinia, in order to reach a lasting agreement with him.[8] This supposed expression of Victor Amadeus's willingness to give up Sicily became the central element in Stanhope's peace plan, but it was based on a distortion of Victor Amadeus's actual intentions, and wrongly ascribed the initiative in suggesting the scheme to him. In fact Stanhope himself seems to have raised the question of a possible exchange of territories between Victor Amadeus and the Emperor, and this certainly suited his wider purpose of improving Britain's relations with the latter. Early in February Trivié broached the question of Sicily, but in an entirely different context; he in fact asked for British naval protection for the island against the Turks, who were attacking the Venetian outposts in the Aegean and threatening to move west. Towards the end of the month Stanhope raised the question again, dwelling at length on the difficulties that Victor Amadeus faced by holding on to the island, and hinting that he might be wiser to surrender it. Trivié immediately rejected this argument and explained that his master had no intention of giving up Sicily, which in any case his agreement with the British government obliged him to retain. The impression of a British initiative designed to persuade Victor Amadeus to cede Sicily for the benefit of the Emperor is strengthened by a parallel approach made at the same time by lord Stair, the British ambassador at Paris, to his Savoyard counterpart, Perrone, exploring Victor Amadeus's views on the desirability of settling his differences with the Emperor; here however the question of Sicily was not mentioned. At no point, it seems, did Victor Amadeus offer to exchange or cede Sicily: Stanhope was merely contriving a convenient fiction to facilitate the conclusion of a Mediterranean peace settlement which would cement the new-found harmony between Britain and the Habsburgs.

In June 1716 George I and Charles VI signed a treaty guaranteeing their respective territories, together with any future acquisitions they might make. This last phrase had an ominous ring: when Trivié questioned Stanhope about its implications he was told that Victor Amadeus might have to resign himself to ceding Sicily to the Emperor.[9] A special Savoyard mission to George I later in the summer failed to secure any promise of British support if the Emperor attacked the island: the hostile drift of British policy was becoming clearer. In November the Anglo-French treaty of Hanover contained secret provisions for a Mediterranean settlement by which Victor Amadeus was to give up Sicily for Sardinia, thus gratifying the Emperor's pretensions, while the latter would be required to recognize the claim of Philip V's sons by Elizabeth Farnese to Parma and Tuscany. This agreement formed the basis of the Triple Alliance, concluded in January 1717, by which the Dutch Republic joined Britain and France in their mediation between Philip V and the Emperor. The treaty itself made no explicit mention of Sicily, but it pointedly omitted the guarantees that Victor Amadeus had requested it should contain.

The Triple Alliance now set about persuading the other powers to accept their peace plan, but for the time being their efforts went unrewarded. The issue of the Spanish Bourbon claim on Parma and Tuscany proved intractable, and as the price of adhering to the Alliance's terms Charles VI demanded that Victor Amadeus hand over to him not only Sicily but Monferrato as well, thus undoing the treaty of 1703.[10] Certain questions arising from that treaty – most notably the matter of the Vigevanasco, still held by the Emperor – were still unresolved, and in the new diplomatic climate the latter evidently intended to reopen the entire question in the hope of recovering the territory ceded to Victor Amadeus during the last war. In an effort to avert this danger Victor Amadeus despatched a secret envoy to Vienna in February 1717, seeking a separate agreement with the Emperor before he could join the Triple Alliance and accept its terms. The basis of this agreement was to be, as before, the marriage of Victor Amadeus's heir to a Habsburg princess, and the cession of the Vigevanasco. These propositions had no chance of success, however; prince Eugene, to whom they were addressed, did not try to gain them a hearing, and by July 1717 the Emperor had decided in principle to adhere to the Triple Alliance.

Just at this moment, however, the Alliance's plans were thrown into confusion by a sudden Spanish attack on Sardinia. Philip V was attempting to recover the former Spanish domains in Italy before the Triple Alliance could forestall him, and while the Emperor's armies were still employed in the war against the Turks. In July 1717 a Spanish force landed at Cagliari, and by November the last Habsburg garrisons in Sardinia had capitulated. This did not deflect the Triple Alliance from its course. In November 1717 the British and French governments proposed to mediate the dispute on much the same terms as before: Charles VI was to drop his claim to the Spanish crown and to recognize the right of Philip V's sons to the successions of Parma and Tuscany, obtaining Sicily in return, while Victor Amadeus would be compensated with Sardinia.[11] In this way a balance of power would be established in the Mediterranean and in Italy, where a new Bourbon presence would check the Habsburg preponderance.

Within a month Victor Amadeus had learned of these plans, and began to work desperately to prevent their implementation, trying to detach both Britain and France from the Triple Alliance, opening negotiations with Philip V's minister Alberoni, and sending yet another mission to Vienna. Alberoni attempted to lure Victor Amadeus into attacking Habsburg Lombardy with tenuous promises of assistance, but this was merely a feint to cover the next Spanish move – the invasion of Victor Amadeus's own kingdom of Sicily. In January 1718 Victor Amadeus sent the conte d'Ussolo to renew his proposals to the Emperor, offering an alliance to be sealed by marriage. Ussolo however became involved in discussions about the possible cession of Sicily, exceeding his instructions, so at the end of April he had to be superseded by another envoy, the *contadore* Fontana, with an entirely new plan to lay before Charles VI.[12] Victor Amadeus now offered to renounce Sicily and his claim on the Spanish throne in return for Sardinia and more territory in Lombardy, including the Vigevanasco. Fontana was also secretly empowered to offer an alternative proposal, in which Victor Amadeus would exchange all his mainland dominions for Naples and Sardinia, to form a united kingdom with Sicily. But by the time these offers reached the Emperor in early June it was too late: he had decided to accept the Triple Alliance's terms. And at this point all diplomatic negotiations were upset by Philip V's surprise attack on Sicily.

On 1 July 1718 Spanish troops landed at Palermo, catching Maffei and the Savoyard army unawares: consummate master of deception that he was, Victor Amadeus had been outwitted on this occasion. The Spanish forces were hailed as liberators and the Savoyard garrisons were quickly expelled from most of the island; only the port of Milazzo held out. This quick success was negated however on 11 August when the British fleet destroyed the Spanish transports and their escorts off Cape Passaro. And in the meantime Charles VI had made peace with the Turks, freeing his army for intervention in Italy if it should be required. On 2 August his envoys formally accepted the Triple Alliance's terms for a Mediterranean settlement, which included the exchange of Sicily for Sardinia. Philip V and Victor Amadeus were now isolated; they were invited to adhere to the treaty, and if they refused, force would be used to make them accept its terms. Faced by the prospect of losing Sicily, Victor Amadeus cast about desperately for a way to salvage something from the wreck of his diplomatic fortunes. On 7 August 1718 he sent Saint-Thomas to Vienna with an offer to exchange Sicily for Parma and Tuscany instead of Sardinia. By now, however, the Emperor was fully committed to the projected peace settlement, and this offer produced no more than the others over the past few years. Savoyard démarches at London and Paris likewise failed to persuade the leaders of the Alliance to change their plans, and so on 8 November 1718 Victor Amadeus agreed to their terms, reluctantly accepting the loss of Sicily.[13] Now only Philip V held out against the Allies' demands, but an invasion from France, the presence of the British fleet cutting off the Spanish forces in Sicily and Sardinia, and a counter-attack in Sicily by a Habsburg army forced him to accede to the terms of the settlement early in 1720.

In May 1719 Maffei handed Sicily over to the commander of the Imperial expeditionary force there, and on 4 August 1720 the Savoyard viceroy Saint-Rémy landed at Cagliari to take possession of Sardinia for Victor Amadeus II. It was a far less desirable island than Sicily. An officer on the British squadron that ferried the Savoyard viceroy to Cagliari judged that the island 'is hardly of any other advantage to the Prince that possesses it than giving him the title of king'.[14] (This title had been created by the Emperor Frederick II in the mid-thirteenth century.) Initial reports from the Savoyard officials sent there echoed this doleful sentiment: to them Sardinia appeared barren and unhealthy, its inhabitants shiftless and given to brigandage. Although almost as large as Sicily in area, Sardinia was more sparsely populated, with a total of just over 300,000 inhabitants at this time.[15] Its economy was pastoral; almost the entire population lived in isolated villages in the inaccessible mountains. Roads hardly existed in the interior; there were no towns worthy of the name besides Cagliari, the capital, and Sassari and Alghero in the north; in these few towns commerce languished, and outside them there was none. There was not even a textile industry; the wool from the island's flocks was woven into rough cloth by the peasants for their own use, and not marketed. The island's chief export was salt from the great salt-pans around Cagliari and at a few other points along the coast. The fear of Barbary pirates prevented the development of fishing and coastal traffic, apart from a few isolated coral fisheries. Communication by sea was as deficient as on land.

In normal years Sardinia was self-sufficient in grain, and in times of abundance (as in 1722) there was a surplus for export. But when Saint-Rémy took over in 1720 the island was threatened by a dire famine, which grew even worse in the following year, and struck again in 1728, necessitating the import of grain and the imposition of controls on the sale or hoarding of cereals. These regulations were extremely difficult to enforce, for most of the island was effectively outside the government's control. With a force of only 2,500 Piedmontese troops and a restricted budget the viceroy could do little to compel obedience in the hinterland. Here the nobles held sway, giving such law as there was to their peasants and prosecuting their centuries-old vendettas. Poverty and oppression drove many peasants from their land to form the bands of brigands who roamed much of the interior of the island, seemingly impervious to the government's efforts to suppress them. Throughout the coming century the Savoyard authorities would grapple unceasingly but vainly with the interrelated problems of appalling poverty, endemic banditry and aristocratic insubordination. Man and nature conspired to keep the island in a state of abject backwardness: to the evils of drought, malaria and locusts were added the lack of communications and the twin legacies of unchecked baronial oppression and perpetual brigandage.

Yet this depressed and backward land in some ways offered a more welcoming terrain for Savoyard rule than had Sicily. With careful management the island's revenues slowly grew, although during the decade that Victor Amadeus reigned they showed a deficit.[16] After the anarchy and successive foreign invasions that had marked the first two decades of the century, Savoyard dominion inaugurated a long period of peace in which the government could begin its first faltering efforts at reform and economic development. The mass of the Sardinian people remained indifferent to – and probably ignorant of – the change of dynasties ruling them; the nobles, although they initially hankered for the days of Spanish rule, offered no serious opposition to the new government. Perhaps because of his experience in Sicily, Victor Amadeus instructed his viceroys to make only gradual changes in the structure of government, and to respect local customs and laws. The system of administrative councils and magistracies headed by the Reale Udienza continued to function as before, under the viceroy, but a new intendant-general was appointed to deal with economic affairs, and the whole local administration was placed under a Supreme Council for Sardinian affairs at Turin. Taxation was supposedly authorized by a Parliament made up of the three estates or *stamenti* of the realm, but this assembly had not met since 1699 and was fast becoming moribund after generations of neglect under Spanish rule, two decades of war and three changes of regime in rapid succession. Saint-Rémy convoked the *stamenti* in August 1720 to swear fealty to Victor Amadeus and to vote the customary taxes, and then summoned them again early in the following year to vote emergency funds to combat an outbreak of plague. Thereafter they did not meet again. Victor Amadeus preferred to deal with the permanent commission of deputies that acted for the *stamenti* between sessions; at his request the commission authorized taxes for further three-year periods, prolonging the mandate of the assembly to collect the taxes and so obviating the need to convoke it again. In this way Victor Amadeus accelerated the demise of the *stamenti* by a policy of deliberate neglect, and began to establish the principle of taxation at the monarch's behest, as in all his mainland domains except for the duchy of Aosta.

The withering-away of the *stamenti* deprived the Sardinian nobles of a rallying-point from which to oppose the government; by 1720 in fact the *stamenti* wielded little political power – far less than the Sicilian Parliament. Nor was the Sardinian aristocracy as politically powerful as the Sicilian. For all their violence and disorderliness (two Spanish viceroys had been assassinated by nobles in the later seventeenth century), the Sardinian feudatories did not possess the power of the great families that ruled Sicily. Few Sardinian nobles could match the riches of the great Sicilian lati-fundists; their country was much poorer, and they had to share the land with a numerous class of lesser gentry. So although the turbulent Sardinian nobles constituted a formidable obstacle to the consolidation of Savoyard authority, they could not oppose it as effectively as the Sicilian barons could. The basic problem facing Savoyard rule in Sardinia was the need to create order in an anarchic, backward society; the nobility, for all its riotousness, represented a crude simulacrum of hierarchy, a structure around which the government could build up its own authority. So Victor Amadeus and his successors did not institute reforms curtailing the political and economic power of the Sardinian baronage, as they were doing on the mainland; they left the feudal structure of society largely intact. Victor Amadeus aimed merely to preserve the peace of the island and to avoid too brutal a transition from Spanish rule; beyond that he does not seem to have been much concerned by his new kingdom and apparently never contemplated visiting it. His viceroys were left to grapple with the fearful problems of the economy and public order; genuine reorganization and reform would begin only under his son and successor.

For some years after the diplomatic reverses of 1718–20 Victor Amadeus II followed a relatively unadventurous foreign policy. His envoys appeared at the Congress of Cambrai, where the European powers were meeting to settle their remaining differences, but played no real part in the discussions, and merely advanced formal claims that their master be compensated for his rights to the Spanish inheritance and for the loss of Sicily. Victor Amadeus's inaction was not the result of his own choice but of the unfavourable position in which he found himself after the realignments of the major powers. His eyes were still fixed on his traditional objectives – acquisitions in Lombardy, or the exchange of the duchy of Savoy for territory in Italy. He kept a close watch on developments in Parma and Tuscany, whose ruling houses were about to die out. He does not seem to have regarded his possession of Sardinia as permanent, and stood ready to exchange it for territory on the mainland if the chance arose. In fact, his attitude to his new kingdom seems to have been extremely ambiguous, and his failure to initiate reforms there may well have stemmed, in part at least, from his considering it only a provisional adjunct to his domains.

This period of diplomatic stasis was brought to a close by the revival of tensions between the great powers, which permitted Victor Amadeus to resume his former role as an ally to be courted by both sides. In May 1725 a sudden treaty between those erstwhile antagonists Philip V and the Emperor unexpectedly reversed the prevailing system of alliances; it was immediately countered by a new pact between Britain, France and the Dutch Republic, to which other states subsequently adhered. For both sets of allies the question of Parma and Tuscany was of prime importance, and if they were to carry out their plans for these disputed territories they would need Victor Amadeus's support. Charles VI, however, would offer no concrete benefits in return for a Savoyard alliance. He turned aside Victor Amadeus's request for concessions in the dispute over the Imperial fiefs of Le Langhe, refused to reconsider the sale of Finale, and did not even respond to a suggestion that the king exchange Sardinia for Tuscany, and guarantee the Pragmatic Sanction in return. Victor Amadeus therefore inclined more and more to the proposals put forward by Britain and France, even though the contradictory nature of these offers, caused by the two governments' failure to coordinate their policies, made their value dubious at best. The British government suggested that Victor Amadeus be restored to Sicily, and in September 1726 despatched an envoy, John Hedges, to make this proposition at Turin. Hedges was also instructed to discuss two other issues that were currently straining Anglo-Savoyard relations: the treatment of the Vaudois, and the vexed matter of rising Savoyard tariffs and tightening restrictions on trade. For its part the French government refused to consider restoring Sicily to Victor Amadeus, but instead proposed a joint attack on Habsburg Lombardy; any conquests there would become part of the Savoyard domains. These different offers left Victor Amadeus profoundly sceptical, but in private correspondence with the French minister Fleury he put forward other ideas which harked back to the negotiations at Utrecht: in return for his alliance he wanted to recover Barcelonnette, extend his frontier along the Rhône, and obtain recognition of his suzerainty over Monaco.

Though none of these proposals bore fruit they indicate an underlying trend in Savoyard policy favourable to Britain and France leading eventually to the treaty of Turin in 1733, which aligned the Savoyard state with the Bourbons for a war of conquest in Lombardy at the expense of the Emperor. This preference is not hard to explain, for Victor Amadeus remained on extremely bad terms with Charles VI as a result of their still

unsettled territorial disputes in Lombardy – most notably the question of
the Vigevanasco – and because of the Emperor's well-grounded apprehension of Savoyard expansionism. French policy could happily encourage these latter ambitions as the easiest way to win Victor Amadeus's
support, particularly since the prospect of conquests in Italy might make
him more amenable to suggestions for ceding the duchy of Savoy. His
longstanding ties with Britain were reinforced by a growing volume of
commercial traffic in both directions, while the British government
recognized the advantages of acting as paymaster to Victor Amadeus in
the event of war; now as before he would form a crucial part of any
system of continental alliances.

These mutual interests were overshadowed for the moment, however,
by British displeasure at Victor Amadeus's policy towards his Vaudois
subjects. The restored Vaudois communities relied heavily on aid from
their friends abroad; without the funds channelled to them by Swiss,
Dutch and British charities they would have found it difficult to pay their
pastors and schoolmasters, assist their poor and indigent members and
survive as a community, for they were heavily burdened by extra taxes
imposed by the Savoyard government. Their chief recourse against
official intolerance was still diplomatic intercession by the Protestant
states. Britain in particular took a strong line in defence of 'the poor
Vaudois', as a way of intervening directly in its ally's affairs. Occasions for
diplomatic protest arose continually, for even though the Vaudois no
longer suffered outright persecution they were still subjected to the full
weight of institutionalized intolerance from the legal system and the
Catholic officials who administered it. In June 1718 the high court at
Pinerolo reaffirmed an earlier edict prohibiting work on Catholic feast-
days.[17] The Vaudois – some of whom were put on trial for violating this
law – appealed to their friends abroad (actually exaggerating the wrongs
done to them), and made direct representations to Victor Amadeus
himself. The king overruled the measure and moderated the zeal of his
officials, decreeing that essential labour could be performed on feast-days
by Catholics and Protestants alike. But in June 1723 the new law code,
the *Costituzioni*, reiterated the ban, so that once more the Vaudois alerted
their protectors abroad and protested to their king. The rulers of Prussia
and Sweden remonstrated on their behalf, but even before their protests
arrived Victor Amadeus had settled the affair by reissuing his earlier order.
A more serious defect of the *Costituzioni* was the omission of the edict of
toleration of 1694, the cornerstone of Vaudois religious liberties, and as
the original instigator of this measure the British government lodged an
official complaint at its omission from the new law code, and at the
inclusion of several laws that plainly discriminated against the Vaudois.

John Molesworth, who was then British minister at Turin, requested an
enquiry into the whole question.[18] Through the summer of 1724 Mellarède,

who as secretary of state for internal affairs was charged with enforcing the laws relating to the Vaudois, rebuffed the British envoy's approaches, until finally Molesworth appealed directly to Victor Amadeus himself. As before, the king took a more tolerant line than his officials and despatched a special magistrate to investigate: his report revealed a number of irregularities in the enforcement of the laws, together with a variety of infractions committed by the Vaudois themselves. Molesworth was invited to help resolve the entire problem by suggesting ways of redrafting the offending passages in the *Costituzioni*, but before he could cooperate in the final revision of the law code he was obliged to return to England in the middle of 1725. The king and his advisers seem however to have believed that he had given his approval to the new regulations they were then drafting for the Vaudois, originally intended as part of the new edition of the *Costituzioni* in 1729, but in fact published as a separate edict in June 1730. This new law was at once branded as discriminatory by the Vaudois, whose distrust of their government had been compounded just at that moment by a new wave of persecution directed against their brother-community in Pragelato, representing the culmination of the policy of systematic intolerance that Victor Amadeus and his officials had pursued there since 1713.[19] The king apparently believed that the legal safeguards enjoyed by the original Vaudois community in his domains did not extend to the newly acquired enclave of Pragelato; as we have seen, he had deliberately avoided giving any guarantee on their behalf during the negotiations for the treaty of Utrecht.

The motives for this seemingly gratuitous intolerance are far from clear. Perhaps he hoped to minimize the intrusive concern of his Protestant allies for the Vaudois of Pragelato by making their position entirely discretionary, unregulated by treaty obligations as was the toleration accorded to the original Vaudois community after 1694; in this way protests from abroad would have no legal foundation. He may also have intended to eliminate what seemed to his authoritarian idea of sovereignty a serious jurisdictional anomaly within the state, an exception to the uniformity he was striving to impose everywhere. He could not destroy the legal standing of the other Vaudois communities since their rights were based on long legal prescription, on his own edicts and on foreign treaties, but he still evidently considered them a nuisance to be limited in every possible way. The Vaudois of Pragelato, however, fell into an entirely different category. No ancient laws safeguarded them, and in the government's official view they were still subject to the harsh laws imposed on them by their former master, Louis XIV, before 1713. Victor Amadeus therefore seems to have felt free to restrict their liberties with increasing severity, leading to a complete ban on Protestant worship in 1720. Further civil disabilities followed over the next few years, provoking a number of conversions and a growing exodus to the Protestant Swiss Cantons. This mounting discrimination forms the background to the British protests over the omission of the 1694 edict of toleration from the *Costituzioni*, but despite the intercession of the Protestant states, the persecution moved inexorably to its conclusion, which was nothing less than the total elimination of the heretical enclave of Pragelato. Early in 1730 the authorities outlawed any profession of Protestantism there, confronting the Vaudois population with the bitter choice between conversion and exile. Most preferred the latter course and withdrew to Switzerland. There they were soon joined by hundreds of refugees from the original Vaudois region whom the edict of 1730 had defined as relapsed heretics, since they had converted to Catholicism in the time of troubles between 1686 and 1694, but had subsequently reverted to their original faith. They were given six months to leave the state or face the death penalty. The destruction of the Vaudois community of Pragelato and the rigours of the new edict led to immediate representations from the Protestant Cantons, the States-General and the kings of Sweden and Prussia; early in 1731 the British government too voiced its outrage. Intercession by the Protestant states, however, failed to help the Vaudois. The Savoyard authorities held to their rigorous enforcement of the law and before long every Protestant had been forced to leave Pragelato.

British displeasure at the unrelenting Savoyard pressure on the Vaudois was exacerbated by disagreements over trade and tariffs, sparked by a dispute over the export of Piedmontese silk. About 1717 a factory in England began producing high-grade spun silk, which threatened to encroach on the market for Piedmontese organzines, the fine spun silks that had hitherto constituted a staple material for the English silk-weaving industry. The new English spinning plant relied heavily on raw silk from Italy, much of it coming from either Piedmont or Monferrato. To undercut the nascent English silk-spinning industry and protect their own exports of spun silk the Savoyard authorities in 1722 banned the export of raw silk from their territories, claiming with some justification that a shortage of cocoons that year left insufficient raw silk for their own spinners. The British government protested, but the ban was upheld, with serious consequences for the new spinning factory in England. The silk embargo became the first shot in a trade war that rapidly escalated. Its prime cause was Victor Amadeus's protectionist economic policy, which aimed to make his state commercially and industrially self-sufficient, by using his state's most valuable export as a weapon in negotiation. The conflict soon involved France as well. In June 1725 the Savoyard government restricted the import of woollen cloth from Dauphiné, since it competed with the coarse and medium-grade cloths produced in Piedmont. A year later these restrictions were extended to other types of cloth, particularly high-quality English woollens. The French government retaliated by halting the export of raw wool to Piedmont in order to create difficulties for the cloth industry there. The British government responded to the raising of the Savoyard tariffs by attempting to reduce the import of Piedmontese spun silk, but in the end it could not carry out its intentions because of lobbying by the powerful silk-weaving interests in England, which depended heavily on Piedmontese spun silk, and which wielded greater influence than the new silk-spinning interests. As Victor Amadeus pointed out to the English ambassador, 'you cannot do without our organzines'.[20]

In the end, however, the British government would not allow either commercial wrangling or religious scruples to stand in the way of its efforts to secure Victor Amadeus as an ally, for he offered the only effective support for British policy in Italy. In 1729 another sudden reversal of alliances quickened the great powers' eagerness for the Savoyard alliance. Britain had effected a rapprochement with Philip V which was crowned by the treaty of Seville in November of that year; central to the treaty's provisions was a pledge of support for the Spanish king's sons by his marriage to Elizabeth Farnese, who were claiming the right to succeed to Parma and Tuscany. Victor Amadeus saw at once that this new situation offered him fruitful possibilities, not the least of which was the isolation of Charles VI, whose Italian ambitions had now received a severe setback. Already in August 1729 Fleury had tried to draw Victor Amadeus into the new alliance as it was forming, but he refused to commit himself, knowing that the British government was conducting parallel negotiations at Vienna in the hope of reaching a peaceful settlement by which the Emperor would accede to the arrangement agreed upon with Philip V, thus removing the principal source of discord in the Mediterranean. Victor Amadeus accordingly waited to see what result these negotiations would produce before he would consider joining the alliance, since its whole purpose would be thrown into question by a separate Anglo-Habsburg treaty. In the meantime he set forth his terms, outlined in the instructions he drafted for his new ambassador to London in November 1729: compensation for the loss of Sicily, and territory in Lombardy.[21] Only in this way, he argued, would the Savoyard state become strong enough to hold the balance of forces in the Italian peninsula and be free from the perpetual threat posed by Habsburg armies on its border. Neither Britain nor France was yet ready to meet these demands, but Victor Amadeus held fast to them, for he knew that the treaty of Seville could not be implemented without his support; his assistance was a *sine qua non* for the installation of a Bourbon candidate on the thrones of Parma and Tuscany. In the end he was proved right. When war came in 1733 the French government had to purchase the Savoyard alliance as the only means of launching an attack on the Habsburgs in Italy.

By then, however, Victor Amadeus no longer guided his state's complex foreign relations; his son Charles Emanuel III reaped the harvest that he had so carefully sown. When Victor Amadeus abdicated in September 1730 he was able to bequeath a fundamentally favourable diplomatic situation to his successor. His alliance was once more sought after by the great powers, and prospects of territorial conquest in Lombardy beckoned invitingly. Although the setbacks inflicted by the Quadruple Alliance in 1718 had not been fully overcome, they were offset by new possibilities. The Savoyard state was now more than a mere pawn on the European chessboard; it possessed a pugnacious army that could measure its performance against greater states, and its diplomats were respected in the courts and chanceries of Europe. This enhanced international standing was the result of the internal reforms that Victor Amadeus II had initiated from the beginning of his reign, and which reached their conclusion in the years after 1713, turning the state into a compact, efficiently governed amalgam of territories in which the ruler's will was strictly obeyed and foreign influences were largely excluded.

XIV
The High Tide of Reform
(1713–1730)

After the peace of Utrecht, as in the years after 1696, the Savoyard state was confronted by urgent problems of internal reconstruction. This time, however, Victor Amadeus II was granted a long interval of peace in which to bring his reforms to fruition. Only the brief and distant campaign in Sicily troubled the later years of his reign, so that he was able to concentrate all his energies on rebuilding the state's administrative and fiscal institutions, and on setting out guidelines for state-sponsored economic development. After 1713 the pace of internal transformation accelerated: the *perequazione* was completed, new law codes were drawn up, the central departments of the state were restructured, government control was imposed on charity and education, the central power was enhanced at the expense of the privileged orders of society.

The pressure of war and the need to maintain a large army helped stimulate these changes, but they were not the sole determinants behind the process of reform. Certainly the army continued to be enlarged and improved, while a new ring of fortresses was constructed at great expense to guard the frontiers gained at Utrecht; along the Alps the newly conquered forts at Exilles and Fenestrelle were refurbished, and Susa was strengthened, while Alessandria became a powerful strongpoint protecting the new province of Monferrato. But after 1713 the government could turn its attention to aspects of policy which it had been forced to neglect in the years of war. Nor were Victor Amadeus II's reforms motivated to any overwhelming extent by the need to assimilate the newly conquered territories. This process was not completed until much later. Under Victor Amadeus Sicily and Sardinia remained separate realms; the new provinces in Lombardy and Dauphiné kept their old tax structures and were not included in the *perequazione*; the Val Sesia (like the Val d'Aosta in the original Savoyard domains) kept its old laws and customs. Islands of local separatism thus survived despite a growing pressure for institutional uniformity. The traditional Savoyard thrust towards tighter central control and greater fiscal efficiency was certainly quickened by war and its inexorable demand for men and money, which the existing state institutions could scarcely furnish, and then only at enormous social cost. But the real dynamic behind the flood of reforms that marked the later years of the reign was Victor Amadeus's determination to bring every activity, every stratum of society, every locality under his personal control in a tradition of state-building that stretched back unbroken for a century and a half, and his resolve to extend his authority against the powers that limited it – the Church, the nobility, the corporate institutions of the state itself, and the local communities.

Reorganization did not start in earnest until Victor Amadeus came back from Sicily late in 1714, for the regency council that governed during his absence had no power to initiate reforms. When the king returned a welter of problems awaited him, above all the ever-present undercurrent of aristocratic opposition. In Piedmont the nobles were by now largely reconciled to the dominance of the state and its bureaucracy, and tended to merge with it rather than resist its advance. But they were alarmed by a series of postwar inquests into their landed properties and tax exemptions, most particularly an order in 1715 for them to make declarations of all their landed possessions. Yet though they might complain at the way their king treated them they did not offer overt opposition. In the duchy of Savoy, however, the nobles were more restive. A decade of French occupation had freed them from the prying of Victor Amadeus's officials and had encouraged their feelings of independence. One sign of their impatience with state control was a perceptible rise in violence and extortion directed against their peasants. Heightened fiscal pressure from the lords provoked stirrings of peasant discontent which the state's officials noted with concern. Noble resentment broke out more directly in sporadic acts of defiance against the representatives of authority. In general the aristocracy's loyalties seemed dubious: Victor Amadeus noted with displeasure how readily the duchy had surrendered to the French, and was always on the alert for disaffection.[1] Savoy thus became the focal point of confrontation where tensions between state and nobles, lords and peasants, attained their most extreme form.

At first the newly restored intendants in the duchy worked merely to palliate the worst excesses of seigneurial lawlessness. A few parish tyrants were brought to book and punished in exemplary fashion, as if to affirm that noble birth did not set a man above law as the aristocracy had always liked to believe. The nobles grumbled at Victor Amadeus's 'tyranny' and muttered that he had no use for his vassals, but only wanted 'soldiers and peasants' for subjects.[2] One disaffected noble, on trial in 1718 for violence to his peasants, went so far as to denounce his sovereign as 'a tyrant who would load us with taxes rather than deliver us from them. The nobles of Savoy made His Highness what he is now, but he is no more than *primus inter pares*. If everyone thought the way I do, we should soon see. . . .'[3] A common complaint among the nobles was that the king's officials – mostly Piedmontese – favoured their peasants against them. Such grumblings betrayed a feeling that the concept of royal authority was changing, that Victor Amadeus was overturning the normal hierarchical order of society; by exalting his own authority he was levelling all classes of society into a single undifferentiated mass in which distinctions of rank and privilege would disappear. There was some foundation for this. Victor Amadeus's policies were assuming a more determinedly anti-aristocratic tone, and the government was beginning to act – albeit tentatively – as a mediator between lord and peasant, privileged and non-privileged. In his instructions for the governor of the duchy of Savoy in 1721 the king specifically enjoined him to protect the common people from the avarice and oppression of their lords.[4] The rigorous new form of absolutism demanded order and obedience even from the privileged classes.

The tension between crown and aristocracy was aggravated by the state's aggressive fiscal policies, which cut at the roots of feudal privilege. In Piedmont the *perequazione* was moving slowly towards completion during these years, threatening to demolish the tax immunities of the privileged orders. The government was also acting decisively to recover lands and revenues it had alienated in the past. After the war all infeudations and grants to the nobles of the right to collect the local *tasso* ceased, and from 1717 many of these grants were redeemed, so that within two years about one-fifth of the crown's alienated fiefs and revenues had been recovered. In 1719 a survey revealed that roughly half the grants of fiefs and revenues made to private parties were without proper justification at law, and could therefore be recovered without compensation. Victor Amadeus now issued an edict ordering the confiscation of all illegally granted fiefs and their reintegration into the royal demesne, adducing as justification the crown's debts incurred during the war and its consequent need for extra revenue. In fact the measure was deliberately intended to reduce the wealth and power of the landed nobility, which had profited from the crown's past financial woes to increase its tax-exempt lands. A special tribunal was set up to judge cases arising from the edict, for Victor Amadeus evidently felt he could not trust the sovereign courts to press his case against the privileged classes.[5] About 800 fiefs were taken away from their outraged holders and in 1722 were offered for sale. Many were repurchased by their previous possessors, but the rest found no takers until Victor Amadeus enhanced their appeal by endowing their purchasers with automatic ennoblement and entry to court. Buyers eager for social advancement then snapped them up, to become known derisively as 'the nobility of 1722'.

The revocation of the fiefs was a profound affront to the aristocracy. One historian (of patrician sympathies) has even called it 'a coup d'état against those families that shed so much blood at Staffarda, Orbassano, Nice and Turin'.[6] As a direct assault on privilege the measure provoked violent opposition from the Chambre des Comptes at Chambéry, which refused to enforce it. The Chambre had regained some of its past splendour during the French occupation, but after 1713 it had to contend once more with Victor Amadeus's intendant-general, now bolstered by six newly created provincial intendants working under his direction. The edict revoking the fiefs thus came at a moment when the Chambre was fast losing ground to the central power, and in defiance it refused to comply. Victor Amadeus in return abolished it outright in January 1720, transferring its functions to the intendant-general and the more docile Camera dei Conti at Turin. These stinging blows to aristocratic and judicial privilege were soon followed by an attack on the clergy. In the summer of 1720 plague broke out at Marseille, quarantine was imposed to halt the spread of infection into the duchy of Savoy, and in June 1721 the Senate levied a special tax to pay for the preventive measures which had saved the duchy from the disease. An assembly of the clergy, however, refused to pay its part of the tax without prior authorization from the Pope, further aggravating Victor Amadeus's struggle with Rome. He therefore moved quickly to stifle the opposition, ordering the Senate to collect the tax without the clergy's consent, and obtaining opinions from the Sorbonne to justify the use of his authority in an emergency to override clerical privilege for the common good. But matters were not as easily disposed of as he had hoped. In some places the clergy resisted, even excommunicating the tax-collectors, and the conflict dragged on for years. As with the revocation of the fiefs and the abolition of the Chambre des Comptes, his assertion of state power left a long undercurrent of rancour.

Victor Amadeus's reforms were thus enacted against a backdrop of constant friction between the crown and the privileged orders. But the government was in a commanding position, and such opposition as there was proved ineffective. It was at this moment that Tillier began his historical studies of the Val d'Aosta with the explicit aim of combating the rising trend of royal 'despotism', for he recognized that the local Estates and other constituted bodies could no longer restrain the crown. The fate of the Chambre des Comptes demonstrated how impotent the sovereign courts had now become to defend privilege and curb the exercise of royal power. To drive the lesson home, any recalcitrance on the part of the magistrates, rare though it had now become, was punished with exile or censure. For a time Victor Amadeus even contemplated abolishing the Senates' right to register royal edicts, even though by now it was hardly used. In the end he allowed the right of registration to subsist and enshrined it in his new law code of 1723, but only as a formality that posed no effective obstacle to his will.

The preparatory studies for the new code or *Costituzioni* were undertaken at the king's order in 1713 by Giovanni Cristoforo Zoppi, a jurist from Pavia; advice on controversial points of law was sought from abroad if necessary, most notably from the legal theorists of the flourishing school of jurisprudence at Utrecht. Initially the king intended to replace the confusion of customary law and old edicts with a simplified recodification that would be valid everywhere in his domains. By 1718 Zoppi's draft was ready, but it apparently did not please the king. He ordered two young officials from Nice to produce a revised version. They excised a vast mass of minor laws, adopted a more logical arrangement by topic, and appended commentaries that took the form of sweeping statements of legal principle. All this was too much for Victor Amadeus's rather tradition-bound views, so it was discarded in favour of another compilation drawn up by a panel of government functionaries and Senators from Turin. This third draft was sent to the Senate of Chambéry for review in 1722, but once again the king intervened and had it reworked by another committee. This fourth and final version of the *Costituzioni* was published on 20 February 1723, in five sections. Book I covered religious law, Book II the conduct of magistrates and officials, Books III and IV civil and criminal procedure, Book V private law, wills and notarial practice. A sixth section on fiefs and land law was left out because of the spate of lawsuits that had followed the revocation of the fiefs in 1719–20.

Despite these endless reworkings – so typical of Victor Amadeus's methods in government – the *Costituzioni* did not fulfil their original purpose of forming a unified law code for the whole state. Important differences persisted between the legal systems of Piedmont and Savoy; the new territories were not included. Moreover, the new code was marred by inconsistencies, by significant omissions – such as the edict of toleration for the Vaudois – by archaisms and obscurities. Almost at once the king realized that modifications would be needed, and so he asked the Senates, the commercial tribunal or Consolato, and various magistrates to submit revisions and additions. Originally these were to form an appendix to the *Costituzioni*, but in the summer of 1726 the king decided instead to redraft the whole code from the beginning, for only in this way did he feel that the necessary clarity and consistency would be achieved. After another painful process of revision the new *Costituzioni* were registered by the Senates of Turin and Chambéry in July 1729. They now included the section on land law omitted in 1723, while the other sections were rearranged and improved. But even after all these changes the *Costituzioni* remained, as Mario Viora has pointed out in his meticulous study of their development, no more than a compilation of existing laws, and not a new codification deriving from a trenchant analysis of legal principle. They reflected the intellectual limitations of the ruler and the legal bureaucrats who had drawn them up; though compiled with enormous labour they still remained tradition-bound in form and conception.[7]

The production of the new *Costituzioni* was an attempt to rationalize the legal system, to render it more uniform, logical and efficient. In the same way the central institutions of the state were subjected to a process of radical renovation, and here the weight of tradition did not impede the application of the kind of rigorous logic that the framers of the *Costituzioni* had sought but failed to bring to their work. Perhaps the most serious structural defect of the old administration was the lack of definition between the elements that composed it; this was true of both the fiscal system and the central political institutions. Spheres of ministerial activity were only loosely mapped out and the merging of both secretaryships of state in the Carron de Saint-Thomas family added to the confusion. A minister's influence depended more upon personal factors than upon a clearly delimited area of responsibility; power was not institutionalized. In a way this suited Victor Amadeus's practice of consulting his ministers separately, but the jurisdictional untidiness at the heart of the state machine interposed a grave obstacle to the transmission of his orders. The successful restructuring of the local administrative system through the creation of the intendants served to focus attention on the problem at the centre; now the real blockage in the chain of command came at the top. Early in 1717, therefore, Victor Amadeus restructured the central organs of the state, aided by Gropello, whose last political achievement this was. On 17 February an edict established a new Council of State made up of eight ministers.[8] This body was honorific rather than functional, and hardly ever met; it served mainly to define the political leadership by setting the ministers apart from the other officials and advisers at the centre of affairs. In conception it was not new. The Savoyard rulers had always had a small council of close advisers to attend them, and its immediate antecedent was probably the council of regency that governed during Victor Amadeus's absence in Sicily; there is considerable resemblance between the organization of the two councils. More significantly, however, the edict of 1717 went beyond such precedents by making drastic changes in the central executive departments of the state. The old secretaryship of state was split into two offices – as it had originally been – one for internal affairs (headed now by Mellarède), the other for foreign affairs (where del Borgo replaced Saint-Thomas). The secretaryship of war was also reorganized. Each of the three secretaries now ran a similarly structured department consisting of three under-secretaries, each with his specific area of competence. The department of internal affairs was divided regionally: one under-secretary and his staff handled Piedmont; another dealt with Savoy, Nice and Aosta; the third looked after Sicily, or Sardinia after 1720. The department of foreign affairs was similarly divided into three offices, one handling general policy, the second dealing with the northern states, and the third with Spain, Italy and the Holy See. Likewise the secretaryship for war was made up of an office for general strategic policy, one to manage troops in the field, garrisons and supplies, and the third to handle finances.

These reforms brought a new rationality to the central departments of the state. They were followed and completed on 11 April 1717 by a

parallel measure reorganizing the financial administration.[9] Here the
central focus was a reformed Council of Finances headed by the Generale
delle Finanze, flanked by the first president of the Camera dei Conti, the
controller-general, the Contadore Generale (who directed the remodelled
Ufficio del Soldo), and the secretary for war. The original Council of
Finances, set up in 1588, had not included these last two officials, and the
new arrangement reflects the heightened importance of the military in
Victor Amadeus's state. It also served to unite the officials at the head of
the military departments, who spent most of the state's revenues, with
those responsible for collecting the taxes and planning the budget. This
orderly, unified central direction was complemented by a reorganization
of the departments immediately below it, all of which now reported
directly to a member of the Council of Finances. These lesser departments
were regrouped into four Aziende. One managed military finance, and
was in fact a revised version of the Ufficio del Soldo, headed by the
Contadore Generale; one ran the royal household, under the grand
chamberlain; one was in charge of artillery and fortifications, under its
intendant-general; one was for general administration and revenue
collection, subsuming all the earlier treasurers and collectors. This last
Azienda was directed by the Generale delle Finanze. To bring the whole
revenue-collection mechanism under his control, he also supervised the
office of the state gabelles and directed the activities of the provincial
intendants, as he had in the past, while the heads of the other Aziende
reported to him. To prevent the diffusion of revenue through separate
treasuries, a cardinal defect of the old system, all taxation now had to pass
through the office of the treasurer-general, who would render daily
accounts to the Generale. Frequent, meticulous accounting thus became
an essential feature of the new system. The Generale would be assisted in
drawing up the annual budget estimates by the controller-general and his
staff, who were to present daily reports of all their transactions to him. In
this way the movement of funds could be followed with ease, and could
be compared at any time with budget projections. All departments had
to submit their accounts within a year for auditing by the Camera dei
Conti.

This radical upheaval in the central administration was the starting-
point for a series of improvements throughout the rest of the eighteenth
century; it in fact marks a watershed in the institutional development of
the Savoyard state. Another major change in the financial administration
was effected by a new regulation issued in June 1730.[10] This strengthened
the Council of Finances' authority over the Aziende by stipulating that
the Council must first approve any order by the head of any of its subordinate departments, before it was carried out. The regulation also
restated the principle of centralizing all tax moneys into a single fund; all
revenue was to be paid directly to the Tesoriere del Piemonte, who would

then disburse funds to the various Aziende in accordance with their budgets. Provincial treasurers were allowed to make payments at the local level, but only with the approval of the Tesoriere del Piemonte, who was thus in a position to keep track of every item of revenue and expenditure. The result of the reforms of 1717 and 1730 was to establish centralized direction and simple, standardized procedures for the conduct of financial policy. Regular auditing assured a high standard of honesty within the system. The regular presentation of accounts ensured that at any given moment the king and his ministers knew precisely how their revenues and expenditures stood. For the first time they could draw up a proper budget and match it against the current disposition of funds; shortages could be detected and funds shifted as required to meet unforeseen expenses.

Through the financial and administrative reforms of 1717 the whole structure of central authority was clearly defined and institutionalized. Domestic policy was directed by the secretary for internal affairs and the Generale delle Finanze; it was executed by the Aziende and the intendants. The secretary for war was in charge of military affairs, while army finance was in the hands of the Contadore Generale. Foreign policy was handled by the secretary of state for external affairs. The central bureaucracy was neatly compartmentalized, the entire system pivoting around the king, who formed the only common denominator between the different components of the state machine. Victor Amadeus's reforms thus endowed the Savoyard state with one of the most efficient administrations in Europe, far ahead of the cumbersome structures of the French and Spanish monarchies, or the outmoded institutions of the other Italian states. The main failing of the system was its rigid centralization, which discouraged initiative from below. Its strength lay in its ability to translate orders swiftly into action, and to extract a surprising amount of revenue from a backward group of territories. Above all the system emphasized the ruler's supremacy within the state, and enhanced his power at the expense of privilege and local interests.

Sweeping changes in the central fiscal institutions were, however, of little value without a corresponding effort to overhaul the local tax structure. Taxation had reached its upper limits during the wars and could not be maintained at that level without ruining the economy. Evidence of financial exhaustion abounded, first and foremost in the parlous condition of the local communities' finances. An order to the intendants of Piedmont in 1711 marked the beginning of a renewed effort to stabilize the overtaxed communal budgets. The intendants were told to report on the problems afflicting communal finance, and their responses were examined by a committee of ministers. But the problem remained intractable. In 1725 a special committee was set up to examine it once more; eight years later yet another committee was established for the same purpose. The running sore of communal debt, caused in part by war and famine but aggravated by mismanagement, corruption and the demands of privileged creditors, was to remain an irremediable malaise sapping the vitality of the Savoyard state throughout the era of absolute monarchy, and beyond.

One obstacle in the way of fiscal reform at the local level was the lack of accurate information at the government's disposal; too little was known about fiscal immunities, about local economic conditions, even about the basic datum of population. Under Victor Amadeus the state began a series of enquiries into these questions, leading finally to the great inquest into population and resources conducted by the intendants in 1750.[11] In 1700 the government had made an initial attempt at a census, under the impetus of the great famine of 1695, but it foundered with the onset of war. In 1718 the Camera dei Conti ordered all local authorities to report the extent of the population under their jurisdiction, as the edict of 1700 had required. The order had to be repeated in 1721, but from that time local censuses seem to have been taken with reasonable regularity. A full census of the whole state, conducted by the central government, was not carried out until 1734, and this laborious effort was repeated only at long intervals later in the century, but the insistence on accurate population figures was part of an important trend that now made itself felt in Savoyard administration. Precise data were now increasingly required as the basis for policy-making, and the scope and accuracy of the state's information-gathering clearly increase from this point, inaugurating a tradition of tireless, thorough enquiry that would be the chief glory of the Savoyard bureaucracy under the Ancien Régime. In 1729 a survey was made of the threatened forest lands, the first of several similar efforts to follow. Inquests were constantly made into trade and manufacturing as the starting-point for decisions in economic policy. There had been sporadic essays at precise fact-gathering in the previous century (the census of 1612 is a case in point), but these had never been carried through to a satisfactory conclusion. What had changed was the government's resolve to obtain accurate information, and also the means for collecting it. Here, as in so many other aspects of institutional development under Victor Amadeus, the intendants were crucial. They became the chief fact-gatherers on whose efforts the central bureaucracy relied for the entire eighteenth century.

From the information flowing in from the provinces Victor Amadeus and his ministers realized that the state's meagre capacity to generate revenue had been strained to its limits. For instance, in 1712 the Estates of the Val d'Aosta rejected the government's pressing demand for a bigger *donativo*; in 1718 they repeated their refusal. In 1720 a new system was adopted for levying the salt gabelle in the duchy of Savoy, but it produced only a fractional increase in taxes; the duchy was evidently producing about as much revenue as could be expected from its thin economic base. An attempt by the intendant-general of Nice to introduce a tax on real property in the city – essayed but not carried through by Mellarède in

1702 – provoked a riot and the intendant-general had to be recalled. There was no great outburst of anti-fiscal protest like the rebellion of Mondovì at the end of the last century, but the lesson was obvious enough: no more could be expected from the social and economic base that sustained the state machine, and any increase in taxation would only imperil the tenuous economic recovery that the government was trying to foster.

If more proof were needed of this, the chronic pauperism afflicting every region of the state provided it. In the crisis years of the late seventeenth and early eighteenth centuries the endemic poverty caused by the marginal nature of the state's agrarian base was overlayed by new waves of beggars driven from their homes by war and famine. By the time peace returned pauperization had reached alarming levels, raising fears of public disorder. In 1716 an inquest (one of many conducted in these years, whose results survive only in part) classified 9.4 percent of the population of the province of Susa as paupers, 7.2 percent in the province of Casale, and a massive 20.2 percent – one person in five – in the province of Cuneo.[12] The existing system of charity and poor relief could not respond to the emergency; buildings were often in sad disrepair, endowments had been frittered away or embezzled, and two decades of war had consummated the ruin caused by neglect. Action by the central government thus became imperative.

The first efforts to resolve the crisis seem to have been made by the Senate of Savoy, which in 1714 invited a well-known reformer of charitable institutions, the Provençal Jesuit Guevarre, to reorganize the overstrained hospital at Chambéry. Guevarre had spent a long career overhauling the *bureaux de charité* of southern France, and his activity there evidently attracted the Senate's attention. His uncompromising methods soon recommended him to Victor Amadeus, and at the king's behest he drew up a handbook to guide the local authorities in the work of reforming their charities.[13] In 1716 Guevarre came to Turin to reorganize the poorhouses there and in the rest of Piedmont. He started by banning all begging and almsgiving, for he contended that the personal dispensation of charity was self-defeating and that relief was best administered through large centralized institutions. Donations were to be given to these foundations rather than to individual beggars, who would consequently be unable to live any longer by crime and casual charity, and would be forced to enter the poorhouses and become productive members of society. Most important for Guevarre in all this was the fact that the poor would now be able to receive regular religious instruction, so that both their moral and material welfare would be assured. The new system appealed to Victor Amadeus because it meant that private, spontaneous Christian charity would be institutionalized under state control, and the secular power would replace the clergy as the dispensers of relief. In any case such methods were part of a tradition long rooted in the Savoyard state. An ordinance of 1627 reforming the central poorhouse at Turin, the Ospizio di Carità, had outlawed begging and private almsgiving, and had ordered (without lasting effect) that all beggars were to be shut up in the institution. Similar measures were re-enacted at regular intervals through the seventeenth century. Guevarre's ideas helped to provide a fresh justification for a concept of poor relief already gaining ground in the Savoyard state, and they harmonized with Victor Amadeus's overwhelming ambition to bring every facet of society under central state control.

In August 1716 the government implemented the first stage of Guevarre's programme by banning begging in the streets of Turin. Meanwhile Guevarre and his assistants preached in the capital's churches, spurring the citizens to make offerings to rebuild the endowment of the Ospizio di Carità. The government contributed its own share to this, and set up a special committee to run the institution. On 7 April 1717 the Ospizio was reopened in a grand public ceremony.[14] A phalanx of uniformed paupers several hundred strong attended Mass in the cathedral, then sat down to an open-air banquet in the main piazza, at which they were served by persons of quality in a spectacular display of Christian humility. Victor Amadeus and the royal family watched the proceedings from the balcony of the royal palace above. Finally the paupers marched in procession to the Ospizio, where they settled into a dire regimen of labour and devotions. Families were split up, the sexes segregated, all were cut off from the outside world. Artisans were hired to teach them useful trades. The government fed them, clothed them and sold their labour at bargain rates to the big textile entrepreneurs who ran the state manufactories. Paupers with homes of their own and the chance of gaining a livelihood were not sent to the Ospizio; instead they were registered by the poor-relief committee, which gave them bread and outdoor relief to supplement their meagre earnings. In this way a two-level system of poor relief was established: the destitute were sent to the poorhouse and put to work, while the indigent were given relief at home.

Between 1717 and 1720 this system was extended to the entire state, except for Sardinia. In the larger cities the old hospitals and almshouses were consolidated into big state poorhouses, and outdoor relief was dispensed by newly founded committees. In the smaller towns and country districts only outdoor relief committees were set up. Charity now became – in theory at least – a state monopoly. Old habits died hard, however. Private almsgiving went on despite the ban, beggars still haunted the streets and convent steps, the new charitable foundations did not win ready acceptance. But Guevarre's harsh methods represent a clear break with traditional Catholic attitudes. Formerly a divinely-ordained condition, poverty had now been redefined as a social evil, a vice to be eradicated by locking up the poor. Private charity was no longer regarded, at least officially, as a Christian duty, but was branded as a social failing that encouraged sloth and crime. The concept of charity had been secularized, brought under state control and harnessed to serve the government's plans for economic expansion.

The parlous state of the economy so dramatically revealed in the high incidence of pauperism meant that the government had to reduce expenditure wherever possible. One way in which this could be done was by diminishing the heavy interest payments on the debts incurred during the past wars. Throughout these conflicts the state's credit had remained sound, and the successive issues of state bonds had always found subscribers. But the total amount of debt was crippling. In the later years of the war Victor Amadeus and Gropello had already started to pay off some of their short-term obligations, partly with the help of the allied subsidies, so that by 1713 the short-term debt had been reduced to less than three million lire, and by 1721 careful management had lowered this to a mere 775,476 lire.[15] The long-term debt, however, (composed of shares in the Monte, infeudations and alienations of the *tasso*) was far more extensive. As the state's credit improved in the later stages of the war some of this was reconverted to lower rates of interest, so that by 1713 bonds in the Monte stood at 4 or 5 percent compared with $7\frac{1}{2}$ or 8 percent at the height of the war. For a time Victor Amadeus toyed with a project advanced by John Law (later to achieve notoriety as the author of a similar scheme in France) for a state bank to consolidate the debt and unify revenues into a central fund, but the plan was too difficult to implement and remained no more than an interesting project. In 1716 and 1718 special commissions were set up to liquidate the state debt, and even though they never fully achieved this aim, state bonds were steadily redeemed or converted to lower rates as they fell due. These measures made the Savoyard state debt one of the lowest in Europe, which not only staunched the drain of interest payments but had broader political overtones. The government's creditors came very largely from the privileged classes – mainly the landed nobility, with a few clerics and religious foundations, and a sprinkling of rich bankers and merchants. A big state debt would have given these powerful groups even greater influence than they already possessed in the making of policy: the neighbouring republic of Genoa, where the state's creditors were organized in a powerful lobby that virtually ran the government, furnishes an extreme instance of how such interests could make themselves felt. The Savoyard state never evolved in this direction: Victor Amadeus's efforts to reduce the state debt were a deliberate policy which should be seen as part of his wider assault on the power of the privileged classes.

Reducing expenditure was part of a two-pronged attack on the state's financial problems; the other part was the campaign to increase revenue by expanding whatever sources were available, and this logic pointed inexorably to an attack on fiscal immunities. The central element in this drive was the completion of the *perequazione*, initiated in the 1690s but interrupted by the outbreak of war in 1703. As soon as Piedmont had been cleared of invaders, work was resumed on this great land-survey, and by 1711 most of it was complete. The method employed in Piedmont was far more rigorous than that used earlier to compile the new *catasto* for the county of Nice. In every province of Piedmont squads of surveyors measured each parcel of land, while other teams of experts estimated its value. But this was only the first step in a long and complex operation. The taxable status of each piece of land had to be determined before it could be entered in the new register, a procedure entailing the detection and eradication of a myriad time-honoured frauds. Inquests conducted in the years after 1711 revealed a vast array of illegal or dubious exemptions, so that the task facing the tax-assessors was enormous. But the work was done: within a few years of the end of the War of the Spanish Succession Victor Amadeus was in possession of the information he needed to carry through his long-contemplated reform of the land tax in Piedmont.

For a long time, however, he hesitated to put it into execution. To some extent the king seems to have been restrained by legitimate doubts about the accuracy of the data from the survey. In 1716 the provincial intendants were instructed to report the value of land in their districts, and their figures were then compared with the land values in the *perequazione*. Some discrepancies emerged, so two years later the government ordered another enquiry. All land sales since 1680 were tabulated and averaged, and then compared with the estimates in the *perequazione*. But even after these exhaustive checks, which tended to confirm the *perequazione*'s reliability, Victor Amadeus still did not enact it. The reasons for this continuing delay were almost certainly political. This was the time of the revocation of the fiefs, and the king may well have wished to avoid outraging his nobles still further by disallowing many of their tax exemptions, as the *perequazione* was bound to do. Moreover, the ticklish question of clerical exemptions remained unresolved until the Concordat of 1727, occasioning further delay. But even when this problem was resolved Victor Amadeus still seems to have entertained doubts about the validity of the figures in the *perequazione*. In 1729 he ordered a special commission to go over the statistics yet again, and a year later still another committee rechecked the data by comparing average land values in three representative provinces with the values in the *perequazione*. All these tests merely showed that the survey, although perhaps inaccurate in some details, could not really be improved, and so in the last months of his reign Victor Amadeus finally determined to implement it. But he abdicated before this final step could be taken; the edict implementing the *perequazione* was actually signed by his successor on 5 May 1731.

The fruit of these labours was a register listing every scrap of land in Piedmont, forest and waste included, under the names of the individual owners, and ranged in grades according to fertility and value. The new *catasto* showed at a glance the landed wealth of each proprietor, at taxable rather than market value; every year his quota of the *tasso* would be assessed at so many soldi per taxable unit of property. This was essentially the same procedure used since the inception of the *tasso*, but the inequities of the old system were now drastically reduced, since the valuation of land was no longer arbitrary, but based on the painstaking classification of every field according to its actual worth. Yet despite this care some injustices remained and had to be eliminated by subsequent adjustments. To keep the *catasto* up to date every change in ownership was to be recorded in a special register (the *libro di mutazioni*) and transcribed into the *catasto* itself. The prodigious effort involved in compiling the new *catasto* was without parallel in Europe at this time, at least until the Austrian government of Lombardy began its own land-survey in 1718; for thoroughness and attention to detail the Savoyard *catasto* would remain a monument to the energy of the ruler who ordered its redaction and to the diligence of the surveyors and bureaucrats who produced it. It cost a considerable amount of money, but it made the *tasso* far more productive than before: revenue from the land tax rose by 6.6 percent in the year after the *perequazione* was enacted, because it did away with so many unjustified tax immunities.[16] This in turn allowed the government to abolish a number of minor taxes without any loss of revenue to itself.

The elimination of a host of illicit tax exemptions aroused a storm of protest from the privileged classes, and the motives behind their fury are not hard to divine. In Piedmont the nobles lost 31.5 percent of their fiscal immunities, the clergy up to 65 percent: a total of 315,736 *giornate* of formerly exempt land was added to the tax-register, increasing the total amount of taxable land by 17 percent. After the *perequazione* the tax-exempt lands owned by the nobility comprised 7.93 percent of the landed wealth in Piedmont, while those owned by the clergy accounted for 8.27 percent, plus a further 7.23 percent of clerical lands that paid the *tasso* but were exempt from other taxes.[17] Nonetheless the landed wealth of the privileged orders remained extremely impressive. They owned rather more than one-fifth of the land in Piedmont tax-free, while also possessing extensive holdings of allodial land (which were not tax-exempt). So although the *perequazione* dealt a severe blow to the fiscal status of the privileged orders it did not really alter the distribution of wealth and political power. Even though it did away with many abuses of fiscal privilege it left intact the edifice of seigneurial rights over the land and the people who tilled it. And in the following years the great landowners moved to recoup their losses by reviving old seigneurial dues, raising rents and shortening leases in a kind of feudal reaction. Victor Amadeus's reform of the tax structure had stopped short of a complete attack on seigneurial privilege, and these limitations in the scope of the reform became even more evident when the *perequazione* was extended to the duchy of Savoy in 1728.

Throughout the seventeenth century the Savoyard government had periodically tried to bring the duchy's tax-registers up to date, but when Gropello examined the tax-system there in the years after 1696 he had been struck by an 'infinity of abuses' in the way the *taille* was levied.[18] In 1700 he ordered the local communities to draw up new *cadastres*, but the opposition of the Chambre des Comptes and then the outbreak of war put a stop to his efforts. At this stage he seems to have envisaged using the same method that was then being employed to revise the *cadastres* in the county of Nice, relying on local knowledge for an assessment of land values, but by 1720 when Victor Amadeus returned to the problem of revising the duchy's tax-registers, the *perequazione* had been carried out in Piedmont, and he decided to use the more rigorous method that had been so successful there, employing the teams of surveyors and assessors who had worked in Piedmont, and who were in many cases now working on the Habsburg land-survey in Lombardy. On 9 April 1728 the king ordered the start of a new land-survey for the duchy of Savoy. The squads of experts worked fast and within about five years the actual measurement and valuation of the land had been finished. But Victor Amadeus's plans went beyond the mere compilation of a register of landed property, as in Piedmont; he apparently now contemplated dismantling the entire structure of seigneurial privilege. Soon after the start of the land-survey he required all possessors of fiefs to produce the titles by which they held them, and declared that only fiefs held since before 1584 would enjoy tax immunity. (In that year Charles Emanuel I had declared all fiefs granted henceforth to be taxable.) Few titles could be traced so far back, so that this principle would effectively wipe out most feudal exemptions. This was sufficient to arouse the nobility's fear and anger, but it was not all. Next year the intendant-general ordered an inquest into all feudal dues levied on the peasantry, apparently as a prelude to abolishing them – a move that anticipated the emancipation of the serfs in Savoy forty years later. One observer commented that 'if one were not convinced of the sovereign's good intentions, one would have to believe that all this was devised more to destroy our fiefs than to confirm them'.[19] But the difficulties involved in checking so many feudal titles and dues proved greater than the king had imagined. The paperwork was immense and the landowners resisted demands that they produce their deeds, slowing the work almost to a standstill. Victor Amadeus was evidently reaching the limit of his power to coerce the nobility of the duchy of Savoy, and soon a softening in the government's attitude became perceptible. In December 1730, just after Victor Amadeus's abdication, Charles Emanuel III gave up the inquest into feudal dues, even though he persevered with the enquiry into fiefs and tax immunities. This was still more than enough to stir up vehement protests from the duchy's nobles; these continued throughout the period in which the new *cadastres* were being compiled, and for decades to come.

The new land-register for the duchy of Savoy took a decade to complete, and Victor Amadeus did not live to see it enacted. On 15 September 1738 the intendant-general of Savoy issued instructions for implementing the new *cadastre*, which was now ready to go into operation. It disallowed about seven-eighths of the immunities formerly claimed by the clergy and nobility. In a compromise with the Papacy the lands owned by the clergy before 1620 were declared exempt from taxation: the rest were to pay.[20] All this was a serious economic setback for the privileged classes, but as in Piedmont, the *péréquation* (to give it the Gallicized name used in Savoy) did not really undercut their preponderant social position. Though they lost many of their fiscal exemptions, they still possessed vast estates; in 1734 the intendant-general calculated that the nobility owned 17 percent of the land in the duchy, and this proportion was not affected by the enactment of the *péréquation* four years later.[21] It left all feudal dues as before, for the government had been forced to give up its plan to do away with them. Moreover, as in Piedmont the privileged classes compensated themselves for their lost fiscal exemptions by raising rents, reviving old feudal incidents and compiling land-registers of their own – in imitation of the *péréquation* – listing all their rents and dues. They also intensified the attack they were already making on the common lands, appropriating large tracts for their own use, often with the connivance of the better-off villagers who acted as syndics of the communities.

While the new *cadastre* distributed taxes more evenly between the different regions of the duchy, gross inequities persisted. After the *péréquation* the average incidence of the *taille* stood at 18.4 percent of agricultural output for the duchy as a whole, but while some districts paid the equivalent of only 8 percent of their production, others paid as much as 35 percent.[22] These injustices were only partially remedied by later adjustments. Furthermore, the *cadastre* in Savoy, as in Piedmont, soon ceased to be an accurate record of property ownership because the transfer of land was rarely inscribed in the registers, as the law required. But despite all these shortcomings Victor Amadeus II's *cadastre* marked a vast advance over the old disorderly land-registers. Above all, by disallowing so many illegal exemptions it eased the burden on the poorer taxpayers, while at the same time increasing global revenue from the *taille*. The land-register was complemented by a large-scale map for each district showing every scrap of property, indexed to a list of owners. These great maps, beautifully drawn and coloured, with every topographical feature minutely recorded, are a triumph of the cartographer's art and a monument to the meticulous labour that went into the land-survey of Savoy. Many survive down to the present day, and until the beginning of this century they still formed the basic documents regulating all property transactions.

While this massive reorganization of the tax-structure was under way, Victor Amadeus was also working to broaden the state's tax-base by sponsoring commercial and industrial development, partly to make the state economically self-sufficient, and partly to increase his subjects' wealth in order to draw more from them in taxes. These policies followed a mercantilist tradition laid down in the sixteenth century, and articulated most clearly by Charles Emanuel II and his minister Trucchi in the 1660s and 1670s. State support for industrial development tended to favour Piedmont: the other regions received little or no attention, so that government intervention helped widen the gap between the state's more dynamic heartland and its less developed fringes. Government policy also failed to promote agricultural development. Techniques remained largely stagnant, vast stretches of land were still uncultivated, irrigation and reclamation proceeded at a laggardly pace. But such disregard for agriculture was typical of mercantilism everywhere and was not a weakness of the Savoyard version alone: given the inertia of the agrarian sector and the enormous amount of capital that would have been needed to transform it, this failure to grapple with the problem becomes more intelligible. Savoyard agricultural policy thus restricted itself to assuring the cities' grain supply under the traditional *annona* system, whose first priority was the maintenance of a steady food supply for the capital, Turin, and which favoured the interests of town-dwellers over rural producers.

Once the crisis of 1708–9 and the ravages of invasion had passed, agricultural production increased gradually, despite the absence of official encouragement. Rising demand (apparently due in the main to the increase in population) pushed up food prices and so led to a slow upward movement in land values. This trend may well have run counter to the government's efforts to stimulate industrial development, as rising prices made land a more attractive investment than the riskier opportunities of commerce or manufacture. Nevertheless, industrial growth seems to have outstripped the general pace of economic development: one recent estimate suggests that while gross production rose by perhaps two and one-half times in the first half of the eighteenth century, industrial production rose fourfold.[23] Victor Amadeus II's reign thus marks a significant moment in the economic history of Piedmont – if not of Savoy or the county of Nice, or Sardinia. It is the starting-point for the growth of certain industries, notably textiles, which despite their initial falterings would progress in the century to come. This type of industrial growth owed a great deal to state protection and subsidies. The government alone possessed the will and the capital to effect a systematic, long-term programme of development: private capital, too easily sidetracked into speculation or landed investment, could not provide the same impetus for sustained growth. Past criticism of Savoyard *dirigisme* by Giuseppe Prato and other liberal economists tended to overlook this fact. More recent work by Quazza and Bulferetti has reminded us that without state backing the pace of industrial development would have been far slower, or might not have taken off at all.[24] These writers also draw attention to the social side-effects of state economic policy, which gradually called forth a small group of entrepreneurs, the embryo of a commercial-industrial class which though not yet strong enough to challenge the established power of landed wealth was nevertheless the portent of changes to come.

It should be noted, however, that this incipient social transformation was not the outcome of deliberate choice by Victor Amadeus II and his successors, but the incidental side-effect of a policy of state-sponsored industrial development undertaken for totally different motives. It would be tempting to place this trend in the wider context of Victor Amadeus's other reforms, which the economic historian Valerio Castronovo recently characterized as 'a clear socio-political programme directed against the nobility', and to view it as part of a grand design to alter the balance of class power in society.[25] But this would ascribe intentions to Victor Amadeus II which he never possessed. Though so much of his policy was 'pro-bourgeois and anti-noble', as Quazza correctly defines it, there were definite limits beyond which he would not press his attack on the privileged classes.[26] Quazza has demonstrated, as has Jean Nicolas, that the aristocracy's ascendancy was never called into question. As long as this was so, the tiny nucleus of rising entrepreneurs tended to be absorbed into the nobility in a familiar pattern of social osmosis. So even though government policy might indirectly encourage the rise of a group of entrepreneurs it did not make them an autonomous class. They depended on state subsidies, contracts and protection, worked in close contact with the economic agencies of the state, and were easily co-opted into the ruling élite of bureaucrats and nobles. Absolute monarchy in Piedmont–Savoy, as in the rest of Europe, thus remained essentially aristocratic in nature. An emergent industrial class perhaps strengthened the monarchy by offering an alternative source of support to be used under certain conditions to offset the power of the aristocracy. But the price that the state exacted for sponsoring industrial development, in the form of controls and regulations, tended to stifle much of the productive force represented by this emergent group of entrepreneurs. Savoyard mercantilism was thus trapped in a circle of contradictions: without state intervention, industrial development could hardly have begun, yet state controls distorted the process and repressed much of the energy that it might otherwise have released.

The central mechanism through which state control was exercised was the Consolato. Its origins can be traced back to a commercial tribunal founded in the sixteenth century and restored in 1676. Victor Amadeus reorganized it in 1687 and again in 1701, during one of the periodic slumps in the silk industry, giving it special powers to enforce bans on the export of raw silk and on the exodus of skilled workers. Further reorganizations in 1713 and 1722 completed its transformation from a commercial court into an agency for supervising economic development; from the latter year it was assisted by three subsidiary branches at Nice, Chambéry and Casale. Appointments to the Consolato were made by the king, in certain instances after nomination by local merchants. Besides still judging commercial disputes by summary procedures it now inspected manufactures to uphold standards of quality, enforced guild statutes and drew up proposals for the advancement of trade. In 1729 the government set up another agency for economic development, the Council of Commerce; its functions, like those of the Consolato, were largely advisory. Policy, once formulated, was implemented by the Generale delle Finanze, acting through the provincial intendants. They produced a constant stream of reports on economic matters, forwarded projects to the government and lobbied on behalf of local interests.

A typical example of how economic regulation operated can be seen in the cotton and fustian industry. The government used the guild of cotton-masters at Chieri to control production and enforce standards of workmanship, and after 1713 expanded production by founding another cotton and fustian factory at Vercelli. Far more attention, however, was lavished on the silk industry, the most vital sector of the Piedmontese economy: it had been carefully regulated since the sixteenth century and Victor Amadeus's measures followed in a well-established tradition. Here the government attempted to accomplish a number of sometimes incompatible ends. First there was the problem of maintaining supplies of silk in a volatile market determined by wide annual fluctuations in the harvest of cocoons. For this reason the export of raw silk was banned in 1691 and many subsequent years because of shortages, and in the period after 1722 the export of both raw and spun silk was prohibited. But these restrictions were more than just measures of conservation. The ban on raw silk exports in 1722 was (as we have seen) also intended to deny raw material to the rival English silk-spinning industry and to stimulate the development of spinning at home. Export bans thus formed part of a protectionist policy intended to raise Piedmont from a primary producer of raw materials to an exporter of high-grade finished goods, to increase profits and create employment.

But it was often difficult to determine the correct line of policy, since the interests of the different sectors of the industry would conflict. A ban on the export of raw silk penalized the farmers who produced it, preventing them from obtaining the highest price for their cocoons, and favoured the spinners and weavers. In the same way a ban on the export of spun silk and fine organzines worked to the advantage of the weaving industry.

But the underlying purpose of government policy was clear enough: to expand manufacturing by all possible means. In 1698 a ducal edict decreed that only spun silk could be exported and that raw silk must be worked up in the state prior to being exported. Although this principle was more often waived than observed, it enunciated a fundamental maxim for the future. Another aspect of this policy was the endless series of enactments to improve the quality of spun silk and to foster technological innovation. By 1722 an official count revealed 429 spinning-plants in the Savoyard state (essentially Piedmont and Monferrato), employing 7,800 people and turning out 796,000 pounds of spun silk a year, of which 130,000 pounds were high-quality organzines for the English market.[27] The silk-weaving industry was husbanded even more carefully. The royal manufacture set up at Venaria Reale in 1671 was the first of several subsidized and privileged factories. Others were established with state support at Turin in 1701 – although it soon foundered during the war – and again in 1710 and 1727; in 1714 another state factory was set up at Cuneo. A new guild was chartered in 1686 for weavers of silken cloth mixed with gold and silver thread, and a factory for producing these luxury textiles was founded at Turin in 1719. Government subsidies encouraged foreign master-craftsmen to settle, either to train apprentices or to introduce technical improvements. Some foreign entrepreneurs benefited from the cheap labour available in the state poorhouses; in 1734 a syndicate of Genevans set up stocking-factories in the Ospizi di Carità at Turin and Pinerolo. In cases like these the Savoyard government was willing to lay aside its customary bigotry and grant *de facto* toleration to foreigners with useful skills: by 1729 there were roughly a hundred Protestants living in Turin, many of them merchants or craftsmen. The government also made continual efforts to entice workers from the great textile centres – especially Lyon – to settle in Piedmont, while trying to prevent the exodus of its own skilled artisans. Much of the regulation in the silk industry was aimed at raising standards of quality in order to compete with the more advanced industries of Lyon and Geneva. The general *Regolamentazione* for the silk industry issued in 1711 (one of several such enactments) was based on a close study of practices at Lyon. These measures seem to have achieved considerable success in laying the foundations of a native silk-weaving industry in the face of stiff foreign competition. By the end of Victor Amadeus II's reign the export of silken cloth was rising, but raw silk, spun silk and organzines would remain the staples of Piedmont's export trade for the rest of the century.

A similar intention to make Piedmont a centre of labour- and capital-intensive manufacturing lay behind the government's efforts to build up the woollen industry. Here regulations were enforced by an inspector-general, appointed in 1698, and by the various guilds. State-supported woollen manufactures were established, again at the Ospizio di Carità in

Turin. As with the silk industry, efforts to build up a self-sufficient industrial base in woollen textiles were impeded by foreign competition, initially from France and later from England. Piedmontese manufacturers had traditionally produced a steady flow of low- and medium-grade cloth for the home market: the problem facing Victor Amadeus and his officials was to stimulate manufacture of the better grades in order to oust imported cloth from the upper reaches of the market. This was done in part by the familiar expedient of bringing in foreign craftsmen and technology. From 1722 various English entrepreneurs and workmen began to settle in Piedmont, the most notable being a certain Coward of Frome who helped the marchese d'Ormea set up his great woollen factory in 1724. This enterprise benefited from its owner's high political position and was for a long time the largest woollen textile factory in the Savoyard state. At the same time, as we have noted elsewhere, the government began systematically excluding foreign woollens. In 1725 Victor Amadeus embarked on his tariff war with France and England, and ordered all merchants within the state to sell a fixed quota of locally-made cloth, even though this was often more expensive and of poorer quality than the imported variety.

The government's efforts to foster industrial development were often undercut, however, by other considerations that might have little to do with economic policy. Regulation tended to protect the smaller masters from competition by larger entrepreneurs, probably out of fear that this would cause unemployment, and add to the problems of pauperism and vagabondage. This policy, though perhaps understandable in social terms, seriously retarded (even though it did not halt) the trend towards concentration in both the woollen and silken industries. Another factor, which bore particularly on the woollen trades, was the desire to keep the industry decentralized, partly to spread employment to every region of the state and partly to serve the needs of the army. Military uniforms were made from local cloth, and by keeping the industry dispersed the government hoped to assure the supply of this strategic commodity even if parts of the state were occupied by an invader. A further motive was the government's aim to limit competition for labour between the silk and woollen industries, particularly in the capital. In 1733 the Consolato decreed that all woollen manufactures must leave Turin, with the sole exception of the official workshop at the Ospizio di Carità, so that they would no longer deprive the silk manufacturers of labour. Several woollen manufactures were forced to relocate or had to close. The silk industry, traditionally favoured by the government, had triumphed and the nascent woollen industry had received a grave setback. This was compounded by another order forbidding manufacturers in the Biellese – the most advanced area of the woollen industry – from producing high-grade cloth. This ban gratified rival manufacturers in other provinces, but it retarded develop-

ment in the most promising sector of the industry. So despite an aggregate
expansion in woollen output the scale of enterprises remained generally
small. In 1721 a survey counted 247 looms making woollen cloth in
Piedmont; by 1757 this total had risen to 1,293 looms, but there was little
sign of concentration. In the latter year the state's fifteen largest workshops
mustered an average of no more than thirteen or fourteen looms each.[28]
Political and military considerations had taken precedence over economic
logic.

The impossibility of reconciling these conflicting social and political
priorities imposed serious limitations on Victor Amadeus's plans for
economic development. His policies did not transform the economic
structure of the Savoyard state, but merely strengthened the thin commercial and industrial sector that overlay its vast and intractable agrarian
substructure. Plans to stimulate manufacturing ran into insurmountable
obstacles that derived from weaknesses of social and economic structure
afflicting not only the Savoyard state but every society of the Ancien
Régime. Victor Amadeus's answers to these problems naturally resembled
those put forward elsewhere, for the difficulties he faced were the same –
shortage of capital, of skilled labour, of good communications, of a broad
and resilient market. As in the rest of Europe, he had to contend with the
entrenched power of the privileged orders, which held back development
at every turn. Large-scale cultivation on the big clerical and noble estates
perpetuated inefficient methods and limited agricultural output. The
capital amassed by the privileged orders was hard to tap for industrial
development, and their traditional prestige inhibited the growth of an
independent class of entrepreneurs, while also sanctifying traditional
economic attitudes.

In certain respects the clergy presented an even greater obstacle to plans
for economic development than did the landed aristocracy. The reform
of charity in 1717 provides a good instance of how Church and state could
collide over economic questions. The local clergy tried to obstruct the
establishment of the new state poorhouses since they wanted to keep
control over the dispensation of charity and retain the social and political
influence that it represented. Their resistance hampered the government's
efforts to tap the reservoir of paupers' labour for industrial development
and it encouraged the king and his advisers to take a sharper view of the
Church's place in society. One official, for instance, went so far as to
describe the clergy as parasites, 'a useless multitude of wandering
priests . . . who not only burden the other subjects by reason of their tax
exemptions, but also cause scandals and disgrace the churches with their
idle and disorderly behaviour'.[29] Indolent clerics and the shiftless paupers
they protected were an affront to the economic discipline that Victor
Amadeus demanded of his subjects, a force of inertia restraining the
economic dynamism he was striving to inject into the state. He would

now judge the Church according to a new criterion, social utility: viewed in this way, the clergy's negative economic role became increasingly evident. And at the centre of the issue, as ever, stood the fiscal privileges that the clergy enjoyed, which were always a central item on the government's agenda and the underlying factor provoking conflict with the Papacy.

The familiar question of fiscal privilege forms the central thread of so many reforms during this period. An inquest in 1711–13 credited the clergy with tax-exempt lands worth 3,201,141 lire per annum, or about 16 percent of the landed wealth in Piedmont. The intendants were therefore instructed to scrutinize clerical immunities with special care: a particular cause of concern was the way in which allodial lands acquired by the clergy imperceptibly took on tax-free status through a perplexing array of fiscal frauds.[30] Abuses like these prompted questions about the whole principle of clerical property rights, and as early as 1701 the chancellor had expressed his belief that 'the perfect state for a Christian, which is what ecclesiastics are, consists in being entirely free of worldly possessions'.[31] This line of argument led to a more restrictive interpretation of the Church's economic rights. When he was drawing up the *Costituzioni* Victor Amadeus asked the jurists of Leyden whether he might legally forbid the transfer of land to the clergy: they replied that the state was justified in preventing the loss of its taxable resources in this way. The issue at stake here forms a direct parallel to the problem of seigneurial rights, and, as he had on the latter issue, Victor Amadeus eventually retreated from his initially rigorous position: the *Costituzioni* of 1723 merely repeated earlier enactments that permitted novices to take one-third of their property with them when they entered the Church, and when the law code was republished in 1729 the king decided against including any formal ban on clerical acquisition of property in it.

The crucial problem of the Church's fiscal status thus figured at the centre of Victor Amadeus's dispute with the Papacy until it was resolved by the Concordat of 1727, but another matter (which also bore on the fundamental issue of state sovereignty) was the question of clerical jurisdiction. This was dramatically highlighted by the conflict with the bishops in Sicily, and in Victor Amadeus's mainland dominions it became a vital problem after Clement XI's condemnation of Jansenism in the Bull *Unigenitus* of 1713. Observing the furore stirred up by the Jansenist controversy in France, the king refused to allow *Unigenitus* to be published in his own states, 'forbidding anyone to raise any question about it on pain of perpetual imprisonment in the castle of Miolans'.[32] This prohibition, which reflected both his habitual authoritarianism and his impatience with any discussion that did not serve immediately practical ends, proved extremely effective. In 1717 the vicar-general administering the archdiocese of Turin admitted that few of his clergy had heard of *Unigenitus*;

he himself knew of the Bull's existence but had never read it. Clerics ill-advised enough to express themselves on this subject were frightened into silence or banished; such was the fate of a Jesuit at Chambéry who broached the topic in his lectures. Yet while Victor Amadeus prevented the Jansenist controversy from erupting into the open, he was ready to use any arguments the Jansenists might devise if they helped him in his dispute with the Pope. Thus the defence of his stand against the Sicilian bishops was published by the French Jansenist Dupin. Jansenist criticisms of Papal authority harmonized with the arguments being put forward by Savoyard officials in defence of secular supremacy in temporal matters; both after all drew on a Gallican heritage that asserted the independence of the state in non-doctrinal questions. Such arguments, however, were reserved for the negotiations with Rome and were not publicized. In public Victor Amadeus carefully dissociated himself from any taint of Jansenist sympathy and stifled any discussion of theological issues. He seems to have been unaware, for instance, that the handbook he had had composed at this time for the prince of Piedmont, *L'Institution d'un Prince*, which he believed was by the abbot of Tamié, was actually by the Jansenist Duguet, exiled from France for his beliefs.[33] Victor Amadeus believed that the function of religion was to ensure social stability: he did not wish to see the peace of his Church disrupted by the polemics of contentious divines, nor did he intend to challenge Papal authority merely to see it replaced by a Jansenist ecclesiology, with its emphasis on episcopal power and its implicit hostility to despotism in both Church and state.

Victor Amadeus's conflict with the Pope was thus strictly legal, fiscal and jurisdictional: it was political but never theological. As if to fortify his position he made a great show of submission to Papal authority and of orthodoxy in doctrinal matters, consonant with his conception of a rigorous dichotomy between the spiritual and temporal spheres. The laws against the Vaudois were enforced with every artifice that the Savoyard bureaucracy could devise, the Protestant community of Pragelato was extinguished, and the status of the Jews deteriorated. Jews in the larger cities were confined to ghettos, after the example already set in the capital. The prohibition on Jewish ownership of real property was extended to the new territories in Monferrato, where it was hitherto unknown. The *Costituzioni* meticulously detailed all the humiliating civil disabilities that had hedged the Jews' existence for centuries. This parade of official intolerance protected the Savoyard government against imputations of heresy and schism which would have undermined the king's jurisdictional position and shifted the locus of debate onto less favourable terrain. It also provides a fitting commentary on the intellectual narrowness and bigotry so characteristic of Savoyard absolutism.

On his chosen ground Victor Amadeus held his own against the Pope and even gained some advantages. But things did not go entirely as he wished. After 1720 the Pope refused to recognize him as king of Sardinia and would not approve his nominees for bishoprics there. In his mainland states too a dangerous number of sees had fallen vacant, including the archbishoprics of Turin and Tarentaise, and the important dioceses of Vercelli, Acqui, Alessandria and Nice. Despite surveillance and intimidation, undercurrents of dissent surfaced from time to time among the clergy, articulated most vigorously by bishop Radicati of Casale, whose strictures were rendered doubly dangerous because he belonged to a powerful feudal clan: clerical and aristocratic discontent threatened to join hands. These considerations made it urgent for Victor Amadeus to reach an accommodation with Rome. In 1724 the newly elected Pope, Benedict XIII, despatched a special envoy to sound out the possibility of bringing the conflict to an end, and Victor Amadeus decided that the time had come for a new initiative. On 7 March 1725 he drew up an instruction for the marchese d'Ormea, who was to conduct the negotiations.[34] Ormea had begun his career as a minor functionary at Carmagnola, where he first attracted Victor Amadeus's attention in 1706. He was soon promoted to intendant of Susa, later worked with Gropello in the central financial administration, succeeding the latter as Generale delle Finanze in 1717, and was a prime mover in the revocation of the fiefs in 1720. The embassy to Rome would test his impressive abilities to the full. He required all his firmness, his quick and supple intelligence, his cynical ruthlessness, his lordly air which overawed and charmed his interlocutors, for the dispute was extremely complex and his orders left him little room for manoeuvre. Victor Amadeus's instructions initially construed the negotiations in the narrowest terms: Ormea was to get the Indult of 1451 extended to the entire state, in order to give his master control over contested clerical appointments in the regions acquired since that date, and to make good the Savoyard claims to the fruits of vacant benefices.

But, as Victor Amadeus knew well, far more was at stake and the negotiations protracted themselves for two years before an agreement could be reached. Ormea benefited from Benedict XIII's desire for compromise, which sprang from apprehensions that Victor Amadeus might adopt a Gallican form of Church governance or lapse into schism. But negotiation proved a lengthy process. For his part, Victor Amadeus was only gradually brought to realize the need for compromise, while at the Papal court a faction worked to obstruct any settlement. Ormea had to isolate these rigorists and win over the less intransigent members of Benedict XIII's entourage – by bribery in certain cases – while flattering the earnestly religious Pope with a show of his own and his master's piety, expressed in appropriate gifts like a relic of Saint François de Sales or a magnificent set of silver candelabra for Benedict's home monastery of Benevento. In January 1726 Ormea was able to reach a preliminary agreement on major ecclesiastical appointments, under which the Pope extended the Indult of 1451 to the lands acquired since that date by the Savoyards, in return for the right to allot pensions on the revenues from certain vacant benefices. The focus of the negotiations now shifted to the question of Sardinia. Victor Amadeus countered the Pope's refusal to recognize him as king by proposing that the signatories of the 1718 treaty that had given him the island should be allowed to mediate. The Pope could not agree to this since it would have involved him in diplomatic relations with Protestant powers, and the discussions languished.

Victor Amadeus was ready, as ever, to make use of aid from any quarter. He had used the Jansenists in the past, but now he turned to a far more radical source of arguments. The young aristocrat Alberto Radicati di Passerano was known for his advanced views: during his travels abroad he had become acquainted with recent critical scholarship in Church history, and probably with English deism. By now he was well on the way to abandoning his faith altogether. In a private interview (probably about the middle of 1725) the king asked him to expound his ideas on the relationship between Church and state, to which Radicati replied that 'the authority of the Pope, far from being divinely ordained, was in fact contrary to the Gospels'.[35] He believed that to restore Christianity to its primitive evangelical form the Church would have to be stripped of its temporal power and its wealth. Out of this conversation (which evidently did not shock Victor Amadeus's religious sensibilities too deeply) came the germ of Radicati's chief work, the *Discours moraux, historiques et politiques*, published in various forms between 1730 and 1736. A first manuscript version was actually submitted to the king in 1729, after Radicati had fled to England, fearing the machinations of the Inquisition and his enemies at court. He postulated a state of primitive equality in the early Church, which had later been corrupted by wealth and political power, creating rank and subordination in place of brotherly love. In later editions of the *Discours* Radicati took these ideas further, drawing an explicit parallel between the early Church and the original state of nature, in which men had lived as political equals. His indictment of the Church thus implicated the civil power as well, allowing no place for subordination and authority in either. Such subversive notions were naturally abhorrent to Victor Amadeus, who now – after initiating Radicati's speculations to serve his own purposes – dismissed him with outrage and contempt, transforming his self-imposed exile in England into perpetual banishment.

By the time Radicati's *Discours* were drafted in 1729 the circumstances that had prompted their composition had completely changed. For a moment Radicati had believed that he might persuade Victor Amadeus to support the great 'reform' of the Church that he was pondering, to restore Christianity to its primeval state. But the king only flirted for an instant with these perilous notions, looking for tactical help in his dispute with the Pope; soon the need for them disappeared, for in the later months of 1726 Ormea had broken the deadlock in the negotiations at Rome. On 9 December Benedict recognized Victor Amadeus as king of Sardinia and extended the Indult to cover the appointment of bishops there. Now only the issues of jurisdiction and of fiscal immunity remained to be settled. The latter question was resolved by making all lands owned by the Church prior to 1620 free from taxation. The dispute over jurisdiction was settled in a preliminary agreement, signed on 27 March 1727, which required foreign bishops whose sees included border regions of the Savoyard state to appoint vicars to administer those areas. The bishoprics of Casale, Acqui and Alessandria, acquired in 1707, were to be included in a special extension of the Indult, which was also to embrace the sees of Fossano, Alba, Asti and Saluzzo, added to the Savoyard state since 1451. In this way Victor Amadeus would have the undisputed right to appoint bishops to all the dioceses in his state. A formal Concordat embodying these different agreements was signed on 29 May 1727.[36]

The Concordat resolved most jurisdictional questions on lines favourable to Victor Amadeus and legitimized his spiritual overlordship in Sardinia. But agreement had been reached only by setting aside the issues on which neither side was willing to compromise, so that many details were left in limbo – certain regalian rights, the sovereignty over various Papal fiefs, the powers of the Church courts. Tension therefore persisted. Early in 1730 the conciliatory Benedict XIII died; his successor Clement XII had been part of the faction that had tried to block the Concordat, and he soon began to undermine it. The old disputes flared up anew, and would not be finally laid to rest until another Concordat was concluded in 1742. In the end the secular authorities were to emerge stronger from the dispute, which led to the establishment of something much closer to a state Church than before: its organization paralleled the secular government more closely, and it was less subject to Papal authority. A striking feature of the conflict had been the submissiveness of the Savoyard clergy; in Piedmont and Savoy, as in Sicily, the Papacy had found it impossible to stir up a counter-current of clerical opposition. The vast majority of the clergy remained loyal to their ruler and asked no questions; the few who stepped out of line were spied upon, bullied or expelled. Clerical acceptance of secular authority was the strongest card that Victor Amadeus had to play in his dispute with the Pope, and the Concordats' strengthening of secular dominion over the clergy merely recognized the fact that their loyalties were already firmly focused on their ruler. But despite this humbling of some of its pretensions and its loss of ground in the face of the rising secular power, the Church remained an all-pervasive presence, with deep roots in popular piety, and enormous political influence: the Savoyard state was still a profoundly Catholic polity, in which a free-thinker like Radicati was a forlorn and aberrant figure, execrated for his ideas. Victor Amadeus could no more have contemplated following his proposals for disestablishing the Church than he could imagine abolishing feudal privilege: both were equally unthinkable to his authoritarian mind and to the dominant elements in the society that he ruled. The Church, like the aristocracy, might be battered by the onslaught of aggressive absolutism, but it stood. Victor Amadeus knew, for all his efforts to circumscribe clerical influence, that his own authority could hardly subsist without the essential buttress provided by the Church.

A quiescent and dutiful clergy, untroubled by doctrinal strife and obedient to the secular power, thus formed a central component of Savoyard absolutism. By precept and example the clergy were expected to inculcate respect for authority, either from the pulpit or in the schools and colleges where they taught. The long conflict with Rome made Victor Amadeus acutely aware of how the clergy dominated education, and he became concerned that they might use this enormous power against him. From 1713 he therefore began planning a complete overhaul of the educational system, starting at the top. He aimed to reduce, if he could not abolish, the clergy's monopoly of teaching, and to this end he envisaged the establishment of a lay system of education. But this should not be taken as implying any tenderness on his part for the minuscule lay intelligentsia, or for intellectual freedom in any case. He set out to create an educational system that would serve the state, in which clerical and lay teachers alike would become in effect an extension of the bureaucracy. The purpose of education in his eyes was not to encourage speculation or innovation, but to train devoted servants for the state and to instil the discipline that held society together.

From about 1711 he started making plans to restore the moribund university of Turin, not merely to resurrect its past glories but to direct its curriculum and intellectual atmosphere along lines he deemed suitable. A site was selected for a new university building in the extension added to Turin in 1669, symbolically close to the royal palace and the government offices adjoining it, as if to emphasize the university's integration into the structure of state power then taking shape. Work on the new building took about five years, and in the interim the king pondered projects for the university's intellectual rejuvenation. Following his usual practice he studied the institutions of other states in order to adapt their best features to his own purposes, examining Padua, Bologna, Paris, Oxford and a number of German universities, even though in tradition and organization all of these differed widely from the old university of Turin. He was assisted by two Sicilian jurists who had come to his attention as zealous and erudite defenders of the monarchy against Rome: Nicolò Pensabene and Francesco d'Aguirre. In 1715 the king ordered Aguirre (then a member of the council for Sicilian affairs at Turin) to draw up plans for the curriculum and organization of the new university. He also commissioned the great Veronese scholar Scipione Maffei to draw up a project, but this proposal was judged to be too heavily weighted towards the humanities and the critical study of history and philosophy, and was accordingly rejected. Aguirre's more functional plan, submitted in April 1717, won the day.[37] It postulated the foundation of twenty-five Chairs distributed between the fields of theology, canon law, Church history, philosophy, mathematics, medicine, science and civil law. Aguirre was careful to stipulate that the university should be independent of the archbishop of Turin, who had formerly been its nominal head, for he wanted it to be free of clerical control. He envisaged it as an autonomous institution governed by the heads of its faculties, who would be responsible to a small council of Conservators under the ultimate authority of the Chancellor. This broadly speaking became the structure established by Victor Amadeus's University Constitutions of 1720.

For a time it seemed as if a new era was about to dawn in the intellectual history of the Savoyard state, hitherto a provincial backwater where traditional Aristotelianism and Thomism had hardly been touched by the revolutionary developments taking place in science, philosophy and historical criticism. The new ideas did not appeal to the Jesuits and Dominicans who controlled Savoyard education, nor did they find an eager reception among such lay intellectuals as there were, who stayed wedded to their old pursuits of law and rhetoric. But the great wars and the struggle with the Papacy served, for a time at least, to open the Savoyard state to external influences. Contact with the Protestant cultures of England and the United Provinces, with Sicilian and Neapolitan anti-curialism, with Cartesian philosophy, Gallicanism and French biblical criticism, all helped to fructify the Savoyard state's sterile intellectual life and began to draw it into the mainstream of European culture. These fresh intellectual currents were invigorated by the arrival of the new professors brought in by Aguirre to teach at the resurrected university of Turin. Aguirre himself was a man of wide culture, corresponding with many of the leading thinkers in Italy, Muratori and Giannone among them, and maintaining contact with the movement of ideas in France. Some of his arguments for freeing the university from clerical control have a Gallican ring to them, and his Jansenist sympathies are revealed by his advocacy of the Port-Royal grammar as a basic instructional text. Not all his chosen candidates came to Turin however. The great Neapolitan legist Grimaldi preferred to remain where he was, the eminent canonist Gravina died before he could take up his appointment, and the Papacy spared no effort to prevent scholars from joining the new university. But by its inauguration in 1720 Aguirre had assembled a competent (if not perhaps brilliant) group of professors to staff it, hailing mainly from the Savoyard domains, but also from other Italian states and from France.

In preparation for the opening of the new university all other institutions of higher learning in the Savoyard state were deprived of their right to grant degrees: thus the Studium at Mondovì and the college at Nice disappeared in 1719. Victor Amadeus tightened up the university of Turin's traditional monopoly of higher education, since it was easier to police academic life when it was concentrated into a single institution. Savoyard subjects were barred from foreign universities, where standards were in fact often lax: in the duchy of Savoy the feeble attainments of the French university of Valence, where many lawyers obtained their qualifications, were proverbial.[38] The affirmation of more rigorous intellectual standards was one of the positive results of Victor Amadeus's university reforms, but the centralization that it entailed caused hardship to students from the more distant parts of the state. In the years immediately after the reform few students from the duchy of Savoy made their way to the university of Turin, so that in 1723 a proposal was mooted for opening a parallel university at Chambéry which would have amalgamated all the colleges in the duchy into a single institution serving students on that side of the Alps. Although this plan was not put into effect, there was some relaxation of the university of Turin's tight intellectual monopoly.

On 17 November 1720 the reformed university of Turin opened its doors to a total of 901 students. Pensabene was appointed Conservator, heading its governing body, the Magistrato della Riforma. The inaugural oration was delivered by Bernardo Andrea Lama, perhaps the most distinguished scholar brought in by Aguirre. He was a follower of Malebranche and had studied at Paris, Naples and Rome. His address was a scathing attack on the obsolete scholasticism taught by the Jesuits and a plea for a more modern curriculum that would embrace recent developments in science and the humanities. His polemical tone aroused his adversaries, who retorted with accusations of heterodoxy directed against him and several of his colleagues. On the day that the university was inaugurated Victor Amadeus issued the new University Constitutions to regulate its operations. The required course of studies and the examinations were rigorous – so much so that in the first years few candidates survived – discipline was stringent, and extensive religious devotions were prescribed for every student. A degree from the university of Turin was made the condition – at least in theory – for access to public employment, the professions or the Church. This regimen of hard work and public orthodoxy, so typical of the ethos that dominated the Savoyard state, was intensified in the new edition of the University Constitutions issued in 1723. Students had to pass through a sequence of three sets of examinations, with a fourth if they contemplated going on to teach at university level, and as if this were not enough, a year later the king intervened personally to make the schedule of examinations even more strict.

By the end of Victor Amadeus's reign the university was functioning efficiently along the lines he had laid down. Each year it turned out a hundred or so graduates to fill positions in the government, the professions and the priesthood. The majority of graduates had studied law, which was the discipline favoured by the upper and middle classes because it offered ready access to state service. The university thus fulfilled its main purpose, which was to train servants for the state. It was also a secular institution, as Victor Amadeus had intended. Although most of its professors were in holy orders, the secular directors who formed the Magistrato della Riforma controlled every detail of its organization and curriculum, keeping it independent of clerical dominance.

The next stage in Victor Amadeus's educational reforms dealt with the school system, where clerical control still persisted after the reform of the university. Primary and secondary education were provided by a heterogeneous array of local schools, colleges and seminaries: standards were often low and curricula varied enormously. Measures were needed to raise the quality of instruction and to enforce some kind of uniformity. Until his dispute with the Pope was settled Victor Amadeus was reluctant to tamper with the school system, for fear of the repercussions this step might have on the negotiations, but once the Concordat was signed he moved quickly to establish lay control and to weld the different types of secondary schools into a coherent system. His efforts constitute what is probably the first deliberate attempt to set up a system of secular education anywhere in Europe, even though in the end its achievements fell short of his intentions. A new set of University Constitutions was promulgated in 1729, giving the Magistrato della Riforma the power to appoint teachers and determine the curriculum in every secondary school.[39] As in the university, an onerous round of devotions was required of every pupil, to disarm any criticism that the new system was anti-religious. Primary education was not much affected; the old parish schools, mainly staffed by the clergy, and the few surviving communal schools seem to have gone on as before. But secondary education underwent sweeping changes. The old provincial colleges and high schools were transformed into thirty-six 'royal schools' with a complement of 128 teachers chosen by the Magistrato and recruited (theoretically at least) exclusively from graduates of the university of Turin. A new College of the Provinces was founded at Turin with 100 places for poor but promising students from all over the state, who would be educated at government expense, taking some of their courses at the university. The new royal schools and the College of the Provinces fed directly into the university; students began at the local level but had to complete their studies and graduate from the university of Turin. In this way central control and uniform standards could be enforced, while the entire structure of secondary education was taken out of the clergy's hands.

The results of this reform varied from place to place. Some Jesuit colleges like the one at Pinerolo closed their doors, but others – at Nice or

Sospel, at Evian or Vercelli – continued to function under the auspices of the state, sending their students on to Turin. The royal schools produced a stream of students destined for the most part to become schoolmasters: in this way Victor Amadeus planned to train a cadre of lay teachers to replace the clerics who had filled the profession up till then. But his intention was not realized. There were never enough lay teachers, and clerics (who could draw on their Church stipends) were content with lower salaries and so were preferred by the impoverished local councils. Moreover as time went on the government moved towards a rapprochement with the Church, and as part of this policy relaxed the original requirement that secondary education be secular in concept and personnel. The number of clerics teaching in the schools thus remained high after the reform and actually increased in the later years of the eighteenth century, so that Victor Amadeus's aim of breaking the clergy's hold on secondary education was never fulfilled.

Retreat from these advanced positions had in fact begun even in Victor Amadeus's last years, after the Concordat of 1727. The king no longer needed the intellectuals he had brought in to combat the Roman curia and to pioneer a new departure in public education. After 1727 they became expendable, to be used as mere bargaining counters in the continuing power struggle with the Church. Moreover they constituted a nucleus of opinion that could not always be trusted to follow the government's prescribed line, and so they were forced to conform, or were discarded. The promise of a freer intellectual life that had seemed to open up after 1713, and which had gathered strength from the government's duel with the Church, was cynically betrayed as first Victor Amadeus and then his son and successor sought a rapprochement with the Papacy and consequently found it necessary to reaffirm their orthodoxy. Royal authority, for all the confidence with which it was now exercised, and despite the more efficient institutions that now bolstered it, could not stand firmly without the support of the Church. To restore this essential bond after a long and wounding struggle Victor Amadeus II and Charles Emanuel III sacrificed the small intellectual élite that they had nurtured for tactical reasons, but whose values had never commanded their allegiance. In 1728 Aguirre left Turin, finding the intellectual climate no longer tolerable, and Pensabene was removed from his post as head of the Magistrato della Riforma; clerical attacks redoubled against the supposed unorthodoxy of certain professors at the university of Turin; in 1730 Lama departed into voluntary exile. Conditions worsened in the next few years, as official prying increased and several professors were purged from the university. The clamp-down reached a symbolic climax in 1736 when in an act of official bigotry coldly calculated to curry favour with the Papacy the anticlerical philosopher Giannone was enticed from Geneva across the Savoyard frontier, arrested and imprisoned until his death. The Piedmont of Victor Amadeus's last years offered little comfort to any man who prized intellectual freedom. In 1728 Muratori congratulated Aguirre on escaping its oppressive atmosphere:

> Things are too mysterious, too delicate, too uncertain in the country you have left behind. I would not have stayed there a moment: a wise man cannot but live uneasily in a land where he encounters so many contrary winds and lives in perpetual danger of a fall. Merely to have one's correspondence intercepted and one's letters opened is enough to make one bid farewell to that country and hasten to some other land of liberty.[40]

The void left by Aguirre and Pensabene was filled by the minions of the state. The Magistrato della Riforma was placed under the rising bureaucrat Caissotti, who with the aid of Mellarède and Ormea implemented the University Constitutions of 1729 and mounted a campaign of surveillance over potential dissidents. Censorship grew more intense and all-pervasive. Everything was subordinated to the need for an orthodox stance in the continuing dispute with Rome, and no latitude was permitted to anyone who might compromise it. Repression of the intellectual revival that had begun to flower before 1727 implied no contradiction for Victor Amadeus. The reform of the educational system, like all his reforms, was intended to fulfil one purpose alone: the strengthening of the state. It had nothing to do with freedom of expression or the widening of intellectual horizons: these might be encouraged for a moment by particular religious and political measures aimed at strengthening the state, but they were not ends in themselves, and were abandoned as soon as the circumstances that had called them into being changed. Then the régime's fundamental hostility to any manifestation of intellectual autonomy at once reasserted itself. The shortcomings of Victor Amadeus's educational reforms thus serve to demonstrate both the strengths and weaknesses of the state that he did so much to create, and of the outlook that lay behind his policies.

Victor Amadeus's reforms radically transformed the Savoyard state and were to have long-lasting repercussions for its economic and social structure. Between the peace of Utrecht and his abdication in 1730 he twice redrafted the laws, streamlined the central administration, reordered the state's finances, established a network of government charities, tightened his control over the clergy and overhauled the system of education from top to bottom. His policies circumscribed religious diversity more tightly than before and rigorously subordinated intellectual autonomy to the exigencies of state policy. As he prepared to abdicate, the *perequazione* (which he himself considered his most notable achievement) stood ready for promulgation in Piedmont, while in the duchy of Savoy a similar comprehensive land-survey was under way. Throughout his domains – save in Sardinia and the Val d'Aosta – the provincial intendants linked the central government directly to the local communities, combating local particularism and enforcing a much higher degree of administrative uniformity than ever before. The long arm of the state now reached out into the remotest areas, where its authority had hardly been known before, and every order of society felt its force. Peasant insurrection had been crushed and driven underground. The privileged classes had been made to respect the Crown instead of challenging it in overt rebellion or covert intrigue as they had traditionally done in the past. A backward, disunited agglomeration of territories had been welded into one of the most efficient political and military machines in Europe, run by a conscientious bureaucracy that enforced the ruler's decrees in their minutest particulars and collected the revenues to support a strong army and a vigilant diplomatic service. Victor Amadeus had forged the political and military instruments to free his domains from French tutelage, to extend their frontiers and to carve out an independent role for his dynasty in the scheme of European power politics. His achievement laid the foundations for the dominant position that the Savoyard state would assume a century and a half later as the nucleus of Italian unification.

Victor Amadeus II's form of absolute monarchy recalls in many ways the classic model of Louis XIV's France in its uncompromising centralization and fast-growing bureaucratic institutions, in its general disregard for the social cost of policies, and in a rigid confessional orthodoxy that however did not preclude bitter jurisdictional wrangling with the Papacy. Some of its features on the other hand prefigure the enlightened despotisms of the century to come: the efforts (limited though they might be) to level fiscal privilege; a dawning secularism in education and an incipient sense of the clergy as a retrograde social force; a growing tendency to seek accurate statistical information as the basis of policy, and to evaluate some policies at least by the yardstick of social utility. But overall the institutions and political values of the Savoyard state under Victor Amadeus II remained rooted in the preceding age, and it is with the régimes of this earlier period that his pattern of absolutism can best be compared. Judged as an exercise in state-building, in disciplining a recalcitrant social fabric and in mobilizing resources from an exiguous economic base, his achievement is undeniable. Few monarchs of the day could match his success in realizing his political objectives through a comprehensive programme of carefully pondered reforms. But this success was bought at considerable cost.

The strength of Victor Amadeus's system of absolute monarchy, which links it to the régimes of the previous age, was its unrelenting insistence on the primacy of the state. But this also constituted its gravest weakness. Uncompromising statism exacted a high standard of obedience and self-sacrifice from subjects and officials alike, but it stifled their initiative and discouraged any independence of thought. Orders emanated from the top and were carried out with exemplary punctuality, but no spontaneous energy flowed from below to rejuvenate the political structure, so that in time it ossified. The indifference, verging on contempt, with which Victor Amadeus and his ministers regarded the free expression of ideas was a symptom of their wider mistrust of speculation or innovation, and of any idea or action not expressly called into being by the state and its needs. Savoyard absolutism thus could not accommodate divergencies of thought or the upsurge of energies from outside the closed circle of those in power. Such displays were feared as threats of disorder and repressed. The ubiquitous soldiers and functionaries, and the dungeons of Miolans or Ceva were always there to deal summarily with those who contravened the ruler's will or who sought to escape the numbing conformity demanded by the régime. The mass of the population was never consulted or involved in policy, even at the most elementary level; it is symptomatic that during this period the last village assemblies ceased to function and the local communities lost their last vestiges of autonomy to the intendants. The king and his ministers did what they held was best for their subjects, whose sole function was to generate wealth and manpower to serve the state's imperious needs. The military virtues of obedience and order were prized; imagination and originality were suspect. These qualities made Piedmont–Savoy one of the most justly and intelligently governed states in Europe, and won it military renown out of proportion to its small size. These are notable achievements. But the state's political and intellectual culture remained backward and provincial. Once Victor Amadeus had turned his back on the broader intellectual horizons that had seemed to beckon in the first decades of the eighteenth century, diversity was stifled and the Savoyard domains were barely touched by the great movement of ideas in the Enlightenment. The few creative, critical minds that it produced – Radicati, Alfieri, Vasco – were driven abroad or proscribed. By the end of the century, for want of new men and new ideas to revivify its deadening political structure, the state had degenerated into a brittle, formalistic shell that easily succumbed to the shock of revolution. Autocratic paternalism at the top, passivity below: the state that Victor Amadeus did so much to create became a *locus classicus* of the strengths and weaknesses of absolute monarchy.

The extreme centralization of power characteristic of Savoyard absolutism, which went beyond the concentration found in most other absolute monarchies, had the further defect of placing an enormous burden on the individual ruler; if he was not equal to the task the system could not function effectively. Under Victor Amadeus II and Charles Emanuel III the sovereign was equal to the crushing task required of him, but after the latter's death this was no longer so, and vitality gradually ebbed from the centre of power. While he reigned Victor Amadeus provided the driving force behind every facet of policy, but in the long run the system that he built around his own powerful personality no longer functioned as he had intended. Deprived of his relentless will urging it on, the action of the state machine gradually degenerated into routine; innovation and élan disappeared. This was to some extent because of the need for consolidation after a period of breakneck change, but the tone of government policy subtly changed, and the searching, daring character of Victor Amadeus's reforms vanished. This is not to say that after 1730 the Savoyard state was overtaken by complacent lethargy; later in the century the government would free the serfs in the duchy of Savoy, reorganize local government and confront the appalling problems of economy and society in Sardinia. To some extent the reformist impulse survived Victor Amadeus II. But in the end the system proved to be too closely dependent on the individual will at its centre. Victor Amadeus's success in concentrating all power into his own hands enabled him to carry through a vast, audacious programme of political and administrative change, but it reinforced the rigidity and authoritarianism that were the gravest underlying defects in the state that he ruled so masterfully and so long.

Epilogue: The Abdication

After 1713 Victor Amadeus's thoughts turned increasingly to the commemoration of his victories and political achievements, and he gave free rein to his passion for architecture, now no longer limited by the financial constraints of war. The progress of his domestic reforms was reflected in the construction or embellishment of the administrative buildings flanking the central piazza of Turin close to the royal palace: the mint, the military academy and the new university. After 1730 these would be completed by the imposing offices of the secretaries of state. The king commissioned other public buildings for the capital, notably a new hospital and lunatic asylum, and the College of the Provinces. To the west of the city, scene of the fiercest fighting during the siege of 1706, a new extension was laid out on the classic rectilinear plan (possibly by Juvarra); soon its empty spaces began to be filled with aristocratic palaces and more modest citizens' houses to accommodate the capital's fast-growing population. At the gate of the new quarter Juvarra built an austere barracks for part of the garrison, and close by he designed the exquisite, airy church of the Carmine. Outside Turin the royal palaces at Rivoli and Venaria Reale had been sacked by the French and urgently needed restoration: Venaria Reale was refurbished, and at Rivoli an ambitious programme of enlargements and decoration was executed under Juvarra's direction. In the very last years of his reign the king decided to build another country palace near Turin, and so in 1729 Juvarra began work on the hunting-lodge at Stupinigi, one of his most brilliant conceptions, radiating from a magnificent domed ballroom extending the full height of the building. Here the dynamism of the baroque begins to be tempered with rococo refinement. Victor Amadeus probably saw no more than the preliminary designs for the palace, and did not live to see it built; to commission it as he did at the end of his reign, when he was already contemplating abdication, seems almost an affirmation of immortality, an act of defiance hurled at old age and the infirmities afflicting him.

By this time he was deeply aware of approaching death and of the need to mark his place in history. Building would ensure that his fame lived on. In 1717 he had ordered work to begin on the great basilica of Superga, on the hill where he and prince Eugene had surveyed the besieging French army before their victory outside the walls of Turin in 1706. Juvarra's proud dome above the church, visible for miles on its steep hilltop, commemorated the decisive victory that had assured the survival of the state and the dynasty. But Superga was planned as more than a triumphal monument: behind the church Juvarra constructed a monastery, modelled it seems after the Escorial, whose crypt was intended to become Victor Amadeus's mausoleum and the resting-place of his successors. The monks would guard the shrine of the Savoyard dynasty, now unequivocally royal, offering perpetual prayers for their rulers both living and dead. A decade of herculean labour was required to complete the great church, for all the materials – dressed stone, plaster, lime, even water – had to be carried up to the barren hilltop on muleback. The consecration of the basilica in 1727 thus became a symbolic triumph over nature itself, epitomizing in the most concrete way the power of the ruler who had ordered it. The superb upward thrust of church and dome presented a dramatic demonstration of Victor Amadeus's unchallenged authority, sited high above his capital for all his subjects to see long after he had passed away.

The old king's intimations of mortality were sharpened by the onset of illness and the advance of old age. Increasingly his mind seems to have turned to the thought of abdication; particular historical examples, notably the abdication of his ancestor Amadeus VIII, and the recent retirement (and subsequent return to power) of Philip V of Spain, evidently impressed him. Abdication would form a fitting conclusion to a reign spent creating order and stability, for instead of allowing death to surprise him with his work still incomplete, he would prepare everything in good time, tidy up every loose thread of policy, and hand the state over to his heir in impeccable order. Having assured a peaceful, logical transition of power in this way, he would retire into private life for the few years that might be left to him. By the beginning of 1730 his mind was made up; his resolution was no doubt confirmed by a growing sense of isolation as many of his closest relatives and advisers died. His mother, Madame Royale, had died in 1724, his faithful consort Anne of Orleans in 1728; of their children, only Charles Emanuel now survived. Mellarède, the last of the old generation of ministers, died in March 1730, and new men now headed the government: Caissotti, Platzaert, Bogino, Maistre, whom he had discovered and raised to prominence, and Ormea, destined to be the most powerful of the new generation.[1] Each of these men had been hand-picked by Victor Amadeus for loyalty and efficiency. An apocryphal story (told of both Caissotti and Bogino) records how the old king would roam the streets of Turin at night in disguise, eavesdropping on his subjects. One night, seeing a lamp burning late in a garret, the king went up to see who was at work so far into the night. He found a young man poring over his law books, questioned him and, impressed by his diligence and quick wit, took him into his service at once, rewarding him with rapid advancement. This anecdote, even though inaccurate in detail, nonetheless conveys something of the old king's methods and well expresses both his secretiveness and his respect for those as single-minded and hard-working as himself. These were the men he selected as his advisers, and by 1730 they had proved their worth and gained experience in a wide variety of state business.

Surrounded by this devoted team of ministers, Charles Emanuel should encounter few difficulties once he assumed power on his own. Meanwhile to ensure that the young prince was well qualified to govern, from 1727 Victor Amadeus had begun training him systematically in every aspect of administration and statecraft. Charles Emanuel attended his father's meetings with his ministers and was then interrogated on the reasons for every decision that they reached. He went over the budget and the daily financial accounts to absorb all the arcane intricacies of state finance. He was sent on tours of inspection in the provinces to familiarize himself with every garrison and fortress, and to study industry and commerce at first hand. By the early months of 1730 Victor Amadeus was satisfied that this thorough political education had fitted his son to take over the reins of power, and he began to prepare for the abdication he had long meditated. Conditions for the transfer of power seemed extremely propitious. The treasury was full, the *perequazione* ready for promulgation, the nobles submissive, the wheels of administration turning faultlessly. Relations with the Papacy, although ruffled by the election of Clement XII, seemed stable. The treaty of Seville seemed to offer a settlement of the tensions in Italy and the Mediterranean, diminishing the risk of war, and the great powers were once more competing for the Savoyard alliance. On 22 April the French envoy Blondel was in the king's study, discussing the conditions on which Victor Amadeus would ally himself with the two Bourbon powers. As if to tempt him with the perennial prospects of conquest, the Frenchman pointed to the view through the palace windows, up the plain of the Po towards Milan. Victor Amadeus merely changed the subject, but later on, when they parted at the door to the royal chapel, he confided: 'Everyone thinks I am ambitious and eager for trouble in order to aggrandize myself, but before the Holy Shroud I swear to you that soon they will see I am only looking for peace and retirement.'[2]

Blondel attributed no importance to this Delphic utterance at the time, but it indicates that Victor Amadeus was now determined to abdicate. Characteristically he kept this resolution to himself and prepared his last dramatic stroke of policy in secret. He commissioned his trusted secretary Lanfranchi to research the circumstances of other abdications, the legal formulae and the ceremonies used. To assure himself of companionship in his retirement, on 12 August he secretly married the contessa di San Sebastiano, whom he had loved long ago when she was a maid of honour to his mother, and who had returned to occupy his affections in recent years.[3] As a wedding gift he settled on her the marquisate of Spigno, a recently acquired Imperial fief. But as yet he did not disclose his plan to abdicate even to her.

On 3 September 1730 Victor Amadeus formally abdicated in a ceremony at the castle of Rivoli attended by all his ministers and the leading figures of the court.[4] In a brief but touching speech he handed over power to his son, expressing confidence in his capacity to rule wisely and justly, and then asked each minister and dignitary in turn to serve their new king as loyally as they had served himself. All wept. The old king now prepared to withdraw into retirement at Chambéry. That night, in an informal conversation with Blondel he explained why he had chosen this moment to abdicate.

> For over a year I have noticed that I am no longer clearheaded when it comes to making decisions, and I often forget essential things. I felt myself declining and I found that my head was frequently muddled, perhaps because of the enormous labours I have undertaken during my lifetime and which I still continued. It might also be the result of my illnesses: half my right side is paralysed to some extent, so that I can hardly raise my arm and use it; I am afflicted with colic every other day, which torments and weakens me, and which affects my work because of the ill humour that it causes me; I have been pissing blood all winter, and can no longer lead an active life or ride on horseback. I am most fortunate to have been able to reflect in good time on this warning from God that death will soon overtake me, so that I have not let myself be blinded by pride and glory, and by all the seductions of power, and have been able to come to a decision which goes against my passions and my character. This decision would have become inevitable within a short space of time anyway, but with the difference that my subjects would have noticed my condition and taken advantage of my weakness. I would have allowed them to mislead me and would have committed follies that my son would have had great difficulty in putting right. Instead at this moment everything is in good order: I am leaving him memoranda on all the business of state and on every contingency that can arise, for him to make use of as he sees fit. In truth these instructions are not meant to be strict commandments for him, because now that I have renounced the throne he is answerable only to his own will. All I can do now is exhort him to trust my advice contained in those memoranda, which are the fruit of experience bequeathed by a father who loves him tenderly, who has reigned for fifty years, and who has found himself in some extremely difficult and dangerous situations.[5]

Victor Amadeus left the next day and took up his residence at Chambéry with the marchesa di Spigno and a modest retinue, intending (as he said) to live out the rest of his days as a simple country gentleman, and merely requesting that his son would send him 'a weekly bulletin of all that was decided in the affairs of the state, to entertain him in his retirement'.[6] This was duly done.

But despite the old king's protestations that he only wanted to live in easy retirement, it soon became apparent to Charles Emanuel and Ormea (who had returned shortly after the abdication from a diplomatic mission to Rome, and had become the new king's leading adviser) that Victor Amadeus had not really lost his interest in high policy. In fact he seemed determined to guide their actions from his rural retreat in an irksome display of paternal solicitude, which threatened to set up a dangerous division of authority within the state. Victor Amadeus was especially preoccupied with two questions, to which he had devoted much of his working life: the final enactment of the *perequazione*, and the Concordat with the Papacy. He watched with concern in December 1730 as Charles Emanuel abandoned the inquest into feudal dues in Savoy, easing the pressure on the nobility, and then as Clement XII began to call the Concordat into question in January 1731. He began to doubt his son's capacity to govern and tried to direct his conduct of affairs by correspondence. Ormea summed up the situation (which threatened his own ascendancy over Charles Emanuel) in a harsh metaphor: 'the play is here at Turin, but the machine that moves the puppets is in Savoy'.[7]

Early in February 1731 word reached Turin that the old king had suffered an apoplectic seizure. He recovered quickly, but it seems clear in retrospect that his mind must have been affected, for his actions now grew increasingly irrational. He became suspicious of those around him and more convinced than ever of his son's political incapacity. During his illness Ormea suppressed the weekly bulletins on state affairs that had been sent to him, to discourage his meddling; Victor Amadeus noted this but made no protest. In March Charles Emanuel paid his father a visit and found him outwardly well and in good spirits. Under the surface, however, the old man's resentments were building up. When his son passed through Savoy again in July 1731, en route to take the waters at Evian, there were stormy scenes between them. Victor Amadeus berated his son for failing to keep him informed of state business, called him 'an imbecile' and accused him of being misled by his ministers. The tirade concluded with a threat: those ministers might have sworn allegiance to Charles Emanuel, but Victor Amadeus had never formally released them from their bond of fealty to himself. He therefore felt free to reassert his claim on their loyalties whenever he pleased.[8]

Charles Emanuel returned post-haste to Turin, arriving on 22 August. His father's savage reproaches had brought back his old fears and sense of inadequacy, leaving him uncertain how to act. Within a week Victor Amadeus followed him across the Alps and settled at the castle of Moncalieri just south of Turin. There Charles Emanuel dutifully visited him, to be greeted with studied coldness. Victor Amadeus demanded to be kept informed of all state business and talked wildly of hanging his son's ministers. Next day he insisted that he should sign all the diplomatic correspondence with Rome, along with his son; his intention was evidently to resume a *de facto* role in running the state. Again he asserted that his abdication was invalid since his subjects had not been released from their oaths of allegiance to himself. All this was duly reported to Charles Emanuel and Ormea, who realized that a confused design to recover the throne was forming in the old king's disordered mind. He spoke freely and wildly to all and sundry, with none of his old circumspection or even the remotest effort at concealment: he believed the state was in venal or incompetent hands, and that he must intervene to prevent the ruin of his life's accomplishment.

His delusions soon crystallized into action. On 16 September Victor Amadeus summoned Caissotti and Ormea to Moncalieri and announced that he had decided to resume power: his son's government was beset by cabals, order must be restored at once. The act of abdication had no legal force and would be set aside. In the meantime Charles Emanuel was to obey his orders and leave at once on a tour of inspection to the fortress of Fenestrelle. Ormea was to begin revising the *perequazione*: Victor Amadeus claimed that the edict implementing it in May 1731 was full of errors and must be corrected. This jumble of paranoid accusations and unfounded assertions, which repeated what Victor Amadeus had been saying ever since his return from Chambéry, indicated that matters were becoming critical. The old king was now manifestly deranged, broadcasting his wild designs and talking of plots. He seems to have regressed to the time when he ruled with unquestioned authority over his ministers and cowed his son into silent obedience, but this was only in his mind and the reality was now far different. It was as if his rational faculties had crumbled away like a husk, leaving only the raw incandescent kernel of will at the centre of his mind, that unquenchable urge to dominate that had always been the mainspring of his actions. But this was more than the private tragedy of a powerful mind falling into ruin, undermined by age and illness: Victor Amadeus's delusions constituted a direct threat to the stability of the state. In his dotage he was about to undo the work of his lifetime, the construction of an orderly, rational structure of state power. On 26 September the exact nature of the threat declared itself: he announced that he would depart for Milan to seek the Emperor's arbitration in his quarrel with his ungrateful son and faithless ministers. To invoke the Emperor's authority in this way was to overthrow the whole concept of independent sovereignty that Victor Amadeus himself had fought to attain. He was inviting intervention by the state's most dangerous foe, who would exploit this admission of overlordship to the full.

Charles Emanuel had hesitated until now, fearful of his terrible old father, and unable to act. On Ormea's advice he had refused to go to Fenestrelle, for this might leave the way open for Victor Amadeus to enter the capital in person and seize power in his absence. But he still could

take no action; his consort noted that he was suffering agonies of inde-
cision and anxiety. His father's design of appealing to the Emperor left
him no choice but to act, however, so at Ormea's urging he called a
meeting of his ministers and the archbishop of Turin to decide what should
be done. This council assembled on the evening of 28 September and
quickly agreed that Victor Amadeus must be arrested: Ormea warned of
plots that might centre on the old king, leading perhaps to civil war and
foreign intervention. He urged Charles Emanuel 'to think of the danger
confronting the state', and insisted, 'Your Majesty, this is a matter of life
and honour for us all'.9 At this Charles Emanuel finally signed the warrant
for his father's arrest, and then broke down.

A picked detachment of grenadiers and dragoons rode at once to
Moncalieri and burst in on Victor Amadeus and the marchesa di Spigno
as they slept. The old king was bundled into a carriage, raging and
threatening, and driven to the castle at Rivoli, while his consort was
transported to cruel and humiliating captivity in a house for reformed
prostitutes at Ceva. When Victor Amadeus arrived at Rivoli he was
scarcely able to walk; observers noticed that his tongue was protrud-
ing and that he was frothing at the mouth. He was shut up in a room whose
windows had been hastily fitted with iron bars, and guarded day and night.

Ormea meanwhile put it about that the marchesa di Spigno had been
the cause of Victor Amadeus's bid to return to power, and that she and
some of her family had conspired to overthrow the new government out
of thwarted ambition. A few unfortunates were imprisoned but soon
released, for there was in fact no plot; the story was a necessary fiction to
hide the true nature of the crisis. After a time the marchesa was allowed to
return to her husband at Rivoli, where he spent the last year of his life in
harsh captivity, denied all contact with the outside world. What was left
of his mind dissolved amid fits of alternate fury and lassitude; he would
lie inert, or from time to time round on the luckless marchesa di Spigno,
blaming her for his misfortune and battering her with his fists. On 31
October 1732 he finally died. He was not laid to rest in the crypt at Superga,
as he had wished, for Charles Emanuel and Ormea did not wish to draw
public attention to the drama of which he had been the centre, and to arouse
passions that might threaten the stability of the state. Only much later in the
century would his grandson, Victor Amadeus III, transfer the king's remains
to the burial-place that he had wished for himself. The marchesa di Spigno
was quietly released from confinement and entered a convent at Pinerolo,
where she lived to a great age, dying in 1769. Ormea retained his ascendancy within the government until his death in 1745, amassing vast wealth
and living in ostentatious luxury. Charles Emanuel survived this traumatic
test and became an effective sovereign, whose prowess on the battlefield
and diligence in state affairs made him a worthy successor to his great
father.

Rumours of the startling events surrounding Victor Amadeus's abdication and abortive attempt to regain power soon spread abroad, arousing passionate curiosity: in decline and death, as in the prime of life and authority, Victor Amadeus was at the centre of public attention. The circumstances of his end offered material for endless speculation and moralizing: here, enveloped in an aura of profound mystery and intrigue, was a tragic drama of father against son, of a great man's fall from absolute power to abject misery and impotence. By a profound irony, Victor Amadeus was destroyed by the power of the state that he had done so much to create. In a last mad gesture he tried fumblingly to overthrow the structure of authority that he himself had established, forcing the new keepers of that sovereign power, whom he had trained in his own ideal of ruthless duty, to crush him. The soldiers who guarded him like mute automata, without compassion, and Ormea, who nerved Charles Emanuel to resistance and procured the old king's downfall, had each in their own ways learned the lesson that he had taught them. To defend the state they unhesitatingly destroyed the man who for so long had been its embodiment but who now, broken and senile, threatened its integrity. In their place he would have done exactly what they did; he died, as he had lived, by the inexorable imperatives of state power. The events he set in motion by endeavouring to regain the throne would have profoundly troubled the inner harmony of the state if it had still been as it was when he first came to power in 1684; then, under the impulse of conflict within the ruling house, faction would have erupted into civil war. By 1731 his futile attempt to regain the throne and subsequent fall occasioned no more than a ripple on the surface of affairs, for the institutions he had built up and the concept of state service he had inculcated were proof against such upheavals. This perhaps is the true measure of his achievement.

1   The Savoyard State, c. 1713

2   Italy, *c.* 1700

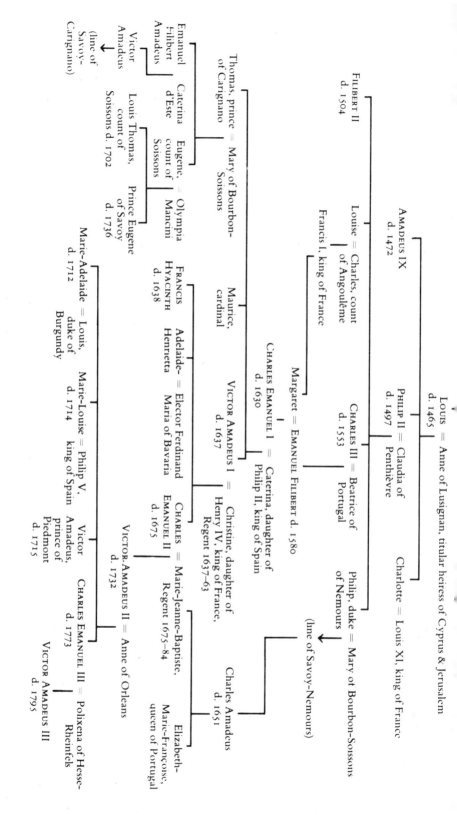

Bibliographical Notes and Notes on the Text

Manuscript Sources

The most important collections of documents bearing on Victor Amadeus II's reign are in the Archivio di Stato at Turin, which is divided into two sections: *Prima Sezione* (at Piazza Castello), and *Sezioni Riuniti* (Via Santa Chiara).

The *Prima Sezione* contains close to 2,000 of the king's letters in the series Lettere di duchi e sovrani. Several times that number of his letters, orders and instructions are to be found in the diplomatic correspondence (Lettere di ministri), arranged country by country. This section of the Archivio di Stato also contains many documents on trade, industry and related matters, in the category Materie Economiche; among these I have used relevant papers in the sub-groupings Annona (provisioning and grain supplies), Censimenti (censuses), and in the Materie di Commercio, which has extensive documentation on the silk industry. Much information on local history is catalogued under the individual provinces (here I have made use of the series Provincia di Torino for the history of the capital city and its immediate area), and there is also the series Paesi per A e B which lists each locality in alphabetical order. It should be noted that there is a vast – and still largely untapped – wealth of material for local history in the numerous local archives throughout Piedmont.

The *Sezioni Riuniti* contain (inter alia) the chief series of documents for the history of the state's finances: the general series Finanze, catalogued in two separate groupings, the Archivio Camerale, or records of the Camera dei Conti which audited payments, and also including the Patenti Controllo Finanze, or payments authorized by the controller-general. The accounts of the state treasurer, or Conti dei Tesorieri, form another series. The best introduction to the use of these different series of documents is in the work of Luigi Einaudi: *Le entrate pubbliche dello stato sabaudo nei bilanci e nei conti dei tesorieri durante la guerra di successione spagnola* (Turin 1909), and *La finanza sabauda all'aprirsi del secolo XVIII e durante la guerra di successione spagnola* (Turin 1908), to be supplemented by E. Stumpo, *Finanza e stato moderno nel Piemonte del Seicento* (Rome 1979).

A certain amount of documentation on Victor Amadeus's reign can be found in the Biblioteca Reale at Turin, particularly scattered through the series Storia Patria; this library has a useful collection of rare printed materials and contemporary pamphlets, many of which are unobtainable elsewhere. The municipal archive of Turin, the Archivio del Comune, is rich and well-arranged but is primarily concerned with the city's history. It does however contain a variety of documents relevant to the history of the state as a whole, for example those on the Monte or state debt, which was administered by the municipality.

Documentation for the history of the regions that formerly comprised the Savoyard state in Savoy and Nice is located in the respective archives at Nice, Chambéry and elsewhere; these I have not been able to consult. Materials relating to the history of these regions formerly held by the Archivio di Stato at Turin have been transferred to Chambéry and Nice. There is a great deal of documentation for the history of Sardinia under Savoyard rule in the Archivio di Stato at Cagliari, although a good deal of material bearing on Sardinian affairs is conserved at Turin.

Printed Sources

The most extensive and representative selection of state papers to be printed from Victor Amadeus II's reign is in the first five volumes of the collective work *Le campagne di guerra in Piemonte (1703–1708) e l'assedio di Torino (1706)* ed. C. Contessa et al., 10 vols. in all (only 9 apparently published) (Turin 1907–1933). Another long series of Victor Amadeus's correspondence is in A. Manno, E. Vayra and E. Ferrero (eds.), *Relazioni diplomatiche della monarchia di Savoia dalla prima alla seconda restaurazione 1559–1814: Francia, Periodo III, 1713–1719* (3 vols. Turin 1886–91: no other vols. in this series were ever published).

An indispensable instrument for research into the history of the Savoyard state is F. A. & C. Duboin (eds.), *Raccolta per ordine di materia delle leggi, cioè Editti, Patenti, Manifesti ecc. emanati negli stati sardi sino all'8 dicembre 1798* (23 vols. Turin 1818–69). This is a collection of laws, as its title implies, but its scope ranges far beyond legal and constitutional history. Its successive volumes each deal with a separate topic – religious law, trade and industry etc. – and within each volume the material is arranged chronologically, and provided with explanatory notes. This collection far exceeds earlier compilations of its kind, such as G. B. Borelli, *Editti antichi e nuovi dei sovrani principi della Real Casa di Savoia . . .* (Turin 1681).

For the history of state finance the works of Einaudi and Stumpo listed above are fundamental. For the economic history of the Savoyard state under Victor Amadeus II the pioneering work of Giuseppe Prato is essential; in particular we may note here *Il costo della guerra di successione spagnuola e le spese pubbliche in Piemonte (1703–1708)* (Turin 1907: actually vol. 10 of *Le campagne di guerra*) and *La vita economica in Piemonte a mezzo il secolo XVIII* (Turin 1908), which although it covers a slightly later period is still extremely valuable for the early eighteenth century. Mention should also be made of S. Pugliese, *Due secoli di vita agricola. Produzione e valore dei terreni. Contratti agrari, salari e prezzi nel Vercellese nei secoli XVIII e XIX* (Turin 1908), which is still the only systematic study of a local economy.

Biographies

The basic – and only – work is D. Carutti, *Storia di Vittorio Amedeo II* (I have used the 3rd ed., Turin 1897). M. Robatto, *Vittorio Amedeo II, primo re sabaudo* (Turin 1913), is a short school text. A useful quick summary of the king's principal achievements is in F. Cognasso, 'Nel secondo centenario della morte di Vittorio Amedeo II', published in the review *Torino* (Dec. 1932), and recapitulated in the relevant chapter of his work on the Savoyard dynasty, *I Savoia* (Milan 1971).

Abbreviations used in the notes

ACT	Archivio del Comune, Turin
AST	Archivio di Stato, Turin
BR	Biblioteca Reale, Turin

AFLN	Annales de la Faculté des Lettres de Nice
AISIEMC	Annuario dell'Istituto Storico Italiano per l'Età Moderna e Contemporanea
AM	Annales du Midi
ASI	Archivio Storico Italiano
BCTH	Bulletin Historique et Philologique du Comité des Travaux Historiques et Scientifiques
BSBS	Bollettino Storico-Bibliografico Subalpino
BSSV	Bollettino della Società di Studi Valdesi (formerly known as the Bulletin de la Société d'Histoire Vaudoise)
CGP	C. Contessa et al. (eds.), *Le campagne di guerra in Piemonte (1703–1708) e l'assedio di Torino (1706)* (10 vols., Turin 1907–1933)
CH	Cahiers d'Histoire (Clermont-Lyon-Grenoble)
CNSS	Congrès National des Sociétés Savantes
CSSS	Congrès des Sociétés Savantes Savoisiennes
DBI	*Dizionario Biografico degli Italiani* (Rome, 1961–, continuing)
Duboin	F. A. & C. Duboin (eds.), *Raccolta per ordine di materia delle leggi . . . emanati negli stati sardi sino all'8 dicembre 1798* (23 vols., Turin 1818–69)
EHR	English Historical Review
Einaudi, *Finanza*	L. Einaudi, *La finanza sabauda all'aprirsi del secolo XVIII e durante la guerra di successione spagnola* (Turin 1908)
HPM	Historiae Patriae Monumenta (Turin)
MAS	Mémoires publiés par l'Académie de Savoie (formerly Académie Royale), Chambéry
MAST	Memorie dell'Accademia delle Scienze di Torino
MSI	Miscellanea di Storia Italiana (Turin)
MSSHA	Mémoires et Documents publiés par la Société Savoisienne d'Histoire et d'Archéologie, Chambéry
NRS	Nuova Rivista Storica
PH	Provence Historique
RGA	Revue de Géographie Alpine
RHES	Revue d'Histoire Economique et Sociale
RR	Recherches Régionales, Côte d'Azur et Régions Limitrophes, pub. by Centre de Documentation des Archives des Alpes-Maritimes, Nice
RSI	Rivista Storica Italiana
RSR	Rassegna Storica del Risorgimento
TSHM	Travaux de la Société d'Histoire de la Maurienne

I The Growth of the State

The most recent general accounts of the growth of the Savoyard state from the Middle Ages are in P. Guichonnet (ed.), *Histoire de la Savoie* (Toulouse 1973), 142 ff., and the collective *Storia del Piemonte* (2 vols., Turin 1961) I, 102 ff. On the Alpine passes see L. Bulferetti, 'Les communications entre Turin et Lyon au XVIIIe siècle', *CH*, V pt. 4 (1960), and idem, 'Il Gran San Bernardo e gli altri valichi alpini del Regno Sardo nel secolo XVIII', *Relazioni del XXXI congresso storico subalpino* (2 vols., Turin 1959); M. Abrate, 'Trasporti transalpini in Piemonte nel secolo XVII), *Economia e storia* (1959), pt. 3.

1 V. Alfieri, *Vita scritta da esso*: Eng. trans. ed. E. R. Vincent (London 1961): especially pt. I, ch. 3.

II The Regions of the Savoyard State

THE COUNTY OF NICE
General: R. Blanchard, *Le comté de Nice, étude géographique* (Paris 1960); R. Latouche, *Histoire du comté de Nice* (2 vols., Paris 1951); A. Compan, *Histoire de Nice et de son comté* (2 vols., Toulon 1973); M. Bordes (ed.), *Histoire de Nice et du pays niçois* (Toulouse 1976); H. Costamagna, 'Nice au XVIIIe siècle: présentation historique et géographique', *AFLN* no. 19 (1973); F. Hildesheimer, 'Nice au XVIIe siècle, économie, famille, société', *RR* (Oct. 1974).
Economy and demography: G. Veyret-Vernier, 'L'industrie attardée d'une région enclavée. Les montagnes du comté de Nice au début du XIXe siècle', *RGA* XXXI, 2 (1943); J. Devun, 'Les dénombrements de la population et des communautés du comté de Nice au XVIIIe siècle', *Actes du 90e CNSS, Nice 1965* (2 vols., Paris 1966) I; H. Costamagna, 'Notes sur les migrations dans le comté de Nice au XVIIIe siècle', *Les migrations dans les pays méditerranéens* (*Cahiers de la Méditerranée*, special series, no. 2: 1973–4); idem, 'Aspects et problèmes de la vie agro-pastorale dans le comté

de Nice (1699–1792)', *RHES* XLIX, 2 (1971); M-H. Siffre, 'Aperçu sur les pratiques communautaires dans le comté de Nice au XVIIIe siècle', *RHES* XLVIII, 2 (1970); idem, 'Un exemple d'ascension sociale au XVIIIe siècle: la famille Foucard de la Rocca', *AM* LXXXV (Ap–June 1973); S. Foà, *La politica economica della Casa Savoia verso gli Ebrei dal secolo XVI fino alla rivoluzione francese. Il porto franco di Villafranca (Nizza)* (Rome 1961); P. Waksmann, 'Les Français à Barcelonnette de 1690 à 1693', *Actes du CNSS, Nice 1965* (2 vols., Paris 1966) I.

Institutions: H. Moris's introduction to *Inventaire sommaire des archives départementales antérieures à 1792. Alpes-Maritimes, archives civiles, série A et B* (Nice 1902); H. Costamagna, 'Libertés communales et tutelle centralisatrice à Nice (1699–1792)', *AM* LXXXIV (1972); idem, 'Budgets communaux du comté de Nice au XVIIIe siècle, essai de typologie), *PH* XCI (1973); idem, 'Ressources financières des communautés dans le comté de Nice au XVIIIe siècle', *PH* XCV (1974); M. Bordes, 'L'originalité des institutions communales du comté de Nice au XVIIIe siècle', *AFLN* XIX (1973); idem, 'Les institutions municipales de Nice au XVIIIe siècle', *PH* LXVI (1966); idem, 'L'administration des communautés d'habitants en Provence et dans le comté de Nice à la fin de l'Ancien Régime', *AM* (Oct–Dec. 1972); E. Hildesheimer, 'Communautés d'habitants et tutelle administrative dans le comté de Nice sous l'Ancien Régime', *Actes du 90e CNSS, Nice 1965* (2 vols., Paris 1966); F. Hildesheimer, 'Nice au XVIIe siècle, institutions locales et vie urbaine', *Bibliothèque de l'Ecole des Chartes* CXXXIII (1975); P. Canestrier, 'L'inféodation des communes du comté de Nice à la fin du XVIIe siècle. Conséquence de la dévaluation monétaire', *Nice historique* (1944).

1 Quoted by P. Canestrier, 'L'oeuvre de Vauban dans les Alpes-Maritimes', *Congrès Vauban, Avallon 1933, Mémoires* (Beaune 1935), 115.

2 Ibid., 113. Modern figures in K. J. Beloch, *Bevölkerungsgeschichte Italiens*

(3 vols., Berlin 1937-65) III, 286; G. Prato, 'Censimenti e popolazione in Piemonte nei secoli XVI, XVII e XVIII', *Rivista italiana di sociologia* X (1906), 365-370.

3 Canestrier, 'Vauban', 114.

4 Figures in F. E. Bollati di St-Pierre (ed.), *HPM* XV (Turin 1884), 360 ff.; R. Bachi, *I bilanci, le scritture, i rendiconti nella monarchia piemontese nel secolo XVIII* (Turin 1896), table of revenue for 1731.

5 H. Costamagna, 'Aspects et problèmes de la vie agro-pastorale', 509-510.

6 Canestrier, 'Vauban', 114.

7 Siffre, 'Aperçu', 196.

THE PRINCIPALITY OF ONEGLIA

8 Einaudi, *Finanza*, 103-106; population figures from Beloch III, 286, and Prato, 'Censimenti', 356-357.

THE DUCHY OF SAVOY

General: M. Bruchet, 'Instructions de Victor-Amédée II sur le gouvernement de son duché de Savoie en 1721', *BCTH* (1900, nos. 1-2); idem, *L'abolition des droits seigneuriaux en Savoie (1761-1793)* (Annecy 1908); G. Pérouse, 'Etat de la Savoie à la fin du XVIIe siècle (1679-1713). Documents inédits recueillis aux archives de Turin', *MSSHA* LXIII (1926); J. Nicolas, *La Savoie au XVIIIe siècle. Noblesse et bourgeoisie* (2 vols., Paris 1977); idem, 'La noblesse et l'état en Savoie au XVIIIe siècle', *CH* XXII (1977); A. Gros, *Histoire de la Maurienne* (6 vols., Chambéry 1946-60).

Social and economic: M. Bruchet, 'L'émigration des Savoyards originaires de Faucigny au XVIIIe siècle', *BCTH* (1896); J. Blache, 'Le troupeau bovin dans les Alpes du Dauphiné et de Savoie au milieu du XVIIe siècle', and F. Gex, 'La clouterie en Bauges', *Mélanges géographiques offerts à Raoul Blanchard* (Grenoble 1932); R. Devos, 'Les maîtres mouliniers de soie d'Annecy au XVIIe siècle', P. Duparc, 'L'industrie textile à Annecy avant la Révolution', and P. Guichonnet, 'La verrerie de Thorens', *Mémoires et documents publiés par l'Académie Salésienne, Annecy* LXXXVI (1976); J.

Nicolas, 'Une ancienne famille de la bourgeoisie annécienne au XVIIIe siècle, les Garbillon', *Revue savoisienne* (1961); M. Mestrellet, 'Les étrangers, les mines savoyardes au XVIIIe siècle. La Compagnie Anglaise (1740-41)', *MSSHA* LXXX (1965); P. Bozon, 'La vallée des Villards aux XVII et XVIIIe siècles d'après les consignes du sel', *TSHM* (1967); idem. *Le pays des Villards en Maurienne* (Grenoble 1970); F. Vermale, *Les classes rurales en Savoie au XVIIIe siècle* (Paris 1911); P. Tochon, *Histoire de l'agriculture en Savoie depuis les temps les plus reculés jusqu'à nos jours* (Chambéry 1871; also pub. in *MAS*, 2nd series, XII: 1872); P. Guichonnet, 'L'émigration saisonnière en Faucigny', *RGA* (1920); idem, 'L'émigration alpine vers les pays de langue allemande', *RGA* XXXVI (1948); idem, 'Exploitation rurale et affermage des terres en Faucigny aux XVIIe et XVIIIe siècles', *Actes du 81e CNSS, Rouen-Caen 1956* (Paris 1956); A. Gorré, 'La vie économique en Maurienne aux XVIIe et XVIIIe siècles', *TSHM* 2nd series, X (1945); P. Dufournet, *Pour une archéologie du paysage. Une communnauté agraire secrète et organise son territoire. Bassy et alentours* (Paris 1978); G. Pérouse, 'Une communauté rurale sous l'Ancien Régime, d'après les archives de Termignon en Maurienne', *BCTH* (1903-4); idem, *Les communes et les institutions de l'ancienne Savoie d'après les archives communales* (Chambéry 1911), which is a reprint of his intro. to *Inventaire sommaire des archives départementales de la Savoie antérieures à 1793. Archives civiles – Série A. I: Archives communales, arrondissement d'Albertville* (Chambéry 1911); idem, 'Histoire d'une population aux XVIIe et XVIIIe siècles (St-Sorlin d'Arves)', *MSSHA* LXVII (1930).

Institutions: H. Arminjon, *De la noblesse des sénateurs au souverain Sénat de Savoie* (Annecy 1971); E. Burnier, 'Histoire du Sénat de Savoie et des autres compagnies judiciaires de la même province', *MAS*, 2nd series, VI-VII (1864), also pub. separately in 2 vols., Paris 1864; J. Chetail, 'Insinuation et tabellion dans l'ancienne

Savoie', *Actes du 85e CNSS, Chambéry-Annecy 1960* (Paris 1961); L. Chevailler, *Essai sur le souverain Sénat de Savoie 1559–1793. Organisation, procédure, compétence* (Annecy 1953); A. Palluel-Guillard, 'L'administration communale de Chambéry au XVIIIe siècle', *MSSHA* LXXVIII (1963).
Religious history: A. Bergès, *Des libertés de l'Eglise savoyarde et du gallicanisme du souverain Sénat de Savoie aux XVIIe et XVIIIe siècles* (Paris 1942); P. Bourban, 'La confrérie de St-Amédée ou des Savoyards', and abbé Poncet, 'Les statuts de la confrérie du Saint Nom de Jésus érigée à Héry-sur-Ugines en 1671', *14e CSSS Evian 1896* (Evian 1897); C. Michel, 'Etienne Fodéré, sculpteur de retables, son oeuvre en Tarentaise', M. Hudry, 'Les communautés de prêtres aux XVIIe et XVIIIe siècles dans l'archidiocèse de Tarentaise', P. Dufournet, 'L'art religieux populaire en Haute-Maurienne', and idem, 'Croix, oratoires, et chapelles de Bessans, Haute-Maurienne', *Actes du 2e congrès des sociétés savantes de la province de Savoie, St-Jean-de-Maurienne 1966* (St-Jean-de-Maurienne 1972); G. Pérouse, 'Les paroisses rurales d'un diocèse de Savoie au XVIIe siècle), *Revue de l'histoire de l'Eglise de France* IV (1913); P. Duparc, 'Confréries du Saint-Esprit et communautés d'habitants au moyen-âge', *Revue historique du droit français et étranger* series 4, XXXVI (1958); M-A. Robbe, *Les retables de bois sculpté en Tarentaise aux XVIIe et XVIIIe siècles* (Chambéry 1939); A. van Gennep, 'Patronages, chapelles et oratoires de la Haute-Maurienne. Etude statistique et critique', in *Revue de l'histoire de l'Eglise de France* XXV (1939), reprinted in his *Culte populaire des saints en Savoie* (Paris 1973).
9 Nicolas, *Savoie* I, 12; Beloch III, 282–284 misquotes figures from 1723 as being from 1734.
10 A survey of 1741 at Chambéry listed 2,004 households, of which 197 were 'merchants' (of whom 92 were 'better-off'); a survey at Annecy in 1743 listed 1,084 households, including 126 belonging to 'merchants' and 367 to 'artisans': ibid., I, 102. In Faucigny

in 1774 the capital, Bonneville, had 775 inhabitants, while Samoëns and Sallanches, the only other towns, had 2,768 and 2,320 respectively: Bruchet, 'Emigration', 817.
11 Nicolas, *Savoie* I, 93.
12 Ibid., I, 142–156, 212–220; for communal lands, 138–139.
13 Bruchet, 'Emigration', 818–820; cf. Bozon, *Pays de Villards*, 85–87, 134–139; Pérouse, 'Histoire d'une population', 33 ff.
14 Marquis Costa de Beauregard, *Essai sur l'amélioration de l'agriculture dans les pays montueux et en particulier dans la Savoie* (Chambéry 1774), 31 note.
15 His view is most clearly enunciated in 'Une communauté rurale', 242–249.
16 Nicolas, *Savoie* I, 506 ff.
17 Ibid., I, 10–14, 274–283; figures in Bruchet, 'Instructions', 285 note 1.
18 Nicolas, *Savoie* I, 23–38.
19 Ibid., I, 250–251.
20 Hudry, 'Communautés de prêtres', 232–236.

THE DUCHY OF AOSTA
In general, see L. Marini, 'La Valle d'Aosta fra Savoia e Piemonte 1601–1730', *Relazioni e comunicazioni presentate al XXXI congresso storico subalpino 1956* (2 vols., Turin 1959) II. On the economy, A. Garino Canina, 'Notizie sulle miniere della Valle d'Aosta', ibid. II. On institutions, M. A. Benedetto, *Documenti per la storia del 'Conseil des Commis' del ducato d'Aosta* (Turin 1965); idem, *Ricerche sul 'Conseil des Commis' del ducato d'Aosta* (Turin 1956).
On Tillier: G. Frutaz, 'Jean-Baptiste de Tillier et ses travaux historiques', *Bulletin de la société académique du duché d'Aoste* (1951); A. Berthet, 'Considérations sur les lettres de Jean-Baptiste de Tillier', ibid. (1949). Tillier's most important historical treatise, the *Historique de la vallée d'Aoste* (written *ca.* 1725–40), was first published at Aosta in 4 parts between 1880 and 1887, ed. S. Lucat. A short excerpt appeared in vol. XV of *HPM* (ed. F. E. Bollati di St-Pierre, Turin 1884), but it was not published in a full, critical edition until 1968 (at Aosta). His treatise on

Le franchigie delle comunità del ducato d'Aosta (written 1734) was published at Turin in 1965. His other historical works remain unpublished.
21 J-B. de Tillier, *Historique de la vallée d'Aoste* (ed. S. Lucat, Aosta 1880–87) I, 61.
22 Marini, 675–677.
23 Beloch III, 265–272; Prato, 'Censimenti', 339–343, 357.

THE PRINCIPALITY OF PIEDMONT
Social and economic: the best starting-point is still G. Prato, *La vita economica in Piemonte a mezzo il secolo XVIII* (Turin 1908), even though it refers to a slightly later period. For general studies see also S. J. Woolf, 'Sviluppo economico e struttura sociale in Piemonte da Emanuele Filiberto a Carlo Emanuele III', *NRS* XLVI (1962); idem, *Studi sulla nobiltà piemontese nell'epoca dell'assolutismo* (Turin 1963); M. Dossetti, 'Aspetti demografici del Piemonte occidentale nei secoli XVII e XVIII', *BSBS* LXXV (1977); L. Bulferetti, *Agricoltura, industria e commercio in Piemonte nel secolo XVIII* (Turin 1963); R. Davico, 'Pauperismo urbano e contadino in Piemonte sotto Vittorio Amedeo II', thesis for Faculty of Modern History, University of Turin, 1962–3; G. Levi, 'Sviluppo urbano e flussi migratori nel Piemonte del 1600', *Les migrations dans les pays méditerranéens au XVIIIe et au debut du XIXe siècle*, edited by Centre de la Méditerranée moderne et contemporaine (Nice 1973).
Industries: G. Arese, *L'industria serica piemontese dal secolo XVII alla metà del secolo XIX* (Turin 1922); M. Abrate, *L'industria siderurgica e meccanica in Piemonte dal 1831 al 1861* (Turin 1961) – its first chapter covers the eighteenth century; V. Castronovo, *L'industria laniera in Piemonte nel secolo XIX* (Turin 1964); idem, *L'industria cotoniera in Piemonte nel secolo XIX* (Turin 1965); L. Giordano, *L'università dell'arte del fustagno in Chieri* (Turin 1895).
Banking: E. Tesauro, *Istoria della veneranda Compagnia della fede cattolica sotto l'invocazione di San Paolo nell'augusta città di Torino* (2 vols., Turin 1701); M. Abrate, *L'Istituto Bancario San Paolo di Torino* (2 vols., Turin 1964); S. Foà, 'Banchi e banchieri ebrei nel Piemonte dei secoli scorsi', *Rassegna mensile di Israël* XXI (1955). On the general status of the Jews, see M. Anfossi, *Gli Ebrei in Piemonte* (Turin 1914).
Local studies: L. C. Bollea, *Storia de Bricherasio* (Turin 1928); D. Carutti, *Storia della città di Pinerolo* (revised ed., Pinerolo 1893); G. Claretta, *Cronistoria del municipio di Giaveno* (Turin 1875); C. Dionisotti, *Memorie storiche della città di Vercelli* (2 vols., Biella 1861–64); G. Doria, *Uomini e terre di un borgo collinare dal secolo XVI al XVIII* (Milan 1968) – deals with the village of Montaldeo; L. Fulcheri, 'I prezzi delle granaglie e dei principali generi di consumo a Mondovì nel secolo XVIII e XIX', thesis for Faculty of Modern History, University of Turin, 1970; F. Gabotto, *Storia di Cuneo* (Cuneo 1898; reprint 1973); R. Menochio, *Memorie della città di Carmagnola* (Turin 1890); S. Olmo, 'Emigrazione e comunità in Val Cervo nella prima metà del '700', *BSBS* LXXV (1977); A. Pittavino, *Storia di Pinerolo e del Pinerolese* (2 vols., Milan 1964); S. Pugliese, *Due secoli di vita agricola. Produzione e valore dei terreni. Contratti agrari, salari e prezzi nel Vercellese nei secoli XVIII e XIX* (Turin 1908) – a classic of its kind.
Turin and its development: F. Cognasso, *Storia di Torino* (Milan 1964); P. Gribaudi, *La posizione e lo sviluppo di Torino* (Turin 1911); C. Boggio, 'Gli architetti Carlo e Amedeo di Castellamonte e lo sviluppo edilizio di Torino nel secolo XVII', *Atti della società degli ingegneri ed architetti di Torino* (1895; printed separately, Turin 1896); L. Cibrario, *Storia di Torino* (2 vols., Turin 1846; reprint 1965); G. M. Busso, 'Evoluzione demografica in una parocchia torinese del '700: S. Maria di Pozzo Strada', *BSBS* LXVIII (1970); M. R. Duglip, 'Alfabetismo e società a Torino nel secolo XVIII', *Quaderni storici* XVII (1971); A. Cavallari-Murat, *Forma urbana ed architettura nella Torino barocca* (3 vols., Turin 1968).
24 *Theatrum Statuum Regiae Celsitudinis*

Sabaudiae Ducis Pedemontii Principis . . ., pub. by J. Blaeu, Amsterdam 1682, and reprinted 1700; cf. F. Rondolino, 'Per la storia di un libro', *Atti della società d'archeologia e belle arti per la provincia di Torino* VII (1907).

25 Figures for the growth of Turin compared to the other Piedmontese cities, from Beloch III, 279, and Prato, 'Censimenti', 354–355. *see chart below*.★

26 W. Blackley (ed.), *The Diplomatic Correspondence of the Rt. Hon. Richard Hill, Envoy Extraordinary from the Court of St James to the Duke of Savoy, in the Reign of Queen Anne: from July 1703 to May 1706* (2 vols., London 1845) II, 814: report on his mission in 1699.

27 Arese, 53; Bulferetti, *Agricoltura, industria e commercio*, 144 note, cites a survey from 1702 listing 423 looms in Turin for silk-weaving, employing 187 masters and 231 workmen, under the direction of 28 entrepreneurs.

28 T. Partenio, *Secoli della città di Cuneo* (Mondovì 1710; reprint Bologna 1968).

29 Figures based on the survey of 1719 for the revision of the land-tax; Einaudi, *Finanza*, 437.

30 Beloch III, 252–270; Prato, 'Censimenti', 335–340, and *Vita economica*, 3–9, 31–37; Woolf, 'Sviluppo', 12.

31 Figures from inquest of 1750; Prato, 'Censimenti', 357:

Biella	153 persons/km²
Ivrea	107
Alba	106
Casale	105
Turin (province)	99
Asti	87

Saluzzo	80
Acqui	73
Mondovì	73
Alessandria	72
Pinerolo	70
Cuneo	64
Susa	63
Vercelli	58
Val Sesia	52
Lomellina	47

32 Pugliese, 40–48; laws limiting cultivation near towns are in Duboin X, 773–780.

33 Einaudi, *Finanza*, 426–429; Pugliese, 123–127.

34 Woolf, *Studi sulla nobiltà piemontese*, passim.

35 L. Bulferetti, 'I Piemontesi più ricchi negli ultimi cento anni dell' assolutismo sabaudo', *Studi in onore di Gioacchino Volpe* (Florence 1958), 49–51.

36 Einaudi, *Finanza*, 426; Woolf, 'Sviluppo', 43 and *Studi sulla nobiltà piemontese*, 11.

37 Pugliese, 66–69. 1 *giornata* = 3,800 sq. metres, or about 0.93 acres.

III The Institutions of Government

General: institutional development is treated in some older histories of the Savoyard state such as E. Ricotti, *Storia della monarchia piemontese* (6 vols., Florence 1861–69); see also F. Sclopis di Salerano, 'Considerazioni storiche intorno alle antiche assemblee rappresentative del Piemonte e della Savoia', *HPM* XV (Turin 1884). More modern

★	1571	1612	1702/3	1725	1745	1765	1785
Turin	14,244	24,410	43,806	63,551	65,869	77,159	87,017

	1571	1612	1734	1774
Asti	8,339	9,592	13,269	14,365
Biella	5,847	7,101	5,487	8,259
Chieri	9,511	10,710	8,387	10,374
Cuneo	6,154	10,566	12,704	18,106
Fossano	8,973	9,997	11,647	14,398
Mondovì	—	10,903	6,975	17,614
Racconigi	4,414	5,085	7,515	11,689
Savigliano	—	9,586	11,101	13,363
Vercelli	8,645	10,257	7,842	12,556

works include P. Bodo, *Le consuetudini, la legislazione, le istituzioni del vecchio Piemonte* (Turin 1950), which despite its title is also concerned with local government; relevant sections in G. Astuti, *La formazione dello stato moderno in Italia* (2 vols., Turin 1957), and his chapter 'Legislazione e riforme in Piemonte nei secoli XVI–XVII' in *La monarchia piemontese nei secoli XVI–XVII* (Rome 1951). The best study is G. Quazza, *Le riforme in Piemonte nella prima metà del '700* (2 vols., Modena 1957); see also the chapter on Piedmont in his *La decadenza italiana nella storia europea. Saggi sul Sei-Settecento* (Turin 1971).

On taxation, besides the work of Einaudi, see M. Abrate, 'Elementi per la storia della finanza dello stato sabaudo nella seconda metà del XVII secolo', *BSBS* LXVII (1969); on the salt gabelle, G. Pérouse, 'Origine de la taille en Savoie, Bresse et Bugey', *Revue savoisienne* LII (1911); P. Baud, 'Une industrie d'état sous l'ancien régime. L'exploitation des salines de Tarentaise', *RHES* XXII (1934–35); M. Blanchard, 'Sel et diplomatie en Savoie et dans les Cantons Suisses aux XVIIe et XVIIIe siècles', *Annales ESC* XV, 6 (1960).

Magistracies: in addition to Burnier's work (already cited) on the Senate of Savoy, see C. Dionisotti, *Storia della magistratura piemontese* (2 vols., Turin 1881); M. Viora, *Il Senato di Pinerolo* (Turin 1927); G. Lombardi, 'Note sul controllo degli atti del sovrano negli stati sabaudi ad opera delle supreme magistrature nel periodo dell'assolutismo', *Annali della scuola speciale per archivisti e bibliotecari dell'*

università di Roma II, 1 (1962); E. Esmonin, 'Les intendants de Savoie au XVIIIe siècle', *Actes du 85e CNSS, Chambéry 1960* (Paris 1961), reprinted in his *Etudes sur la France des XVIIe et XVIIIe siècles* (Paris 1964); E. Stumpo, 'La vendita degli uffici nel Piemonte del '600', *AISIEMC* XXV–XXVI (1973–74); idem, *Finanza e stato moderno nel Piemonte del Seicento* (Rome 1979).

On representative institutions: H. G. Koenigsberger, 'The Parliament of Piedmont during the Renaissance, 1460–1560', *Recueil de travaux d'histoire et de philologie*, 3rd series, XLV (1952), pub. by University of Louvain (reprinted in his *Estates and Revolutions*, Ithaca N.Y. 1971).

1 Pérouse, 'Etat de la Savoie', 6–8.
2 Nicolas, *Savoie* II, 606–608: 8 Piedmontese, 1 Niçard, 4 French (appointed during the occupations), the rest Savoyards.
3 Pérouse, 'Etat de la Savoie', 13.
4 Nicolas, *Savoie* II, 606.
5 Einaudi, *Finanza*, 340–341.
6 Figures from ibid., 44, combined with population estimates from Beloch III, 286, and budget for 1700, give these proportions, *see chart below.*★
7 Pérouse, 'Etat de la Savoie', 46; cf. Einaudi, *Finanza*, 432–433.
8 Edict of 12 Jan. 1624, Borelli, 472; Bodo, 90; on the relationship between *referendarii* and intendants, Stumpo, 'Vendita', 193–196; Esmonin, 139; Duboin III, 1280 ff.; L. Bulferetti, 'L'elemento mercantilistico della formazione dell'assolutismo sabaudo', *BSBS* LIV (1956), 280, derives the intendants from the earlier provincial *direttori*.

★	*Population*		*Direct taxes*	
Piedmont	950,000	68%	3,404,017 lire	77.7% of total
Savoy	300,000	21%	871,834	20%
Nice	70,000	5%	50,000	1%
Aosta	60,000	4%	41,666★	1%
Oneglia	16,000	1%	ca. 15,000	0.3%
	1,396,000		4,382,517	

★Taxes for the duchy of Aosta doubled in 1701.

9 On the *sopravvivenza*, see E. Stumpo, art. 'Giuseppe Gaetano Giacinto Carron', in *DBI*.

10 Idem, art. 'Giovanni Carron' ibid.; 'Vendita', 198–199, 225–226.

11 This concept is developed in a series of articles by Bulferetti; in addition to the one cited in note 8 above, see 'Sogni e realtà nel mercantilismo di Carlo Emanuele II', *NRS* XXXVII (1953); 'Considerazioni generali sull' assolutismo mercantilistico di Carlo Emanuele II (1663–1675)', *Annali della Facoltà di Lettere e Filosofia e di Magistero della Universita di Cagliari* XIX, 2 (1952); 'La feudalità e il patriziato nel Piemonte di Carlo Emanuele II', ibid., XXI, 1 (1953); 'Assolutismo e mercantilismo nel Piemonte di Carlo Emanuele II', *MAST* 3rd series, II, 2 (1953).

12 Quazza, *Riforme* I, 94.

13 Nicolas, *Savoie* I, 30–38; Stumpo, 'Vendita', 248 note 1 gives these figures for the creation of offices, *see chart below*.★

IV The Ruler

Main sources for this character-study are Hill's correspondence (ed. Blackley) cited in ch. II, pt. 5, note 25; comte de Tessé, *Mémoires* (2 vols., Paris 1806); L-A. Blondel, 'Memorie aneddotiche sulla corte di Sardegna (Anecdotes sur la cour de Sardaigne)', ed. V. Promis, *MSI* XIII (1871). See also G. de Léris, *La comtesse de Verrue et la cour de Victor-Amédée II de Savoie* (Paris 1881).

1 Quazza, *Riforme* I, 13.

2 J-J. Rousseau, *Les confessions*, in *Oeuvres complètes* (ed. B. Gagnebin & M. Raymond; 3 vols., Paris 1959–64) I, 187.

3 Quoted by Léris, 11.

4 The line of Savoy-Nemours descended from Philippe, duke of Nemours, son of duke Philip II of Savoy, who established himself in France in the early sixteenth century. The dukes of Nemours were also counts of Genevois, and barons of Faucigny and Beaufort; on the death of Marie-Jeanne-Baptiste's uncle Henri, last duke of Nemours, in 1659, these appanages reverted to the ducal line; Carutti, *Vittorio Amedeo II*, 7.

5 On assuming power in 1684 Victor Amadeus banished his mother's reputed lover, the conte di Masino, to his estates and subsequently exiled him to Milan for life: M. Grosso & M. F. Mellano, 'Su una vicenda di Carlo Francesco Valperga conte di Masino', in their *Spunti e profili nella storia del Piemonte nei secoli XVII e XVIII* (Turin 1961), 76–81.

6 C. Rousset, *Histoire de Louvois et de son administration politique et militaire* (6th ed., 4 vols., Paris 1879) III, 182.

7 Tessé, *Mémoires* II, 2.

8 Hill, *Correspondence* II, 811.

9 Sourdis to the controller-general, 29 Dec. 1696, A. de Boislisle (ed.), *Correspondance des contrôleurs-généraux des finances avec les intendants des provinces* (3 vols., Paris 1874–97) I, 440.

10 Blondel, 'Anecdotes', 641, 644–645.

11 Tessé, *Mémoires* I, 151 (letter to Louis XIV, 20 Jan. 1699).

12 Blondel, 'Anecdotes', 508.

13 Ibid., 487, 647–648; cf. Tessé, *Mémoires* I, 166: 'the essential condition for succeeding with this prince is to seem inferior to him.'

14 Ibid. I, 153.

15 Blondel, 'Anecdotes', 481, 617. This story concerns Charles Emanuel's second wife, Polixena of Hesse-Rhèinfels, whom he married in 1724.

16 Tessé, *Mémoires* I, 168; cf. Léris's work on this love-affair.

17 V. Dainotti, 'Veggenti ed astrologhi intorno a Vittorio Amedeo II', *BSBS* XXXIV (1932).

18 M. Viora, *Le Costituzioni piemontesi 1723, 1729, 1772. Storia esterna della compilazione* (Turin 1928), chs. 20–21.

19 On music, M-T. Bouquet, 'Musique

★					
	1600–30	288 offices	(average	9.6 per year)	
	1631–50	197	(	10.4	)
	1651–70	167	(	8.8	)
	1671–90	104	(	5.5	)

et musiciens à Turin de 1648 à 1775', *MAST*, 4th series, XVII (1968); on painting, V. Viale, 'La pittura in Piemonte nel '700', *Torino* XXII, 6–11 (June–Nov. 1942); on architecture there is the classic work of A. E. Brinckmann, *Theatrum Novum Pedemontii* (Düsseldorf 1931); R. Wittkower, *Art and Architecture in Italy 1600–1750* (2nd ed., Harmondsworth 1965), esp. 275–282, with excellent bibliography; R. Pommer, *Eighteenth-Century Architecture in Piedmont: the Open Structures of Juvarra, Alfieri and Vittone* (New York 1967); L. Rovere et al., *Filippo Juvarra* (Milan 1937); A. Telluccini, *L'arte del architetto italiano Filippo Juvarra in Piemonte* (Turin 1926).

V The Regency and the 'Salt War' at Mondovì (1675–1684)

On the internal politics of the regency: A. Ferrero della Marmora, *Le vicende di Carlo di Simiane, marchese di Livorno poi di Pianezza tra il 1672 ed il 1706* (Turin 1862); idem, *Notizie sulla vita e sulle gesta militari di Carlo Emilio San Martino di Parella, ossia cronica militare aneddottica delle guerre in Piemonte dal 1672 al 1706* (Turin 1863); J. Lemoine, 'Le marquis de Saint-Maurice', *La revue de Paris* XVII, 5 (Sep. 1910), together with extracts from his correspondence in the next four numbers; idem (ed.), *Marquis de Saint-Maurice, lettres sur la cour de Louis XIV* (2 vols., Paris 1911–12); C. Contessa, 'Progetti economici della seconda Madama Reale fondati sopra un contratto nuziale (1678–1682)', *MSI* XLVIII (1915); idem, 'Aspirazioni commerciali intrecciate ad alleanze politiche della Casa di Savoia coll'Inghilterra nei secoli XVII e XVIII', *MAST*, 2nd series, LXIV, 3 (1914) – also pub. separately, Turin 1914; idem, 'La congiura del marchese di Parella (1682)', *BSBS* XXXVIII (1936). French policy can be followed in Rousset, cited above, and in H. de Beaucaire (ed.), *Recueil des instructions données aux ambassadeurs et ministres de France depuis la paix de Westphalie jusqu'à la Révolution: Savoie-Sardaigne*

et Mantoue (2 vols., Paris 1899).

On the 'Salt War' at Mondovì: T. Canavese, *Memoriale istorico della città di Mondovì dalla sua origine sino ai nostri tempi* (Mondovì-Breo 1851); G. Grassi, *Memorie istoriche della chiesa vescovile di Monteregale in Piemonte dall'erezione del vescovato sino a' nostri giorni* (2 vols., Turin 1789); S. Lombardini, 'Demografia e agricoltura nel Monregalese durante la guerra del sale', thesis for Faculty of Modern History, University of Turin (1972–73); idem, 'Equilibrio demografico e comunità in rivolta nel Piemonte del '600', *Miscellanea storica ligure* IX, 1 (1978); A. Michelotti, *Storia di Mondovì* (Mondovì 1920); F. Valla, *Saggio intorno alla guerra del sale, contributo alla storia di Mondovì* (Mondovì 1894). Details of military events can be found in A. de Saluces, *Histoire militaire du Piémont* (5 vols., Turin 1859).

1 Beaucaire, *Recueil* I, 110: Estrades to Louis XIV, 17 Jan. 1682. On the question of Casale, see C. Contessa, 'Per la storia di un episodio della politica italiana di Luigi XIV al tempo della pace di Nimega', *Rivista di storia, arte, archeologia della provincia di Alessandria* VI (1897).

2 Louvois to Pianezza, 16 Oct. 1681, Rousset III, 140.

3 Same to same, 26 Nov. 1681, ibid. III, 142.

4 Ibid. III, 118.

5 Contessa, 'Progetti', 157.

6 Edict by bishop Trucchi of Mondovì, 16 May 1668, forbidding clergy from carrying firearms, smuggling salt and harbouring bandits; Grassi, II, 484.

7 Rousset III, 151.

8 On 21 May 1682 Estrades offered troops and the regent suggested an alliance; ibid. III, 147.

9 Orders for Estrades to conclude the alliance, 20 Sep. 1682, in Beaucaire, *Recueil* I, 111–116; it was to last six years, and Louis XIV would pay 300,000 livres p.a. to increase the Savoyard army from 800 horse and 6,700 foot to 1,800 horse and 7,200 foot. French cavalry would be quartered in Piedmont until Casale's walls were complete. Once the Savoyard army was up to strength, the French forces in Piedmont would be reduced by one-third.

10 Ibid. I, 118: in Dec. 1682 Louis XIV proposed Mlle. de Valois, second daughter of the duke of Orleans, as Victor Amadeus's bride; cf. Rousset III, 165.

11 Contessa, 'Congiura di Parella', 120–123.

12 Rousset III, 179–181.

VI The First Years of Personal Rule and the Massacre of the Vaudois (1684–1687)

On foreign policy: D. Carutti, *Storia della diplomazia della corte di Savoia* (4 vols., Rome 1875–80) – vol. III and part of IV cover Victor Amadeus II's reign; R. Moscati (ed.), *Direttive della politica estera sabauda da Vittorio Amedeo II a Carlo Emanuele III* (Milan 1941).

On the Vaudois: A. Armand-Hugon, *Bibliografia valdese* (Turin-Torre Pellice 1952); A. Armand-Hugon & E. Rivoire, *Storia dei Valdesi* (2 vols., Turin 1974; vol. III not pub.) is the most recent general work. The first modern history of the Vaudois is A. Muston, *L'Israël des Alpes* (4 vols., Paris 1851; Eng. trans. Glasgow 1857), which despite its sometimes polemical tone is still valuable; E. Montet, *Histoire littéraire des Vaudois du Piémont* (Paris 1885; reprint Geneva 1977) is also useful. The best studies are a long series of articles by A. Pascal titled in general 'Le valli valdesi negli anni del martirio e della gloria (1686–1690)', in *BSSV* from vol. LXVIII (1937) onwards, each article titled individually. The final sections of this series were pub. separately as *Le valli durante la prigionia dei Valdesi* (pt. III: Torre Pellice 1966); *Le valli durante l'esilio dei Valdesi (1687–1689)* (pt. IV: 1966); *Le valli durante la guerra di rimpatrio dei Valdesi* (pt. V, 1–2, 1967). On the military aspects see E. A. de Rochas d'Aiglun, *Les vallées vaudoises. Etude de topographie et d'histoire militaire* (Paris 1880). The work of M. Viora is also essential, in particular his *Storia delle leggi sui Valdesi di Vittorio Amedeo II* (Bologna 1930); idem,

'Notizie e documenti sugli interventi diplomatici dell'Inghilterra in favore dei Valdesi durante il regno di Vittorio Amedeo II', *Studi Urbinati* I (1928); idem, 'Documenti sulle assistenze prestate dall'Olanda ai Valdesi durante il regno di Vittorio Amedeo II', *BSBS* XXX (1928).

1 A. Manno (ed.), 'Un mémoire autographe de Victor Amédée II', *Revue internationale* (Florence) I (1884), 95–96.

2 Report by Pighetti, envoy from Parma, 26 May 1686; Moscati, *Direttive*, 34–35.

3 On the prince of Carignano's marriage, Carutti, *Vittorio Amedeo II*, 107–109, and *Diplomazia* III, 127–132.

4 M. Viora, 'Su Innocenzo XI e la persecuzione dei Valdesi nel 1686', *BSSV* LV (1930).

5 On English interest in the Vaudois, see S. J. Woolf, 'English Public Opinion and the Duchy of Savoy', *The English Miscellany* (Rome) XII (1961).

6 Armand-Hugon & Rivoire, *Storia dei Valdesi* II, 139.

7 H. Arnaud, *Histoire de la glorieuse rentrée des Vaudois dans leurs vallées* (Cassel 1710; reprint Geneva 1879), 322. On Arnaud himself, P. Lantaret, 'Henri Arnaud', *BSSV* (1889).

8 Duboin II, 239; Viora, *Storia delle legge*, 37.

9 Louis XIV to d'Arcy, 7 Dec. 1685; Muston, *L'Israël des Alpes* III, 473.

10 Duboin II, 240–242; Viora, *Storia delle leggi*, 48; Pascal, 'Le valli valdesi negli anni del martirio e della gloria', *BSSV* LXIX (1938), 40 ff.

11 Armand-Hugon & Rivoire, *Storia dei Valdesi* II, 139, 142–147 (figures based on Pascal); A. Pascal, 'Valdesi a Torino sulla fine del secolo XVII', *BSBS* XXVI (1924); A. Pittavino, 'I prigionieri Valdesi nella cittadella di Pinerolo', *BSSV* LXXIII (1940).

12 M. Viora, 'Vercelli e la persecuzione dei Valdesi nel 1687', *Bollettino storico per la provincia di Novara* XX, 3 (1926); A. Pascal, 'Il confinamento dei Valdesi catolizzati nelle terre del Vercellese', ibid., XXIX, 1–3 (1935); Armand-Hugon & Rivoire, *Storia dei Valdesi* II, 145–166; cf. the same authors' *Gli esuli Valdesi in Svizzera 1686–1690* (Torre Pellice 1974), for details on the Vaudois in Switzerland.

VII Rupture with France (1687–1690)

Background: on relations with the Holy Roman Empire, G. Tabacco, *Lo stato sabaudo nel sacro impero romano* (Turin 1939); S. Pugliese, *Le prime strette dell'Austria in Italia* (Milan 1932); on relations with Venice, G. Claretta, 'Delle principali relazioni fra Venezia e Savoia nel secolo XVII', *Nuovo archivio veneto* IX–X (1895); C. Contessa, 'Per la storia della decadenza della diplomazia italiana nel secolo XVII. Aneddoti di relazioni veneto-sabaude', *MSI*, 3rd series, XI (1905); on Milan, C. Morandi, 'Lo stato di Milano e la politica di Vittorio Amedeo II', *AISIEMC* IV (1938: actually pub. 1940); cf. in general, idem, *Problemi storici italiani ed europei del XVIII e XIX secolo* (Milan 1937). On French policy in 1688–89, G. W. Symcox, 'Louis XIV and the Outbreak of the Nine Years War', R. M. Hatton (ed.), *Louis XIV and Europe* (London 1976).

1 V. Dainotti, 'Vittorio Amedeo II a Venezia nel 1687 e la lega di Augusta', *BSBS* XXXV (1933), explains the real purpose of the journey.

2 N. Brancaccio, *L'esercito del vecchio Piemonte. Gli ordinamenti. Parte I: Dal 1560 al 1814* (Rome 1923) 187–198, 219–220; cf. Saluces I, 258–263.

3 The regiments concerned were Nizza, Aosta, Marina.

4 Rousset IV, 280.

5 On the Glorieuse Rentrée, see Arnaud's account, cited above (ch. VI, note 7); T. G. Pons, 'Il ritorno dei Valdesi in patria secondo la relazione di Francesco Huc', *BSSV* LXXII (1939); G. Martinat, 'Il grande capo di una grande impresa militare' (Henri Arnaud), ibid.; A. Pascal, 'Lo sbarramento militare di Val Susa e la vittoria di Salbertano', and 'Il marchese Antonio di Feuquières e le sue campagne militari contro i Valdesi', ibid.; some of Feuquières's correspondence is in E. Gallois (ed.), *Lettres inédites des*

Feuquières, tirées des papiers de famille de madame la duchesse Decazes* (5 vols., Paris 1846); cf. B. le Bouyer de St-Gervais, *Mémoires et correspondence du maréchal de Catinat* (3 vols., Paris 1819), for this and subsequent campaigns.

In addition, Pascal's *Le valli durante la guerra di rimpatrio dei Valdesi*, cited above (ch. VI) is essential; cf. also his 'I Valdesi nei Grigioni ed il loro tentativo di rimpatrio (1689–90)', *BSBS* LXIV (1966), LXVII (1969).

6 Beaucaire, *Recueil* I, 135–142.

7 Rousset IV, 291–293.

8 Ibid. IV, 305–307.

9 Ibid. IV, 310–311; Pascal, *Guerra di rimpatrio* pt. 2, 708 ff.

10 Victor Amadeus II to conte Govone, 6 May 1690, ibid. pt. 2, 803–804.

11 Ibid. pt. 2, 919–953.

12 Treaties in Solar de la Marguérite, *Traités publics* II, 121–131. The governor of Milan was to provide 3,000 cavalry and 8–9,000 infantry; the Emperor was to support Victor Amadeus with 5–6,000 of his 'best troops'.

VIII The War in Piedmont (1690–1696)

General: there is no collection of Savoyard documents for the Nine Years War, comparable to the CGP for the War of the Spanish Succession. See F. Guasco, 'Vittorio Amedeo II nelle campagne dal 1691 al 1696 secondo un carteggio inedito', C. Contessa et al., *Studi su Vittorio Amedeo II* (Turin 1933); see also the memoirs of Tessé and Catinat, cited above. For the policies of Victor Amadeus and his allies, see H. J. van der Heim (ed.), *Het archief van den Raadpensionaris Anthonie Heinsius* (3 vols., The Hague 1867–80); C. F. Sirtema van Grovestins, *Guillaume III et Louis XIV. Histoire des luttes et rivalités politiques entre les puissances maritimes et la France dans la dernière moitié du XVIIe siècle* (8 vols., Paris 1868); N. Japikse (ed.), *Correspondentie van Willem III en van Hans Willem Bentinck, eersten Graaf van Portland* (5 vols., The Hague 1927–37); M. A. Thomson, 'Louis XIV and William III 1689–1697', *EHR* LCCVI (1961); useful narratives can be found in M. Braubach, *Prinz Eugen von Savoyen* (5 vols., Munich 1963); D. McKay, *Prince Eugene of Savoy* (London 1977); A. Legrelle, *La diplomatie française et la succession d'Espagne* (2nd ed., 6 vols., Braine-le-Comte 1895–99); comte d'Haussonville, *La duchesse de Bourgogne et l'alliance savoyarde sous Louis XIV* (4 vols., Paris n. d.); E. A. de Rochas d'Aiglun, *Documents inédits relatifs à l'histoire et à la topographie militaire des Alpes. La campagne de 1692 dans le Haut-Dauphiné* (Paris 1874); on the negotiations between Louis XIV and Victor Amadeus, besides Tessé's memoirs, see P. Canestrier, 'Comment M. de Tessé prépara en 1696 le traité de paix entre Louis XIV et Victor-Amédée II de Savoie', *Revue d'histoire diplomatique* XLVIII (1934); R. D. Handen, 'The End of an Era: Louis XIV and Victor Amadeus II', R. M. Hatton (ed.) *Louis XIV and Europe* (London 1976).

1 Clause XVI of the treaty with Spain, repeated in the treaties with Leopold I and William III.

2 Heinsius to Schomberg (William III's envoy at Turin), 11 Mar. 1692, van der Heim I, 206.

3 Solar de la Marguérite, *Traités publics* II, 144–154; the secret clause is on pp. 153–154. Anglo-Dutch subsidies totalled 15,775,480 lire (an average of 2,253,354 lire p. a.) for the years of war; Stumpo, 'Vendita', 256 note 1.

4 Tessé, *Mémoires* I, 18–25; Catinat, *Mémoires* II, 65–76; Handen, 244–245; Legrelle I, 438–440.

5 L. Winkler, *Der Anteil der Bayerischen Armee an den Feldzügen in Piemont 1691 bis 1696* (2 vols., Munich 1886–87) II, 125–126, prints the 'Mémoire' by prince Eugene outlining these plans.

6 Tessé, *Mémoires* I, 43.

7 Ibid. I, 55.

8 The edict had been drawn up already in 1692, but Innocent XII had warned Victor Amadeus not to publish it; Viora, *Storia delle leggi*, 202–241. Text of the edict is in Duboin II, 257–259.

9 Contessa, 'Aspirazioni', 21–25. The original Anglo-Savoyard trade treaty of 1669 is in Duboin XV, 1304–1313; the 1690 treaty did not mention trade. On the growth of English trade, R.

Davis, 'England and the Mediterranean 1570–1670', F. J. Fisher (ed.), *Essays in the Economic and Social History of Tudor and Stuart England in honour of R. H. Tawney* (Cambridge 1961): by 1669 one-third of English silk imports came from Italy; see also idem, 'English Foreign Trade 1660–1700', *Economic History Review*, 2nd series, VII (1954); further information may be gleaned from *The Journals of the House of Commons* (75 vols., London 1803) X, 359, 382, 700 ff.; XI, 9; XII, 210–230; *Calendar of State Papers, Domestic Series, William III* (11 vols., London 1895–1937) III, 253–254, 286–287.

10 Summary of Galway's letter, ibid. VI, 16.

11 Documentation on this crisis in AST 1a Sezione, *Annona*, mazzo 1 d'addizione; cf. A. Fossati, 'Una "società annonaria" per gli ammassi granari sotto Vittorio Amedeo II', *Torino* XXI, 12 (Dec. 1941); idem, 'Consegne ed ammassi nella politica granaria dello stato subaudo', ibid. XXI, 7 (July 1941); idem, 'La politica annonaria e degli ammassi di Vittorio Amedeo II', ibid. XXII, 1 (Jan. 1942); idem, 'Ricorsi storici di due secoli fà: nuovi tentativi sabaudi di una politica di ammassi', ibid. XXII, 2–3 (Feb-Mar. 1942).

12 Carutti, *Diplomazia* III, 223–227; Legrelle I, 446–449; Sirtema van Grovestins VI, 435.

13 Tessé, *Mémoires* I, 57–60; Handen, 251–252.

14 Instructions for conte Vernone, 2 May 1695, in C. Morandi (ed.), *Relazioni di ambasciatori sabaudi, genovesi e veneti durante il periodo della grande alleanza e della successione di Spagna (1693–1713)* (Bologna 1935), xxxiii–xxxiv.

15 Galway to Heinsius, 11 July 1695, van der Heim I, 222. Galway suspected a secret agreement between Victor Amadeus and the French garrison, but was not sure.

16 Tessé, *Mémoires* I, 70–72; Legrelle I, 451–454; Carutti, *Vittorio Amedeo II*, 194–200; Haussonville I, 65–76; treaty in J. Dumont, *Corps universel diplomatique du droit des gens* (8 vols., The Hague 1731) VII, pt. 2, 368–371;

marriage contract on pp. 371–375.

17 On 21 July 1696, van der Heim I, 226; cf. William III to Heinsius, 29 June 1696: 'je suis fort alarmé de cette négociation séparée dans le Piémont', Sirtema van Grovestins VI, 557.

18 Treaty in Dumont VII, pt. 2, 309–317; details of allied evacuation in Guasco, 309–317. See also Carutti, *Diplomazia* III, 248–249.

IX The First Period of Reform (1696–1703)

For state institutions see the items listed for ch. III. On the question of Church-state relations, P. C. Boggio, *Lo stato e la Chiesa in Piemonte* (2 vols., Turin 1854). For education, A. Bersano, 'Per la storia delle scuole medie negli antichi stati sardi', *Rivista pedagogica* XXVIII, 5 (Sep. 1935); P. Boccard, 'Simples notes historiques sur le collège d'Evian avant la Révolution française', *14e CSSS, Evian 1896* (Evian 1897); A. de Jussieu, *Histoire de l'éducation primaire en Savoie*, Chambéry 1875; D. Féliciangeli, 'L'éducation dans le comté de Nice sous l'Ancien Régime sarde', *L'information historique* XXXVII (May 1975); J. F. Gonthier, 'L'instruction publique dans le diocèse de Genève (aujourd'hui d'Annecy) avant 1789', *8e CSSS, Thonon 1886* (Thonon 1886); G. Mantellino, *La scuola primaria in Piemonte e particolarmente in Carmagnola dal secolo XIV alla fine del secolo XIX* (Carmagnola 1909).

1 J. Addison, *Remarks on Several Parts of Italy, & C. In the Years 1701, 1702, 1703* (London 1705), 444.

2 Davico, 'Pauperismo', 10–68.

3 Stumpo, 'Vendita' 262: interest payments totalled 1,553,368 lire p.a., or 21 percent of revenue.

4 On Gropello, Einaudi, *Finanza*, 5 note 2; Quazza, *Riforme* I, 23–26.

5 On Mellarède, ibid. I, 26–32; D. Carutti, 'Relazione sulla corte d'Inghilterra del consigliere di stato Pietro Mellarède', *MSI* XXIV (1885); Frutaz, 51; art. 'Mellarède' by C. Morandi in *Enciclopedia italiana* (36 vols., Milan 1929–39).

6 Duboin IX, 8–14.

7 Quazza, *Riforme* I, 65; cf. Esmonin, 139–140; Duboin III, 1387 & IX, 6. Stumpo, 'Vendita', 146 observes that 'nothing prevents us from concluding that already in 1624 the office of intendant was well defined and extremely important'.

8 'Istruzioni agl' intendenti delle provincie di Piemonte', 31 Mar. 1697, Duboin IX, 20–23.

9 Quoted in Burnier II, 108–109; cf. Nicolas, *Savoie* I, 73, & II, 606.

10 Einaudi, *Finanza*, 93–97.

11 Figures for 1700 from ibid., 340–341; for 1689 from Abrate, 'Elementi', 397; cf. Stumpo, *Finanza e stato moderno*, 38–40.

12 Quoted in Marini, 651.

13 Einaudi, *Finanza*, 68–71, 230–236.

14 Patenti, 12 June 1697, Duboin XX, 149–150; Einaudi, *Finanza*, 65.

15 On the *catasto* for the county of Nice, ibid., 98–101; Bordes (ed.), *Histoire de Nice*, 170–172; Costamagna, 'Libertés communales', 411–412; M. Bloch, 'Les plans parcellaires. Le cas de la Savoie et du comté de Nice', *Annales* I (1929). The method to be used is detailed in the instruction for Mellarède, 15 Jan. 1702, Duboin XX, 988–999.

16 Quoted in Carutti, *Vittorio Amedeo II*, 243.

17 Bergès, 54–60.

18 Quoted in Boggio I, 57.

19 Duboin XX, 149–154, XXIII, 214–218, for these documents; cf. Carutti, *Diplomazia* III, 593–594; Einaudi, *Finanza*, 56–57.

20 For events at Mondovì, Michelotti, 410 ff.; Canavese, 247 ff.

21 Davico, 'Pauperismo', 113 note 1.

X The Spanish Succession and the Approach of War

Much of the bibliography for this chapter is listed in chs. VII & VIII above, but for the negotiations at this time see P. Grimblot (ed.), *William III and Louis XIV. Letters of William III and Louis XIV and their Ministers 1697–1700* (2 vols., London 1848); C. Contessa, 'I regni di Napoli e di Sicilia nelle aspirazioni italiane di Vittorio Amedeo II', in *Studi su Vittorio Amedeo*

II (Turin 1933); A. Bozzola, 'Giudizi e previsioni della diplomazia medicea sulla Casa di Savoia durante la guerra di successione spagnuola', ibid. On the problems of nearby fiefs and enclaves, see V. Barale, *Il principato di Masserano e il marchesato di Crevacuore* (Biella 1966); A. D. Perrero, 'Un carceriere vercellese del tempo antico. A proposito dell'acquisto per parte della Casa di Savoia del feudo di Desana 1683–1701', *Curiosità e richerche di storia subalpina* III (Turin 1879).

1 In response to an approach from Victor Amadeus, Louis XIV suggested in Ap. 1698 that the former be given Milan; Louis XIV to Tallard, 17 Ap. 1698, Grimblot I, 387; in a letter to Portland, 24 Ap., William III dismissed this as 'une raillerie', Japikse I, 1, 292–293.

2 Hill, *Correspondence* II, 810–811.

3 Instruction for la Tour, July 1700, Moscati, 63–67.

4 Solar de la Marguérite, *Traités publics* II, 194–203: in return for subsidies of 600,000 écus a year Victor Amadeus was to provide 8,000 infantry and 2,500 cavalry.

5 Carutti, *Vittorio Amedeo II*, quoting the duke's letter to Priè of 11 Ap. 1701. Nevertheless the Aulic Council at Vienna declared him a felonious vassal for allying with France (though his status as a vassal was doubted by certain members of the court): Pugliese, *Prime strette*, 200.

6 *CGP* IV, xxx: Auersperg's mission had been decided in May 1703.

7 Hill's Instructions, 26 July 1703 (OS), Hill, *Correspondence* I, 2–6; new instructions were issued 9 Nov. 1703 (OS), ibid., 57–60. On the importance that the British government attached to these negotiations, see Marlborough to Godolphin, 8/19 July & 2/13 Aug. 1703, H. Snyder (ed.), *The Marlborough-Godolphin Correspondence* (3 vols., Oxford 1975) I, 218–219.

8 Estimated figures in *CGP* I, 24–46.

9 On the difficulties in concluding the treaty, ibid. IV, xxxi–xxxiii; this accounts for the difference between the texts of the treaty printed by G. de Lamberty, *Mémoires pour servir à l'histoire du XVIIIe siècle* (14 vols.,

Amsterdam 1725–40) II, 547–562, and Solar de la Marguérite, *Traités publics* II, 203–219.

10 Louis XIV to Phélipeaux (ambassador at Turin), 5 Oct. 1703, H. Fazy, *Les Suisses et la neutralité de la Savoie 1703–1704* (Geneva 1895), 5; cf. C. Morandi, 'La politica di Vittorio Amedeo II e le proposte francesi di pace', in his *Problemi storici*.

XI The War of the Spanish Succession in Piedmont

See the bibliographies for chs. VII, VIII and X. For the conduct of the war by the Habsburgs, see (in addition to Braubach), C. W. Ingrao, *In Quest and in Crisis: Emperor Joseph I and the Habsburg Monarchy* (W. Lafayette, Ind., 1977); K. O. von Aretin, 'Kaiser Joseph I zwischen Kaisertradition und österreichischer Grossmachtpolitik', *Historische Zeitschrift* CCXV, 3 (1972). On British policy, see F. Sclopis di Salerano, 'Delle relazioni politiche tra la dinastia di Savoia e il governo britannico 1240–1815', *MAST* XIV (1854); H. Richmond, *The Navy as an Instrument of Policy 1558–1727* (Cambridge 1953); J. H. Corbett, *England in the Mediterranean 1603–1713* (2nd ed., 2 vols., London 1917). The campaigns in northern Italy can be followed in J. J. G. Pelet & F. E. de Vault, *Mémoires militaires relatifs à la succession d'Espagne sous Louis XIV* (11 vols., Paris 1835–62); cf. also the duke of Berwick's *Mémoires écrits par lui-même* (Paris 1778) for the later campaigns. On the siege of Turin, A. Manno, 'Relazioni e documenti sull'assedio di Torino nel 1706', *MSI* XVII (1878), and vol. VI of *CGP* for various accounts and bibliography; C. Pio de Magistris (ed.), 'Lettere di Vittorio Amedeo II nel periodo dell'assedio di Torino del 1706', C. Contessa et al., *Studi su Vittorio Amedeo II* (Turin 1933). The most recent account of the campaign of 1706 is P. Pieri, 'L'evoluzione dell'arte militare nei secoli XV, XVI e XVII e la guerra del secolo XVIII', in *Nuove questioni di storia moderna* (2 vols., Milan 1966). For particular aspects of the war, E. Bonjour, *Die Schweiz und Savoyen im Spanischen Erbfolgekrieg* (Berne 1927); E. Mosca, 'La provincia di Alba e la comunità di Bra durante la guerra di successione spagnola', *BSBS* LV (1957); A. Armand-Hugon, 'La repubblica di San Martino', *BSSV* LXXXIV (1945).

1 Brancaccio I, 184–212; Saluces I, 272.

2 Hill's letters (Dec. 1703–Mar. 1704) list payments of 100,000 écus, in addition to the regular bi-monthly subsidies, which began in Oct. 1703: Hill, *Correspondence* I, 300 ff.

3 Instruction for Maffei, 29 Oct. 1703, *CGP* V, 273–276; treaties in Solar de la Marguérite, *Traités publics* II, 220–239, 248. The treaty with the States-General was not signed until 21 Jan. 1705.

4 Hill's second instructions, 9 Nov. 1703 (OS), Hill, *Correspondence* I, 59.

5 Nottingham to Hill, 19 Nov. 1703 (OS), ibid. I, 62; cf. also pp. 66 and 80. Victor Amadeus was reluctant to join the embargo: Hill to Nottingham, 1 Feb., 5 Feb., 25 Mar. 1704, pp. 311, 315, 336.

6 Solar de la Marguérite, *Traités publics* II, 235–236; cf. Viora, *Storia delle leggi*, 250–253.

7 Instructions for Mellarède, 4 Oct. 1703, *CGP* VI, 398–400; cf. Bonjour, 13 ff.; D. Carutti, 'Della neutralità della Savoia nel 1703. Narrazione e documenti', *MAST*, 2nd series, XX (1863).

8 Hill to Hedges, 25 July 1704; Hill, *Correspondence* I, 391.

9 Hill to Marlborough, 30 June 1704, ibid. I, 375.

10 Instruction for Maffei, 15 Jan. 1706, *CGP* V, 450–459.

11 Hill estimated in Nov. 1705 that Victor Amadeus had 11,800 men, including the Imperial contingent; Hill, *Correspondence* II, 660–661.

12 Figures from Pieri, 1159 ff. Braubach II, 153, says that by mid-May Eugene's army had 'only half its strength of 60,000 men'. Cf. also the figures in *CGP* V, xcviii.

13 Victor Amadeus to conte Tarino (envoy at Vienna), 17 Nov. 1706, ibid. V, 74–75.

14 On this agreement, the Pactum Mutuae Successionis of 1703, see Ingrao, 91–93.

15 Joseph I to Victor Amadeus, 22 Jan. 1707, *CGP* V, 242.

16 Revenues in Einaudi, *Finanza*, 306–319; Beloch III, 275–276, estimates the area of the new territories as 4,328 sq. km. Contessa, 'Regni', 72 note 1, cites budget figures from 1710, which show that the new territories provided 849,721 lire out of a total of 8,804,778 lire, or 9.65 percent.

17 A. Forneron, 'L'articolo segreto sul Pragelato nel trattato di alleanza colle Potenze Marittime', *BSSV* LXX (1938); Muston III, 470 ff.

XII Negotiations for the Peace of Utrecht (1709–1713)

Besides the works listed in chs. VII, VIII, X and XI, see A. Baudrillart, *Philippe V et la cour d'Espagne* (5 vols., Paris 1890–1901); M. Gasco, 'La politica sabauda a Utrecht nella "relazione Mellarède"', *RSI* (1935); A. Bozzola, 'Venezia e Savoia al congresso di Utrecht (1712–1713)', *BSBS* XXXV (1933); E. Robiony, 'Un' ambizione mal nota della Casa di Savoia' *ASI*, 5th series, XXXII (1903). On French policy, F. Masson (ed.), *Journal inédit de Jean-Baptiste Colbert, marquis de Torcy . . . pendant les années 1709, 1710 et 1711* (Paris 1884); Torcy, *Mémoires* (ed. A. Petitot & L. J. N. Monmerqué, in *Collection des mémoires relatifs à l'histoire de France*, LXVIII–LXIX, Paris 1828); P. Léon, 'Economie et diplomatie. Les relations commerciales delphino-piémontaises au début du XVIII siècle (1700–1713)', *CH* V, 3 (1960). For English policy, B. C. Brown (ed.), *The Letters and Diplomatic Instructions of Queen Anne* (London 1935); L. G. Wickham Legg (ed.), *British Diplomatic Instructions 1689–1789: vol. II: France 1689–1721* (London 1925); H. N. Fieldhouse, 'St John and Savoy in the War of the Spanish Succession', *EHR* L (1935); idem, 'A Note on the Negotiations for the Peace of Utrecht', *American Historical Review* XL (1935); A. D. MacLachlan, 'The Road to Peace 1710–1713', G. Holmes (ed.), *Britain after the Glorious*

Revolution 1689–1714 (London 1969); anon., *Memoirs of the Life and Ministerial Conduct of the late Lord Viscount Bolingbroke* (London 1752); R. Walpole, *A Report from the Committee of Secrecy appointed by the House of Commons to examine several Books and Papers . . . relating to the late Negotiations of Peace and Commerce* (London 1715).

1 Decree of English and Dutch representatives, 27 June 1712, Solar de la Marguérite, *Traités publics* II, 272–275.

2 On British trade, see the statistics in E. B. Schumpeter, *English Overseas Trade Statistics 1697–1808* (Oxford 1960), which are however only roughly indicative. W. Cobbett, *Parliamentary History* (36 vols., London 1806–1819) VI, 631, prints a report of 1708 that states the duties on trade with Venice, Genoa and Livorno amounted to £300,000 p.a. Some figures on British trade at Livorno are in G. Naselli, 'Legazione a Londra del conte G. A. Gazzola dal 1713 al 1716', *Atti e memorie della R. deputazione di storia patria per le provincie modenesi e parmensi* VII (1874). On trade to Genoa, L. Bulferetti & C. Costantini, *Industria e commercio in Liguria nell'età del Risorgimento 1700–1861* (Milan 1966), 121–133; on trade with southern Italy, H. G. Koenigsberger, 'English Merchants in Naples and Sicily in the Seventeenth Century', *EHR* LXII (1947).

3 Boyle to Townshend, 24 June 1709 (OS), Wickham Legg, 14.

4 Victor Amadeus to del Borgo, 13 Ap. 1709, Contessa, 'Regni', 66.

5 Ibid., 68–71.

6 Peterborough to St John, 7 May 1711, Sclopis, 'Delle relazioni', 145–150; Victor Amadeus's reflections are in Moscati, 112–117; cf. Carutti, *Vittorio Amedeo II*, 360–364.

7 Instructions for lord Strafford and bishop Robinson, 11 Nov. 1711, Wickham Legg, 31–32; wrongly dated to 1712 by Brown, 385–389.

8 Quoted in Carutti, *Diplomazia* III, 404.

9 Ibid. III, 415–416; cf. the 'Mémoire' (1700) on the diversion of Alpine traffic, Beaucaire, *Recueil* I, 273.

10 Baudrillart I, 505–507; Torcy,

Mémoires (Petitot & Monmerqué LXIX), 158–160.

11 Carutti, *Diplomazia* III, 430.

12 Quoted in Walpole, *Report*, 26; cf. *Memoirs of . . . Bolingbroke*, 237.

13 This claim was through his wife, Anne of Orleans, granddaughter of Charles I. Her protest against the Act of Succession (Ap. 1701) is in Lamberty I, 503; Carutti, *Vittorio Amedeo II*, 359 note 1, quotes Mellarède's 'Relation' of the Utrecht negotiations on 'the favourable sentiments that she has for Your Royal Highness, not only in recognition of the important services that you have rendered to the Common Cause, . . . but also because Your Royal Highness, my lady the Duchess Royal and my lords the Sovereign Princes are her closest relatives'.

14 Despatch of 16 Nov. 1712, quoted in Walpole, *Report*, 26.

15 Contessa, 'Aspirazioni', 29–30.

16 Solar de la Marguérite, *Traités publics* II, 281–294.

17 See the pamphlet *Compendioso ragguaglio delle solenne feste*, ACT, 1176, and also nos. 1178–79; G. A. Gianelli, *Fedele, e distinta relazione . . .* (1713), BR, Misc. 302, no. 5.

18 P. de Rege di Donato, 'Stato generale dei danni patiti dal Piemonte nella guerra di successione di Spagna dall'ottobre 1703 a tutto il 1710', *CGP* X, 367–436; in general, G. Prato, *Il costo della guerra di successione spagnola e le spese pubbliche in Piemonte (1703–1708)* (Turin 1907), for the effect on the Piedmontese economy. For the evidence from local councils' records, F. Gaziello, 'Les régistres d'*Ordinati di Consiglio* de Saorge et la guerre de succession d'Espagne', *RR* VIII, 3 (1968); F. Eusebio, 'Alba e suo territorio nella guerra del 1703–1710. Cronaca composta degli estratti dagli "Ordinati Generali" del Comune', *CGP* X. Einaudi, *Finanza*, 364–367, sums up the effects of war taxation.

19 On Pietro Micca, Carutti, *Vittorio Amedeo II*, 324–325: his widow was refused a pension and granted merely a double ration of army bread for life as the reward for his sacrifice; the legend came later. On disaffection at

Mondovì in 1706, when the city greeted the French with joy, see Saluces V, 185. On resistance to the new tax of the *macina* imposed for the war, Einaudi, *Finanza*, 159.

20 Brancaccio I, 184.

21 G. Quazza, *Il problema italiano e l'equilibrio europeo 1720-1738* (Turin 1965), estimates the cost of the army at 54.2 percent of state expenditure in the 1720s. The table of revenue for 1731 printed by Bachi shows that the army, artillery and fortifications accounted for 7,161,050 lire out of a total of 15,880,051; Abrate, 'Elementi', 397, indicates 2,577,808 lire for the military out of a total of 7,534,841 lire in 1689.

22 Figures for subsidies in Einaudi, *Finanza*, 350-358; cf. also pp. 278-283.

XIII Sicily, Sardinia and Foreign Relations to 1730

Many works cited in the preceding chapter are relevant here, particularly Quazza, *Il problema italiano*. See also A. Baraudon, *La maison de Savoie et la triple alliance (1713-1722)* (Paris 1896); A. Bazzoni, 'Relazioni diplomatiche tra la Casa di Savoia e la Prussia nel secolo XVIII', *ASI*, 3rd series, XV (1872); D. Carutti, 'Lettere di Vittorio Amedeo II al conte Morozzo della Rocca, ambasciatore a Madrid dal 1714 al 1717', *MSI* X (1870); E. Morozzo della Rocca, 'Lettere di Vittorio Amedeo II a Gaspare Maria conte di Morozzo ... suo ambasciatore a Madrid dal settembre 1713 al principio del 1717', ibid. XXVI (1887); L. la Rocca, 'Una proposta di lega italiana al re di Sicilia nel 1719', *Archivio storico siciliano*, new series, XXXII (1907); R. Moscati, 'La politica estera degli stati italiani dalla caduta di Alberoni al terzo trattato di Vienna (1720-1731)', *RSR* XXXV (1948); C. A. Garufi (ed.), *Rapporti diplomatici tra Filippo V e Vittorio Amedeo II di Savoia, nella cessione del regno di Sicilia ... 1712-1720* (Palermo 1914); A. Tallone, *Vittorio Amedeo II e la quadruplice alleanza* (Turin 1914: reprinted

in *Studi su Vittorio Amedeo II*, Turin 1933); F. Venturi, 'Il Piemonte dei primi decenni del Settecento nelle relazioni dei diplomatici inglesi', *BSBS* LIV (1956).

For relations with France the diplomatic correspondence edited by A. Manno et al. (cited above) is essential. For relations with Britain, see G. C. Gibbs, 'Parliament and the Treaty of Quadruple Alliance', J. S. Bromley & R. M. Hatton (eds.), *William III and Louis XIV. Essays by and for Mark A. Thomson* (Liverpool 1968); R. M. Hatton, *Diplomatic Relations between Great Britain and the Dutch Republic 1714-21* (London 1950); idem, *George I, Elector and King* (London 1978); D. McKay, 'Bolingbroke, Oxford and the Defence of the Utrecht Settlement in Southern Europe', *EHR* LXXXVI (1971); L. G. Wickham Legg (ed.), *British Diplomatic Instructions 1689-1789. Vol. VI: France 1727-1744* (London 1930); B. Williams, *Stanhope, a Study in Eighteenth-Century Diplomacy* (Oxford 1932).

On Savoyard rule in Sicily, see V. E. Stellardi (ed.), *Il regno di Vittorio Amedeo II di Savoia in Sicilia dall'anno 1713 al 1719* (3 vols., Turin 1862); G. Catalano, *Studi sulla legazia apostolica in Sicilia* (Reggio Calabria 1973); I. la Lumia, 'La Sicilia sotto Vittorio Amedeo di Savoia', *ASI* 3rd series, XIX, XX, XXI (1874-75); L. la Rocca, 'Relazione al re Vittorio Amedeo II di Savoia sulle condizioni economiche, sociali e politiche della Sicilia alla fine del dominio spagnuolo', *Archivio storico per la Sicilia orientale* XI (1914); G. Raffiotta, *Gabelle e dogane a Palermo nel primo trentennio del '700* (Palermo 1962); P. Revelli, 'Vittorio Amedeo II e le condizioni geografiche della Sicilia', *Rivista geografica italiana* XVII, XVIII (1910-11); L. Riccobene, *Sicilia ed Europa dal 1700 al 1735* (Palermo 1976); G. Spata (ed.), 'I primi atti costituzionali dell'augusta Casa di Savoia ordinati in Palermo', *MSI* X (1870).

On Sardinia the best study is R. Palmarocchi, *Sardegna sabauda. Vol. I: Il regno di Vittorio Amedeo II* (Cagliari 1936: subsequent vols. never apparently pub.); idem, 'Il regno di Vittorio Amedeo II', *RSR* XXII (1935); see also A. Bernardino, *Tributi e bilanci in Sardegna nel primo ventennio della sua annessione al Piemonte (1721–1740)* (Turin 1921); L. la Rocca, 'La cessione del regno di Sardegna alla Casa Sabauda', *MSI*, 3rd series, X (1905); A. Marongiù, *I Parlamenti di Sardegna nella storia e nel diritto pubblico comparato* (Rome 1931); there are relevant chapters in recent general histories, notably F. Loddo Canepa, *La Sardegna dal 1478 al 1793* (2 vols., Sassari 1974), and R. Carta Raspi, *Storia della Sardegna* (Milan 1977). There is a good survey of the economy in A. Boscolo, L. Bulferetti & L. del Piano, *Profilo storico economico della Sardegna dal riformismo settecentesco al "Piano di Rinascita"* (Padua 1963).

1 'Breve ragguaglio del Reale ingresso in Palermo' (1713), BR, Misc 302, no. 6; see also nos. 9–11, 13; anon., *Récit de l'entrée royale que leurs Majestés Victor Amédée roi de Sicile et la Reine Anne de France ont faite à Palerme le 21 Décembre 1713* (Turin 1714).

2 Revelli XVIII, 68; la Lumia XX, 133–134, gives a total of 1,123,163.

3 Ibid. XIX, 92, and XX, 101–102, 145; Garufi, xv–xvii, explains the anomalous position of these fiefs; map of their location in Revelli XVIII, 81.

4 The turbulent bishop Tedeschi of Lipari is probably the author of the anon. *Istoria della pretesa monarchia di Sicilia* (Rome 1715); the monarchy's position is defended by G. B. Caruso, *Discorso istorico-apologetico della monarchia di Sicilia* (ed. G. M. Mira, Palermo 1863). This was originally pub. in 1715, and was then reissued, along with another treatise by a Sicilian cleric (Settimo's *Discorso della sovranità dei re di Sicilia*) in the Gallican canonist Dupin's *Défense de la monarchie de Sicile* (Amsterdam 1716).

5 M. Martin, 'The Secret Clause, Britain and Spanish Ambitions in Italy 1712–1731', *European Studies Review* VI, 4 (Oct. 1976).

6 A. Tallone, 'Diritti e pretese sul marchesato del Finale al principio del secolo XVIII', *BSBS* I (1896); idem, 'La vendita del marchesato del Finale

nel 1713 e la diplomazia piemontese', ibid. I–II (1896–97).

7 Victor Amadeus to Morozzo, 1 Feb. 1716, Carutti, 'Lettere', 212–213; Baraudon, 116.

8 Williams, 277, accepts Stanhope's account, as does Hatton, *George I*, 222–223, 233; Trivié's despatches, 16 & 29 Feb. 1716, are in AST, Prima Sezione, *Lettere Ministri: Gran Bretagna*, mazzo 20. (I am most grateful to Dr. Sandro Lombardini for checking these references for me.) Stair's approaches in Paris may be followed in A. Manno et al., *Relazioni diplomatiche della monarchia di Savoia . . . 1559–1814. Francia, Periodo III, 1713–1719* (3 vols., Turin 1886–91) II, 101–123, especially Perrone (Savoyard ambassador) to Victor Amadeus, 31 Jan. 1716.

9 Tallone, 'Quadruplice alleanza' (1933 ed.), 189.

10 Ibid., 194.

11 Baraudon, 230–238.

12 Tallone, 'Quadruplice alleanza' (1933 ed.), 226–237.

13 Carutti, *Diplomazia* III, 550.

14 J. L. Cranmer-Byng (ed.), *Pattee Byng's Journal 1718–1720* (London 1950), 292.

15 Carutti, *Vittorio Amedeo II*, 437, gives a total of 309,996.

16 Bernardino, 101–102.

17 M. Viora, 'Note sulla quistione dell'osservanza delle feste della Chiesa cattolica per parte dei Valdesi dopo il ristabilimento del 1690', *BSSV* LII (1928), 61–64; idem, 'Due interventi di Federico di Svezia presso Vittorio Amedeo II in favore dei Valdesi', *ASI*, 7th series, XII (1929).

18 Venturi, 'Il Piemonte', 247 ff.; Viora, 'Interventi diplomatici dell' Inghilterra', 105 ff.

19 T. Gay, 'Les derniers Vaudois du Pragela', *BSSV* XXVII (1910); Muston III, 537 ff.; Viora, *Storia delle leggi*, 265 ff.

20 Quoted in Venturi, 'Il Piemonte', 244. On trade relations see G. H. Jones, 'English Diplomacy and Italian Silk in the Time of Lombe', *Bulletin of the Institute of Historical Research* XXXIV (1961); G. Prato, 'L'espansione commerciale inglese nel primo Settecento in una relazione di un inviato sabaudo',

Miscellanea di studi storici in onore di A. Manno (2 vols., Turin 1912).
1 Quazza, *Problema italiano*, 135–136.

XIV The High Tide of Reform (1713–1730)

Many of the works listed in chs. III and X will be relevant here. On the *perequazione*, see also M. Bruchet, *Notice sur l'ancien cadastre de Savoie* Annecy 1896; reprint 1977); P. Gui-chonnet, 'Le cadastre savoyard de 1738 et son utilisation pour les recherches d'histoire et de géographie sociale', *RGA* (1955); J. Nicolas, 'Mobilité foncière et cadastre en Savoie au XVIIIe siècle', *Actes du 90e CNSS, Nice 1965* (2 vols. Paris 1966).

On charity reform, C. Joret, 'Le père Guevarre et les bureaux de charité au XVIIIe siècle', *AM* IV (1889); G. Prato, 'Il problema dell'assistenza legale in Francia e in Piemonte prima della rivoluzione', *Rivista di diritto pubblico* (1909); I. Bernardi, *Il Regio Ospizio di Carità in Torino e ordinamenti negli stati sardi per prevenire e soccorrere la indigenza* (Turin 1857); A. Guevarre, *La mendicità sbandita col sovvenimento dei poveri* (Turin 1718).

On the intellectual background and educational reform, F. Venturi, *Studi sull'Europa illuminista. I. Alberto Radi-cati di Passerano* (Turin 1954); G. Ricu-perati, 'Bernardo Andrea Lama professore e storiografo nel Piemonte di Vittorio Amedeo II', *BSBS* LXVI (1968); idem, 'L'università di Torino e le polemiche contro i professori in una relazione curialista del 1731', ibid. LXIV (1966); T. Vallauri, *Storia delle università degli studi del Piemonte* (4 vols., Turin 1845–46); F. Cognasso, 'I primi risultati della riforma vittoriana dell'università di Torino in una relazione del d'Aguirre', *Atti dell'Accademia delle scienze di Torino* LXXVII, 2 (1941–42); M. Roggero, 'La scuola secondaria nel Piemonte da Vittorio Amedeo II a Carlo Emanuele III. Crescita ed involu-zione di un modello innovativo', *BSBS* LXXII (1974); L. Falco, R. Plantamura & S. Ranzato, 'Le istitu-zioni per l'istruzione superiore in Torino dal XV al XVIII secolo. Il

Collegio dei Nobili', ibid. LXXI (1973); and the same authors' 'Il Collegio delle Provincie', ibid. LXXII (1974); see also vol. LXXVI (1978), which is entirely devoted to the University of Turin in the eighteenth century, and has articles by D. Car-panetto, D. Balani and F. Turletti.

On the Church, L. Allegra, *Ricerche sulla cultura del clero in Piemonte* (Turin 1978); G. della Porta, 'Appunti di bibliografia giurisdizionalista piemon-tese', *Miscellanea di studi storici in onore di Antonio Manno* (2 vols., Turin 1912); P. Stella, *Il Giansenismo in Italia. Piemonte* (vol. I, 1–2; Zurich 1966–70); idem, *Studi sul giansenismo* (Bari 1972); idem, *Giurisdizionalismo e giansenismo all'università di Torino nel secolo XVIII* (Turin 1958); P. Zovatto, *Introduzione al giansenismo italiano* (Trieste 1970); A. Barbero, F. Ramelli, A. Torre, *Materiali sulla religiosità dei laici. Alba 1698–Asti 1742* (Turin-Cuneo 1981).

1 Nicolas, *Savoie* II, 622–628.
2 Vermale, 154–157.
3 Nicolas, *Savoie* II, 630.
4 Bruchet, 'Instructions', 286–287.
5 Patenti, 16 June 1719, Duboin III, 1006–1008; Carutti, *Vittorio Amedeo II*, 452–455.
6 A. Manno, *Il patriziato subalpino* (reprint, Bologna 1972, 2 vols.) I, vii.
7 Viora, *Le costituzioni*, ch. 20.
8 Editto, 17 Feb. 1717, Duboin VIII, 331–348; Quazza, *Riforme* I, 55–60.
9 Editto, 11 Ap. 1717, Duboin VIII, 567–608; Quazza, *Riforme* I, 60–64.
10 Regolamento, 28 June 1730, Duboin VIII, 619–676.
11 Prato, *Vita economica*, 3–18.
12 Davico, 'Pauperismo', tables VI–VIII; Beloch III, 259, notes that 2.4 percent of the population were listed as paupers in the census of 1734.
13 A. Guevarre, *La mendicità sbandita*.
14 Ibid., 46–56.
15 Einaudi, *Finanza*, 192 ff., 385–390, 441–442. On Law's plan for a state bank, G. Prato, 'Un capitolo della vita di Giovanni Law', *MAST* 2nd series, LXIV (1914).
16 Quazza, *Riforme* I, 149.
17 Idem, *Decadenza*, 154–155; Einaudi, *Finanza*, 65–66.
18 Nicolas, *Savoie* I, 122–125.

19 Ibid. II, 603.

20 Ibid. II, 633.

21 Ibid. I, 156.

22 Bruchet, *Cadastre*, 25–30.

23 Quazza, *Decadenza*, 159.

24 Thus G. Prato, *Il problema del combustibile nel periodo pre-rivoluzionario come fattore della distribuzione topografica delle industrie* (Turin 1912), 43–44; cf. Quazza, *Decadenza*, 158, and Bulferetti, 'Elemento mercantilistico', passim.

25 V. Castronovo, art. 'Caissotti' in *DBI*.

26 Quazza, *Decadenza*, 147–152; idem, *Riforme* I, 123, 203.

27 'Ricavo della quantità . . . degli organzini 1721–1725', 'Nota delle piante di filatori da seta' 13 Aug. 1722, Duboin XVI, 109–110.

28 Castronovo, *Industria laniera*, 5.

29 Anon. memo. of July 1722, quoted in Venturi, *Radicati*, 73.

30 Einaudi, *Finanza*, 59, 65–66; cf. the orders to the intendants, 21 June 1711, and to the indendant-general of Nice, 9 Jan. 1718, Duboin IX, 39, 52.

31 Quoted in Venturi, *Radicati*, 81.

32 Blondel (ed. Promis), 615; cf. Marini, 664.

33 P. Stella, *Itinerari portoregalistici: Jacques-Joseph Duguet (1649–1733) e le sue fortune in Italia* (Turin 1966), 4–7; Duguet's treatise was pub. at Leyden in 1729.

34 Quazza, *Riforme* II, 367; on Ormea, ibid. I, 33–43, and Carutti, *Vittorio Amedeo II*, 456.

35 Venturi, *Radicati*, 152.

36 These agreements are in Solar de la Marguérite, *Traités publics* II, 418–443; cf. Carutti, *Diplomazia* III, 603 ff.; Boggio I, 118–121.

37 S. Maffei (ed. G. B. Giuliari), *Parere sul migliore ordinamento della R. Università di Torino a Sua Maestà Vittorio Amedeo II* (Verona 1871); F. d'Aguirre, *Della fondazione e del ristabilimento degli studi generali in Torino (anno 1717)* (Palermo 1901). For background, F. Cordova, *I Siciliani in Piemonte nel secolo XVIII* (Palermo 1913); A. Lattes, 'Francesco de Aguirre e Scipione Maffei', *MSI*, 3rd series, XIII (1909); S. Romano, 'Francesco d'Aguirre e la sua opera manoscritta sul riordina-

mento degli studi generali in Torino' *Archivio storico siciliano* XXVII (1902) G. Pensabene Perez, 'Nicolò Pensabene giureconsulto palermitano ministro di stato di Sua Maestà Vittorio Amedeo II di Savoia', ibid XXXVII (1913).

38 'C'est un avocat de Valence, longue robe et courte science', Nicolas, *Savoi* I, 80.

39 *Costituzioni di Sua Maestà pe l'Università di Torino* (Turin 1729); cf Roggero, 457 ff.; Vallauri III, 46–51 Féliciangeli, 'L'éducation', 126 ff. Carpanetto et al., 22–25.

40 Quoted in Carutti, *Vittorio Amedeo II*, 469. For a similar judgment on Victor Amadeus's methods and outlook, F. Torcellan Ginolino, 'Il pensiero politico di Paolo Mattia Doria e un interessante profilo storico di Vittorio Amedeo II', *BSBS* LIX (1961) On Giannone's arrest, P. Giannone (ed. S. Bertelli), *La vita di Pietro Giannone* (2 vols., Turin 1977) II 320–336; F. Venturi, *Settecento riformatore. I. Da Muratori a Beccaria* (Turin 1969), 24–25.

Epilogue: The Abdication

Best narrative is in Carutti, *Vittorio Amedeo II*; the main contemporary source that I have used is Blondel. See also A. Reumont, 'Lettere di Polissena regina di Savoia sull'abdicazione e prigionia di Vittorio Amedeo II', *ASI*, 4th series, XI (1883). An important contemporary assessment of Victor Amadeus, with an account of his abdication, is in L. A. Muratori, *Annali d'Italia* (25 vols., Rome 1788) XXIII, 213–225. Radicati wrote a pamphlet on the abdication, with critical comments on Victor Amadeus's government, which he pub. under the pseudonym of Wicardel de Trivié as *Histoire de l'abdication de Victor Amédée Roi de Sardaigne et C. De sa Détention au Château de Rivoli. Et des Moyens qu'il s'est servi pour remonter sur le trône. A Turin de l'Imprimerie Royale MDCCXXXIV* (false imprint).

1 Arts. 'Bogino' (by G. Quazza), 'Caissotti' (by V. Castronovo), in

)BI; on Platzaert, Viora, *Le costi-
uzioni*, 123.
  Blondel, 'Anecdotes', 501.
  Grosso & Mellano, 153 ff. She was
orn Anna Carlotta Teresa Canalis di
Cumiana in 1680; maid of honour to
Madame Royale in 1695; married 1703
o the conte di San Sebastiano, who
ccepted paternity of the child she was
hen expecting (probably by Victor
Amadeus), and by whom she had
even other children. Her husband

died in 1724; she was later named lady-
in-waiting to Charles Emanuel's new
consort. After Victor Amadeus's death
she withdrew to the convent of the
Visitation at Pinerolo, where she died
in 1769.
4 Blondel, 'Anecdotes', 509–510.
5 Ibid., 639–640.
6 Ibid., 513.
7 Ibid., 527.
8 Carutti, *Vittorio Amedeo II*, 557.
9 Ibid., 571.

List of Illustrations

Maps drawn by Bryan Woodfield

Index

Dates given for sovereigns are for regnal years; dates for other persons are for lifetimes. Numbers in italics refer to illustrations.